Intelligent Decision Making Through Bio-Inspired Optimization

Ramkumar Jaganathan
Sri Krishna Arts and Science College, India

Shilpa Mehta
Auckland University of Technology, New Zealand

Ram Krishan
Mata Sundri University Girls College, Mansa, India

A volume in the Advances in Computational Intelligence and Robotics (ACIR) Book Series

IGI Global
PUBLISHER of TIMELY KNOWLEDGE

Published in the United States of America by
IGI Global
Information Science Reference (an imprint of IGI Global)
701 E. Chocolate Avenue
Hershey PA, USA 17033
Tel: 717-533-8845
Fax: 717-533-8661
E-mail: cust@igi-global.com
Web site: http://www.igi-global.com

Library of Congress Cataloging-in-Publication Data

CIP Pending

Intelligent Decision Making Through Bio-Inspired Optimization
Ramkumar Jaganahan, Shilpa Mehta, Ram Krishan
Information Science Reference 2024

ISBN: 979-8-3693-2073-0
eISBN: 979-8-3693-2074-7

This book is published in the IGI Global book series Advances in Computational Intelligence and Robotics (ACIR) (ISSN: 2327-0411; eISSN: 2327-042X)

British Cataloguing in Publication Data
A Cataloguing in Publication record for this book is available from the British Library.

For electronic access to this publication, please contact: eresources@igi-global.com.

Advances in Computational Intelligence and Robotics (ACIR) Book Series

Ivan Giannoccaro
University of Salento, Italy

ISSN:2327-0411
EISSN:2327-042X

Mission

While intelligence is traditionally a term applied to humans and human cognition, technology has progressed in such a way to allow for the development of intelligent systems able to simulate many human traits. With this new era of simulated and artificial intelligence, much research is needed in order to continue to advance the field and also to evaluate the ethical and societal concerns of the existence of artificial life and machine learning.

The **Advances in Computational Intelligence and Robotics (ACIR) Book Series** encourages scholarly discourse on all topics pertaining to evolutionary computing, artificial life, computational intelligence, machine learning, and robotics. ACIR presents the latest research being conducted on diverse topics in intelligence technologies with the goal of advancing knowledge and applications in this rapidly evolving field.

Coverage

- Fuzzy Systems
- Computer Vision
- Machine Learning
- Algorithmic Learning
- Cyborgs
- Robotics
- Synthetic Emotions
- Artificial Life
- Computational Logic
- Natural Language Processing

IGI Global is currently accepting manuscripts for publication within this series. To submit a proposal for a volume in this series, please contact our Acquisition Editors at Acquisitions@igi-global.com or visit: http://www.igi-global.com/publish/.

The Advances in Computational Intelligence and Robotics (ACIR) Book Series (ISSN 2327-0411) is published by IGI Global, 701 E. Chocolate Avenue, Hershey, PA 17033-1240, USA, www.igi-global.com. This series is composed of titles available for purchase individually; each title is edited to be contextually exclusive from any other title within the series. For pricing and ordering information please visit http://www.igi-global.com/book-series/advances-computational-intelligence-robotics/73674. Postmaster: Send all address changes to above address.

Titles in this Series

For a list of additional titles in this series, please visit:
www.igi-global.com/book-series/advances-computational-intelligence-robotics/73674

Exploring the Ethical Implications of Generative AI
Aftab Ara (University of Hail, Saudi Arabia) and Affreen Ara (Department of Computer Science, Christ College, Bangalore, ndia)
Engineering Science Reference • © 2024 • 295pp • H/C (ISBN: 9798369315651) • US $300.00

Secure and Intelligent IoT-Enabled Smart Cities
Sushil Kumar Singh (Marwadi University, India) Sudeep Tanwar (Nirma University, India) Rajendrasinh Jadeja (Marwadi University, India) Saurabh Singh (Woosong University, South Korea) and Zdzislaw Polkowski (Wroclaw University of Economics, Pland)
Engineering Science Reference • © 2024 • 434pp • H/C (ISBN: 9798369323731) • US $325.00

Using Real-Time Data and AI for Thrust Manufacturing
D. Satishkumar (Nehru Institute of Technology, India) and M. Sivaraja (Nehru Institute of Technology, India)
Engineering Science Reference • © 2024 • 343pp • H/C (ISBN: 9798369326152) • US $345.00

AI Approaches to Smart and Sustainable Power Systems
L. Ashok Kumar (PSG College of Technology, India) S. Angalaeswari (Vellore Institute of Technology, India) K. Mohana Sundaram (KPR Institute of Engineering and Technology, India) Ramesh C. Bansal (University of Sharjah, UAE & University of Pretoria, South Africa) and Arunkumar Patil (Central University of Karnataka, India)
Engineering Science Reference • © 2024 • 432pp • H/C (ISBN: 9798369315866) • US $300.00

Wearable Devices, Surveillance Systems, and AI for Women's Wellbeing
Sivaram Ponnusamy (Sandip University, Nashik, India) Vibha Bora (G. H. Raisoni College of Engineering, Nagpur, India) Prema M. Daigavane (G. H. Raisoni College of Engineering, Nagpur, India) and Sampada S. Wazalwar (G. H. Raisoni College of Engineering, Nagpur, India)
Engineering Science Reference • © 2024 • 321pp • H/C (ISBN: 9798369334065) • US $335.00

Methodologies, Frameworks, and Applications of Machine Learning
Pramod Kumar Srivastava (Rajkiya Engineering College, Azamgarh, India) and Ashok Kumar Yadav (Rajkiya Engineering College, Azamgarh, India)
Engineering Science Reference • © 2024 • 296pp • H/C (ISBN: 9798369310625) • US $300.00

IGI Global
PUBLISHER of TIMELY KNOWLEDGE

701 East Chocolate Avenue, Hershey, PA 17033, USA
Tel: 717-533-8845 x100 • Fax: 717-533-8661
E-Mail: cust@igi-global.com • www.igi-global.com

Table of Contents

Detailed Table of Contents

With the technological developments in the fields of natural language processing (NLP) and opinion mining (OM), many real-time applications are concentrating on analyzing the opinions of the people. The opinions or reviews given by the people through the internet are collected for summarization or classification based on the need. The feature selection typically saves the operating time, eliminates irrelevant features and redundancy. For feature selection, a semantic based feature selection algorithm called information gain (IG) is used. Naive Bayes, bagging, support vector machines (SVM), classification and regression trees (CART), and algorithms along with optimization techniques like ant colony optimization algorithms are used to optimize and classify the opinions. Also, in this chapter, the state-of-the art machine learning technique, deep learning, is also involved with the convolution neural networks (CNN) algorithm to identify the positive and negative opinions in different fields such as movie reviews, emojis and medical data.

Swarm intelligence is inherent in many living things and is inspiring new ways of thinking among computer scientists. Scientists from all walks of life including software corporates are interested in it because of its ties to collective intelligence behaviour. Bugs are an expensive and quality killer in software development. The development of DP models was driven by the critical need to predict defects early on. Classifying modules as either defect-prone or non-defect-prone relies heavily on machine learning algorithms. Improving software quality relies on defect prediction. SI improves the accuracy and efficacy of bug predictions by modelling their actions after the social group behaviour of insect colonies. The objective of this chapter is to outline swarm intelligence-based bug prediction in order to assist software engineers and QA teams with increased accuracy.

This chapter thoroughly explores the versatile applications of genetic algorithms (GAs) in decision optimization across diverse domains. GAs, inspired by natural selection, adeptly navigate solution spaces, adapting to complex objectives and revealing near-optimal solutions. The exploration encompasses theoretical foundations, customizations for decision optimization, and a variety of GA algorithms demonstrated through real-world case studies, showcasing their adaptability. The GA process iteratively evolves populations, incorporating multiple tailored algorithms that address conflicting objectives and intricate variables. GAs, positioned as optimization keys, redefine decision-making for complex problems where traditional methods fall short. The chapter provides a concise yet comprehensive overview, offering valuable insights into the nuanced applications of GA algorithms in decision optimization.

Nature has all healing powers. Same way, nature is a basis of spur for resolving rigid and multifaceted problems Bio-inspired represents the parasol of diverse studies of computer science, mathematics, and biology in the last years. Bioinspired optmization algorithm is a developing approach that is based on the philosophies and motivation of the biological evolution of nature to develop new and robust challenging techniques. Biologically enthused computing and optimization is a foremost subclass of natural computation. This chapter presents a life-threatening survey of bio-inspired optimization techniques. Diabetic long-lasting disease upsets several organs of human body including the retina. Diabetic retinopathy datasets are taken and machine learning techniques are used to determine the detection of DR (diabetic retinopathy). Feature extraction and classification phases are involved, optimal results for composite problem are found, and correctness is predicted by using the GA.

Ant colony optimization is a popular metaheuristic algorithm inspired by the foraging behavior of ants. It's often used to solve complex optimization problems. Train scheduling is a challenging problem involving the allocation of train resources, routes, and timetables to optimize various objectives like minimizing travel time, energy consumption. In train scheduling, this usually involves defining nodes and arcs to represent railway stations, tracks, and possible connections to optimize, well-defined, such as minimizing the total travel time or energy consumption. The process of ant movement and pheromone update is repeated for a predefined number of iterations or until a termination condition is met. Vehicle routing problem with time frames, the time dependent VRP, the VRP with pickup and delivery, and the dynamic VRP were developed to bring the VRP closer to the types of situations found in the real world. The optimum route serving all clients utilizing a driver's maximum working hours and minimizing total transportation cost is one solution to this problem.

gecko's ability to actively control adhesion has spurred biomimetic innovation. In healthcare, where surgical adhesives play a critical role, traditional solutions often suffer from biocompatibility issues, weak bonding, and limited adaptability.

Deep learning, a subset of AI, has gained popularity in various fields, including computer vision and NLP. It is based on artificial neural networks, which process multiple layers of data and extract high-level features automatically. Unlike traditional ML algorithms, deep learning can process large unstructured data and complex algorithms better than traditional methods. The human brain inspires neural networks, which contain artificial neurons similar to biological neurons. These networks are made up of three layers: input, hidden, and output. Deep learning maps inputs to outputs and finds correlations, making it a "universal approximator." It can be combined with other AI methods to perform more complex tasks, such as deep reinforcement learning. Top companies using ANN include Nvidia Corp., Alphabet, Salesforce.com, Amazon.com, Microsoft Corp., Twilio, IBM, and Facebook. Deep learning uses ANN to analyze data and make predictions and has found applications in almost every business sector.

In the realm of robotics and artificial intelligence, researchers often draw inspiration from the intricate and efficient systems found in the animal kingdom. For instance, the study of swarm intelligence, inspired by the collective behavior of insects like ants or bees, has led to the development of algorithms for autonomous drones and robotic systems that can collaboratively solve complex problems. The adaptation of nature's strategies for smart systems showcases the potential for interdisciplinary collaboration between biology and technology. By understanding and emulating the efficiency, adaptability, and sustainability observed in natural systems, scientists and engineers continue to push the boundaries of innovation, creating smart systems that are not only technologically advanced but also environmentally conscious and resilient.

The rapid proliferation of networking and wireless communication technologies has led to the development of low-cost unmanned aerial vehicles, which will soon occupy a significant amount of the sky. UAVs may be effectively used to complete complicated missions when arranged as an ad hoc network, leading to the

Preface

Welcome to *Intelligent Decision Making Through Bio-Inspired Optimization*, a comprehensive exploration of the dynamic intersection between bio-inspired optimization techniques and the evolving landscape of decision-making. Edited by Ramkumar Jaganathan, Shilpa Mehta, and Ram Krishan, this reference book brings together a wealth of knowledge from the realms of computer science, artificial intelligence, optimization, and decision science.

In today's rapidly advancing technological landscape, the need for intelligent decision-making tools is more critical than ever. This book aims to bridge the gap between theory and application, offering a multidisciplinary perspective on bio-inspired optimization principles and their practical implementation in diverse decision-making scenarios.

The journey begins with an in-depth introduction to the foundations of bio-inspired optimization and decision-making, providing readers with a solid conceptual framework. The subsequent chapters delve into specific techniques, such as Evolutionary Algorithms, Swarm Intelligence, Genetic Algorithms, Particle Swarm Optimization, Ant Colony Optimization, and Evolutionary Strategies, exploring their applications and adaptability to complex decision-making challenges.

The editors have meticulously curated a collection of chapters that not only elucidate the theoretical foundations of bio-inspired optimization but also showcase real-world case studies across domains such as finance, engineering, and healthcare. The inclusion of Hybrid Approaches, combining bio-inspired optimization with machine learning, adds a contemporary dimension to the book, reflecting the ongoing synergy between these two powerful paradigms.

Designed with a diverse audience in mind, this book is intended for researchers, graduate students, and professionals eager to delve into cutting-edge approaches to decision-making and optimization. Each chapter provides a blend of theoretical insights and practical considerations, ensuring that readers can not only understand the conceptual underpinnings but also apply bio-inspired techniques to solve complex decision-making problems.

As editors, our main objective is to present a cohesive and insightful exploration of the application of bio-inspired optimization techniques in the realm of intelligent decision-making. We believe that this book will serve as a valuable resource for those seeking to navigate the ever-expanding landscape of bio-inspired algorithms and their transformative potential in decision science.

We express our gratitude to the contributors who have shared their expertise and experiences, making this book a collaborative endeavor at the forefront of the evolving field of intelligent decision-making. We hope that you find "Intelligent Decision Making Through Bio-Inspired Optimization" to be an enriching and inspiring journey into the exciting world of bio-inspired optimization and its profound impact on decision science.

ORGANIZATION OF THE BOOK

Chapter 1, "Performance Evaluation of Deep Learning and Machine Learning Techniques for Opinion Mining" by K. Saraswathi, Renukadevi N T, Nandhinidevi S, explores the application of natural language processing (NLP) and opinion mining in real-time scenarios. The chapter emphasizes the importance of feature selection, utilizing the Information Gain (IG) algorithm, and applies machine learning techniques such as Naive Bayes, Bagging, SVM, and CART. Deep learning, specifically Convolutional Neural Networks (CNN), is introduced for identifying positive and negative opinions in diverse fields like movie reviews, emojis, and medical data.

Chapter 2, "Swarm Intelligence Empowered Bug Prediction Strategy for Decision Support in Software Defect Prediction" by Medhunhashini DR, Jeen Marseline KS, delves into the use of swarm intelligence techniques, such as Ant Colony Optimization (ACO), Bee Algorithm (BA), and Particle Swarm Optimization (PSO), to enhance bug prediction strategies in software development. The chapter addresses the critical need for defect prediction and classifying modules as defect-prone or non-defect-prone, integrating swarm intelligence to improve accuracy and efficacy in bug predictions.

Chapter 3, "Genetic Algorithms for Decision Optimization: Genetic Algorithm" by Sakshi Patni, Bharti Sharma, thoroughly explores the versatile applications of Genetic Algorithms (GAs) in decision optimization across diverse domains. The chapter provides a comprehensive overview of GAs, showcasing their adaptability through theoretical foundations, customizations for decision optimization, and real-world case studies.

Chapter 4, "Acute Analysis of Bioinspired Optimization Algorithms for Diabetic Debrecen" by Suchitra B, Valarmathi V, presents a critical survey of bio-inspired optimization techniques applied to address the challenges of diabetic retinopathy (DR). Machine learning techniques, including Genetic Algorithms (GA) and Ant Colony Optimization (ACO), are employed for feature extraction and classification to determine the detection of DR.

Chapter 6, "Nature Inspired Optimized Artificial BEE Colony for Decision Making in Energy Efficient Wireless Sensor Network" by Dr. J.Viji Gripsy, Dr. M. Sasikala, focuses on the application of nature-inspired algorithms, specifically Optimized Artificial Bee Colony (OABC), for decision-making in energy-efficient wireless sensor networks. The chapter addresses challenges in WSNs, such as low energy consumption, network lifetime improvement, and data rate enhancement, showcasing the superiority of OABC over existing algorithms.

Chapter 7, "Making Healthcare Decisions: An Evolution" by Venkata Tulasiramu Ponnada, Venkata Tulasikrishna Ponnada, Narendra Kumar Rao B, Rama Krishna Raju Sammeta, Hymavathi Jasti, explores the transformative evolution in healthcare decision-making processes. The chapter analyzes factors contributing to this evolution, emphasizing the integration of technological advancements with ethical principles, patient empowerment, and effective communication.

Chapter 8, "Bio-Inspired Design in Healthcare: The Gecko-Inspired Surgical Adhesive" by Kaushalya Thopate, Krishna Jaiswal, delves into bio-inspired design in healthcare, focusing on a surgical adhesive inspired by geckos. The chapter explores the hierarchical structure of gecko toe pads and their application in surgical adhesives, highlighting the potential of bio-inspired decision-making in addressing challenges in patient care.

Chapter 9, "Neural Network and Neural Computing: Neural Network and Neural Computing" by Partha Ghosh, Suradhuni Ghosh, provides an overview of deep learning, a subset of AI, based on artificial neural networks. The chapter discusses the applications of neural networks in various fields, emphasizing their ability to process large unstructured data and extract high-level features automatically.

Chapter 10, "Evolutionary Computation in Artificial Intelligence: Adapting Nature's Strategies for Smart Systems," focuses on the development of algorithms for autonomous drones and robotic systems that can collaboratively solve complex problems. The adaptation of nature's strategies for smart systems showcases the potential for interdisciplinary collaboration between biology and technology. By understanding and emulating the efficiency, adaptability, and sustainability observed in natural systems, scientists and engineers continue to push the boundaries of innovation, creating smart systems that are not only technologically advanced but also environmentally conscious and resilient.

Chapter 11, "Comprehensive Study on Routing in Fanet" by Mylsamy R, Jaikumar R, offers an extensive investigation of routing in Flying Adhoc Networks (FANETs). The chapter compares and analyzes current FANET routing protocols, addressing the challenges posed by the diverse flying limits and highly dynamic topology of FANETs.

Chapter 12, "Intelligent Routing Scheme for FANET Using Bio-Inspired Optimisation" by Nandhini S, Jeen Marseline K.S., focuses on the application of bio-inspired optimization techniques for routing in Unmanned Aerial Vehicle (UAV) networks, specifically in Flying Adhoc Networks (FANETs). The chapter highlights the importance of intelligent routing decisions in dynamic multi-UAV systems, proposing bio-inspired optimization algorithms for enhanced efficiency.

Chapter 13. "Biospheric Reverie: Unraveling Indoor Air Quality through Bio-Inspired Textiles, Awareness, and Decision-Making" by Rita Komalasari. explores the themes of indoor air quality, a crucial but often underestimated aspect of our daily lives. The authors embark on an exploration of this issue, providing a distinctive perspective by incorporating the transformative influence of bio-inspired textiles. The chapter's primary objective is to illuminate the significance of indoor air quality, fostering awareness and empowering individuals to optimize their living spaces.

IN CONCLUSION

As we bring the chapters of *Intelligent Decision Making Through Bio-Inspired Optimization* to a close, it is with great satisfaction that we reflect on the diverse and enlightening journey we have undertaken. This edited reference book, curated by Ramkumar Jaganathan, Shilpa Mehta, and Ram Krishan, transcends traditional boundaries, exploring the innovative intersection of bio-inspired optimization techniques and decision-making across various domains.

The collection begins by laying a strong foundation in the introductory chapters, providing readers with a holistic understanding of bio-inspired optimization principles. From there, the subsequent chapters delve into specific techniques such as Evolutionary Algorithms, Swarm Intelligence, Genetic Algorithms, and more, showcasing their adaptability and applications in decision optimization.

The chapters not only contribute to the theoretical understanding of these bio-inspired approaches but also present real-world case studies that demonstrate their practical efficacy. From the realms of healthcare to software defect prediction, from energy-efficient wireless sensor networks to indoor air quality improvement through bio-inspired textiles, each chapter addresses unique challenges and offers valuable insights.

We extend our heartfelt appreciation to the contributing authors who have shared their expertise, providing readers with a rich tapestry of knowledge at the intersection of bio-inspired optimization and intelligent decision-making. The intended audience, including researchers, graduate students, and professionals, will find this book to be a valuable resource in navigating the evolving landscape of decision science.

In conclusion, *Intelligent Decision Making Through Bio-Inspired Optimization* stands as a testament to the collaborative efforts of the authors and editors, seeking to unravel the potential of bio-inspired techniques in shaping intelligent decision-making across diverse domains. As we look towards the future, we anticipate that this reference book will inspire further exploration and innovation in the fascinating and dynamic field of bio-inspired optimization. May the insights contained within these pages ignite curiosity, spark innovation, and guide readers on their own journeys of discovery in the world of intelligent decision-making.

Ramkumar Jaganathan
Sri Krishna Arts and Science College, India

Shilpa Mehta
Auckland University of Technology, New Zealand

Ram Krishan
Mata Sundri University Girls College, Mansa, India

Chapter 1
Performance Evaluation of Deep Learning and Machine Learning Techniques for Opinion Mining

K. Saraswathi
Kongu Engineering College, India

Renukadevi N. T.
Kongu Engineering College, India

Nandhinidevi S.
https://orcid.org/0000-0001-8893-6556
Kongu Engineering College, India

ABSTRACT

With the technological developments in the fields of natural language processing (NLP) and opinion mining (OM), many real-time applications are concentrating on analyzing the opinions of the people. The opinions or reviews given by the people through the internet are collected for summarization or classification based on the need. The feature selection typically saves the operating time, eliminates irrelevant features and redundancy. For feature selection, a semantic based feature selection algorithm called information gain (IG) is used. Naive Bayes, bagging, support vector machines (SVM), classification and regression trees (CART), and algorithms along with optimization techniques like ant colony optimization algorithms are used to optimize and classify the opinions. Also, in this chapter, the state-of-the art machine learning technique, deep learning, is also involved with the convolution neural networks (CNN) algorithm to identify the positive and negative opinions in different fields such as movie reviews, emojis and medical data.

DOI: 10.4018/979-8-3693-2073-0.ch001

1. INTRODUCTION OF OPINION MINING AND THE ISSUES FACED

1.1 Introduction to Opinion Mining

A subset of natural language processing (NLP) called opinion mining (OM) is used to monitor public sentiment toward a certain good, service, or subject. Sentiment analysis (SA) is another name for it, and it entails creating a system to gather and analyze opinions and feelings about a product, service, or issue expressed in blog posts, reviews, comments, or tweets. Remarkably, there isn't much confusion among academics and researchers on the distinction between sentiment and opinion, or if the discipline belongs under the umbrella of opinion mining or sentiment analysis. According to Merriam-Webster, an opinion is a perspective or judgment made in the mind about a certain issue, whereas sentiment is defined as an attitude, thinking, or judgment caused by feeling. There is a noticeable difference.

Opinion mining has various applications. For instance, in marketing, it assists in assessing the performance of an advertising campaign or the debut of a new product, ascertains which of several iterations of a good or service is the most well-liked, and even pinpoints the demographics that find certain aspects objectionable or appealing. (Vinodhini & Chandrasekaran 2012).

One area of research that examines people's opinions, feelings, assessments, appraisals, attitudes, and emotions about goods, services, people, groups, problems, occasions, subjects, and their characteristics is called opinion mining. It encompasses a vast array of issues. In addition, it goes by various names and involves quite varied duties. Some of them are affect analysis, emotion analysis, sentiment mining, opinion extraction, subjectivity analysis, sentiment analysis, review mining, and so forth. Nevertheless, sentiment analysis and opinion mining encompass all of them. (Liu 2012).

Opinion mining automates the process of extracting opinions from the internet. Individuals write blog entries, reviews, comments, and tweets about many subjects to share their opinions. It is possible to monitor companies and items on the internet and ascertain whether people have a favorable or negative opinion of them. Sentiment analysis research has focused on several key topics, including opinion summarization, feature-based sentiment classification, and sentiment categorization (Buche et al. 2013).

Facts and opinions are the two types of textual information that are typically referred to from the standpoint of sentiment and opinion mining.

- Facts: See the objective descriptions of a product's nature. The majority of studies have focused on factual information extraction, including information retrieval, web searches, and numerous other text mining and natural language processing tasks.
- Opinions: Describes attitude, evaluations, and emotional extraction of a good, service, subject, or problem.

Opinion analysis is a relatively recent field of study. Researchers have developed a number of methods up to this point for resolving various issues. These days, sentiment analysis, also known as opinion mining, is a branch of information retrieval (IR) and natural language processing (NLP) that shares some traits with other domains like text mining and information extraction (IE), including extraction, categorization, and concept linking

People, and even companies, are generally curious about other people's opinions. For example, when someone wants to buy a new product or learn more about a topic, they first try to look up reviews online to see what other people think about the product and the topic. Based on these reviews, they decide which product to buy. Similar to this, businesses go through the reviews they have gathered on the internet for customer feedback. For the same, the digital ecosystem offers a wealth of resources in the form of blogs, reviews, and more. A fundamental stage in sentiment analysis and opinion mining is feature extraction (Singh & Husain 2014).

The opinions or reviews are collected as a huge document. Firstly, feature extraction is done from the huge document for classification purpose. Based on the features extracted, the opinions are analysed that it represents favourable (positive) opinion or unfavourable (negative) opinion. Different classification methods are applied for the classification process. The analyzed review is measured by some existing metrics such as accuracy, precision, recall and root mean squared error.

Opinion mining, or extracting opinions from text, has gained a lot of attention lately because to its many practical applications. These include automated recommender systems, extracting consumer sentiments, and determining public attitudes about a certain product, issue, or service for businesses and organizations. Sentiment mining has these two primary objectives:

1. To determine whether a particular text is true or objective, or if it contains an opinion.
2. To determine a text's viewpoint about a specific topic by categorizing it as positive, negative, or neutral.

In addition, opinion mining can be performed at the sentence level or document level. In general, sentence level mining is made complex by the fact that the semantic orientation of words is mostly context dependent, and document level mining is made complex because there is a chance that one document contains several contradictory opinions about the same target (Farra et al. 2010).

There are a number of difficulties in sentiment analysis. First, a common NLP difficulty is Word Sense Disambiguation (WSD), which is observed frequently. For instance, "an unpredictable steering wheel" is seen negatively, whereas "an unpredictable plot in the movie" is seen positively. There are various interpretations of the word "unpredictable" in opinion. Second, as stated in "The movie has a great cast, superb storyline and spectacular photography; the director has managed to make a mess of the whole thing" (Chandrakala & Sindhu 2012), the opinionated term addresses the issue of sudden deviation from positive to negative polarity

1.2 Issues in Opinion Mining

Opinion mining is a relatively new field, therefore there are a number of issues to take into account. The methods now in use, such as standard text processing, are outdated when it comes to opinion extraction, identification, and comparison. These issues primarily concern the veracity of the data that was gathered and the techniques applied during the opinion mining process (Seerat & Azam 2012). The following is an overview of opinion mining's drawbacks:

1. Since product reviews, comments, and feedback may be written in a variety of languages (such as English, Urdu, Arabic, French, and so forth), it can be difficult to approach each language in accordance with its orientation.
2. Verbs and adjectives can also be utilised as feature words, however they are more challenging to recognise than nouns, which are thought of as feature words.

3. On a mobile phone, a consumer would remark, "The voice quality is excellent," and another customer might remark, "The phone's sound quality is very good." Although they are using different language, both are discussing the same functionality. Sorting the words that are synonymous is another difficult challenge.
4. Opinion words would have varying orientations depending on the circumstances. For instance, "The mobile phone's camera is small." The word "small" is used positively in this context. In contrast, if a consumer remarks that "the battery time is also small," the word "small" denotes a negative attitude towards the phone's battery. Determining the polarity of the same adjectives in various contexts is therefore also a difficult issue.
5. The customer may use short words, acronyms, and Roman language in their reviews as long as they are provided in an unrestricted format. "U" stands for you, "cam" for a camera, "pic" for a picture, "f9" for fine, "b4" for before, "gud" for good, and so forth are a few examples. Managing this kind of language to extract opinions takes a lot of work.
6. Since various people write in different ways, it can be challenging to categorise a sentence as positive or negative when using sentence-level opinion mining. There may be both good and negative opinions in the same sentence.
7. Opinions may only be divided into two categories: positive and negative. A neutral opinion, which only recognises adjectives as opinion words, can also be expressed. Additionally, an opinion can be expressed as an adverb, adjective, or verb. For instance, "like" is both an opinion word and a verb. Because it extracts the sentences that have at least one feature word, this method detects the implicit features. Customers' indirect comments about some features are disregarded.
8. The lexicon-based approach used in opinion mining is ineffective for handling terms that depend on context. For instance, the word "small" might convey a favourable or unfavourable perception of a product's attributes. One customer remarks that the "size of mobile phone is small" for a mobile phone. It's unclear from this line whether the magnitude is seen favourably or unfavourably.
9. Opinion mining is primarily used to identify duplicates in order to detect spam and fraudulent reviews.
10. The reputation of the reviewer, the comparison of qualitative summary evaluations, and the identification of outliers are done.
11. In order to evaluate data and provide additional insight into data expressed before opinion, opinions are linked with behaviour.
12. According to Sharma and Chitre (2014), there is a constant need for mining systems to be more user-friendly and usable.

2. FEATURE EXTRACTION AND FEATURE SELECTION USING INVERSE DOCUMENT FREQUENCY AND INFORMATION GAIN

For feature extraction and feature selection, a variety of methods are employed, including Stemmed Terms, Based on minimal, Dependence Y-relation, Graph Distance, TF-IDF, Opinion Words, Document Frequency (DF), MI, Information Gain (IG), CHI, and N-gram.

In machine learning-based sentiment categorization, one of the most important tasks is extracting the best feature in an appropriate quantity. Various studies have attempted to select comparative feature selection approaches and extract complex features. The majority of current studies concentrate on basic features, such as single words, character and word N-grams, such as bigrams and trigrams, or combinations of the aforementioned features. Classifying text documents according to their sentiments is more difficult than classifying them according to topics since it entails making judgements based on the attitudes, ideas, and feelings that the text contains. Online content that is subjective or opinionated is frequently semi-structured or unstructured (Sharma & Dey 2012).

Document Frequency (DF)

Document frequency is the number of papers that make up a specific phrase. Using this method, the document frequency is first compared to the upper and lower specified Document Frequency Thresholds. Terms and phrases with frequencies below the threshold are removed, as are those with frequencies beyond the upper threshold. The most unusual words—and even those that are overly common—are thought to be either unimportant in affecting overall performance or unhelpful in identifying the best feature categories to predict. This is the most straightforward—yet efficient—selection technique for text classification. (Patel & Kothari, 2015).

DF, CHI, and IG are significant feature selection approaches in the filter area of feature selection. The frequency of a word across all categories is tallied by DF. Finally, the features at the top and bottom of the list are eliminated. The degree to which a given trait is irrelevant for a certain class is determined by CHI. Features are arranged according to how applicable they are to a specific class. IG uses the likelihood that a word will appear in a given class to determine how relevant a feature is. Categorical Proportional Difference is another feature selection technique (CPD). The existence of a feature in a class is taken into account in the calculations.

$$CPD\left(t\right) = \frac{\left|FP_i - FN_i\right|}{DF_i} \tag{2.1}$$

where FP_i is the total number of feature i in the positive class, FN_i is the total number of feature i in the negative class while DF_i is the total number of document where feature i exists.

- Optimizing the classification using Support Vector Machine and Ant Colony Optimization (ACO) along with Medical opinions

The genetic approach would result from optimisation techniques and has a small probability of being trapped at local minima. The synthesis of neural network designs, scheduling, numerical optimisation, and other issues requiring efficient and effective search are finding extensive applications in genetic techniques, which produce globally optimal or nearly optimal solutions. Artificial Neural Networks (ANN) use genetic algorithms for topology optimisation, genetic training methods, and control parameter optimisation

A feature (term) goodness criteria in machine learning-based categorization is Information Gain (IG). By determining if a feature is present in each given text content, it calculates the amount of information (in bits) needed for class prediction. It is determined by how much the characteristic contributes to lowering the total entropy.

IG is a decision tree-based feature ranking technique that generates fewer features and performs well in classification. IG aims to choose attributes that provide the most insights into the classes. Every feature has an individual IG value that dictates whether or not it should be chosen for the classification task. The features are checked using a threshold value; if a feature's IG value is higher than the threshold value, it is selected; if not, it is not. Assume that C is the set of k classes and S is the set of n instances. symbolises the segment of the S example with class Ci. Next, the anticipated data for this class membership are derived as given by Equation (2.2).

$$Info(S) = -\sum_{i=1}^{k} P(C_i, S) \times \log(P(C_i, S)) \tag{2.2}$$

If an attribute A has v distinct values, the decision tree with A as its root will yield the expected information, and the weighted sum of the expected information of the subsets of A will be determined by the distinct values v. Consider that in Equation (2.3), Si is the set of instances and Ai is the value of attribute A.

$$Info_A(S) = -\sum_{i=1}^{v} \frac{|S_i|}{|S|} \times Info(S_i) \tag{2.3}$$

Then the difference between $Info(S_i)$ and afford the knowledge obtained from dividing S based on test A in Equation (2.4).

$$Gain(A) = Info(S) - Info_A(S) \tag{2.4}$$

The probability of finding pure classes in a target class would increase with increasing information gain.

Though few words in the corpus truly indicate sentiment, many words that are employed as features are taken into account for processing when classifying a document. These extra words and features must be removed because they slow down the document classification process by using more words than are necessary. Moreover, using more features for classification decreases the classifier's accuracy because every feature should be taken into account when classifying a document. In machine learning-based sentiment categorization, one of the most important tasks is extracting the best feature in an appropriate quantity.

Removing superfluous features is required since using fewer characteristics is advantageous. This is why selection is used. With feature selection, a classifier may quickly fit a model to the issue set because there is less data to take into account, improving text classification accuracy.

Experiments are conducted in the preliminary inquiry to classify opinions based on varying numbers of features sorted by IG. The acquired classification accuracy is shown in Figure 2.1.

Text-based categorization is essentially what sentiment classification is. In contrast to traditional text classification, which uses topic-related terms as key characteristics to categorize various topic-based texts like those in politics, science, or sports, sentiment classification places greater weight on sentiment/ opinion words that express positive or negative opinions.

Figure 1. Classification accuracy with IG-based feature selection

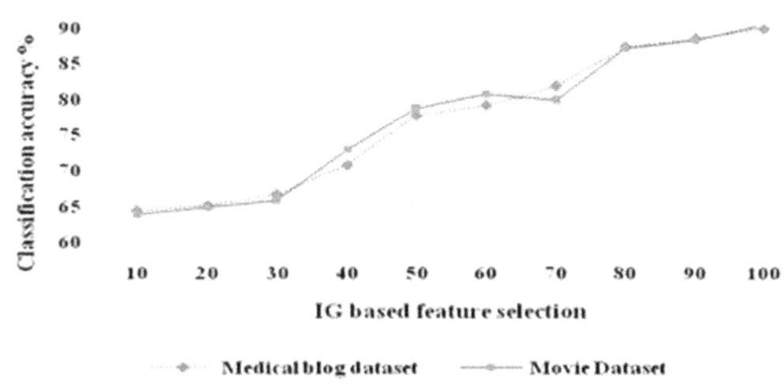

Two methods are used in sentiment classification to categorize the content of documents and sentences. These are the Lexicon Based Approach and the Machine Learning Approach. Text classification in particular and supervised learning in general are related to machine learning. It is also known as "Supervised Learning" as a result. Numerous techniques are included in it, including ID3, C5, Neural Networks, K-Nearest Neighbor, Winnow Classifier, Centroid Classifier, N-gram Model, Naïve Bayes, Maximum Entropy, SVM, and so on.

3. DATASET

A movie review data set containing 2,000 reviews—1,000 positively and 1,000 adversely rated by classification algorithms—was obtained by Pang & Lee (2004). Pang et al. (2002) also utilize an earlier version with 700 good and 700 negative evaluations. A subset of 300 occurrences from the Internet Movie Database (IMDB)—150 positive and 150 negative—as well as a 300-item medical opinion dataset are used to test various categorization algorithms.

3.1. Evaluation Metrics

Another name for precision is positive predictive value. It is the percentage of retrieved instances that are relevant. Equation (3.1) provides it.

$$\text{Precision} = TP/\,(TP + FP) \tag{3.1}$$

Another name for recall is sensitivity. It is the percentage of pertinent examples that have been found out of all the relevant occurrences. Recall is the percentage of pertinent documents that are successfully recovered in information retrieval. Equation (3.2) provides it.

$$\text{Recall} = TP/\,(TP + FN) \tag{3.2}$$

Grouping When both high precision and high trueness are attained, high accuracy is attained. If the values in a particular set of data points from a series of measurements are reasonably close to the true value of the quantity being measured, the set is considered accurate. Equation (3.3) provides an expression for it.

$$\text{Accuracy} = (TP+TN) / (TP+TN+FP+FN) \quad (3.3)$$

The following methods are assessed: IG-CART, IG-Naïve Bayes, IG-bagging, IG-SVM-Poly, IG-SVM-RBF (10,0.01), and IG-SVM-RBF (100,0.1).

The IMDB dataset's classification accuracy is displayed in Tables 1 and 2.

Table 1. Results for IMDB dataset using IG-based feature selection

Techniques	Classification Accuracy	Recall -Positive	Recall -Negative	Precision -Positive	Precision -Negative
IG-CART	64.67	0.7156	0.5778	0.6289	0.6701
IG-Naïve Bayes	66.22	0.7222	0.6022	0.6448	0.6843
IG-Bagging	68.56	0.7444	0.6267	0.666	0.7103
IG-SVM – Poly	70.67	0.7578	0.6556	0.6875	0.7302
IG-SVM RBF (10,0.01)	71.78	0.7667	0.6689	0.6984	0.7414
IG-SVM RBF (100,0.1)	76.89	0.8267	0.7111	0.741	0.804

Figure 2. Classification accuracy results with different classifiers to IMDB dataset with IG based feature selection

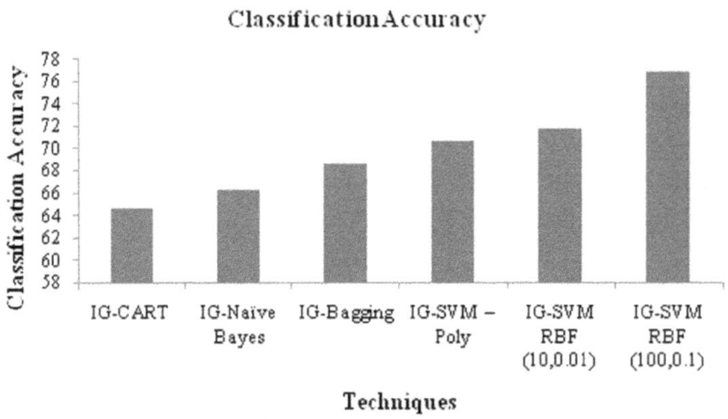

It is observed from Figure 3.4 that the classification accuracy of IG-SVM RBF (100,0.1) is better by 17.26% than IG-CART, by 14.91% than IG-Naïve Bayes, by 11.45% than IG bagging, by 8.43% than IG-SVM-Poly and by 6.87% than IG-SVM RBF (10,0.01) for IMDB dataset.

3.3 Medical Opinion Dataset

It can be noticed from Figure 2 that the classification accuracy of IG-SVM RBF (100,0.1) performs better by 18.97% than IG-CART, by 16.63% than IG-Naïve Bayes, by 11.47% than IG bagging, by 11.63% than IG-SVM-Poly and by 8.83% than IG-SVM RBF (10,0.01) for medical opinion dataset.

Table 2. Results received for medical opinion dataset with IG-based feature selection

Techniques	Classification Accuracy	Recall for Positive	Recall for Negative	Precision for Positive	Precision for Negative
IG-CART	65.22	0.7244	0.58	0.633	0.6779
IG-Naïve Bayes	66.78	0.7289	0.6067	0.6495	0.6911
IG-Bagging	70.33	0.7511	0.6556	0.6856	0.7248
IG-SVM – Poly	70.22	0.7556	0.6489	0.6827	0.7264
IG-SVM RBF (10,0.01)	72.22	0.76	0.6844	0.7066	0.7404
IG-SVM RBF (100,0.1)	78.89	0.84	0.7378	0.7621	0.8218

Figure 3. Classification accuracy to medical opinion dataset with IG based feature selection

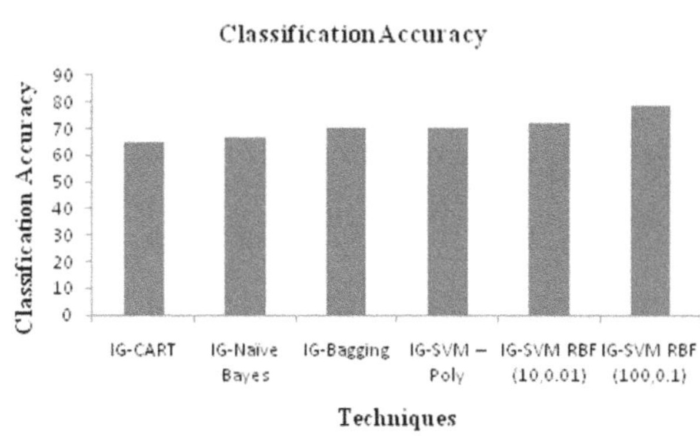

3.4 Results

Opinion mining and sentiment analysis automatically retrieve and categorize user thoughts from the internet. The most often used data mining approach is classification. Using the provided predictive attributes and the stated set of attributes, it is used to forecast the likely result from the given data set. TF-IDF is used to extract the features, and IG selects the most useful feature subsets. The methods CART, Naïve Bayes, Bagging, and SVM are employed to categorize feature sets from reviews as positive or negative. SVM uses RBF kernel and Polykernel to classify features. For evaluation, a bespoke medical opinion dataset and a subset of 300 instances—150 positive and 150 negative—from the Internet Movie Database (IMDB) are employed.

The classification accuracy of IG-SVM-RBF (100,0.1) using the IMDB dataset is 17.26% better than IG-CART, 14.91% better than IG-Naïve Bayes, 11.45% better than IG bagging, 8.43% better than IG-SVM-Poly, and 6.87% better than IG-SVM RBF (10,0.01). Likewise, for the medical opinion dataset, the classification accuracy of IG-SVM RBF (100,0.1) is superior to that of IG-CART by 18.97%, IG-Naïve Bayes by 16.63%, IG bagging by 11.47%, IG-SVM-Poly by 11.63%, and IG-SVM RBF (10,0.01) by 8.83%. To improve feature subset selection and SVM kernel optimization, further work Ant colony optimization technique is applied.

4. ANT COLONY OPTIMIZATION:

There are fifteen ants that were chosen for ACO in the current study project. Kernel function parameters are adjusted via ACO. The goal of the termination condition is to optimize the total accuracy of classification. Several implementations of SVM are available, including SVM with poly kernel, SVM with RBF kernel (10,0.01), SVM with RBF kernel (100,0.1), and SVM with RBF kernel with ACO. Prior to using CART, Naïve Bayes, and SVM, MOFACO is used to improve feature selection. In the end, parameter optimization is done using ACO.

The ACO optimization method aims to provide subsets of significant features with lower sizes. A hybrid search strategy combining wrapper/filter techniques is used in ACO feature selection. Based on these methods, it adjusts the conventional pheromone update and heuristic information measurement principles. It places emphasis on limiting the quantity of prominent aspects and selecting only a few. It selects the prominent aspects of a reduced number by applying a subset size determination algorithm. The overall classification accuracy is maximized by the termination condition.

This study proposes a novel multi-objective fitness function, denoted by Equation (4.1),

$$f(c) = \frac{\left[\dfrac{e-1}{e^{\delta-t}-1}\right]}{N_L} \tag{4.1}$$

where N_L is the number of left out features; δ is give by $\dfrac{\text{wrongly classified instances}}{\text{Total number of training instances}}$; and e is 2.713.

A fitness function with exponential growth was chosen for quicker convergence. A constructive heuristic for probabilistic solution constructions is the foundation of any ACO algorithm. Solutions are put together as element sequences

ACO uses transition probability, which is a trade-off between heuristic information (which expresses move desirability), ηi, and pheromone intensity, τi. This strikes a trade-off between exploitation and exploration. To strike the ideal balance between exploration and exploitation, the α and β are employed. When $\alpha = 0$, no pheromone information is utilised, meaning that past search history is not taken into account. After a while, the search becomes stochastic and greedy. The potential advantage or attractiveness of a move is disregarded if $\beta = 0$.

Following the ants' arrival to their solutions, pheromone evaporation occurs on the nodes. Equation (4.2) states that each ant k leaves a certain amount of pheromone on a node after it has used it.

$$\Delta\tau_i^k(t) = \begin{cases} \phi.\gamma(S^k(t)) + \frac{\varphi.(n-|S^k(t)|)}{n} & if\ i \in S^k(t), \\ 0 & otherwise, \end{cases} \quad (4.2)$$

where $|S^k(t)|$ is the length of the feature subset $S^k(t)$, which was obtained by ant k at iteration t. The parameters are selected based on the assumption that the classifier's performance is equally significant to the subset length. To add pheromone, values ϕ=0.5, φ=0.5 are chosen in Equation (4.4).

$$\tau_i(t+1) = (1-\rho)\tau_i(t) + \sum_{k=1}^{m} \Delta\tau_i(t) + \Delta\tau_i^g(t) \quad (4.3)$$

where m is the number of ants at each iteration and $\rho \in (0,1)$ is a pheromone trail decay coefficient. In this, g indicates the best ant at each iteration.

5. HYBRIDIZATION OF ANT COLONY OPTIMIZATION TECHNIQUES

The relevance in optimization technique leads to the genetic approach which may lead to the problem of local minima. In solving problems, requiring efficient and effective search.

5.1 Proposed ACO-2 OPT Algorithm

In this research work, a supervised feature selection technique is proposed to overcome some of the disadvantages of statistical based feature selection techniques. Features are extracted using TF-IDF and perform optimization in feature selection using a new hybrid method Ant Colony Optimization with 2 Opt (ACO-2OPT) is proposed for feature selection.

The best performing ACO algorithms progress through the application of local search algorithms which are hybrid algorithms. They combine and achieve probabilistic solution construction by an ant's colony with standard local search algorithms.

The 2-opt algorithm systematically tests whether a current solution can be improved by replacing two edges simultaneously.

A local search algorithm is essential for a neighbourhood examination scheme. It defines how a neighbourhood is searched and which neighbour solution replaces the current one. In iterative improvement algorithms, this process is called as pivoting rule.

This 2-OPT algorithm eliminates the long edges and it changes the solution.

ACO based feature selection and proposed ACO (ACO2-OPT) based feature selection are investigated.

Figure 4. Classification accuracy with ACO and proposed ACO (ACO2-OPT)

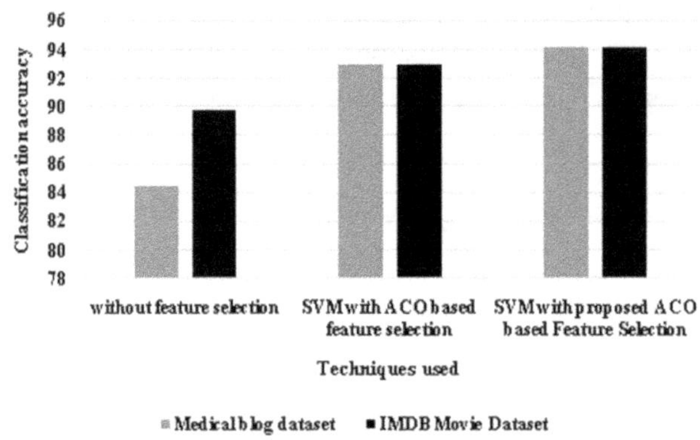

Figure 5.2 depicts that comparing to without feature selection method and SVM with ACO feature selection, proposed ACO based feature selection method improves classification accuracy by 9.48% and 10.8% for Medical dataset. Similarly, for the IMDB Movie Dataset, the improvement is measured as 3.48% and 4.80% which is statistically significant. Figure 5.3 depicts the average precision obtained.

5.2 Proposed Cooperative ACO (CACO) Algorithm

In this research work, an improved ACO algorithm by a collection of cooperative agents named as Co-operative ACO (CACO) is proposed. The ants cooperate using an indirect form of contact mediated by pheromone trails of scent and find the best solution to their responsibilities guided by both the information called exploitation, which has been acquired, and the search called exploration for the new route. A new set of chaotic variables with the same number of optimization variables is generated. Then the chaotic search method is utilized to improve the quality of the individual, and the chaos is considered into optimization variables in order to take on the chaotic state. The chaotic motion characteristics are referred to realize the optimization search. The ergodicity, randomness and regularity of chaotic search method are utilized to solve longer search time, to avoid falling into the local extremum in the starting stage and also to improve the search accuracy in the late search.

The pheromone structure of the `best' performing colony is copied to the other colonies and it leads to the utilization of time effectively. The best performing colony is defined as a number of different measures could be used for getting the optimized result. The drawback of using this method is that the communication cost can be quite high due to the necessity of broadcasting the entire pheromone structures, which can be large for many problems.

It can be observed that Hybrid ACO converges in about 238 iterations whereas MOFACO requires 289 iterations. Similarly, Hybrid ACO creates a feature subset of 24% of overall features.

5.3. Result and Discussion

Experiments are carried out using the IMDB movie dataset and medical blogs collected from various websites. The MOFACO-2OPT-SVM-ACO, MOFACO-2OPT-SVM-ACO-2OPT, CACO-SVM-ACO and CACO-SVM-CACO methods are evaluated.

Tables 3 and Figure 3 show the classification accuracy, recall and precision of Medical dataset

Table 3. Results for medical opinion dataset using ACO-2OPT and CACO

Techniques	Classification Accuracy	Recall -Positive	Recall -Negative	Precision - Positive	Precision-Negative
MOFACO-2OPT-SVM-ACO	92.78	0.9156	0.94	0.9385	0.9176
MOFACO-2OPT-SVM-ACO-2OPT	93.33	0.92	0.9467	0.9452	0.9221
CACO-SVM-ACO	94.78	0.9444	0.9511	0.9508	0.9448
CACO-SVM-CACO	96	0.9489	0.9711	0.9705	0.95

Figure 5. Classification accuracy for medical opinion dataset using ACO-2 OPT and CACO

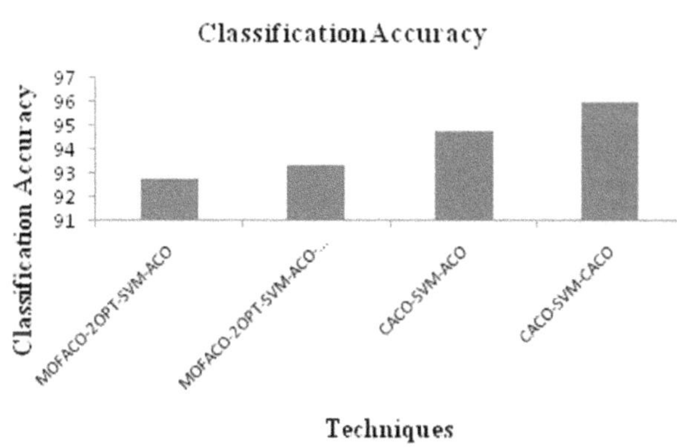

It is observed from Figure 4 that classification accuracy of CACO-SVM-CACO performs better by 3.41% than MOFACO-2OPT-SVM-ACO, by 2.82% than MOFACO-2OPT-SVM-ACO-2OPT, by 1.28% than CACO-SVM-ACO respectively by using Medical opinion dataset. Table 4 shows the Comparison result of proposed methods with other technique found in the literature.

Table 4. Comparison of proposed methods with other technique found in the literature

Author	Technique Used	Classification Accuracy Obtained (%)
Kumar et al. (2014)	Naïve Bayes with Swarm Intelligence optimization	88.5
MOFACO-SVM-ACO	MOFACO with SVM and ACO	90.89
MOFACO-2OPT-SVM-ACO-2OPT	MOFACO-2OPT with SVM and ACO-2OPT	93.89
CACO-SVM-CACO	**CACO with SVM-CACO**	**95.78**

6. CONVOLUTION NEURAL NETWORK

The neural network classifier can be trained on large dataset. We report series of experiments conducted on Convolution Neural Network (CNN) by training it on two different datasets. Neural network model is trained on top of word embedding. Softmax layer is applied to calculate loss and mapping of semantically related words. Gathered results can help justify the fact that proposed hypothetical QAS is feasible.

We further propose a method to integrate Convolutional Neural Network Classifier to an open domain question answering system. The idea of Open domain will be further explained, but the generality of it indicates to the system of domain specific trainable models, thus making it an open domain.

Deep learning models have achieved remarkable results in computer vision and speech recognition in recent years. Within natural language processing, much of the work with deep learning methods has involved learning word vector representations through neural language models and performing composition over the learned word vectors for classification. Word vectors, wherein words are projected from a sparse, 1-of-V encoding (here V is the vocabulary size) onto a lower dimensional vector space via a hidden layer, are essentially feature extractors that encode semantic features of words in their dimensions.

The implemented Convolution Neural Network model has three layers. Basic functionality of convolution neural network resembles to the visual cortex of the animal brain. In text classification task convolution neural network gives promising result. Criteria for text classification is similar to image classification only difference is that instead of pixel values we have matrix of word vectors. Proposed model is implemented in python using tensorflow library

Text classification is an essential task in natural language processing (NLP) because it allows you to automatically organize and structure text data, extract useful information from it, and use it to solve real-world problems.

CNNs are a type of deep learning algorithm particularly well-suited for text classification tasks. They work by applying convolutional filters to the input data to extract features and then using fully connected layers to classify the data based on the extracted features.

CNN Hyperparameters

When building Convolution Neural Networks, deep learning frameworks will usually allow you to tune some of the items discussed above. These include:

The kernel size, The number of filters, The height and width of the strides, The activation function to be used, How the kernel should be initialized, The way the bias will be initialized.

7. CONCLUSION AND FUTURE ENHANCEMENTS

7.1 Conclusion

Opinion mining is performed for movies available in an online database by classifying the users' review comments as positive/negative. Similarly, a custom dataset for medical blog opinion mining is also investigated. A novel hybrid ACO based feature selection technique with local search (ACO-2 OPT) and an improved ACO(CACO) based feature selection technique are proposed using the ACO-2OPT algorithm and CACO algorithm. Results prove that the classification accuracy of CACO-SVM-CACO performs better by 3.44% than MOFACO-2OPT-SVM-ACO, by 1.99% than MOFACO-2OPT-SVM-ACO-2OPT and by 1.64% than CACO-SVM-ACO by using IMDB dataset. Likewise, the classification accuracy of CACO-SVM-CACO performs better by 3.41% than MOFACO-2OPT-SVM-ACO, by 2.82% than MOFACO-2OPT-SVM-ACO-2OPT and by 1.28% than CACO-SVM-ACO respectively by using medical opinion dataset. Hybridization of Deep learning techniques can be made for better results with huge data set.

7.2 Scope for Future Work

In future, the following can be attempted:

- The proposed CACO-SVM-CACO with CNN method can be evaluated for different opinion mining datasets and the efficiency can be checked in a larger dataset.
- Different hybrid optimization algorithms can be used in future to improve the accuracy and to decrease RMSE of the existing result.

REFERENCES

Agarwal, B., & Mittal, N. (2012). Categorical probability proportion difference (CPPD): a feature selection method for sentiment classification. *Proceedings of the 2nd workshop on sentiment analysis where AI meets psychology,* 17-26.

Agarwal, B., & Mittal, N. (2013a). Optimal feature selection for sentiment analysis. In *International Conference on Intelligent Text Processing and Computational Linguistics.* Springer Berlin Heidelberg. 10.1007/978-3-642-37256-8_2

Agarwal, B., & Mittal, N. (2016). Machine Learning Approach for Sentiment Analysis. In *Prominent Feature Extraction for Sentiment Analysis* (pp. 21–45). Springer International Publishing. doi:10.1007/978-3-319-25343-5_3

Agarwal, B., Mittal, N., & Cambria, E. (2013c). Enhancing sentiment classification performance using bi-tagged phrases. *IEEE 13th International Conference on Data Mining Workshops*, 892-895. 10.1109/ICDMW.2013.80

Agarwal, B., Poria, S., Mittal, N., Gelbukh, A., & Hussain, A. (2015). Concept-level sentiment analysis with dependency-based semantic parsing: A novel approach. *Cognitive Computation*, *7*(4), 487–499. doi:10.1007/s12559-014-9316-6

Agarwal, B., Sharma, V. K., & Mittal, N. (2013b). Sentiment classification of review documents using phrase patterns. *International Conference on Advances in Computing, Communications and Informatics (ICACCI),* 1577-1580. 10.1109/ICACCI.2013.6637415

Ahmad, S. R., Bakar, A. A., & Yaakub, M. R. (2015). Metaheuristic algorithms for feature selection in sentiment analysis. In *Science and Information Conference (SAI)* (pp. 222–226). IEEE. doi:10.1109/SAI.2015.7237148

Alazab, M., Venkatraman, S., Watters, P., & Alazab, M. (2011). Zero-day malware detection based on supervised learning algorithms of API call signatures. *Proceedings of the Ninth Australasian Data Mining Conference*, 121, 171-182.

Alsaffar, A., & Omar, N. (2014). Study on feature selection and machine learning algorithms for Malay sentiment classification. *International Conference on in Information Technology and Multimedia (ICIMU),* 270-275. 10.1109/ICIMU.2014.7066643

Alwan, H. B., & Ku-Mahamud, K. R. (2012). Optimizing support vector machine parameters using continuous ant colony optimization. *7th International Conference on in Computing and Convergence Technology (ICCCT),* 164-169.

Anitha, N., Anitha, B., & Pradeepa, S. (2013). Sentiment classification approaches–A review. *International Journal of Innovations in Engineering and Technology*, *3*(1), 22–31.

Anuprathibha, T., & Kanimozhi Selvi, C. S. (2014). Opinion mining for camera reviews. *International Journal of Advanced Research in Data Mining and Cloud Computing, 2*(5), 1-9.

Asghar, M. Z., Khan, A., Kundi, F. M., Qasim, M., Khan, F., Ullah, R., & Nawaz, I. U. (2014). Medical opinion lexicon: An incremental model for mining health reviews. *International Journal of Academic Research*, *6*(1), 295–302. doi:10.7813/2075-4124.2014/6-1/A.39

Baccianella, S., Esuli, A., & Sebastiani, F. (2014). Feature selection for ordinal text classification. *Neural Computation*, *26*(3), 557–591. doi:10.1162/NECO_a_00558 PMID:24320850

Bagheri, A., Saraee, M., & De Jong, F. (2013). Care more about customers: Unsupervised domain-independent aspect detection for sentiment analysis of customer reviews. *Knowledge-Based Systems*, *52*, 201–213. doi:10.1016/j.knosys.2013.08.011

Banati, H., & Bajaj, M. (2012). Promoting products online using firefly algorithm. In *2012 12th International Conference on Intelligent Systems Design and Applications (ISDA)* (pp. 580-585). IEEE. 10.1109/ISDA.2012.6416602

Basari, A. S. H., Hussin, B., Ananta, I. G. P., & Zeniarja, J. (2013). Opinion mining of movie review using hybrid method of support vector machine and particle swarm optimization. *Procedia Engineering*, *53*, 453–462. doi:10.1016/j.proeng.2013.02.059

Bhonde, S. B., & Prasad, J. R. (2015). Sentiment Analysis-Methods, Applications & Challenges. *International Journal of Electronics Communication and Computer Engineering*, *6*(6), 634.

Brindha, G. R., & Santhi, B. (2012). A novel opinion mining technique for product review based on preferences. *Research Journal of Applied Sciences, Engineering and Technology*, *4*(23), 5084–5088.

Buche, A., Chandak, D., & Zadgaonkar, A. (2013). Opinion mining and analysis: A survey. *International Journal on Natural Language Computing*, *2*(3), 40–48. doi:10.5121/ijnlc.2013.2304

Chandrakala, S., & Sindhu, C. (2012). *Opinion Mining and sentiment classification asurvey*. ICTACT Journal on Soft Computing.

Chaudhari, M., & Govilkar, S. (2015). A survey of machine learning techniques for sentiment classification. *International Journal on Computational Science & Applications*, *5*(3), 13–23. doi:10.5121/ijcsa.2015.5302

Cho, S. W., Cha, M. S., Kim, S. Y., Song, J. C., & Sohn, K. A. (2014). Investigating temporal and spatial trends of brand images using twitter opinion mining. *International Conference on Information Science & Applications (ICISA),* 1-4. 10.1109/ICISA.2014.6847417

Choi, J., Kim, D., Kim, S., Lee, J., Lim, S., Lee, S., & Kang, J. (2012). Consento: a new framework for opinion based entity search and summarization. *Proceedings of the 21st ACM international conference on Information and knowledge management*, 1935-1939. 10.1145/2396761.2398547

Farra, N., Challita, E., Assi, R. A., & Hajj, H. (2010). Sentence-level and document-level sentiment mining for Arabic texts. *IEEE International Conference on in Data Mining Workshops (ICDMW),* 1114-1119. 10.1109/ICDMW.2010.95

Liu, B. (2012). Sentiment analysis and opinion mining. *Synthesis Lectures on Human Language Technologies*, *5*(1), 1–167. doi:10.1007/978-3-031-02145-9

Padmaja, S., & Fatima, S. S. (2013). Opinion Mining and Sentiment Analysis–An Assessment of Peoples' Belief: A Survey/ *International Journal of Adhoc. Sensor & Uboquitos Computing*, *4*(1), 21.

Seerat, B., & Azam, F. (2012). Opinion mining: Issues and challenges (a survey). *International Journal of Computer Applications*, *49*(9), 42–51. doi:10.5120/7658-0762

Sharma, A., & Dey, S. (2012). Performance investigation of feature selection methods and sentiment lexicons for sentiment analysis. *IJCA Special Issue on Advanced Computing and Communication Technologies for HPC Applications*, *3*, 15–20.

Sharma, N. R., & Chitre, V. D. (2014). Opinion mining, analysis and its challenges. *International Journal of Innovations & Advancement in Computer Science*, *3*(1), 59–65.

Singh, P. K., & Husain, M. S. (2014). Methodological study of opinion mining and sentiment analysis techniques. *International Journal of Soft Computing*, *5*(1), 11–21. doi:10.5121/ijsc.2014.5102

Vinodhini, G., & Chandrasekaran, R. M. (2012). Sentiment analysis and opinion mining: A survey. *International Journal (Toronto, Ont.)*, *2*(6).

Chapter 2
Swarm Intelligence-Empowered Bug Prediction Strategy for Decision Support in Software Defect Prediction

Medhunhashini D. R.
Sri Krishna Arts and Science College, India

Jeen Marseline K. S.
Sri Krishna Arts and Science College, India

ABSTRACT

Swarm intelligence is inherent in many living things and is inspiring new ways of thinking among computer scientists. Scientists from all walks of life including software corporates are interested in it because of its ties to collective intelligence behaviour. Bugs are an expensive and quality killer in software development. The development of DP models was driven by the critical need to predict defects early on. Classifying modules as either defect-prone or non-defect-prone relies heavily on machine learning algorithms. Improving software quality relies on defect prediction. SI improves the accuracy and efficacy of bug predictions by modelling their actions after the social group behaviour of insect colonies. The objective of this chapter is to outline swarm intelligence-based bug prediction in order to assist software engineers and QA teams with increased accuracy.

1. INTRODUCTION

The success of any software application depends on making sure the quality has not been compromised in any way. Accomplishing quality requires a rigorous defect prediction mechanism. The continuous growth of the software features and its changing nature it makes the prediction challenging with traditional software defect prediction models. Software development is a complex procedure that raises bugs at the final stage making it the most pervasive part. These defects may jeopardize system functionality

DOI: 10.4018/979-8-3693-2073-0.ch002

or even put users' security at risk, among other serious consequences. The intricacy of defect prediction is increased by the dynamic nature of software systems, changing requirements, and frequent updated (Guo et al., 2023).

1.1 Software Engineering

The complex field of software engineering starts with a thorough examination of requirements, which is followed by stakeholder involvement in defining features and limitations. The software's architecture and structure are described in a high-level system design. The coding process takes this idea and turns it into code that can be executed by using languages such as Python or Java. Subsequently, comprehensive testing is conducted, including unit, integration, and system testing, to detect and fix errors and guarantee conformity with predetermined standards. The software is released for use after successful testing, and it is essential to perform continuing maintenance to fix bugs, add upgrades, and adjust to new requirements. Agile methodologies are commonly used in modern software engineering (Butt et al., 2023). These methodologies stress collaborative and iterative development, and they include practices such as continuous integration/deployment, documentation, security considerations, and version control systems like Git. Software systems that are dependable, scalable, and of high quality can be more easily created when team members effectively communicate, use collaboration tools, and follow best practices (Pereira et al., 2021).

1.2 Software Quality

The word "software quality" refers to the overall level of perfection of a piece of software, which is dependent on a number of factors. Software quality is a reflection of how effectively a software system satisfies the defined criteria and the expectations of its users. Structural quality is concerned with the inner workings of the system and its architecture, with an emphasis on things like scalability, maintainability, and modularity, whereas functional quality is concerned with how well the system does its designated functions. Overall quality is greatly influenced by non-functional elements like as performance, reliability, and security. These aspects guarantee that the program runs well in all kinds of situations. Software quality is heavily dependent on the development process, making it imperative to follow best practices, code standards, and thorough testing procedures (Prabha & Shivakumar, 2020).

There are many steps in the Software Development Life Cycle (SDLC) that must be carefully attended to to maintain quality standards. These steps include requirements analysis, design, coding, testing, and deployment. Unit, integration, system, and user acceptance testing are all parts of rigorous testing that help find and fix bugs so the product works as it should. Automated testing, code reviews, and routine inspections are all examples of continuous quality assurance procedures that help find and avoid errors early on. Maintenance, upgrades, and adaptation to changing requirements are also part of quality assurance, which goes beyond development. Because the perceived value of software is heavily influenced by factors like an easy-to-navigate interface and the capacity to meet or surpass expectations, customer satisfaction is a crucial criterion for assessing software quality. By including continuous improvement and feedback loops, which are common in agile approaches, developers can respond quickly to changing requirements and user needs, which in turn enhances software quality. In the end, achieving software quality isn't a one-and-done deal; it's a continuous process that calls for a comprehensive strategy that includes technical prowess, following best practices, extensive testing, and a commitment to satisfying user expectations through the software's lifespan (Kartha et al., 2017).

1.3 Software Defects

Software flaws, often called bugs or issues, are deficiencies in the code that cause it to behave differently than it should, which can lead to failures or malfunctions. These issues can arise at any point in the software development life cycle and can be caused by faulty design, incorrect code, or a failure to properly understand the requirements. The software engineering process revolves around finding, analysing, and fixing bugs. Imperfections in the specification could impact later phases of development if requirements phase misconceptions or omissions are not addressed. Problems with the system's architecture or user interface could creep in during the design process and cause problems later on (Zheng et al., 2021). Errors, such as those in grammar or logic, are more likely to occur during the coding phase.

The testing step which includes testing at the unit, integration, system, and user acceptance levels, is essential for finding bugs. Based on complicated connections, limited test coverage, or unexpected scenarios, problems may still persist despite these efforts. Issues that were missed during testing could manifest themselves during deployment or real use, leading to interruptions and impacting the user experience. Not all flaws are of the same type; some affect performance, security, or reliability, while others affect the system's intended operations. Depending on the software's type and the degree of the flaw, its impact might range from a little annoyance to a catastrophic failure. Tracking, prioritizing, and resolving problems is an integral part of defect management, which occurs throughout the development lifecycle (Shi et al., 2023).

Bug tracking systems and similar tools make this process easier by letting engineers work together, delegate tasks, and keep tabs on how far along the defect resolution process is. Both software quality and the idea of a software fault go hand in hand (Mauša et al., 2014). There should be fewer bugs, more resistance to error, and more robustness in different operating situations in a high-quality software product. By encouraging good development procedures and early detection, best practices like continuous integration, code reviews, and automated testing try to minimize problems. Agile development practices emphasize iterative development, which enables the rapid detection and correction of errors in reaction to evolving needs (Rosa & Jardine, 2023).

To reduce the total cost of repairing issues, the idea of shift-left testing promotes early testing in the development cycle to find and cure faults closer to their source. There will always be some bugs in software, no matter how careful you are throughout development and testing. To find and fix problems in real-world situations, continuous improvement procedures and monitoring after deployment are essential. Analytics, input from users, and error reporting methods all help with software improvement by fixing bugs that can crop up in real-world settings. Due to the intricate nature of software development, software faults are unavoidable (Cai et al., 2019; Mondal et al., 2022). To provide high-quality software that works reliably in many environments and lives up to user expectations, you need a defect management strategy that incorporates testing, collaboration, and continuous improvement approaches.

1.4 Importance of Bug Prediction

Effective bug prediction strategy is must to articulate the early identification of defects in the developmental life cycle. Several factors influence and speak about the importance of bug prediction. Foremost the unexpected bugs that appear after release may need to be fixed right away, necessitating hasty and expensive remedies. Extended periods of downtime caused by unforeseen problems or system breakdowns can negatively affect revenue and productivity. A proactive bug prediction is necessary in these scenarios (Leberruyer et al., 2023). It is less likely that important bugs will surface in the post-release phase when preventive measures are put in place in anticipation of probable concerns.

1.5 Swarm Intelligence in Software Engineering

Swarm intelligence has shown promise in some fields, and when applied to software engineering, it can solve challenging issues in novel ways. One prominent application is process optimization for software development, where swarm intelligence's decentralized and self-organizing properties complement software projects' dynamic and ever-evolving nature. Swarm intelligence techniques, like bee-inspired algorithms, ant colony optimization, and particle swarm optimization, have been used in software engineering for tasks like feature selection, software testing, and code optimization (Piotrowski et al., 2024).

Ant colony optimization has been used to optimize software project schedules, work allocation, and resource management. It is based on the foraging behavior of ants. Ant colony optimization is a useful strategy for increasing project efficiency since it resembles how developers collaborate when looking for food sources.

Inspired by the coordinated movements of fish schools and bird flocks, particle swarm optimization has been used to solve software engineering issues like feature selection in machine learning models. The swarm collectively searches the feature space to find the best subsets for training the model. Inspired by how bees forage, bee-inspired algorithms have been used in software testing to find potential flaws or weaknesses in the codebase by having the swarm take different paths through it (Alam et al., 2023).

All things considered, the incorporation of swarm intelligence into software engineering represents a change towards flexible, self-organizing, and effective methods to address difficulties in the processes of testing, optimization, and decision-making in the software development lifecycle. The investigation of swarm intelligence approaches has the potential to improve the overall efficacy and robustness of software engineering procedures as software systems get more sophisticated.

Applications of swarm intelligence in software engineering

- Project Management Optimization
- Feature Selection in Machine Learning Models
- Software Testing with Bee-Inspired Algorithms
- Code Optimization and Search Algorithms
- Dynamic Resource Allocation
- Fault Tolerance and Self-Healing Systems
- Software Maintenance and Bug Prediction
- Dynamic Code Analysis
- Potential benefits for bug prediction.

1.6 Challenges in Software Defect Prediction

Among the many difficulties in effectively finding and forecasting software faults is the inherent complexity of bug prediction in software development. One prominent issue is the frequently unbalanced distribution of bugs in datasets, which can result in biased models because the number of non-defective examples greatly exceeds the number of real bug occurrences. The dynamic nature of software projects, which is marked by regular code modifications and changing requirements, also makes it challenging to keep bug prediction models current and useful over time (Babalola et al., 2023). Another challenge is identifying and extracting pertinent features from a variety of dynamic codebases. There is noise in development data that can include false or missing information.

2. OBJECTIVE

Swarm intelligence is opposite to conventional centralized methods, and makes use of the decentralized decision-making process.SI allows collective intelligence to arise from the interactions between the individual agents, each of which usually has limited information and processing capability (Yu et al., 2022). This nature of Swarm Intelligence helps in software defect prediction to address and achieve several objectives as given below.

- Improved Prediction Accuracy
- Adaptability to Dynamic Environments
- Handling Imbalanced Data
- Dynamic Feature Selection
- Real-time Decision Support
- Enhanced Context Sensitivity
- Fostering Collaboration and Collective Intelligence

This book chapter focuses on Ant Colony Optimization which helps in real-time decision support process for software defect prediction.

3. BP: DECISION SUPPORT IN SOFTWARE DEFECT PREDICTION

BP can enhance decision-making processes by providing a probabilistic framework for assessing the likelihood of defects in software code.

3.1 Bug Prediction Framework

A bug prediction framework is a structured and methodical strategy combining different approaches to estimate the probability of defects or bugs in software systems used in real-time. These kinds of frameworks are essential for improving software quality assurance because they enable developers to anticipate problems and take proactive measures to fix them before they arise in real-world settings (Hirsch & Hofer, 2022). The key components of the proposed bug prediction framework are described below

3.2 Data Collection and Preprocessing

Collect pertinent information, such as previous problem reports, code modifications, and other project-specific data. To ensure that the data is suitable for analysis, preprocess it to address problems like missing values, outliers, and data normalization.

3.3 Feature Extraction

Determine and take out of the software development process any pertinent features or metrics that could have an impact on the likelihood of defects. Code complexity, developer experience, code churn, and previous defect history are a few examples of these characteristics.

3.4 Swarm Intelligence Integration

The developers and project stakeholders get a quick insight into potential software defects as they arise during the development lifecycle. Real-time decision support plays a critical part in the software defect prediction process. This dynamic technique incorporates swarm intelligence or other predictive models, continuously monitors code changes, and adjusts to the dynamic nature of software projects. A promising Ant Colony Optimization method is chosen for the decision support system (Sulaiman & Mustaffa, 2023; Yuan et al., 2024).

3.5 Ant Colony Optimization

An algorithm called Ant Colony Optimization (ACO) is inspired by nature and is based on how ants forage for food. This method was first presented by Marco Dorigo in the early 1990s and belongs to a larger category of algorithms called swarm intelligence. ACO has been effectively used to address several combinatorial optimization issues. The pseudocode of ACO is given as in below algorithm Table 1.

Table 1. Algorithm I: Pseudocode of ant colony optimization

```
Initialize necessary parameters and pheromone trials
while not end condition do:
Generate ant population
Calculate fitness values associated with each ant
Find best solution through selection methods
Update pheromone trial
end while
end procedure
```

The basic idea of ACO is to follow the ant trail as it leaves it nest in order to find the fastest way to get food. Ants reside in colonies. First step in their quest for food, ants begin to wander aimlessly around their nests. Numerous pathways leading from the nest to the food source are made possible by this random search. Ants take a piece of food with them on their way back, and the amount and quality of that food determine how much pheromone concentration the ants use. These pheromone trials would determine the likelihood that subsequent ants would follow a certain path to the food source. The likelihood is dependent on both the pheromone concentration and its rate of evaporation. The rate of pheromone evaporation is also a determining factor in explaining the length of each trail (Monga et al., 2022). The ant colony works phase wise

Phase 1: Every ant made it back to its nest. The surroundings do not contain any pheromones.

Phase 2: The ant colony starts its search with a half-probability along each path. Because the curved path is obviously longer, ants must spend more time on it in order to reach their food source.

Phase 3: The ants reach the food source earlier by taking the shorter path. Now it's clear that they're in a similar selection dilemma, but this time, the shorter path is provided by a pheromone trail, therefore the chances of selection are higher.

Phase 4: A higher concentration of pheromones is a direct result of more ants returning via the shorter route. The longer route has a lower chance of being selected for subsequent phases because the pheromone concentration decreases with evaporation. The shorter path is eventually used by the entire colony with a higher probability. The path is optimized.

The algorithm is designed as given with help of weighted graph. The given graph $G=(V,E)$, where V and E are the graph's edges and vertices. The analysis indicates that the ant colony (Vs) and food supply (Vd) are the two vertices, and that the two edges, $E1$ and $E2$, have lengths $L1$ and $L2$, respectively. It can be assumed that the related pheromone values, which indicate their strength, are $R1$ and $R2$, respectively, for vertices $E1$ and $E2$.The below is the expression of the initial probability of path selection between $E1$ and $E2$ for each ant as in Eq (1):

$$P_i = \frac{R_i}{R1 + R2} \quad (i=1,2,\ldots) \tag{1}$$

Choosing $E1$ is more likely when $R1>R2$ and vice versa. This shortest path Ei is used to update the pheromone value for the related path when it returns. Factors such as route length and pheromone evaporation rate inform the updating process. The following is the step to implement the update as in Eq (2):

$$R_i < -R_i + \frac{K}{L_i} \tag{2}$$

The model parameter K is used in the previous update, with $i=1$ and 2. The path length determines the update. A shorter path results in a higher addition of pheromones. The evaporation rate of pheromone is calculated as in below Eq (3):

$$R_i < - (1 - v)*R_i \tag{3}$$

to control the rate of pheromone evaporation the parameter 'v' is in the interval (0, 1]. When $i=1$ and 2 the starting point of each iteration is the ant colony, or source vertex Vs. In phase 1 the ant colony will proceed to the second, where it will seek out nourishment. The ants then make their way back to the nest, reinforcing the route they took.

3.6 Training Bug Prediction Model

Labelled training data should be used to train the chosen ML model. The model becomes adapt at recognizing patterns and correlations between features and the probability of errors. The model learns to minimize prediction errors by adjusting its parameters during training. The most out of ACO-BP model is obtained modifying its hyper parameters. The parameters learning rate, regularization, and ensemble size that had not been learnt during training but have an impact on the learning process is dealt in tuning (Rabani et al., 2023).

4. APPLICATIONS OF ACO IN SOFTWARE DEFECT PREDICTION

Software defect prediction has made use of Ant Colony Optimization (ACO)a metaheuristic approach to overcome specific obstacles and enhance the precision of prediction models. The application of the same is given in the below Table 2.

Table 2. ACO application

Metric	Problems	Applications in SDP
Feature Selection	Find the most significant features and minimizing dimensionality both depend on feature selection.	To find the subset of features that improves the model's predictive performance the most, ACO can be used to search over the space of feature subsets. Defect prediction metrics can be better identified in this way.
Parameter Tuning	For optimal performance, it is necessary to modify the hyperparameters of machine learning models used for	ACO used by one to traverse the hyperparameter space in search of the optimal parameter configuration for a specific defect prediction model. The model's performance can be optimized with this.
Data Sampling	When it comes to defect prediction it is not uncommon for the dataset to be imbalanced with more instances of non-faulty items than defective ones.	By optimizing the sample method with ACO, one can ensure that the training dataset contains an equal number of defective and non-defective cases. The defect prediction model may be able to generalize and perform better.
Instance Selection	When training a model it is crucial to choose a subset that is representative of the whole dataset and some instances may provide more useful information for defect prediction than others.	ACO is used by one to maximize the likelihood of accurately predicting defects by selecting training cases for the model based on their likelihood of contributing to such accuracy.
Ensemble Learning	Improving prediction accuracy and adaptability can be achieved by combining different models into an ensembled one.	Improving the defect prediction system's overall performance is possible with the help of ACO by optimizing the selection and weighting of individual models in an ensemble.

5. CONCLUSION

Software Defect Prediction is an essential part of software engineering. Design mistakes, coding mistakes, and misunderstandings of requirements are just a few of the many potential sources of defects that can arise during the software development life cycle. To provide high-quality software that lives up to user expectations and works consistently in a variety of situations, proactive defect management is essential. Metaheuristic methods like Ant Colony Optimization (ACO) and decision support systems like Bug Prediction System (BPS) are among the strategies that aid in the prediction and management of defects. Optimizing solutions to hard combinatorial problems has been made possible by Ant Colony Optimization, which draws inspiration from the foraging behavior of ants. Features selection, parameter tuning, and data sampling strategy optimization are all areas where ACO can be used for software fault prediction. In difficult problem areas, ACO aids software engineers in finding near-optimal solutions by emulating the collective intelligence of ants. Bug Prediction System provides a probabilistic framework to aid with software defect prediction decisions. The modeling is made possible by the ACO - BP technique, which updates forecasts when new data becomes available. With the help of adaptive learning, which BPS enables, fault predictions can be improved over time. Benefiting from an adaptive and probabilistic decision-making framework, BPS helps optimize resources and improves software development overall by measuring uncertainty (Li et al., 2022).

By effective flexibility, teamwork, and data-driven decisions, ACO and BPS both show how software engineering approaches are changing. To guarantee the dependability, safety, and efficiency of software applications, it is essential to systematically and proactively address bugs as software systems grow more intricate. Creating high-quality software that can adapt to changing industry demands and customer expectations is made possible by incorporating these sophisticated approaches into the software development life cycle. Implementing cutting-edge methods such as ACO and BPS demonstrates the industry's unwavering commitment to improving software quality and pushing software engineering forward.

REFERENCES

Alam, S., Zhao, X., Niazi, I. K., Ayub, M. S., & Khan, M. A. (2023). A comparative analysis of global optimization algorithms for surface electromyographic signal onset detection. *Decis. Anal. J.*, *8*, 100294. doi:10.1016/j.dajour.2023.100294

Babalola, S. A., Mishra, D., Dutta, S., & Murmu, N. C. (2023). In-situ workpiece perception: A key to zero-defect manufacturing in Industry 4.0 compliant job shops. *Computers in Industry*, *148*, 103891. doi:10.1016/j.compind.2023.103891

Butt, S. A., Ercan, T., Binsawad, M., Ariza-Colpas, P.-P., Diaz-Martinez, J., Piñeres-Espitia, G., De-La-Hoz-Franco, E., Melo, M. A. P., Ortega, R. M., & De-La-Hoz-Hernández, J.-D. (2023). Prediction based cost estimation technique in agile development. *Advances in Engineering Software*, *175*, 103329. doi:10.1016/j.advengsoft.2022.103329

Cai, Y., Xiao, L., Kazman, R., Mo, R., & Feng, Q. (2019). Design Rule Spaces: A New Model for Representing and Analyzing Software Architecture. *IEEE Transactions on Software Engineering*, *45*(7), 657–682. doi:10.1109/TSE.2018.2797899

Guo, J., Long, K., Yang, K., Jiang, K., Lu, L., & Wang, C. (2023). A novel prediction method for vulnerability outbreak trend. *Computers & Electrical Engineering*, *108*, 108743. doi:10.1016/j.compeleceng.2023.108743

Hirsch, T., & Hofer, B. (2022). Using textual bug reports to predict the fault category of software bugs. *Array (New York, N.Y.)*, *15*, 100189. doi:10.1016/j.array.2022.100189

Kartha, G. P., Anjali, C., Nair, R. V., & Venkateswari, S. (2017). Prediction of defect susceptibility in object Oriented Software. *2017 International Conference on Networks & Advances in Computational Technologies (NetACT)*, 467–472. 10.1109/NETACT.2017.8076817

Leberruyer, N., Bruch, J., Ahlskog, M., & Afshar, S. (2023). Toward Zero Defect Manufacturing with the support of Artificial Intelligence—Insights from an industrial application. *Computers in Industry*, *147*, 103877. doi:10.1016/j.compind.2023.103877

Li, L., Wang, B., Feng, P., Li Liu, D., He, Q., Zhang, Y., Wang, Y., Li, S., Lu, X., Yue, C., Li, Y., He, J., Feng, H., Yang, G., & Yu, Q. (2022). Developing machine learning models with multi-source environmental data to predict wheat yield in China. *Computers and Electronics in Agriculture*, *194*, 106790. doi:10.1016/j.compag.2022.106790

Mauša, G., Grbac, T. G., & Bašić, B. D. (2014). Software defect prediction with Bug-Code analyzer - A data collection tool demo. *2014 22nd International Conference on Software, Telecommunications and Computer Networks (SoftCOM)*, 425–426. 10.1109/SOFTCOM.2014.7039122

Mondal, A. K., Schneider, K. A., Roy, B., & Roy, C. K. (2022). A survey of software architectural change detection and categorization techniques. *Journal of Systems and Software*, *194*, 111505. doi:10.1016/j.jss.2022.111505

Monga, Sharma, & Sharma. (2022). A comprehensive meta-analysis of emerging swarm intelligent computing techniques and their research trend. *J. King Saud Univ. - Comput. Inf. Sci.*, *34*(10), 9622–9643. . doi:10.1016/j.jksuci.2021.11.016

Pereira, J. D., Ivaki, N., & Vieira, M. (2021). Characterizing Buffer Overflow Vulnerabilities in Large C/C++ Projects. *IEEE Access : Practical Innovations, Open Solutions*, *9*, 142879–142892. doi:10.1109/ACCESS.2021.3120349

Piotrowski, A. P., Napiorkowski, J. J., & Piotrowska, A. E. (2024). To what extent evolutionary algorithms can benefit from a longer search? *Information Sciences*, *654*, 119766. doi:10.1016/j.ins.2023.119766

Prabha, C. L., & Shivakumar, N. (2020). Software Defect Prediction Using Machine Learning Techniques. *2020 4th International Conference on Trends in Electronics and Informatics (ICOEI),* (48184), 728–733. 10.1109/ICOEI48184.2020.9142909

Rabani, S. T., Ud Din Khanday, A. M., Khan, Q. R., Hajam, U. A., Imran, A. S., & Kastrati, Z. (2023). Detecting suicidality on social media: Machine learning at rescue. *Egypt. Informatics J.*, *24*(2), 291–302. doi:10.1016/j.eij.2023.04.003

Rosa, W., & Jardine, S. (2023). Data-driven agile software cost estimation models for DHS and DoD. *Journal of Systems and Software*, *203*, 111739. doi:10.1016/j.jss.2023.111739

Shi, H., Song, Z., Bai, X., Hu, Y., Li, T., & Zhang, K. (2023). A novel digital twin model for dynamical updating and real-time mapping of local defect extension in rolling bearings. *Mechanical Systems and Signal Processing*, *193*, 110255. doi:10.1016/j.ymssp.2023.110255

Sulaiman, M. H., & Mustaffa, Z. (2023). Using the evolutionary mating algorithm for optimizing the user comfort and energy consumption in smart building. *Journal of Building Engineering*, *76*, 107139. doi:10.1016/j.jobe.2023.107139

Yu, H., Song, J., Chen, C., Heidari, A. A., Liu, J., Chen, H., Zaguia, A., & Mafarja, M. (2022). Image segmentation of Leaf Spot Diseases on Maize using multi-stage Cauchy-enabled grey wolf algorithm. *Engineering Applications of Artificial Intelligence*, *109*, 104653. doi:10.1016/j.engappai.2021.104653

Yuan, J., Liu, H.-L., & Yang, S. (2024). An adaptive parental guidance strategy and its derived indicator-based evolutionary algorithm for multi- and many-objective optimization. *Swarm and Evolutionary Computation*, *84*, 101449. doi:10.1016/j.swevo.2023.101449

Zheng, W., Tan, L., & Liu, C. (2021). Software Defect Prediction Method Based on Transformer Model. *2021 IEEE International Conference on Artificial Intelligence and Computer Applications (ICAICA)*, 670–674. 10.1109/ICAICA52286.2021.9498179

Chapter 3
Genetic Algorithms for Decision Optimization

Sakshi Patni
Gachon University, South Korea

Bharti Sharma
MMDU, India

ABSTRACT

This chapter thoroughly explores the versatile applications of genetic algorithms (GAs) in decision optimization across diverse domains. GAs, inspired by natural selection, adeptly navigate solution spaces, adapting to complex objectives and revealing near-optimal solutions. The exploration encompasses theoretical foundations, customizations for decision optimization, and a variety of GA algorithms demonstrated through real-world case studies, showcasing their adaptability. The GA process iteratively evolves populations, incorporating multiple tailored algorithms that address conflicting objectives and intricate variables. GAs, positioned as optimization keys, redefine decision-making for complex problems where traditional methods fall short. The chapter provides a concise yet comprehensive overview, offering valuable insights into the nuanced applications of GA algorithms in decision optimization.

1. INTRODUCTION

Scientist of various fields are looking forward towards nature to find out the solution of complex problems. The process of natural selection, the combination of alleles at specific locations of chromosomes, DNA sequences, the genetic makeup of an organism and the way genes are organized at specific locations on chromosomes and mutation diversity have attracted scientists from various fields to see solutions to complex problems in their domains. Computer science is no exception (Gen & Lin, 2023). This chapter will enhance an understanding of various biological concepts of genetics and their conversion into genetic algorithms to solve problems of optimization, cloud and machine scheduling, game playing, robotics, and other fields. The genetic makeup or "genetic constitution" is the genetic information of an organism. It includes the entire set of genes, including both the expressed (coding) and non-expressed

DOI: 10.4018/979-8-3693-2073-0.ch003

(non-coding) regions of an organism's DNA. The organism's traits, characteristics, and overall functioning entirely depend on the genetic constitution (Polo-Mendoza et al., 2023). The important key points related to genetic constitution are genes and chromosomes, alleles, mutation, and inheritance. Genes are segments of DNA responsible for specific traits. Their organization on chromosomes determines the genetic constitution of an organism. Alleles are different versions of a gene that can exist at a specific location on a chromosome. The combination of alleles at various gene loci contributes to an organism's genetic diversity and determines its traits (Jia et al., 2023). The genetic constitution is inherited from one generation to the next through reproduction. Changes in genetic material, known as mutations, can alter the genetic constitution. Mutations can occur spontaneously or be induced by external factors. They contribute to the evolution of species over time. Genetic algorithms (GAs) represent optimization and search techniques inspired by principles found in natural selection and genetics. Part of the broader category of evolutionary algorithms, these computational models draw inspiration from biological evolution. Genetic algorithms prove valuable in approximating solutions for optimization and search challenges, especially in cases where conventional methods may prove impractical or inefficient (Bülbül, 2023). The optimization problem's solutions are encoded as chromosomes, typically portrayed as binary strings (0s and 1s). Each chromosome denotes a potential solution, and selection is based on fitness, gauging how effectively a solution addresses the problem. Those with higher fitness are more likely to be chosen. Pairs of selected solutions (parents) undergo crossover or recombination, where parts of their chromosomes are exchanged to create new offspring (solutions) (Fathi et al., 2021; Mahjoob et al., 2022). The new offspring (solutions) replace some of the less fit individuals in the population. The process continues for a set number of generations or until a termination condition (the best possible solution) is met.

2. GENETIC ALGORITHM AND ITS TYPES

The primary role of genetic algorithms encompasses optimization, search and exploration, parallelism, distributed computing, handling complex and nonlinear problems, parameter optimization, feature selection, and evolutionary robotics. Genetic algorithms prove valuable in finding optimal solutions to intricate problems where traditional methods may prove impractical or inefficient. Such problems often involve a vast search space, non-linearity, and multiple constraints. Genetic algorithms excel in exploring extensive solution spaces by generating and evaluating a population of potential solutions. This capability to traverse widely across the solution space proves particularly beneficial in addressing complex and multimodal problems (Alejo-Reyes et al., 2020).

Genetic algorithms inherently support parallelization. Multiple candidate solutions can be evaluated simultaneously, resulting in the efficient use of parallel and distributed computing resources. Genetic algorithms adeptly handle nonlinear, non-continuous problems with multiple objectives. They are well-suited for scenarios where the relationship between variables is not well-defined or dynamically changes. Genetic algorithms are also effective in parameter tuning, optimizing parameters of algorithms or models. For instance, they find application in optimizing hyperparameters of machine learning models to enhance performance. In the field of evolutionary robotics, genetic algorithms play a crucial role in evolving the structure and behavior of robots across successive generations, leading to the development of robots with improved performance in specific tasks. Genetic algorithms are employed to evolve strategies for playing games, encompassing board games, video games, and simulations where an optimal strategy needs development. Genetic algorithms prove useful in solving combinatorial optimization problems, where the goal is to find the best combination of elements from a finite set. They are applied in designing algorithms, evolving solutions that optimize the performance of algorithms in specific problem domains. In essence, genetic algorithms offer a flexible and robust approach to solving complex problems by mimicking the process of natural selection and evolution to iteratively improve and refine solutions over successive generations. Genetic algorithms can be categorized based on their applications and specific characteristics. Examples of common categories include:

(i) **Standard Genetic Algorithms (SGA):** Follows fundamental genetic algorithm principles, including selection, crossover, and mutation operations.
(ii) **Binary Genetic Algorithm**: Represents each gene as a binary value (0 or 1).
(iii) **Real-valued Genetic Algorithm (ECGA):** Deals with individuals represented by real-valued parameters, suitable for continuous optimization problems.
(iv) **Permutation Genetic Algorithms**: Designed for problems where the solution involves arranging a set of elements in a specific order, as seen in the traveling salesman problem or job scheduling.
(v) **Parallel Genetic Algorithms**: Distribute the evaluation of individuals and the evolution process across multiple processors or threads, facilitating faster convergence and handling larger problem spaces.
(vi) **Steady-State Genetic Algorithm**: Maintains a constant population size, replacing only a subset of the population in each generation.
(vii) **Adaptive Genetic Algorithms**: Dynamically adjust parameters during the optimization process based on the algorithm's performance and progress.
(viii) **Self-Adaptive Genetic Algorithms**: Evolve not only solutions to the problem but also the parameters of the genetic algorithm itself over time.
(ix) **Island Model**: Utilizes multiple subpopulations (islands) evolving independently with occasional migration of individuals between them, improving exploration and exploiting local optima.
(x) **Hybrid Genetic Algorithms**: Combine genetic algorithms with other optimization or machine learning techniques to enhance performance, often combining GAs with local search methods or other evolutionary algorithms.
(xi) **Cultural Algorithms**: Integrate cultural knowledge into the evolutionary process by incorporating a belief space that guides evolution for a more informed search.

These categories underscore the adaptability and versatility of genetic algorithms, making them applicable to a broad spectrum of optimization and search problems across diverse domains. The specific type of genetic algorithm chosen depends on the nature of the problem being addressed.

3. WORKING OF GENETIC ALGORITHM IN DECISION OPTIMIZATION

In genetic algorithms, "genes" serve as fundamental units of information, encoding various traits or characteristics within a population's potential solutions. These algorithms, inspired by natural selection and genetics, optimize solutions by mimicking evolutionary processes. Within the genetic algorithm framework, a "chromosome" embodies a potential solution, comprising individual genes that correspond to specific parameters or features. Genes can assume diverse values, and the combination within a chromosome represents a unique candidate solution to the given problem. Genetic algorithms operate by considering the best solutions, treating them as parents to generate the first generation or F1 progeny (Klinmalee et al., 2020). While F1 progeny may share similarities with their parents, the second generation or F2 Progeny must exhibit solutions distinct from the F1 generation, adhering to Mendel's Law of Inheritance. This process introduces the possibility of expressing previously discarded, recessive traits. Through genetic crossover, an un-inherited error known as mutation occurs, ensuring diversity in subsequent generations. The core operations in genetic algorithms involve manipulating and evolving these genes. Genetic operators like crossover (recombination) and mutation facilitate the creation of new solutions by combining or modifying existing genes. The likelihood of a solution's genes being passed on to the next generation is determined by its fitness, representing how effectively it addresses the problem's objective. Drawing inspiration from the principles of crossover and mutation, genetic algorithms continually iterate, with each generation reproducing offspring and evolving the overall solution. This evolutionary approach ensures the algorithm's adaptability and prevents premature convergence, enhancing the generality and effectiveness of the solutions obtained.

Figure 1. Working of genetic algorithm

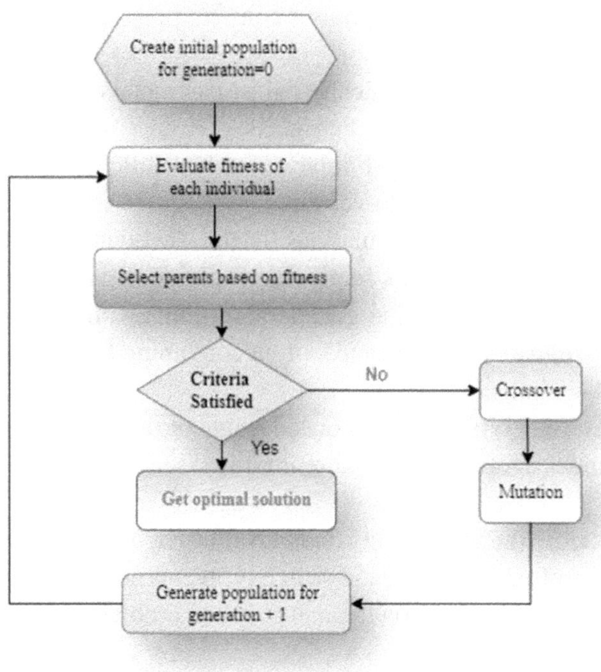

3.1 Initiate the Population

Let us first understand what population means in GA.

- **Population (or Generation)**: It is a set of all possible solutions (candidate solutions) to initiate the search. GA will iterate over multiple generations until it finds an optimized solution.

- **Chromosome**: It represents one particular(candidate) solution present in the population.
- **Gene**: It is a single element of the decision variable that contains the value(allele) and position(locus) of the particular Chromosome.

Figure 2. Offspring

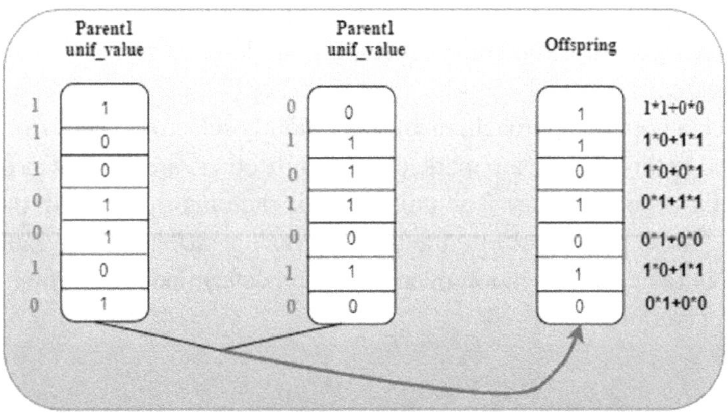

The initial generation is typically initialized randomly (Random Initialization) as the genetic algorithm commences. This involves creating a population through random generation, with the population's size influenced by the problem's characteristics and determined by the decision variable's size. The population size remains constant across all generations. Alternatively, there is an option for initiating the population using a known heuristic for the problem (Heuristic Initialization). However, this approach is generally discouraged due to the potential outcome of generating a population with similar solutions and minimal diversity.

3.2 Evaluate the Fitness

The fitness function assesses the suitability of a candidate solution for the defined objective, assigning a probability value as a fitness score for each individual. This score determines the likelihood of an individual being chosen for reproduction. While the fitness function is akin to an objective function, in complex problems with multiple objectives and constraints, it may be uniquely designed. A well-constructed fitness function should possess the following attributes:

- Efficiency: The fitness function should be computationally efficient.
- Quantification: It must quantitatively measure the fitness of a given solution or the potential for generating fit individuals from that solution.
- Parent Selection is the pivotal process of identifying the fittest solution within a population for the reproduction of the next generation of solutions. This process ensures that favorable traits are naturally passed on. In the initial generation (generation 0), parents are selected from the initiated population. The selection of parents is crucial, driving individuals toward superior and fitter solutions and contributing to algorithm convergence. Maintaining good diversity within the population is a key characteristic of selected parents. Various methods exist for parent selection.

3.3 Crossover

Crossover is a fundamental mechanism in Genetic Algorithms (GAs) responsible for generating new offspring. Given the random nature of GAs, the quantity of genes inherited from each parent is randomly determined. This involves overlapping or mixing certain genes from both parent chromosomes to create a new generation. The resulting offspring inherits characteristics from both parents, with the distribution of genes varying—sometimes half from one parent and half from the other, with potential variations in this percentage. Various methods, including single-point crossover, double-point crossover, and uniform crossover, exist.

Uniform crossover, a popular approach, involves randomly selecting genes from the parent chromosome. Genes inherited in this process are marked as 1, while others are marked as 0, based on a uniform distribution (referred to as unif_value). The unif_value is then multiplied with the gene value of each parent chromosome. These parent selection and crossover operations iterate multiple times until the number of solutions in the next generation matches the predetermined population size, which remains constant across all generations.

Figure 3. Offspring

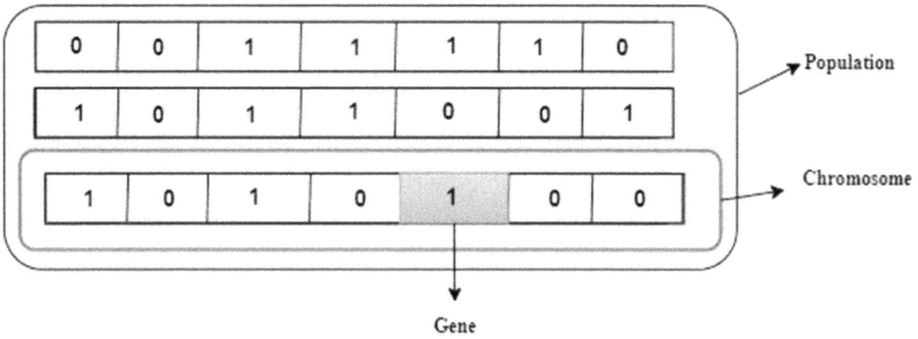

Mutation plays a crucial role in introducing novel characteristics into genes, thereby preserving diversity within the population and averting premature convergence in the process. Unlike crossover, which is primarily concerned with "exploitation" of the search space, mutation is integral to the "exploration" aspect of the Genetic Algorithm (GA), contributing to the algorithm's convergence.

Termination Criteria: The GA concludes its execution when it achieves convergence, meaning it no longer generates offspring significantly different from earlier generations. Common termination conditions include:

- No fitness improvement in the population for the next X iterations.
- Attainment of the optimal or pre-defined value in the objective function.
- Completion of the maximum specified number of generations.

4. ADVANTAGES/DISADVANTAGES OF GENETIC ALGORITHM

Genetic Algorithms (GAs) demonstrate a notable capacity to swiftly provide satisfactory solutions in large-scale problems where traditional algorithms might falter. Offering a generic framework for addressing complex optimization challenges, GA brings several advantages:

a) Overcoming Traditional Algorithm Limitations: Traditional optimization algorithms, relying on derivatives for optimization in differentiable functions, face challenges in complex, non-convex scenarios. GAs, in contrast, do not require derivatives and prove effective in problems with multiple peaks and valleys, offering a robust solution approach (Kurade & Latpate, 2021; Tan et al., 2024).
b) Parallelization Feasibility: GAs lend themselves to easy parallelization, facilitating efficient computation and resource utilization.
c) Speed and Exploration Efficiency: GAs demonstrate speed and the ability to explore the search space rapidly, making them suitable for time-sensitive optimization tasks.
d) Handling Multiple Objectives: GA accommodates multiple complex optimization objectives simultaneously, providing a versatile solution to multifaceted problems.

Limitations:

a) Convergence Challenges: Proper implementation is crucial, as GAs might not converge to an optimal solution if not executed with care.
b) Computational Intensity: Repeated calculation of the fitness function can lead to computational expenses in GA implementations.
c) Handling Constraints: GAs might face challenges with hard constraints, necessitating their representation as penalties in the objective function. Penalty functions are employed to reduce the fitness of infeasible solutions, aligning their fitness with the degree of constraint violation or distance from the feasible region.

4.1. Use of Genetic Algorithm in Inventory Optimization

Define Inventory problem

An inventory problem encompasses the intricate challenges of overseeing the stock of goods or materials within a business, necessitating strategic decisions on quantity, timing, and location to meet customer demand efficiently (Konak et al., 2024). A comprehensive approach to addressing these challenges involves recognizing the diverse factors influencing inventory management within a business. One effective strategy is to employ GAs, optimization techniques inspired by natural selection and genetics. Let's delve into how GAs can be associated with the general methods of defining and solving inventory problems:

1. **Demand Uncertainty:**
    - **Inventory Problem**: Fluctuations in demand can lead to overstocking or stockouts, impacting operational efficiency.

- **Genetic Algorithm Perspective**: GAs can dynamically adapt to uncertain demand patterns by evolving solutions over generations. Robustness in solution space allows for effective handling of varying demand scenarios.

2. **Supply Chain Variability:**
   - **Inventory Problem**: Unpredictable changes in the supply chain, including delays or disruptions, can disrupt inventory levels.
   - **Genetic Algorithm Perspective**: GAs excel in optimizing solutions under dynamic conditions. They can evolve inventory strategies that consider supply chain variability, ensuring adaptability and resilience.
3. **Ordering and Replenishment Policies:**
   - **Inventory Problem**: Poorly defined or outdated ordering policies can lead to suboptimal inventory levels.
   - **Genetic Algorithm Perspective**: GAs can optimize decision variables related to ordering policies, considering constraints and objectives. This allows for the discovery of effective replenishment strategies.
4. **Storage and Holding Costs:**
   - **Inventory Problem**: High storage costs and holding costs can erode profitability if not managed efficiently.
   - **Genetic Algorithm Perspective**: GAs can optimize inventory levels by considering cost parameters. The algorithm can explore the solution space to find a balance that minimizes holding costs while meeting demand requirements.

In the context of mathematics and operations research, inventory problems are often formulated using mathematical models to optimize decision-making related to inventory management. The key components involved in defining inventory problems mathematically include variables, constraints, and an objective function. If we have a problem in hand then by applying a number of constraints on the objective function f(x) like equality constraint, inequality constraints or applying lower bond or upper bond to achieve the desired points. *Minimize f(x)*

Subject to:

g(x) = 0 (equality constraint)

h(x) <= 0 (inequality constraint)

lb <= x <= ub (lb: lower bound, ub): upper bond

4.2 EOQ Model

The Economic Order Quantity (EOQ) model stands as a classical inventory management approach, meticulously designed to identify the optimal order quantity that minimizes the overall cost incurred in ordering and holding inventory (Darmawan, 2024; Delshad et al., 2024). The EOQ formula, derived from the delicate trade-off between ordering costs and holding costs, is expressed as follows:

Q∗=2DS/H
Q* is the economic order quantity
D is the annual demand
S is the ordering cost per order
H is the holding cost per unit per year

As a deterministic model, the EOQ model doesn't incorporate evolutionary algorithms like genetic algorithms. Instead, it relies on mathematical optimization techniques, particularly calculus and algebra. The primary goal of the EOQ model is to pinpoint the order quantity that strikes a balance between the costs associated with holding inventory and initiating orders.

5. IMPLEMENTATION FOR INVENTORY PROBLEM USING GA

In the realm of inventory management, finding an optimal balance between predicted demand, actual demand, and various constraints is crucial for efficient operations. The implemented Genetic Algorithm leverages the capabilities of the R programming language to address this challenge. The Genetic Algorithm implementation in R presents a comprehensive approach to inventory optimization. By combining predictive modeling, constraint handling, parallel processing, and experimental evaluation, the algorithm provides a robust and adaptable solution for addressing the complexities of inventory management.

5.1 Simulation

In both the GA and EOQ models, the total cost is a crucial metric depicted on the y-axis. This comprehensive cost encompasses holding costs, ordering costs, and potentially other relevant expenses. The decision variable common to both GA and EOQ is the order quantity, representing the quantity of items to be procured each time an order is placed. In the EOQ model, the total cost forms a U-shaped curve with the order quantity on the x-axis. At a specific point on this curve, the total cost is minimized, and this quantity is known as the EOQ. The curve indicates a range where the total cost is relatively stable around the EOQ. Conversely, the GA approach yields multiple points on the graph, each representing a potential economic order quantity. The x-axis denotes order quantities, and the y-axis signifies corresponding costs. Notably, the GA results may exhibit a wider range of costs for a given order quantity. For instance, at an order quantity of 10, the costs may vary significantly from approximately 150 to 5. This variability illustrates the versatility of solutions provided by the GA, accommodating diverse cost scenarios. The GA optimization is configured to determine optimal order quantities for three products, though it can be adapted for a different number of products. The objective is to minimize the total cost. The outcome of the GA includes not only the optimal order quantities but also the maximum total cost observed during the optimization process. Comparatively, the EOQ model tends to exhibit a narrower range of costs around the EOQ, typically varying between 60 and 100 for a given order quantity. In essence, while the EOQ model converges on a single optimal solution, the GA explores a broader solution space, offering versatility in addressing various cost scenarios associated with different order quantities. Fig 4 shows the difference between two methods ECQ and GA.

Figure 4. Optimization between various cost and orders

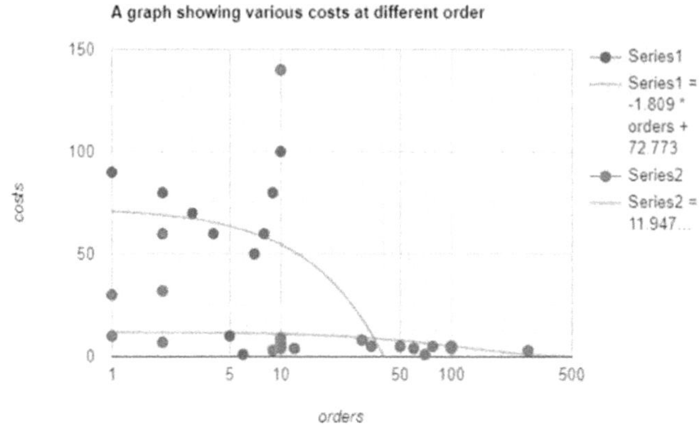

6. CONCLUSION

In conclusion, the selection between the EOQ model and GAs is contingent on the specific characteristics of the inventory management problem. The EOQ model suits well-defined scenarios with stable parameters and clear mathematical representations. In contrast, GAs thrive in dynamic, complex situations lacking precise formulations, accommodating multiple objectives. Understanding the fundamental principles of Genetic Algorithms, including their adaptability, exploration of diverse solution spaces, and applicability to real-world challenges, is essential for making informed choices in addressing the complexities of inventory management. The decision should be driven by a nuanced consideration of the problem's characteristics and the strengths of each approach.

REFERENCES

Alejo-Reyes, Mendoza, & Olivares-Benitez. (2020). Inventory replenishment decision model for the supplier selection problem using metaheuristic algorithms. *Openaire*.

Bülbül, M. A. (2023). Optimization of artificial neural network structure and hyperparameters in hybrid model by genetic algorithm: iOS–android application for breast cancer diagnosis/prediction. *The Journal of Supercomputing*, 1–21.

Darmawan, A. (2024). Evaluating proactive and reactive strategies in supply chain network design with coordinated inventory control in the presence of disruptions. *Journal of Industrial and Production Engineering,* 1-17.

Delshad, M. M., Chobar, A. P., Ghasemi, P., & Jafari, D. (2024). Efficient Humanitarian Logistics: Multi-Commodity Location–Inventory Model Incorporating Demand Probability and Consumption Coefficients. *Logistics*, *8*(1), 9. doi:10.3390/logistics8010009

Fathi, M., Khakifirooz, M., Diabat, A., & Chen, H. (2021). An integrated queuing-stochastic optimization hybrid Genetic Algorithm for a location-inventory supply chain network. *International Journal of Production Economics*, *237*, 108139. doi:10.1016/j.ijpe.2021.108139

Gen, M., & Lin, L. (2023). Genetic algorithms and their applications. In *Springer handbook of engineering statistics* (pp. 635–674). Springer London. doi:10.1007/978-1-4471-7503-2_33

Jia, X., Zhou, X., Bao, J., Zhai, G., & Yan, R. (2023). Fusion Swarm-Intelligence-Based Decision Optimization for Energy-Efficient Train-Stopping Schemes. *Applied Sciences (Basel, Switzerland)*, *13*(3), 1497. doi:10.3390/app13031497

Klinmalee, S., Naenna, T., & Woarawichai, C. (2020). Application of a genetic algorithm for multi-item inventory lot-sizing with supplier selection under quantity discount and lead time. *International Journal of Operational Research*, *38*(3), 403–421. doi:10.1504/IJOR.2020.107540

Konak, F., Bülbül, M. A., & Türkoğlu, D. (2024). Feature Selection and Hyperparameters Optimization Employing a Hybrid Model Based on Genetic Algorithm and Artificial Neural Network: Forecasting Dividend Payout Ratio. *Computational Economics*, 1–21. doi:10.1007/s10614-023-10530-z

Kurade, S. S., & Latpate, R. (2021). Demand and deterioration of items per unit time inventory models with shortages using genetic algorithm. *Journal of Management Analytics*, *8*(3), 502–529. doi:10.1080/23270012.2020.1829113

Mahjoob, M., Fazeli, S. S., Milanlouei, S., Tavassoli, L. S., & Mirmozaffari, M. (2022). A modified adaptive genetic algorithm for multi-product multi-period inventory routing problem. *Sustainable Operations and Computers*, *3*, 1–9. doi:10.1016/j.susoc.2021.08.002

Polo-Mendoza, R., Martinez-Arguelles, G., & Penabaena-Niebles, R. (2023). A multi-objective optimization based on genetic algorithms for the sustainable design of Warm Mix Asphalt (WMA). *The International Journal of Pavement Engineering*, *24*(2), 2074417. doi:10.1080/10298436.2022.2074417

Tan, N. D., Kim, H.-S., Le Ngoc, B. L., Nguyen, D. A., & You, S.-S. (2024). Optimization and inventory management under stochastic demand using metaheuristic algorithm. *PLoS One*, *19*(1), e0286433. doi:10.1371/journal.pone.0286433 PMID:38180984

Chapter 4
Acute Analysis of Bioinspired Optimization Algorithms for Diabetic Debrecen

Suchitra B.
https://orcid.org/0000-0001-6692-5098
Sri Krishna Arts and Science College, India

Valarmathi V.
Sri Krishna Arts and Science College, India

ABSTRACT

Nature has all healing powers. Same way, nature is a basis of spur for resolving rigid and multifaceted problems Bio-inspired represents the parasol of diverse studies of computer science, mathematics, and biology in the last years. Bioinspired optmization algorithm is a developing approach that is based on the philosophies and motivation of the biological evolution of nature to develop new and robust challenging techniques. Biologically enthused computing and optimization is a foremost subclass of natural computation. This chapter presents a life-threatening survey of bio-inspired optimization techniques. Diabetic long-lasting disease upsets several organs of human body including the retina. Diabetic retinopathy datasets are taken and machine learning techniques are used to determine the detection of DR (diabetic retinopathy). Feature extraction and classification phases are involved, optimal results for composite problem are found, and correctness is predicted by using the GA.

1. INTRODUCTION

Retinopathy became a common problem in today's world. Its affects the eye nerve and sometimes lead to blindness. Common symptoms are blurred vision. Patients who have high power also face the issue. Retionopathy actually caused by damaging the blood vessel.

DOI: 10.4018/979-8-3693-2073-0.ch004

Retionopathy, will start from no symptoms, and move towards mild symptoms. Diabetic Retinopathy will occur with the patients whose sugar level is increased and belong to type 1 and type 2 diabetics.

Normal and Diabetic Images

Figure 1. Source taken from Google images

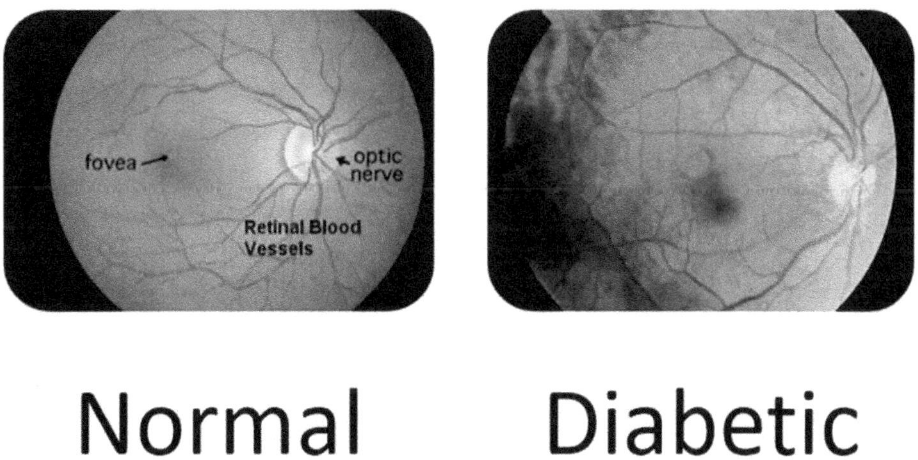

Symptoms of Diabetic Retinopathy

There are many symptoms for diabetic retinopathy.Each patient has never experience the symptoms at first stage. Later, they will found floaters in the eye. Floaters can be small in number, or it can be fly like or ring like which will be surrounded by eyes[4]. People Start experiencing the floaters in the eyes. Vision loss will have suddenly if they not treating it. Some will experience Central vision to become black color and some people will face difficulty in seeing night times

2. RELATED WORKS

Sakthi KarthiDurai and Benadict Raja(2003) proposed the method for an programmed detection of DR with more correctness, fewer recall and compact computation time.

Ahmed Hamza Azad and Aboul-Ella Hassaanien (2016) proposes the method and strongly state about the classification complexity, time and maximizes its accuracy. The primary detection can be accomplished by computerized dissection of blood vessels in retinal images which is two-class classification problem; vessel-like or non-vessel.

Qingqing Xu et al.(2020) conduct limited trainings conveyed predictive prototypes for diabetic retinopathy, nephropathy and neuropathy using ML specifically for T1D patients

Victor Vives and Daniel Ruiz-Fernandez (2021) showed in their previous work that .CNN with synaptic meta plasticity are appropriate for primary detection of diabetic retinopathy due to their wanton conjunction rate, training ease and high enactment.

Figure 2. Symptoms of diabetic retinopathy

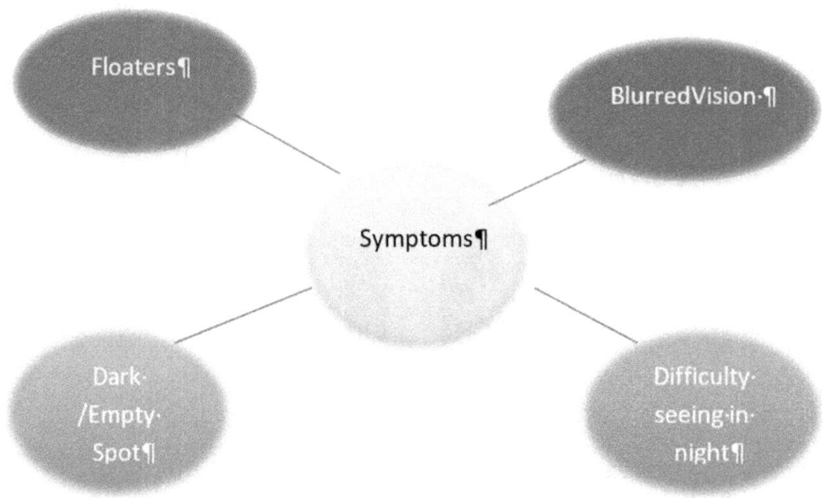

Jo-Hsuan Wu et al. (2021) did a study to methodically scrutinize the overall indicative precision of ML in spotting DR of diverse classes constructed on color fundus photographs and to define the state-of-the-art ML approach.

Sauad Larabi et al. (2021) provides perceptions on how these processes are improved to image-dissection combinatorial hitches, which assist scholars to start the first hands-on application. It also converses their locale parameters and the vastly used systems such as PSO, GA, ACO, and ABC.

MayoClini (2023) talks about the disease, how the people will suffer, what are the stages that we need to consider. There is no cure or medicine till now . Researches are keep on doing researchers based on retina and optic nerve. If optic nerve is damaged,there is no alter patient has to be blind for future.

Suneetha et al. (2023) suggested a model for predicting retinal diseases and also say about the segmentation of images .

3. METHODOLOGY

Diabetic Retinopathy can be classified as 4 types. They are:

1. Mild non-profilerative: In this, small blood vessels will be bulged.
2. Moderate non-proliferative retinopathy: Blocking of retina with small amount.
3. Severe non-proliferative retinopathy: In this, clot will happen, bleeding in side the veins and there show many abnormalities which lead to poor.
4. Proliferative retinopathy: This is the advanced stage and new blood vessels will be trigger.

All these are used in the dataset and various algorithms are used to classify, extract the feature and optimization is done using Cat Optimization Technique.

The Proposed Model Will Have Processed to Following Steps

a. Dataset

In this proposed model, the datasets are taken from UCI Repository. The dataset consists of 1151 instances and attributes of 19. The Instances is based on Medical Patients. It was well-known dataset provided by University of Debrecan. Diabetic retinopathy was diagnosed by using a binary result function.

b. Data Preprocessing

Data can be gathered from different patients. When data are combined there may be a chance of missing value. This paper accumulates different forms of data, and accuracy can be achieved so that early prediction can be done.

c. Feature Extraction

Feature Extraction can be done by ICA. It doesn't emphasis on the issue of inconsistency among data points. Data can be non-Guassain distribution.

d. ML Algorithms

In this paper, three type of ML algorithms are used for predicting retinopathy. Naiye Bayes, and KNN.

e. Confusion Matrix

Gauging a confusion matrix will give a clearer thoughtful of what the classification archetypal is going to do and mistake can be easily find out. true positive, true negative, false positive and false negative are examined and further metrics are used.

d. Classification

Classification are done based on people age, type of disease they have apart from diabetic and also multiple issues are facing which leads to diabetic retinopathy

e. Optimization

Bio-inspired Optimization Techniques are used to find out which algorithm suits best with the dataset and their accuracy are given.

Figure 3. Steps involved in proposed technology

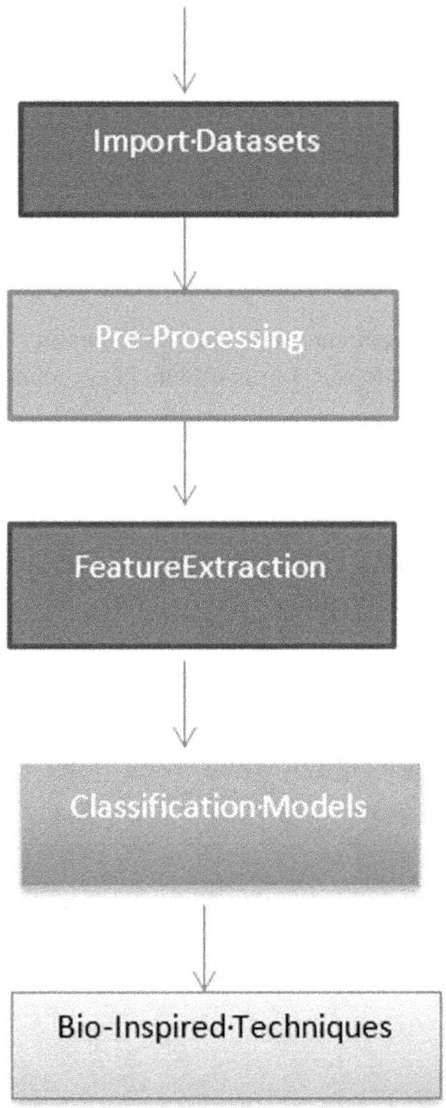

4. EXPERIMENTAL RESULTS

Consider an image of an eye which contains the pixels of points. We factorize the eye picture into two matrices, one comprising the entire eye set which can be denoted as weighted matrix such as Matrix [Weight] and other contain each pixel of the eye. This can be denoted as Matrix[S].Precise programming problem can be indicated as shown in Equation.

Such that

$$A(:, l) \approx \sum weight(:,m) + S(m,l) = weight * S(:,l) \qquad (1.1)$$

NMF can be used for feature reduction. Here, reduction can be done based on pixels of points where it indicates the floaters or any block in the retina of an eye.

t-SNE

t-SNE is another way of reducing the dimensionality. While taking OCT scan of an eye . all these can be determined in the format of 2D or 3D plane. This helps to find out where there is edema in the eye and also it specifies how much leakage of blood vessels are there, and also its specificies the acute positions in the eye. This algorithm support the randomized approach to reduce the high dimension and focus on only exact pixel points of an eye.

t-SNE find similarities in data based on pattern of data points with features, it is based on conditional probability .

NBC

Naive Bayes Classifiers (NBCs) are a traditional of probabilistic classifiers on which Bayes' theorem is pragmatic with conventions about objectivity between features. They are highly mountable, challenging a number of parameters linear to the number of features/predictors in a learning problem. The closed-form expression estimated in Maximum-likelihood training takes linear time, rather than iterative approximation like other types of classifiers.

This method of classification is used for constructing models that assign class labels taken from some finite set to problem instances. The models are denoted as vectors of feature values. There is no specific algorithm for training such classifiers, but a set of algorithms are involved. They are based on a common principle that given the class variable, the value of a particular feature is independent of the value of any other feature.

Performance Metrics

CV:Cross Validation are done by splitting the dataset into training and testing phase.For 5-cross-fold validation, the dataset is divided into 5 equal size folds and 5 iterations are done.In this way at the conclusion of five iteration steps, each record in the datasets is used once for testing purpose.

Classification Accuracy

It is a important measure for determining the performance of classifiers. It is the degree of numeral of correct prophecies made by a model over a data set .

Sensitivity and Specificity

Sensitivity is the true positive rate, and specificity is the true negative rate. They can be alleged as in (1.2), (1.3) and (1.4)

$$\text{Accuracy} = \text{TPR+NR / TPR+TNR+FPR+FNR} \tag{1.2}$$

Sensitivity = TPR / TPR+FNR (1.3)

Specificity = TNR / FPR+TNR (1.4)

KNN

K-Nearest Neighbour (KNN) algorithm is the simplest classification algorithm and the greatest widely used learning algorithms. KNN is well defined as a non-parametric, lazy learning algorithm. A database in which the data points are separated into several classes is used in classification of a new sample point. In short, K-NN is a type of instance-based learning or lazy learning, where the function is approximated locally and the computations are deferred until classification.

Let (Xi, Ai) where i = 1, 2……., n be data points.
'Xi' - Feature values
'Ai' - Labels for 'Xi' for each 'i'
Assuming the number of classes as 'c'
ci ∈ {1, 2, 3, ……, c} for all values of 'i'. Let 'x' be a point for which label is unknown, the label class is to be found using KNN algorithm

Box 1.

Early Diabetic Retinopathy	KNN	NBC
Accuracy (%)	77.21	83.45

Box 2.

Advanced Diabetic Retinopathy	KNN	NBC
Accuracy (%)	60	72

Figure 4. Accuracy of KNN and NBC algorithm

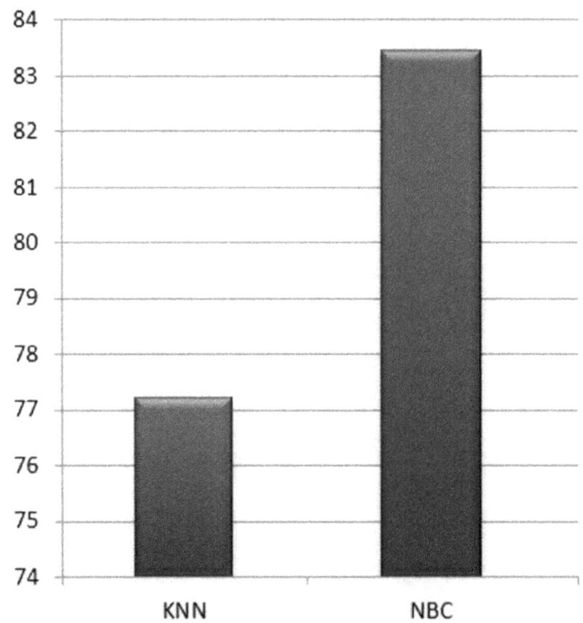

Figure 5. Accuracy of KNN and NBC algorithm for advanced diabetic

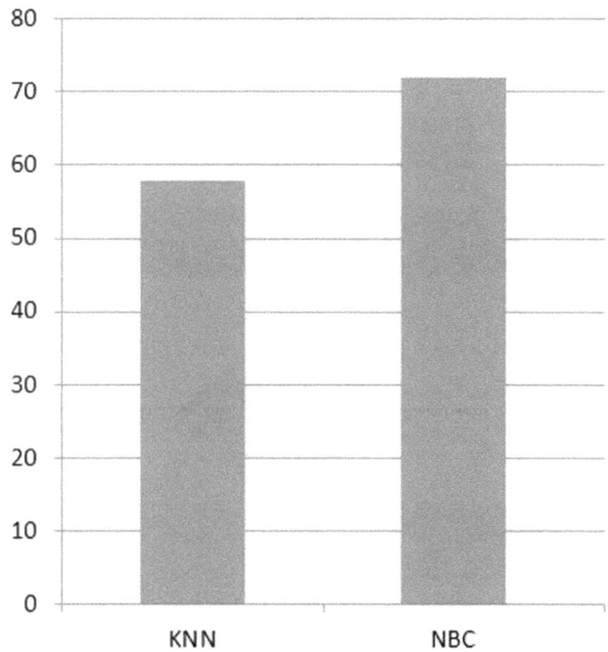

5. OPTIMIZATION TECHNIQUES

Bio-inspired Algorithms are castoff to grab complex problems based on the biotic systems of species living in earth. It plays a vital role for bringing up the solution for different types of issues surrounding us. They Evidenced their proficiency by using in different dataset.

5.1 Genetic Algorithm

It is founded on the concept of Darwinian theory of Evolution that brings optimized solution for a problem. The GA Algorithm (2021), comprise of set of iterations for a random population. Each Person is assessed by Fitness Function and the choice process is enabled by selecting some individuals. Crossover and mutation are used to replicate a unique population for the use in next iteration. The algorithm stops when it reaches the maximum fitness value.

For the experiment, people who have complaints of diabetic and age macular degeneration can be taken and people with pre-diabetic can also be involved. Randomly people are selected from the given population and iterations are repeated until objective are found.

People with Diabetic who are in control, chances of getting DR is 50%. So random selection of all people are taken and this optimized algorithm can be used in order to predict earlier.

Figure 6. Flowchart Of GA

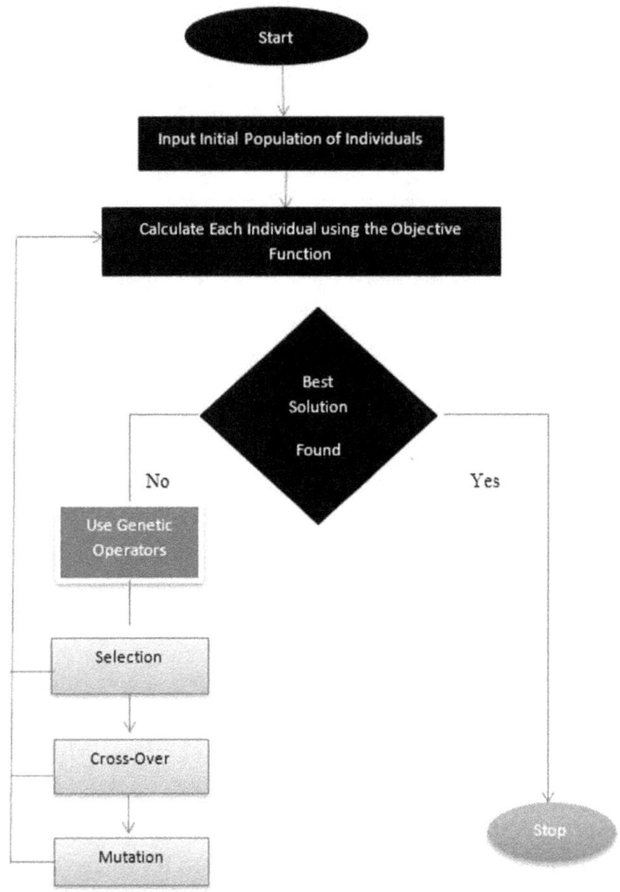

5.2 ACO (Ant Colony Optimization)

In the year 1992. ACO was Launch by Marco Doringo. He inspired by the insect ant and how they are survived. Based on this, he got an idea which we call as bioinspired algorithm. ACO Technique is used to find the shortest path. Here, pheromones are used to decipher many glitches in major application areas. The working nomenclature involves in searching a set of artificial ants. At the early stage, each ant handpicked arbitrarily a node and moves on the next node by allowing pheromone behind it from trial. The trail fascinates another ant. The more path is taken, the more pheromone is enticed by other ants.

Pseudocode

```
1.Begin
2.Intialize the Pheromone=0
3.Intialize the ant position =0
4.For each ant complete the tour
5 Travel node m to n
6. update the pheromone(increment by 1)
```

```
7. Analyse the tour, if solution is found go to step 8, otherwise go to step 4
8.Return to the best tour
9.If best solution found, if yes Goto Step
10.Repeat the Procedures from Step 4 to step 7
11.End
```

6. COMPARISON OF STUDY

Here the comparison study is made by using two algorithms based on KNN, NBC and optimization is found out by using GA and ACO. In this, study we found that ACO gives the best solution for detection of Diabetic Retinopathy

Early Diabetic Retinopathy

Figure 7. Accuracy of early retinopathy using KNN-NBC-GA

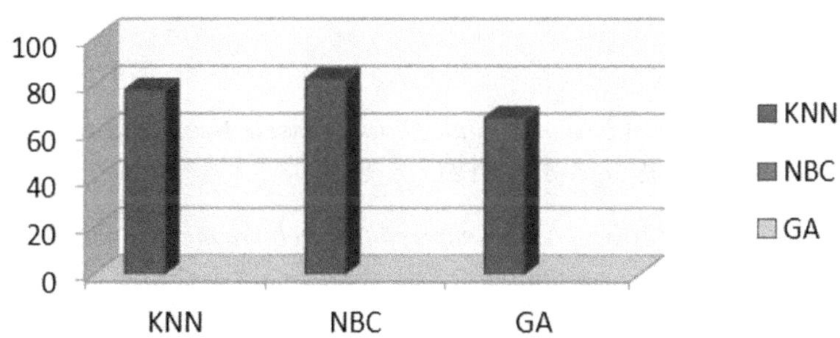

7. CONCLUSION

In this paper, we have presented different types of algorithm and bio-inspired optimization technique. Bio-inspired Algorithm are used in major applications of computer science and it provides the best solution for a variety of problems. Different Bio-inspired algorithms are used by different researchers. In the above algorithm, the KNN-NBC-ACO algorithm produce the better result and also by changing the objective function, searching techniques and updating the strategies can be a modification can be carried out. Other way is by conjoining the algorithms and show the performance of individuals. Using the bio-inspired procedures for optimization complications has recognized to be effective as they help to evade dipping into a narrow bottom. This has upheld its efficiency when handling image dissection as an optimization delinquent.

Figure 8. Accuracy of acute retinopathy-advanced KNN-NBC-ACO

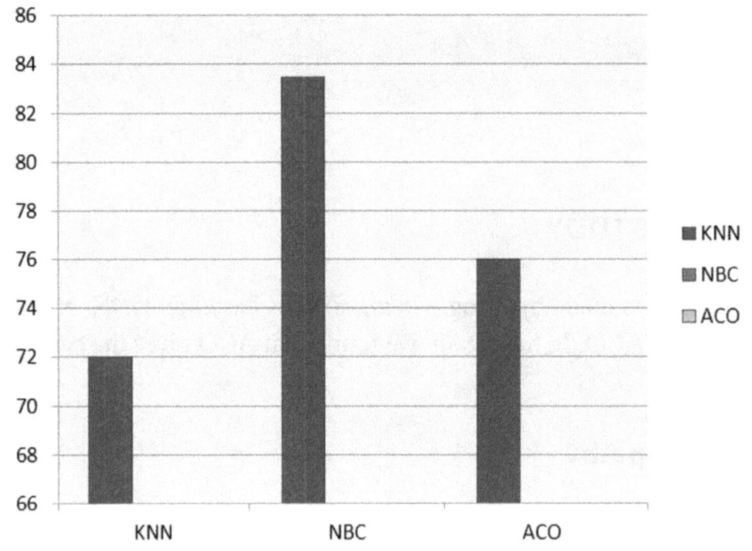

REFERENCES

Azad, A. H., & Hassaanien, A.-E. (2016). *Retinal Blood Vessels Segmentation Based on Bio-Inspired Algorithm*. Springer. doi:10.1007/978-3-319-21212-8_8

Durai, S. K., & Benadict Raja, J. (2003). *A bio-inspired fall webworm optimization algorithm for feature selection and support vector machine optimization for retinal abnormalities detection*. Multimedia Tools.

Larabi-Marie, Sainte, & Saswan. (2021). *Emerging Applications of Bio-Inspired Algorithms in Image Segmentation*. MDPI.

Mayo Clinic. (2023). *Preventing and treating disease to save your eyesigh* (3rd ed.).

Suneetha, Naaz. Dubey, & Panwar. (2023). Classification of inherited Retinal Conditions with Machine Learning and Bio-inspired Algorithms. *International Journal of Intelligent Systems and Applications in Engineering*.

Vives, V., & Ruiz-Fernandez, D. (2021). *Diabetic retinopathy detection through convolutional neural networks with synaptic metaplasticity* (Vol. 20-6). Elsevier.

Wu, Liu, Hsu, Ho, & Lee. (2021). Performance and Limitation of Machine Learning Algorithms for Diabetic Retinopathy Screening: Meta-analysis. JMIR Publications.

Xu, Q., Wang, L., & Sansgiry, S. S. (2020). A systematic literature review of predicting diabetic retinopathy, nephropathy and neuropathy in patients with type 1 diabetes using machine learning. *Journal of Medical Artificial Intelligence*, *3*, 1–15. doi:10.21037/jmai.2019.10.04

Chapter 5
Intelligent Decision Making Through Bio-Inspired Optimization:
Ant Colony Optimization for Real-World Scenarios

J. Angel Ida Chellam
Sri Ramakrishna Engineering College, India

Preethi Muthukumar
Sri Ramakrishna Engineering College, India

M. Senthamil Selvi
Sri Ramakrishna Engineering College, India

ABSTRACT

Ant colony optimization is a popular metaheuristic algorithm inspired by the foraging behavior of ants. It's often used to solve complex optimization problems. Train scheduling is a challenging problem involving the allocation of train resources, routes, and timetables to optimize various objectives like minimizing travel time, energy consumption. In train scheduling, this usually involves defining nodes and arcs to represent railway stations, tracks, and possible connections to optimize, well-defined, such as minimizing the total travel time or energy consumption. The process of ant movement and pheromone update is repeated for a predefined number of iterations or until a termination condition is met. Vehicle routing problem with time frames, the time dependent VRP, the VRP with pickup and delivery, and the dynamic VRP were developed to bring the VRP closer to the types of situations found in the real world. The optimum route serving all clients utilizing a driver's maximum working hours and minimizing total transportation cost is one solution to this problem.

DOI: 10.4018/979-8-3693-2073-0.ch005

ANT COLONY OPTIMIZATION FOR REAL WORLD SCENARIOS

The algorithmic domain is stunning, with several ideas and tools being developed around the clock to suit the demand for high-performance computing. In actuality, algorithms that are inspired by natural principles produce fascinating results. This class of algorithms includes evolutionary algorithms. These algorithms are designed to simulator particular functions and evolutionary characteristics of human DNA. Furthermore, such algorithmic design is not restricted to humans, but can also be stimulated by the natural behaviour of firm animals. The fundamental purpose of developing such practices is to provide practical, related, and low-cost solutions to problems that were previously insoluble using conventional methods.

Several optimisation strategies have emerged based on such evolutionary algorithms. So metaheuristics is introduced into the picture. Metaheuristic is imitative from two Greek words: meta, meaning "one level above," and heuriskein, meaning "to find." Particle Swarm Optimisation (PSO) and Ant Colony Optimisation (ACO) are swarm intelligence and metaheuristic algorithms, respectively. Swarm intelligence seeks to create intelligent multi-agent systems based on the cooperative behaviour of social insects such as ants, termites, bees, and wasps, as well as other animal societies such as bird flocks or fish schools.

Marco Dorigo invented the Ant Colony Optimisation approach in the 1990s, which was fully inspired by ant colonies' foraging behaviour. Ants are eusocial insects, meaning they choose collective endurance and sustainability over each species survival. They communicate using voice, touch, and pheromones. Ants create organic chemical substances called pheromones, which cause members of the same species to engage socially. These are compounds that can impact the behaviour of recipients by functioning as hormones outside of the secretor's body. Because most ants dwell on the ground, they consent pheromone trails on the soil surface for other ants to follow (smell).

Ants live in open nests, and the basic assumption of ACO is to perceive ants' drive away from their homes in order to obtain food in the shortest possible pathAnts begin to wander aimlessly in hunt of food around their nests. This randomised search enables multiple routes from the nest to the food supply. Now, depending on the class and measure of the food, ants transport a portion of it back with the appropriate pheromone concentration on its return voyage. Depending on the results of these pheromone trials, the chance of the next ants taking a specific path will serve as a pointer to the food source. Clearly, this likelihood is governed by the pheromone's concentration and rate of evaporation. It is also worth mentioning that, because the pheromone's evaporation rate is a key factor, the length of every path can be easily calculated.

Ant Colony Optimisation (ACO) is a nature-inspired optimisation technique that excels at solving combinatorial optimisation problems. It is based on the foraging activity of real ants, which seek the shortest route between their nest and a food source. ACO has been effectively utilised in a variety of real-world contexts, including train scheduling and vehicle routing algorithms.

Ant Colony Optimization Pseudocode

```
procedure AntColonyOptimization()
initialize pheromone levels on all edges
repeat until termination criteria are met:
create a population of artificial ants
for each ant in the population:
construct a solution using pheromone levels and heuristic information
```

```
evaluate the solution
update pheromone levels on the solution components
evaporate pheromone on all edges
end repeat
select the best solution found during the optimization process
end procedure
```

Background Study

Train scheduling is a critical aspect of railway operations, aiming to efficiently manage the movement of trains on a network while optimizing various parameters such as travel time, resource utilization, and overall system performance. The development of effective train scheduling algorithms is essential to address the complexities and challenges associated with railway systems. Efficient train scheduling is crucial for maximizing the use of railway infrastructure, reducing delays, and improving overall system capacity. It plays a key role in enhancing safety by minimizing the risk of collisions and ensuring the smooth coordination of trains.

The challenges in train scheduling is:

- The real-time nature of train operations introduces complexities, and schedules need to adapt to unforeseen disruptions.
- Limited resources such as track availability, platform space, and maintenance windows must be considered.
- Optimizing for one parameter (e.g., minimizing delays) may adversely affect another (e.g., resource utilization).

Examination of successful train scheduling implementations and case studies showcasing improvements in efficiency and performance. Learning from failures or challenges faced during the implementation of scheduling algorithms. Exploring emerging technologies such as blockchain, IoT, and AI for enhancing train scheduling processes. Addressing environmental concerns and sustainability in scheduling algorithms.

In conclusion, train scheduling algorithms play a pivotal role in optimizing railway operations, ensuring safety, and enhancing overall efficiency. The field is dynamic, with ongoing research aimed at addressing emerging challenges and incorporating advanced technologies for more robust solutions.

The Vehicle Routing Problem (VRP) is a classic optimisation difficult that seeks to determine the most efficient method of delivering goods or providing services to a set of destinations utilising a fleet of vehicles. Ant Colony Optimisation (ACO) is a nature-inspired metaheuristic algorithm that has been used to address combinatorial optimisation issues, such as VRP.

The VRP involves establishing the best routes for a fleet of vehicles to provide goods or services to a group of clients while minimising total distance travelled, expenses, or other objective functions. Variants of VRP include the Capacitated VRP (CVRP), Time-Dependent VRP (TDVRP), and Multiple Depot VRP (MDVRP), each posing unique challenges. ACO is a nature-inspired optimisation method based on ants' foraging behaviour. It employs a population of artificial ants to solve combinatorial optimisation issues. ACO's key components are pheromone trails, which represent path desire, and exploration-exploitation methods inspired by ant communication. In VRP, ACO is used to iteratively design and enhance routes by modelling ant foraging behaviour.

Pheromone levels are efficient based on the quality of solutions, with ants preferring routes with higher pheromone concentrations. ACO algorithms involve parameters like pheromone evaporation rate, exploration-exploitation trade-off, and heuristics. Tuning these parameters is crucial for the algorithm's performance.

In conclusion, the combination of ACO and VRP addresses the challenges of finding optimal routes for a fleet of vehicles, making it a widely researched area with numerous applications in logistics and transportation optimization. Ongoing research continues to refine and extend ACO algorithms for more complex and dynamic VRP scenarios.

1. TRAIN SCHEDULING PROBLEM

In the Indian railways environment, train scheduling is done between the source and destination stations. It practices the Ant Colony Optimisation (ACO) technique, which is based on ants' food-finding behaviour. The algorithm's iteration-wise junction process and convergence time are explored and compared. Lastly, the Ant Colony Optimisation Train Scheduling (ACOTS) and Standard Train Scheduling (STS) algorithms were evaluated in terms of run time.

In the Indian Railway situation, all types of trains share the same track: mail, passenger, express, superfast, and cargo. The whole territory is separated into zones. Zones are further divided. There are several ways to go from one region to another across multiple partitions. Furthermore, the number of tracks inside the divisions is limited, while the number of trains increases. As a result, effective scheduling is critical for cost optimisation (possibly in terms of time). In the Indian railway system, all types of trains use the same track: mail, passenger, express, superfast, and cargo. The entire territory is divided into regions. Zones are further subdivided. There are various options for moving from one zone to another across multiple divisions.

Optimization techniques can be used to efficiently tackle the train scheduling problem. The train scheduling problem was solved using a heuristic method, and the results were satisfactory. The scheduling is based on a single track with a constant speed. We attempted to circumvent the limitation of uniform speed, and collision-free single track scenarios were evaluated on different positions of trains to keep the problem's complexity, as double track can pass two trains at the same time without colliding.

Pheromones are specific chemicals that ants leave on the earth and on substances. All ants' behaviour is mostly impacted by the pheromones that they detect along the way. Ants employ various quantities of pheromones to organize every motion required by their colony. The discoverer ant searches the surroundings for food at random. When it locates a food cause, it turn to the nest, placing a adjustable quantity of pheromone that is proportionate to the food source's richness. Other ants determine their movements probabilistically, preferring locations with difficult levels of pheromone. The slow evaporation of pheromone reduces the quantity on disused and less regularly used pathways. Their method of message by pheromone is to find the shortest path is known as Ant Colony Optimization (ACO) technique.

The experiment was carried out with two connections of varying lengths placed between the ants' nest and a food stock. The ants initially choose random courses, and their likelihood of picking each connection is 0.5.

Though, with time, the pheromone tracks became more numerous, the ants meant to take the shortest path to the food. Because the ants need less time to travel the distance on the shorter bridge, the pheromone trail grew with regard to time, and the ant population rose on the shortest path.

Figure 1. Ant's food-finding strategy: (A) ants using a pheromone to move between food and their nest, (B) trail closure due to an obstruction, (C) identifying two trail movement paths, (D) determining the most advantageous route

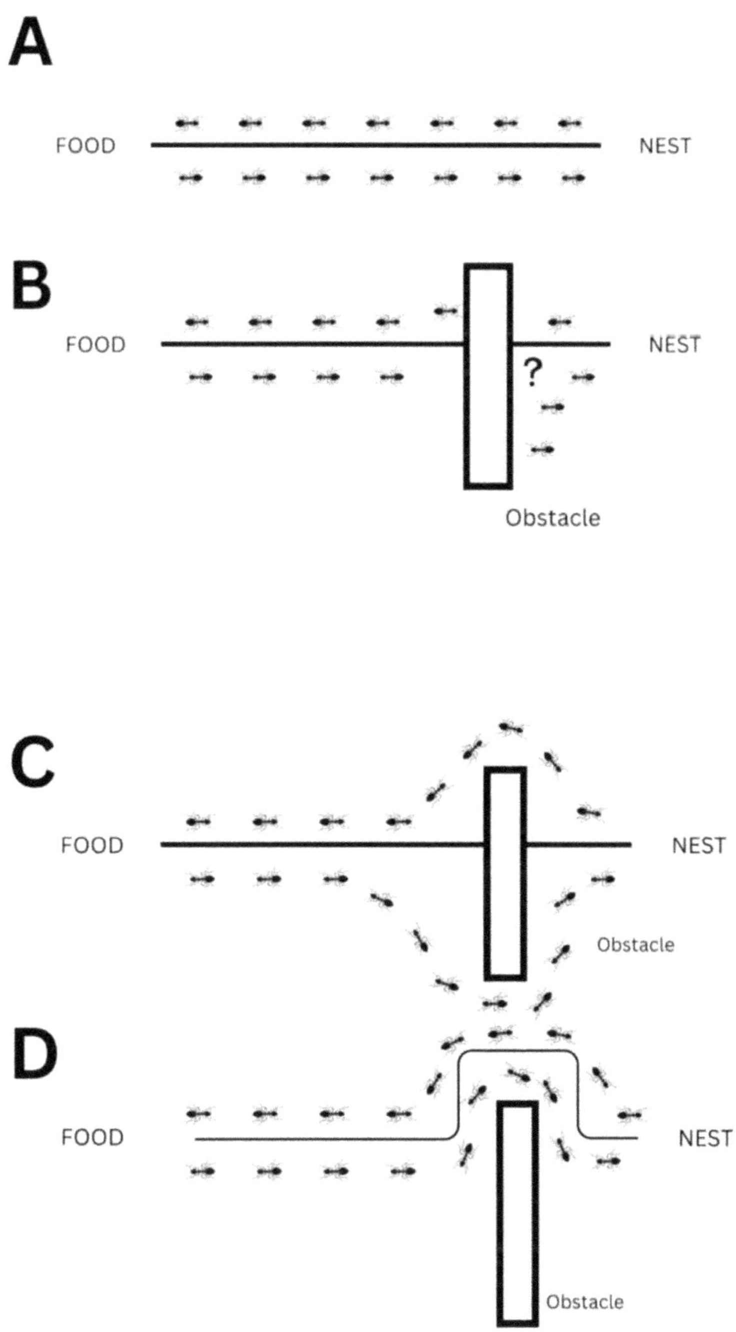

1.1 The Ant Colony System

The Ant Colony System (ACS) is a metaheuristic optimisation algorithm based on the hunting behaviour of ants. It falls under the broader category of Swarm Intelligence, which draws inspiration from the cooperative behavior of social insect colonies, such as ants, bees, and termites, to solve complex problems (Sahana et al., 2014).

The algorithm was announced by Marco Dorigo in the early 1990s and is based on the observation of real ant colonies' ability to find the shortest path amid their nest and a food source. ACS has been successfully smeared to several combinatorial optimization problems, including the traveling salesman problem, job scheduling, and network routing.

Figure 2. A diagram of the original (biological) ant experiment

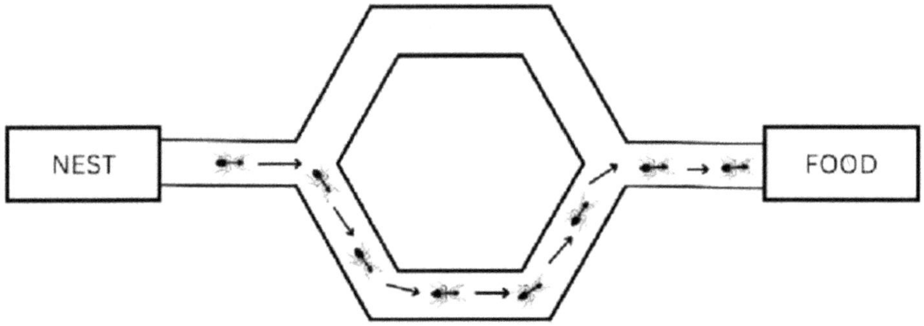

Ant Colony System (ACS) uses mathematical formulas to implement its rules. Here are the key formulas associated with the rules of ACS:

1. Pheromone Update:

The quantity of pheromone (ΔTij) deposited by an ant on track i→j is given by: ΔTij= Cost of solution Q where:

- Q is a constant on behalf of the total quantity of pheromone deposited by an ant.
- The Cost of the solution is the unbiased function value associated with the solution.

2. Local Pheromone Update:

Optionally, a native pheromone update can be performed on the path just traversed by an ant. The update is given by: $Tij=(1-\rho)\cdot Tij+\rho\cdot\tau 0$

Where:

- Tij is the pheromone level on the path i→j.
- ρ is the evaporation rate (a constant between 0 and 1).

- 0τ0 is the first pheromone level on all paths.

3. Global Pheromone Update:

After all ants have completed their construction, perform a global update to adjust the pheromone levels on paths: $Tij= (1-\alpha)\bullet Tij+\sum k= 1m\Delta Tijk$ where:

- α is the pheromone persistence parameter (a constant between 0 and 1).
- m is the Total amount of ants.
- ΔTijk is the amount of pheromone placed by ant k on path i→j.

These formulas ensure that shorter and better solutions receive more pheromone, guiding subsequent ants toward promising areas of the solution space. The evaporation processes help prevent stagnation, allowing the algorithm to explore a variety of solutions. The global update reinforces good solutions found by multiple ants.

It's important to note that the precise parameters and formulas may vary in different versions of ACS or its variants (e.g., Max-Min Ant System, Ant System) depending on the problem characteristics and desired algorithm behavior. Adjustments to these parameters might be necessary for optimal performance on different problem instances (Ghoseiri, 2006).

1.2 Single Track Design

Designing a single-track railway system for train scheduling is a complex optimization problem. The aim is to efficiently allocate time slots for trains on a single track, minimizing conflicts and delays (Sahana et al., 2014). Ant Colony System (ACS) can be applied to find near-optimal solutions for this problem. Here's a basic outline of how ACS can be used for single-track train scheduling:

Problem Representation:

1. Encoding:
   - Represent the train schedule as a sequence of time slots on a single track.
   - Each solution (ant's solution) corresponds to a feasible train schedule.
2. Objective Function:
   - Define an objective function that captures the quality of a schedule.
   - Consider factors such as minimizing delays, maximizing utilization of the track, and reducing conflicts between trains.
3. Ant Movement:
   - Place artificial ants at the starting point of the track.
   - Ants move sequentially, choosing time slots based on pheromone levels and a heuristic factor.
4. Solution Construction:
   - As ants move, they construct train schedules by selecting time slots on the single track.
   - The choice of the next time slot is influenced by the amount of pheromone on the track and a heuristic factor that may consider factors like distance to the destination, upcoming conflicts, etc.

5. Pheromone Update:
    - Deposit pheromone on the selected time slots.
    - Pheromone update is based on the eminence of the solution (schedule) start by the ant.
6. Local Pheromone Update:
    - Optionally, perform local pheromone update on the time slots just traversed by an ant to encourage exploration.
7. Solution Evaluation:
    - Evaluate the class of the complete train schedule constructed by each ant using the defined objective function.
8. Global Pheromone Update:
    - After all ants have completed their schedules, perform a global update to adjust the pheromone levels on time slots.
    - The amount of global pheromone update is influenced by the class of the schedules found by all ants.
9. Iteration Conclusion:
    - Repeat the process for a predefined number of iterations or until a termination criterion is met.
10. Best Solution Update:
    - Keep track of the best train schedule found during the iterations.
11. Parameters:
    - Adjust parameters such as the pheromone evaporation rate, exploration-exploitation trade-off (alpha and beta parameters), and initial pheromone levels for optimal performance.

Applying ACS to single-track train scheduling requires careful consideration of problem-specific details and tuning of parameters to achieve good performance. The algorithm's ability to balance exploration and exploitation can help find solutions that minimize conflicts and delays in the train schedule.

In conclusion, the implementation of Ant Colony Optimization (ACO) for train scheduling represents a promising and efficient approach to optimizing complex railway systems. By harnessing the collective intelligence of artificial ants, ACO effectively addresses the challenges associated with scheduling trains, primary to improved resource utilization, reduced delays, and improved complete system performance. This approach not only demonstrates the capability of nature-inspired algorithms in solving real-world problems but also underscores the potential for ACO to contribute significantly to the advancement of railway scheduling, ultimately fostering a more reliable and streamlined transportation infrastructure.

2. VEHICLE ROUTING PROBLEM

Since at least the early 1960s, the vehicle routing problem (VRP) has been a significant issue in distribution and logistics. During the 1990s, VRP research intensified. Researchers may be able to create and apply more complicated search algorithms as microprocessor capacity and availability improve. During this time, the term meta-heuristics was coined to describe a class of search methods for addressing VRPs and other combinatorial optimization issues.

Affording to the technical description of the vehicle routing problem (VRP), m vehicles originally placed at a depot are to convey discrete quantities of commodities to n consumers. A VRP's goal is to determine the best path for a group of vehicles to take when serving a group of users. The goal of VRP is to reduce the complete transportation cost. The standard VRP solution is a established of routes that all activate and finish in the depot and satisfy the restriction that all customers are assisted only once. Transportation costs can be reduced by reducing the overall distance travelled as well as the number of vehicles required.

Evolutionary algorithms and swarm intelligence-based algorithms are two key types of population-based optimization methods. On VRP, a swarm intelligence-based algorithm is chosen. Swarm intelligence-based algorithms are developed by researching collective intelligence in nature, such as cockroaches, fish, ants, bees, birds, and so on. An algorithm can be used to depict the pattern of their survival (Rizzoli et al., 2004).

The traditional Travelling Salesman Problem (TSP) is extended by Vehicle Routing Problem (VRP). One or more vehicles go around a network, leaving from and returning to a depot node in this problem. Customers are located throughout the network, and each client must be visited just once. Customers are typically found at network nodes. The VRP's goal is to determine the vehicle routing(s) with the lowest cost, or to minimize total route length (Rizzoli et al., 2004). It is defined as determining the shortest distance or the lowest cost of the joint routes of a number of vehicles m that must facility a number of customer's n.

2.1 Mathematical Calculation of VRP

The Vehicle Routing Problem (VRP) includes discovery the optimal routes for a navy of vehicles to deliver goods or provide services to a set of locations while minimizing total costs. To formulate the VRP mathematically, you can use a combination of decision variables, constraints, and an objective function.

Let's define some variables:

- $i,j \in N$ are indices expressive the locations (customers and depot).
- N is the fixed of locations, including the depot.
- V is a set of vehicles, where $v \in V$ is a specific vehicle.
- cij is the cost (distance, time, etc.) to travel from location i to location j.
- di is a demand at location i.
- Qv is a capacity of vehicle v.
- xijv is a binary decision variable specifying whether vehicle v travels straight from i to j (xijv=1) or not (xijv=0)
- ui is a continuous variable representing the cumulative demand served up to location i.
- wiv is a binary decision variable indicating whether location i is visited by vehicle v(wiv=1) or not (wiv=0)

Now, let's formulate the VRP mathematically:

1. Objective Function:
   Minimize the total cost of the routes:

$$Minimize \sum_{v\in V}\sum_{i\in N}\sum_{j\in N} cij\ xijv$$

2. Constraints:
   2.1 Each location is visited by exactly one vehicle:

$$\sum_{v\in V} \mathrm{wiv} = 1 \quad \forall \mathrm{i} \in \mathrm{N}$$

   2.2 Each vehicle leaves and arrives at the depot:

$$\sum_{i\in N} \mathrm{x0iv} = \mathrm{j} \in \mathrm{N} \sum \mathrm{xijv} = 1 \quad \forall \mathrm{v} \in \mathrm{V}$$

   2.3 Flow conservation:

$$\sum_{i\in N} xijv - k \in N \sum xikv = 0 \forall \mathrm{v} \in \mathrm{V}, \mathrm{j} \in \mathrm{N} \setminus \{0\}$$

   2.4 Vehicle capacity constraint:

$$\sum_{i\in N} x\mathrm{di}\ \mathrm{wiv} \leq \mathrm{Qv}\ \forall \mathrm{v} \in \mathrm{V}$$

   2.5 Subtour elimination to prevent cycles:

$$ui - uj + Qv \cdot xijv \leq Qv - dj \forall i, j \in N, v \in V, i\square = j, i, j\square = 0$$

   2.6 Binary variables:

$\mathrm{xijv}, \mathrm{wiv} \in \{0,1\} \forall \mathrm{i,j} \in \mathrm{N}, \mathrm{v} \in \mathrm{V}$

Solving this mathematical formulation will give you the optimal solution to the Vehicle Routing Problem. The constraints guarantee the routes satisfy the problem requirements, and the objective function minimizes the total cost. Keep in mind that solving large instances of the VRP optimally may be computationally challenging, and heuristic methods like Ant Colony Optimization are often employed for larger, real-world instances.

2.2 Vehicle Routing Heuristic Based on ACO

Ant Colony Optimization (ACO) is a prominent metaheuristic based on ant searching behavior. It has been positively used to solve a variety of combinatorial optimization issues, including the Vehicle Routing Problem (VRP). The purpose of VRP is to discover the best set of routes for a navy of vehicles to help a specific regular consumers.

ACO can be applied to the Vehicle Routing Problem in following ways

- Represent a problem as a graph, where nodes represent customers and a depot, and edges represent possible routes between customers and the depot.
- Each edge has associated information such as distance or cost.

Figure 3. Vehicle routing as a graph

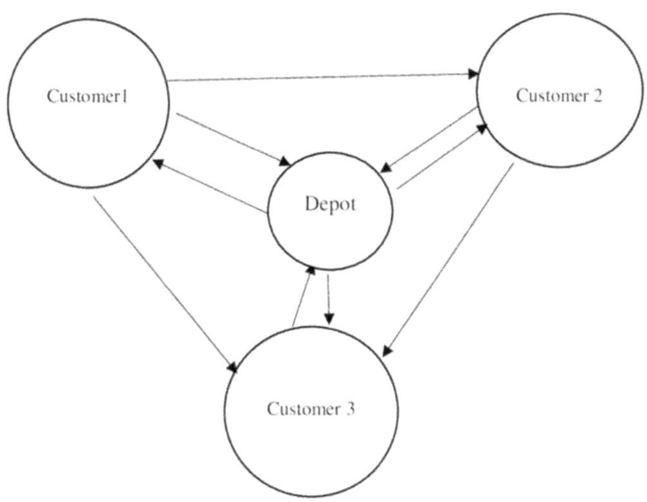

- Define limitations such as the quantity of ants, pheromone evaporation rate, exploration-exploitation trade-off parameters (alpha and beta), etc.
- Initialize pheromone levels on all edges with a small amount.
- Each ant starts its route from the depot and moves to the next customer based on a probabilistic decision influenced by both pheromone levels and the desirability of the move (e.g., inverse of distance).
- The probability of moving from node i to node j is often calculated using the formula:

$$Pij = \sum k \in Ni\tau ik\alpha \bullet \eta ik\beta\tau ij\alpha \bullet \eta nj\beta$$

Where:

- Pij is the chance of affecting from node i to node j,

- τij is the volume of pheromone on the edge (i, j),
- ηij is a measure of the appeal of moving from node i to node j,
- α and β are parameters that control the comparative importance of pheromone and appeal.
- After all ants finish their travels, update the pheromone levels on each control based on the feature of the solutions.
- Evaporate pheromones on all edges to simulate the natural decay of pheromones.
- Repeat the ant movement and pheromone update steps for a certain number of iterations or until convergence.
- Stop when a end condition is met (e.g., a maximum number of iterations, no improvement in solutions).
- Extract the best solution(s) found by the ants.
- Fine-tune parameters based on performance on a validation set.
- Consider additional mechanisms such as local search to enhance the algorithm's exploitation capability.
- Handle constraints specific to the VRP, such as capacity constraints for each vehicle.

Implementing ACO for the VRP requires careful tuning of parameters and adaptation to the specific features of the problem instance. Additionally, ACO can be enhanced with hybridization techniques or other metaheuristics for improved performance on complex problem instances.

2.3 Fundamental Vehicle Routing Issues

The Vehicle Routing Problem (VRP) is a compound combinatorial optimization problem with various real-world applications, and it comes with its own set of challenges. Here are some of the basic problems associated with the VRP:

Combinatorial Complexity

VRP is an NP-hard issue, which means that the number of possible routes rises exponentially in proportion to the number of locations (customers). This makes determining the ideal solution computationally difficult.

Capacity Constraints

Most VRP variants include capacity constraints, meaning that each vehicle has a limited capacity to deliver goods or services. Managing these constraints adds an additional layer of complexity to the problem.

Time Windows

Many VRP instances involve time constraints, where each customer must be served within a certain time range. Ensuring timely deliveries while optimizing routes is a significant challenge.

Dynamic and Stochastic Elements

In real-world scenarios, demands, travel times, and other factors may be dynamic or subject to uncertainty. Dynamic VRP deals with changes in customer demands or service times, while Stochastic VRP considers probabilistic variations in parameters.

Heterogeneous Fleet

VRP often assumes a fleet of vehicles with different capacities, speeds, and costs. Optimizing routes for a heterogeneous fleet adds an extra layer of complexity.

Multiple Objectives

VRP may have numerous conflicting goals, such as reducing trip distance, delivery time, or the number of vehicles used. Balancing these objectives presents a multi-objective optimisation issue.

Depot Location

Determining the optimal location for the depot, from which all vehicles start and end their routes, can significantly impact the solution. The choice of depot location may affect travel distances and overall solution quality.

Geographical Constraints

Real-world VRP instances often include geographical constraints, such as road networks, traffic conditions, or one-way streets. Incorporating these constraints into the optimization model can be challenging.

In conclusion, while the Vehicle Routing Problem presents computational challenges, ongoing research and advancements in optimization techniques continue to improve our ability to find high-quality solutions for real-world routing scenarios, contributing to more sustainable and cost-effective transportation and logistics operations.

REFERENCES

Ghoseiri, K. (2006). *A new idea for train scheduling using ant colony optimization* (Vol. 88). WIT Transactions on The Built Environment. doi:10.2495/CR060591

Rizzoli, Oliverio, Montemanni, & Gambardella. (2004). *Ant Colony Optimisation for vehicle routing problems: from theory to applications.* Academic Press.

Sahana, S. K., Jain, A., & Mahanti, P. K. (2014). Ant Colony Optimization for Train Scheduling: An Analysis. *International Journal of Intelligent Systems and Applications*, *2*(2), 29–36. doi:10.5815/ijisa.2014.02.04

Chapter 6
Nature-Inspired Optimized Artificial Bee Colony for Decision Making in Energy-Efficient Wireless Sensor Networks

J. Viji Gripsy
PSGR Krishnammal College for Women, India

M. Sasikala
PSGR Krishnammal College for Women, India

ABSTRACT

In recent times, there has been a surge in the popularity of nature-inspired algorithms (NIAs) for addressing challenging and complex nonlinear difficult problems. Wireless sensor networks (WSNs) provide a wide range of concerns and challenges that must be addressed when formulating methodologies and algorithms aimed at conserving energy and enhancing the overall lifespan of the network. This chapter examines and analyzes optimization-based energy-efficient strategies for clustering and routing using optimization algorithms. The major challenges in WSNs are to provide low energy consumption, enhancing network lifetime, minimizing interference in communication, improving data rate, balancing network load and quality network functioning, etc. The chapter improves the quality of service of the network by lengthening network lifetime for more packet transmission. The proposed optimized artificial bee colony (OABC) outperformed in comparison to the existing algorithms in terms of less packet loss, higher network lifetime, minimum energy consumption, and lesser average execution time.

DOI: 10.4018/979-8-3693-2073-0.ch006

INTRODUCTION

The significance of optimization in addressing numerous engineering problems is essential in recent situations. In an overview, optimization techniques may be used to minimize a specific function while considering a range of both equal and unequal constraints. Generally, these functions exhibit a nonlinear and offer significant difficulties in terms of finding solutions. There is an extensive variety of algorithms, including several types like linear, quadratic, convex, conjugate, inner point, trust area, numerous, etc. These algorithms have the competence to successfully report difficult iterative challenges, ranging from traditional techniques to evolutionary approaches and nature-inspired meta-heuristic methods. In current times, there has been a recent increase in the popularity of nature-inspired algorithms (NIAs) for solving interesting and complex nonlinear problems. This may be due to their obvious features, such as flexibility, improved efficiency, and openness. The algorithms mainly trust on swarm intelligence, which pursues to duplicate the miscellaneous characteristic realized in nature. Although the research on optimization is extensive, there is a substantial deviation between hypothetical and experiential characteristics.

The practical use of nature-inspired algorithms has shown to be effective in solving a wider range of real-world challenges. While conventional algorithms demonstrate strong performance in executing many tasks and solving a broad range of issues, comprehending their precise mechanisms may be somewhat challenging (Liu, 2019). It is necessary to possess a comprehensive understanding of multi-disciplinary numerical, mathematical, dynamic system investigation, as well as proficiency in computational complexity analysis and the associated tools. This task creates a significant challenge. In contrast, nature-inspired algorithms primarily concentrate on the examination of the fundamental attributes of the methodology, its constituent parts, search patterns, and approaches used to get optimal solutions. Usually, NIAs are characterized by initial steps, search characteristics and dynamics of algorithm. All algorithms use population size or numerous search agents, such as ants, bees, bats, swarms, and so on. Every search agent establishes communication with a designated key vector and typically has a fitness goal that represents the best-known optimal solution. The presence of several solutions within a population size contributes to the variety seen, as well as the existence of distinct fitness goals.

There are various algorithms that exhibit significant differences in terms of their random size and distinct behavior when applied to local and global search scenarios. The process of selecting optimal solutions is often conducted using a "fit to survive" approach, which aims to maintain a population of the most beneficial individuals for the purpose of encouraging the whole population to converge into an integrated and well-structured unit, while minimizing variability (Mood, 2019). WSNs provide a wide range of concerns and challenges that must be addressed when formulating methodologies and algorithms aimed at conserving energy and enhancing the overall lifespan of the network. Network optimization performs a dynamic part in the area of WSN, subsequently it includes the use of optimization methods to get a perfect solution for this specific problem. The variety of a suitable algorithm is of utmost importance in any optimization method, given the reality of numerous optimization algorithms intended to concentrate various tasks (Oren, 2017).

Optimization denotes to the organized method used to obtain the optimal result within a specific set of conditions. The term "optimum" is frequently recognized to denote to either the highest or minimal value, varying the particular situations. When generating a WSN, it is important to focus the issues associated to energy efficiency, cost, and application necessities. Attaining effectiveness in WSNs contains the optimization of both hardware and software mechanisms. There is a diversity of optimization methods that are intended to focus several issues areas. The selection of a suitable algorithm has substantial position in the framework of any optimization procedure. The assignment of sensor nodes in WSNs is frequently restricted to two possibilities: within the monitoring section or in close vicinity to it, owing to the inadequate organization accessible for WSNs. The batteries which are used in the sensor nodes are not manageable to alternative or recharging depend to their deployment in geographically challenging sensing situations. Hence, the loss of a battery's energy in a node indicates the close of the network as a whole. Thus, optimizing the use of battery energy is imperative in order to increase the lifespan of the network.

WSNs have been progressively employed in a diversity of application fields like engineering, to resourcefully monitor remote locations at a reduced cost. WSNs contain essential confines like organize battery life, limited memory resources, and inadequate computing capacity (Wang, 2013). Thus, the conservation of energy and the increasing of network lifespan are vital issues that essential to measure while structure and refining the performance of these networks. The main concern that merits consideration is energy consumption, which may be considerably decreased by the use of effective clustering and routing algorithms (Singh, 2016). Clustering is an essential method used in WSNs with the purpose of achieving energy efficiency, enhancing network lifespan, and enhancing network scalability (Singh, 2016). The utility of clustering and routing is vital in the design of energy-efficient WSNs (Ullah, 2020).

This chapter examines and analyzes a range of conventional and optimization-based energy-efficient strategies for clustering and routing, using optimization algorithms. Nature-inspired algorithms are a class of heuristic approaches that derive inspiration from natural events to address problem-solving challenges. The design of the nature-inspired algorithm encompasses the appropriate formulation of the issue, the evaluation of solution quality via the use of a fitness function, and the generation of a new set of solutions by defining novel operators.

1. BACKGROUND

This section reviews the entire collection of literature in the following manner:

Famila et al. (Famila, 2019) established an additional progressive clustering method in their research. The objective of this method is to cover the durability of the network by minimizing the energy use though selecting cluster heads (CH). The selection process is established by the optimal combination of examination and manipulation values. This method used a integrated system to cluster data into clusters and a disseminated process to select a CH. The IABCOCT protocol utilizes the demand distance vector algorithm for multipath routing, while the CH communicates the combined data to the sink node. The outcomes recognized that the proposed method outperformed the HCCHE, CCT, and EPSPCT methodologies in terms of energy efficiency clustering. Precisely, the proposed approach attained a decreasing of around 23% in average residue energy, 16% in average energy consumption, and 18% in increasing residue energy.

Karthick et al. (Karthick, 2019) offered a novel Krill Herd approach tailored for enhancing clustering difficulties. This procedure utilizes a fusion of genetic algorithm (GA) and K-means clustering algorithm (KH) to select CH depending on their remaining energy. Clusters are formed by the use of the KH algorithm, which intentionally positions nodes throughout each iteration. The selection of the CH is resolved by a GA that consider the node's available energy. The data collection process contains investigative both the intra and inter cluster distance to agree the selection. When comparing LEACH & GA to KH,

KH had a superior Packet Delivery Ratio (PDR). In addition, KH proved a 5.73% and 2.21% enhancement in optimizing the cost of residual energy and refining network lifespan for a network size of 3K.

S. Chavan et al. (S. Chavan, 2019) established an IBeeCup, which is a clustering protocol inspired by biological principles and intended to improve energy efficiency, explicitly for route computing. The suggested technique enhanced the network's performance by attaining the value of the RSSI and extending the network's lifespan. The experimental outcomes enhanced numerous metrics, including average energy consumption, network longevity, overhead reduction, and increased residual energy in the Ch nodes.

S M Daneshvar et al. (Daneshvar, 2019) presented a GWO algorithm that attractions inspiration from the behaviour of grey wolves. The resolution of this method is to optimize energy consumption in wireless networks. The clustering approach used in this research successfully predicted the energy usage of individual nodes throughout numerous iterations. It proficient this by using the persisting energy of each node to proficiently save energy inside the network. The experimental results attained from the proposed singular objective function, successfully avoided the unnecessary collapse of energy throughout the initialization phase and enhanced the complete energy utilization of the network, while concurrently achieving evenness between the Ch nodes and relay nodes.

N. Parkash et al. (Parkash, 2020) employed the SA-AOA select the CH in a cluster. They then compared this method with other existing algorithms such as ALO (Antlion Algorithm), GOA (grasshopper optimization algorithm), FFOA (Fruitfly Optimization Algorithm), and PSO. The outcomes established that the method shows that an extended network lifespan, lower validity, and a superior number of active hubs.

T. A Alghamdi (Alghamdi, 2021) presented an advanced organization for clustering in WSN to select CH. The selection of the head is generally reliant on measures like delay, energy, security, and distance. Firefly Position Update in Dragonfly (FPUDA) associates the dragonfly and firefly optimization algorithms. The performance was evaluated by adjusting the weight factor to expand the selection of CH via 2000 iterations. The simulated results established that the FPUDA model outperformed K-means, FCM, and SOM by 9% in attaining a extended network lifespan. The FPUDA technique outperformed FF, GWO, DA, and WOA by 45.95%, 18.92%, 24.32%, and 24.32% correspondingly, by containing a weight aspect and convergence rate. FPUDA offered a minimum amount compared to FF by 16.93%, GWO by 26.64%, DA by 27.1%, and WOA by 27.7%. The simulated research displayed that the network lifespan was 6% greater to K-mean, 4% superior to FCM, and 24% greater to SOM.

C Mahapatra et al. (Mahapatra, 2020) presented a centralized clustering solution for localization and coverage issues in WSNs using swarm intelligence (SI). The purpose was to generate a network that is extremely scalable, consumes less energy, and attains an admirable packet delivery rate. The research investigations were showed on numerous conditions including large-scale WSN considered by slight heterogeneity. Various sets of nodes, containing 100, 300, and 500, were observed to assess the performance. The centralized approach based on the SI (Swarm Intelligence) algorithm verified greater performance compared to present approaches in WSN in terms of the total amount of information carried to the Base Station (BT), energy consumption, and network scalability.

L. Chan et al. (Chan, 2020) inspected the significant existing research led on routing methods in WSN. The research aims to conduct a systematic investigation of hierarchical routing protocols and classify them depend on the recent state of the art. The protocols were compared and examined in terms of their particular advantages and disadvantages concerning the interest of each routing approach. The aim of this study was to improve the longevity of the network and optimize data delivery by evaluating several protocols based on LEACH.

N. Lavanya et al. (Lavanya, 2019) projected a hybrid squirrel harmony search algorithm (HSHSA) that associates the harmony and squirrel search techniques to efficiently discover energy efficient CH. The procedure being discussed measures the energy reduction in the initial and final nodes, and quantifies the performance of the WSN depend on the remaining energy in the node, which is condensed by 31.02%, and the throughput, which is increased by 85.69%, in comparison to the PSO technique. The simulated results validated that the Hybrid Self-Healing Simulated Annealing (HSHSA) method exceeds the LEACH, HSA, SSA, direct, and PSO algorithms in terms of energy efficiency when selection the head during clustering.

Ali Khan et al. (Ali Khan, 2020) offered a hybrid clustering method that integrates the bio-inspired behavior of krill herd (KH) with gravitational search optimization (GSO) for unmanned aerial vehicles (UAVs). Moreover, a proposed method for attaining energy efficiency by clustering utilizing the KH algorithm. The suggested technique pays a method to establish the locations of UAVs and compute the route using a combination of weighted-residue energy, distance between UAVs, and the number of surrounding nodes. This is done to simplify efficient data discussion. The findings confirmed greater performance in terms of cluster formation execution time, cluster durability, successive packet delivery, and minimized energy consumption compared to GWO and ACO.

2. ENERGY-EFFICIENT WSN

Subsequently the sensors are battery powered, the power consumption of sensors to be organized in WSN should be reduced. To preserve energy, sensors should have their own power supplies, which should get turned off when not in use (Mohammad, 2019). Due to this constraint, extending the lifetime of WSNs by promising the quality of coverage is doubtful. Thus, the wide research and examination about this problem is significant (Hema, 2016).

Figure 1. Energy consumption in WSN

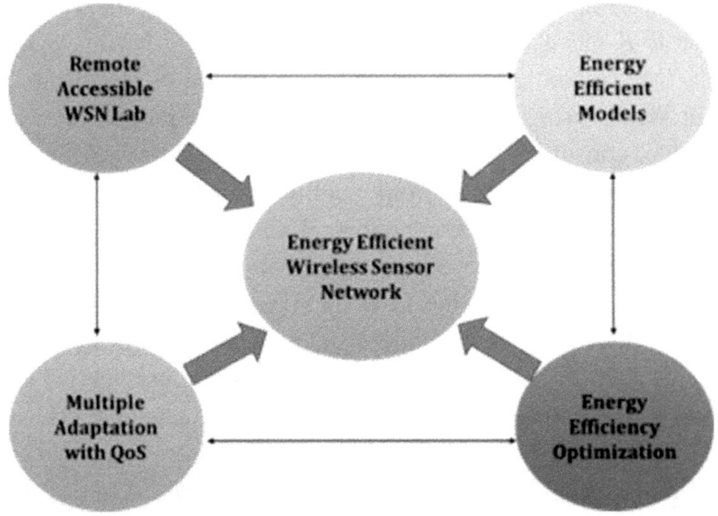

The overview of Energy Harvesting Wireless Sensor Networks (EHWSNs) rather than conventional battery powered WSNs, may cause exploit the network lifetime (Luis A Moncayo, 2016). Though, in repetition, the comprehensive confidence on nodes prepared with energy harvesting strategies in WSNs is not viable due to its extreme cost. Figure 1 demonstrates energy consumption in WSN.

The classification of approaches for exploiting network lifespan is shown in Figure 2. The resourceful transmission system contains the use of explicit sensors in a network. These sensors modify their communicate power depend on the channel state and residual battery charge information to enhance the network's lifetime (Fengben, 2019).

The selection of routing paths has a substantial impact on the duration for which a network may remain operational (Ayesha Siddiqua, 2019). Constructing routes that consider the lifespan of the network is essential for increasing network longevity. This involves creating dynamic routes based on the sensors with the highest remaining battery charge, which may be advantageous.

As an importance of the frequent consumption of these sensors to transmit data to the destination node, the dominant technique of data collection at the sink node commonly indicates to congestion in the routing procedure. As a result, the battery capacity of sensor nodes reduces, eventually resulting in a decrease in the network's overall lifespan (Srivastava, 2015). A determination to the problem has been attained over the deployment of measured mobility, which employs mobile containers or sensors. (Li, 2019) To guarantee that the traffic load is dispersed justifiably, it is the concern of each individual mobile sensor to separately ascertain its own heading. Thus, the cumulative volume of traffic is equitably spread across the network. The phrase "consideration" relates to the process of management and assessing the level of skill established by precise existences within a designated area, at an elected observation opinion, or within a sensor-protected limit. Assuming that each node is prepared with sensors and has been assigned a different set of tasks (Sharma, 2020).

Figure 2. Classification of network lifetime maximization techniques

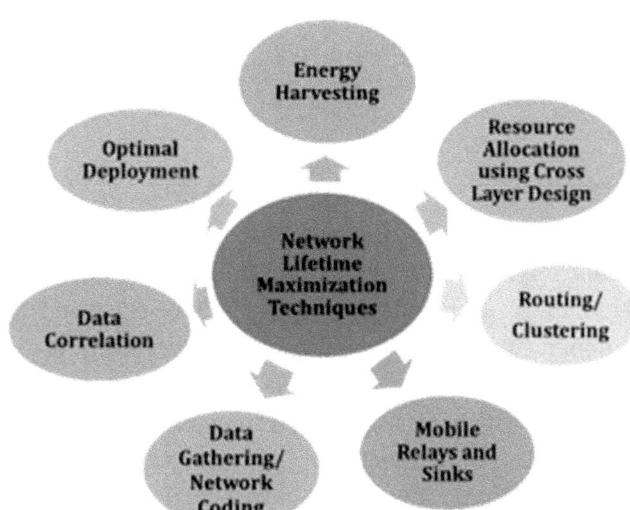

One crucial function of WSNs is to gather the data from sensors and transmit it to the designated node. Data aggregation may be used during data collection to merge data from many sensors, hence preventing unnecessary data transfer and improving the network's lifespan (Mainak Adhikar, 2019).

The sensor nodes in a WSN may experience failure as a result of energy depletion and hardware malfunctions. Therefore, ensuring fault tolerance is regarded as a crucial concern in WSNs (Qiu, 2013).

By implementing appropriate sleep strategies, the longevity of a network may be optimized. Sleeping strategies have been used to mitigate energy usage and enhance the longevity of the network. Enhancing energy efficiency may be achieved by activating the node based on a predetermined wakeup schedule (Oussama, 2019). The sensor node exhibits either standard or intensive sleep patterns based on the designated duty-cycle. The WSN can leverage the effects of implementing sleep mechanisms in data transmissions from the industrial area to the base station. It then compares the number of transmissions resulting from aggressive sleep behavior to that of the usual sleep behavior method.

The longevity of WSNs is contingent upon the battery's capacity. In a multihop WSN, each node serves as both a data source and a data relay. Node failure may result in changes to the network topology, necessitating the reorganization of the network. Key considerations include power saving and management, which have led to the development of various technologies such as energy-aware protocol design and hardware improvements. The research and development efforts have resulted in the creation of many commercially accessible motes or wireless radio modules (PatiBibudhendu, 2017).

The limited energy capacity of the sensor hinders the use of WSN for real-time applications. Integrating renewable energy sources with the sensor nodes may enhance the energy backup and prolong the lifetime of the WSN (Pal, 2015). The total longevity of the network is likewise influenced by these distances. In the relay or multihop transmission paradigm, intermediate routers are used to extend the network's distance, which may have an impact on power usage and the longevity of the network.

Typically, power optimization in WSN focuses on enhancing the efficiency of the networking and sensing components. Node components require a significant amount of energy even when they are not in use. Therefore, power management strategies are used to temporarily deactivate node components. The subsystem responsible for communication uses more energy than the subsystem responsible for computation. According to analysis, transferring a single bit might need a large number of resources, the same as carrying out several thousand instructions.

3. NATURE INSPIRED OPTIMIZATION ALGORITHMS

Optimization is important for solving many engineering problems in the present scenarios. Generally, optimization can be used to minimize a function subject to various equal and unequal constraints. Typically, these functions are nonlinear and very challenging to solve. There is diverse spectrum of many such algorithms including linear, quadratic, convex, conjugate, inner point, trust region and many more. Such algorithms can be used easily solving big iterative problems from traditional simple methods to evolutionary techniques and nature inspired meta-heuristic approaches (Agbehadji, 2021).

In recent times, nature-inspired algorithms (NIAs) have gained popularity for addressing challenging and intricate nonlinear difficult problems due to their outstanding characteristics such as adaptability, superior effectiveness, and straightforwardness. These algorithms primarily rely on swarm intelligence, which seeks to replicate the varied and distinct characteristics seen in nature (Bangotra, 2022). Although optimization is a broad field of research, there exists a substantial disparity between theoretical and observational aspects.

Mostly real-world problems can be successfully solved using practical approach of nature inspired algorithm. Though the traditional algorithms work well in performing various tasks and able to compute a wide variety of problems but very difficult to understand their functioning exactly. This is essential to have the knowledge of multidisciplinary numerical, mathematical, dynamic system study and computational complexity analysis along with the respective tool knowledge. So, this is very challenging task. On the other hand, nature inspired algorithms have focus on investigating the essential characteristics of the technique, their elements, searching behavior and method to achieve the best solution (Brahim, 2019). Usually, NIAs are characterized by initial steps, search characteristics and dynamics of algorithm. All the algorithms utilize population size or multiple search agents such as ants, bees, bats, swarms etc. Each search agent communicates to a key vector and usually has best optimum solution known as fitness objective (Devassy, 2022). Multiple solutions in a population size presented diversity as well as different fitness objectives.

Population development is often achieved by mutation and crossover, following an iterative process that yields many solutions with diverse features. The procedure is considered to have converged after a satisfactory number of relevant solutions have been produced. The search agents' movement in space is characterized by a crisscross pattern, which is referred to as semi deterministic movement. The random technique is often used to generate new potential solutions (Kumar, 2020). This stochastic mechanism enables the solution to avoid being trapped in local optima. All algorithms strive to identify both local and global search solutions. If the search is limited to a certain area, there is a chance of relocating inside that area and being unable to leave. Conversely, if the search is conducted on a global scale, the rate of convergence decreases to some extent.

Various algorithms have significantly different random size and behave differently for local and global search. Selection of best solutions are simply carried out by "fit to survive" so as to keep the best next generation population that is actually act as motivation for driving the miscellaneous population into a unite population with minimized diversity in a well-organized manner. Table 1 shows characteristics and role of nature inspired algorithms.

When building approaches and algorithms for energy conservation in WSN, it is eminent to concentrate the many concerns and obstacles in order to expand the network lifespan of WSN. Network optimization is an essential element of wireless sensor networking, and optimization methods are used to get the most efficient solution for this issue. Given the existence of several optimization algorithms tailored to specific situations, the selection of an appropriate algorithm is crucial in any optimization approach.

4. ALGORITHMS FOR OPTIMIZATION IN WSN

The primary emphasis of sensor network protocols must be on power saving concerns. Additional concerns include the attainment of superior Quality of Service (QoS), restricted bandwidth, and constrained processing and storage capabilities in each individual node. These concerns are closely linked with the optimization problem.

Some of the Nature inspired optimization algorithms are summarized as per Table 1 as follows:

Table 1. Nature-inspired optimization algorithms

S. No.	Nature Inspired Algorithms	Performance Significance
1.	Swarm based Optimization (Jumani, 2020)	• Swarm behavior is an occurrence observed in animals of comparable size, when they come together or move in a coordinated manner along a certain route. • A distributed system consisting of autonomous agents that communicate with each other to improve performance, optimize processes, and allocate tasks in a distributed manner.
2.	Bat Optimization Algorithm (BOA)	• It resolves single- or multi-objective nonlinear global optimization issues. • These bats' excellent echolocation skills, which are made up of a highly competent manner, enable them to locate their roosting niches in the dark, avoid obstructions, and detect prey.
3.	Genetic system Optimization (GA)	• The GA is an optimization technique that explores the decision space by using selection, crossover, and mutation processes. The primary function of this system is to retain the most superior or elite chromosome for the subsequent generation. • Proficiency in managing intricate challenges and parallel processing. GA are capable of optimizing several types of objective functions, including both stable and transient ones, as well as linear and nonlinear ones, and continuous and discontinuous ones. • Parallel implementation of GA may accommodate multiple genes.GA may be used in WSN for tasks like as clustering, deployment, routing, and aggregation.
4.	Particle Swarm (Bird Flocks) Optimization (PSO)	• The PSO algorithm is a computer technique that uses a population of potential solutions, referred to as particles, known as a swarm. • The motion of the particles depends on both the location of the whole swarm as well as their individual best-known position inside the search area. The swarm moves according to this collective instruction, and the process is repetitive until an acceptable outcome is achieved. • PSO is a multi-dimensional optimization method with applications in data aggregation, energy-aware clustering, localization, node placement, and more.
5.	Ant Colony Optimization (ACO) (Li, 2016)	• The ACO approach is inspired by the behavior of ant species. Ants engage in food foraging by locating the food source and then returning to the nest, while leaving a trail of pheromones behind. • All other ants follow various paths without discrimination, thus reinforcing the runway will lead to the quickest route. Ants follow the most direct path and cease to leave scent markers while traveling large distances. • The approach is designed to solve discrete optimization issues in several domains of WSN. ACO has a greater degree of flexibility and decentralization, and it also shares similarities with the foraging and routing behaviors of ants. ACO may be used to address the complex and decentralized routing challenges in networks.
6.	Whale Optimization Algorithm (WOA) (Yue, 2021)	• The WOA models the hunting behavior of whales, specifically the bubble-nut feeding approach. • This foraging method involves targeting little fish that are located near the water's surface. The hunting phenomena is achieved by establishing circular routes among separate clusters. There are two types of drills used for bubble net feeding, namely 'upward spirals' and 'double-loops'.
7.	Cuckoo Search Optimization (CS)	• This study was inspired by the behaviour of cuckoo species and how they deposit their eggs in the nests of other host birds. The primary impulse for the design of this innovative evolutionary optimization approach. • Addressing optimization difficulties in WSN and exploring methods to enhance performance and efficiency by analyzing the node placement in graphs and trees.
8.	Antlion Algorithm (ALO)	• ALO is emulating the hunting tactics used by Antlions in their natural habitat.
9.	Sine cosine Algorithm (SCA) (Pandey, 2018)	• The SCA operates on a population of candidate solutions as an optimisation technique. The SCA algorithm produces a number of initial random solutions and employs a mathematical model that utilises sine cosine functions to direct them towards the optimal solution. • At various phases of optimisation, this method enhances both exploration and exploitation of the search space by incorporating a large number of adaptive and stochastic variables. • Numerous adaptive and stochastic variables aided the SCA method by permitting both divergence and convergence of the search agents.
10.	Fish School Search Optimization (FSO) (Li, 2016)	• An aggregation of fish refers to any group of fish that have gathered together in a certain area. • These aggregations may be either organized or disorganized. • This concept is used in node deployment algorithms, where nodes cluster together for various uses, such as Traffic Monitoring Systems.

Table 1 continued

S. No.	Nature Inspired Algorithms	Performance Significance
11.	Wasp Swam Optimization (WSO)	• A collective of persons collaborating for the preservation of the colony. • Synchronize their activity to construct intricate nest structures.
12.	Chameleon Optimization (CHO)	• The inspiration for this was derived from the adaptive color-changing behavior seen in chameleon animals. • Utilizing dynamic modeling techniques to ascertain the resemblance between clusters in pairs.
13.	Archimedes Optimization Algorithm (AOA)	• AOA employs search techniques such as random sampling of volumes, densities, and accelerations to generate initial candidate solutions. • Each item is placed in the fluid at random positions and its initial fitness is assessed repeatedly. AOA adjusts the density and volume of each item until the termination requirements are satisfied.
14.	Termites Colony Optimization (TCO)	• Termites transition from an uncoordinated state to a coordinated one only when their density exceeds a certain threshold. In order to achieve stability in the distribution of network traffic and extend the lifespan of the network without compromising performance.
15.	Salp Swarm Optimization Algorithm (SSOA)	• Salps belong to the family Salpidae and are marine organisms. • They have a cylindrical form with holes at the ends, which they use to move by pumping water through their gelatinous bodies. • Salps feed by using internal feeding filters. Salps exhibit behaviors that enhance their mobility and foraging capabilities.
16.	Mouth Flame Optimization (MFO)	• The motivation for MFO is derived from the transverse direction recognition approach used by moths in their surroundings. • The MFO algorithm, also known as Moths Fly at Night, utilizes a set angle in relation to the moon's position to efficiently move in a straight line over large distances. • These animals are trapped in a lethal spiral around artificial light.
17.	Honey Bees Optimization (HBO)	• Efficiently integrate replication and evasion techniques to enable the network to sustain data delivery for an extended duration under a congestion assault. • An energy-efficient security mechanism to counteract BT congestion attacks in WSN.
18.	Chimp Optimization Algorithm (ChoA) (Khishe, 2020)	• ChoA is driven by the behavioral traits and sexual drive associated with hunting within chimpanzee social groupings. This technique is used to exploit local optima and mitigate the issue of weak convergence inside their own clusters. • There are four distinct categories of chimpanzees known as attacker, barrier, chaser, and drivers, which are used to simulate hunting, driving, blocking, and assaulting. • ChoA is used for resolving high-dimensional optimization problems across several engineering disciplines.

5. KEY ISSUES AND CHALLENGES

The major technical challenges and issues to be addressed for the effective implementation of WSN are listed below:

- **Resource constraints:** The energy, memory and processing power are the major resources which affect the design and implementation of WSNs. Since WSN is a continuous process, the sensor nodes should be in active mode during the entire session. Hence, the battery to be provided in WSN should have the capability to manage the power requirement. At the same time, the size of the memories is limited and the processor should have the ability to perform the computation.
- **Environmental conditions:** The functionality of sensor nodes may be compromised under adverse environmental conditions. In industrial settings, network connection might be compromised

as a result of route obstructions and failures of sensor nodes. Moreover, the performance of the sensors may also be affected due to electromagnetic and Radio Frequency (RF) interference effects, corrosive environments, vibrations etc. The operation of sensor nodes may also get affected due to environmental conditions and network topologies.

- **Data Transmission Accuracy:** Data transmission accuracy states to the level of precision in the data sent to the destination compared to the real data present in the sensor field. Timely reception of data at the base station is crucial for promptly initiating alarm messages in critical circumstances. If the data is not received in time due to processing or communication delay then wrong decisions may be taken.
- **Security in data transmission:** Ensuring secure data transmission in WSN is a crucial aspect of the design process to provide protected communication, protecting against Denial of Service (DoS) attacks and intrusion (Gill, 2014). WSN facilitate a range of passive security threats, such as intercepting and monitoring signals. It is essential to take into account active attacks.
- **Area of Coverage and Large-scale deployment:** WSNs are comprised of a substantial number of sensor nodes that are sent in a stochastic fashion across the environment. Hence, it is essential to carefully analyze the strategic positioning of sensor nodes in order to achieve effective deployment. During the implementation phase, the sensor nodes have the capacity to spread out over a large geographic area. Moreover, the lack of pre-existing network infrastructure leads to the WSN autonomously forming connections and controlling network topology. To broaden the coverage area, it is important to use appropriate wireless technology which is combined with the routers.
- **Power Optimization and maximization network lifetime:** Continuous monitoring has been conducted in WSNs. Given that sensor nodes rely on battery power, power consumption is a critical aspect to be consider in WSNs. The depletion of energy in a sensor node leads to its shutdown and disconnection from the network, hence impacting the performance of the WSN application (Ray, 2016). Maximizing the network lifespan is crucial, since it is influenced by the number of active nodes and the network's structure. Therefore, power optimization is necessary.

6. THE PROPOSED OPTIMIZED ARTIFICIAL BEE COLONY OPTIMIZATION (OABC) FOR REDUCING ENERGY CONSUMPTION

The integration of the ABC with the stochastic gradient descent (SGD) method is used in a hybrid manner. The suggested method aims to choose a Cluster Head (CH) dynamically for hierarchical clustering (HC) in WSNs by using random deployment. This technique is designed to enhance the performance characteristics of the WSNs. The OABC method, which has been proposed for optimisation purposes, offers the following contributions:

- An optimised technique called OABC, which incorporates features from ABC and SGD, is suggested.
- The OABC method is established for choosing CH in WSNs to improve performance. The selection is based on factors like lasting energy and distance between the node and load on the node.
- The approach involves selecting CH via many processes, including random deployment for HC, using the OABC process to choose cluster heads, and employing the SGD priority vector to construct fitness.

- Data transmission is facilitated by the use of shortest route routing.
- The current algorithms, namely GA, PSO, ACO, and WOA, are subjected to comparative simulation analysis.

Integration of ABC and SGD for Optimized Bee Colony Algorithm (OABC)

OABC is a hybrid methodology that combines the ABC and SGD algorithms. ABC has the capacity to investigate and address intricate issues by exploring solutions that may be local minima. Furthermore, ABC is characterised by its simplicity, resilience, adaptability, and ease of implementation in managing objective costs. However, it is prone to early convergence. The SGD algorithm can be easily accommodated in memory and processed by the network. The system has rapid computational capacity and achieves rapid convergence in updating the parameters. The issue of premature convergence is overcome by using Stochastic Gradient Descent (SGD) with Adaptive Batch Control (ABC). The hybrid strategy OABC is used for CH selection because to the significant advantages offered by both algorithms.

The design of WSN is a complex undertaking due to its application-specific nature and the need to address low power limitations. The primary design criteria are deployment, scalability, energy efficiency, data aggregation, cost, network longevity, and on-chip storage, among others. This study effort proposes the integration of SGD with ABC to concentrate the problems of early convergence and local entrapment in ABC. OABC is used for CH selection and calculating the characteristics required for developing energy-efficient WSN, including energy usage, execution time, packet loss, and network lifespan. The performance is evaluated in comparison to established algorithms such GA, PSO, ACO, and WOA.

The OABC technique is designed for CH selection with the primary objective of maximising network lifespan and minimising energy use. The mathematical properties have been elucidated using the following equations: Initially, the network deploys sensors, referred to as bees, throughout the search region in a random manner. The mean energy of each sensor is determined using equation (1).

$$En_{avg} = \frac{En_{sn1} + En_{sn2} + En_{sn3} + \ldots En_{snN}}{N_L} = \frac{\sum_{i=1}^{N} En_{sni}}{N_L} \quad (1)$$

where $En_{sn(i)}$ is the energy of the node and NL the living node number Then all the nearby locations of the nodes from the node $sn(i)$are computed and the distance between these nodes and $sn(i)$is evaluated as weight (w) of $sn(i)$ parameter by equation (2).

$$weight\,of\,sn(i) = \frac{En_{sn}}{\sum_{dis=p}^{dis=q} dis(sn(i), sn(p)) + \ldots + dis(sn(i)\,sn(q))} \quad (2)$$

Where dis is the distance among the node $s(i)$ and its neighbors (i.e. nodes $sn(p)$ & $sn(q)$), En_{sn} is residual energy of the node $sn(i)$.

Thereafter $SNL_{s(i)}$ is computed depending upon living nodes and neighboring nodes. CH is elected on the highest value of $SNL_{s(i)}$ and is given by equation (3):

$$SNL_{sn(i)} = \frac{Nebr\left(sn\left(i\right)\right)}{N_L} \tag{3}$$

Where $SNL_{s(i)}$ is the neighbor life of $sn(i)$ and $Nebr$ is the number of neighbors of node $sn(i)$. Then following equation (4) is implemented after computing the value of $SNL_{s(i)}$ to validate the solution.

$$P\left(sn\left(i\right)\right) = \begin{cases} \dfrac{C_p}{1 - C_p * \left\{ round\, mod\left(\dfrac{1}{C_p}\right)\right\}} sn\left(i \in g\right) \\ 1 sn\left(i \notin g\right) \end{cases} \tag{4}$$

Where CP represents the chance of CH in each round, calculated as the ratio of the entire number of CHs to the total number of nodes. Round refers to the current round value, while g represents the group of nodes that have not been chosen for $\frac{1}{C_p}$ rounds.

After these three different parameters considered such as energy i.e. dependent upon residue energy and health of the node, distance vector depending upon coverage vector and the load on the node. The energy is calculated as per equation (5):

$$\text{Energy} = E_i \times h_i \tag{5}$$

Where E_i=residue energy of the node and h_i = health of the node whether it is alive or node. Thereafter, the distance weight vector w_K, may be computed by D as per equation (6) by using locations of the nodes p & q and also calculated the coverage vector C_w as per equation (7).

$$D = \sqrt{\left(\left(\left(p_2\right) - \left(p_1\right)\right)^2 - \left(\left(\left(q_2\right) - \left(q_1\right)\right)^2\right.\right.} \tag{6}$$

$$C_w = Max \sum_{s=0}^{w_{K,i}} W_{K,s} \tag{7}$$

Now load on the node is calculated as the rate of routed packets in specific time and expressed by equation (8) as:

$$Load\left(i\right) = \sum_{k=0}^{m} \frac{RP_k}{time} \tag{8}$$

Where RP_k is the packet on the route, and k = 0, 1, 2 ….. m is number of packets for the specific *time* period.

Depending on the Load and on the node, health of the node and residue energy the fitness value of the function is calculated by equation (9) as follows:

$$Min\left(\left(c,i\right)\right)=\sum_{i=1}^{N}\frac{E_i\times h_i\times C_w}{Load\left(i\right)} \tag{9}$$

The final CH is further optimized using SGD on the basis of priority vector by expression given by equation (10):

$$Q_j=Q_j-\propto\left(\hat{q}^i-q^i\right)p_j^i \tag{10}$$

Where Q_j is the head node and *i* is the range of sensor data.

The optimisation of CH is achieved by the calculation of SGD derivatives, making it simpler to process and fit in memory inside the network.

The SGD optimisation must be applied to all sensor data samples in each round until the minimum value is reached. SGD employs a single randomly selected sample for each iteration.

The function is computed for the CH chosen by using a derivative approximation instead of summing the gradients over all samples. At first, the weight for CH is used and the error is computed to get the minimum coverage weight. Adjusted weights are iteratively updated until the optimal value for CH is reached.

Pseudocode for proposed OABC for Cluster Head Selection

```
Input: Nodes of clustered network simulation
Output: Optimized cluster-head
// Processing phase 1
Step 1: Start
// Initialization process of network nodes and parameters
Step 2: N = total number of nodes.
Step 3: For all-nodes-of-network do
Step 4: Init. Positions=true
C_distance_matrix= √(((p2) − (p1))^2 − (((q2) − (q1))^2
Step 5: end
// Processing phase 2
Step 6: For all-clusters k do
Step 7: For all-placed-node i do
Step 8: If node_k,i not in dead-vector then
w_k, = C_distance_matrix_i.
// Calculated distance vector weight
```

$$L_i=\sum_{r=0}^{w_{k,i}}\frac{RP_r}{t}$$

```
// Calculated load vector
```

$$\text{Calculate-weight}_i=\sum_{i=1}^{n}\frac{\left(E_ih_i*Max\left(\sum_{s=0}^{w_{K,i}}W_{K,s}\right)\right)}{L_i}$$

```
Step 9: Find-priority-vector= SGD(Calculate-weight_i)
// Processing phase 3
Step 10: If cost.node>Find-priority-vector //then node become head
Step 11: end
Step 12: end
Step 13: end
Step 14: end
Step 15: end
```

7. RESULTS AND DISCUSSIONS

This discussion focuses on the design of a WSN, specifically the clustering module and routing module of the proposed network architecture. Initially, network parameters are generated and demonstrated in Table 1 to start the network design process.

Table 1. Network parameters

Parameters	Proposed Protocol
Network size	100 m x 100 m
No. of nodes	100
No. of clusters	Variable
Initial energy of nodes	5 J
Position of nodes	Range between (0, 0) and (100, 100)
Round time	20 sec
Simulation time	3600 sec
Packet size	2000 bits

Here, we provide the results of the simulated assessment of the proposed OBCA algorithm for analysing different factors, including network lifespan, execution time, packet loss, and energy consumption. The findings indicate that the proposed OABC significantly enhances the network lifespan by 61% compared with existing optimisation algorithms such as GA (17%), PSO (13%), ACO (4%), and WOA (42%), as shown in Figure 3.

The CH is chosen based on its much lower execution time, which is just about 2% compared to other existing optimisation algorithms such as GA (7%), PSO (8%), ACO (40%), and WOA (41%), as shown in Figure 4. The proposed OABC algorithm displays a shorter processing time in comparison to other methods, resulting in enhanced network speed and reduced average computing time.

The proposed OABC displays a packet loss rate of just 2%, which is much lower than the packet loss rates of existing optimization algorithms like GA (6%), PSO (11%), ACO (38%), and WOA (43%), as shown in Figure 5. This makes it very suitable for network data aggregation.

Figure 3. Execution time

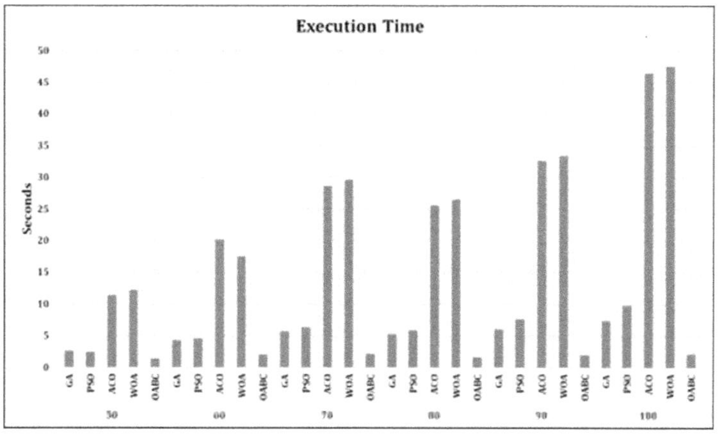

Figure 4. Network lifetime

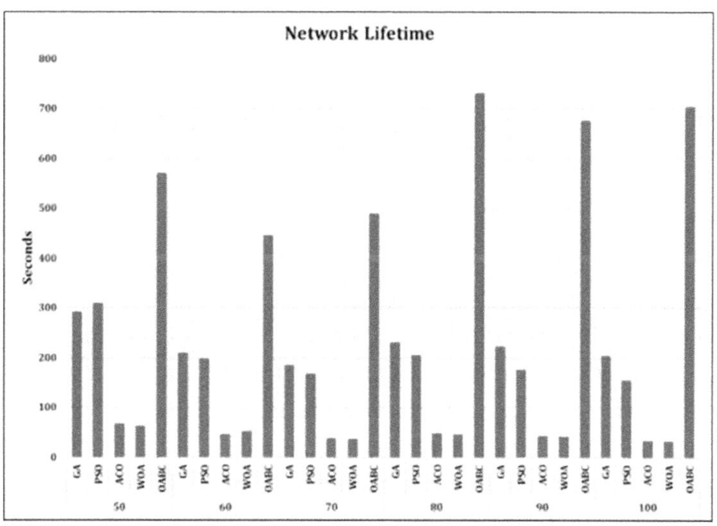

Figure 5. Packet loss

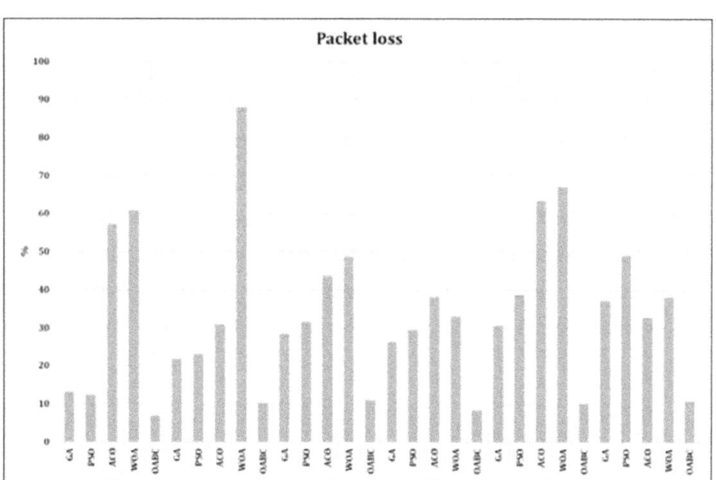

The energy consumption of the proposed OABC is much lower compared to other approaches. It improves the network's lifespan by spending just 6% of the energy, in contrast with existing optimisation algorithms such as GA (28%), PSO (35%), ACO (15%), and WOA (16%), as shown in Figure 6.

Figure 6. Energy consumption

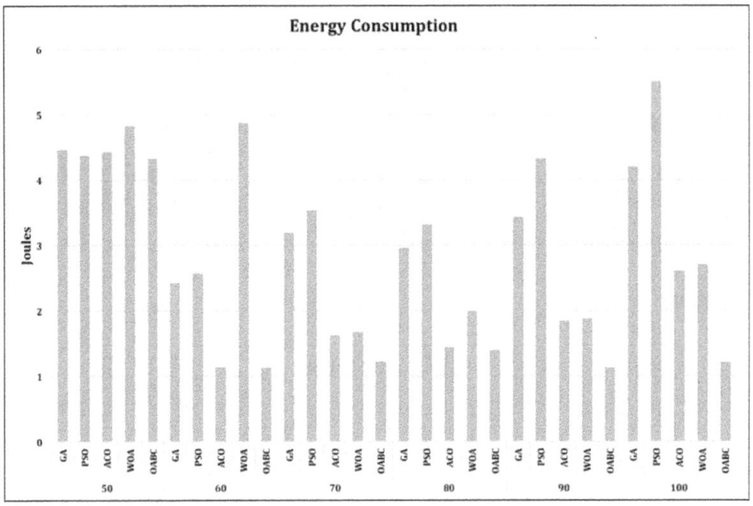

8. CONCLUSION

This chapter presented the introduction of WSN detailed study of the design of an energy efficient WSN that includes background and introduction, taxonomy of energy efficient WSN, classical and optimization approaches. Also, optimal path routing and literature summary is presented, significance of energy consumption, applications and challenges related to WSN. Apart from this, energy efficient WSN, need for optimization, nature inspired algorithms, and key challenges are discussed. Additionally, the network uses less energy to function longer. This work offers an improved bee colony algorithm to improve WSN energy consumption and execution time for better performance. CH selection is chosen using the OABC algorithm, and heads are randomly changed each iteration. The simulation findings reveal that OABC executes quicker, transmits more packets, and uses less energy, extending network longevity. GA, PSO, ACO, and WOA take longer than OABC. The proposed OABC outperforms current packet transfer techniques in execution time. The suggested OABC uses less energy than GA, PSO, ACO, and WOA, according to simulations. OABC maximises data speed and system operability with lesser complexity. Network longevity, another simulation parameter, influences WSN endurance without sacrificing service quality. Compared to GA, PSO, ACO, and WOA algorithms, the suggested technique increases network longevity. Clustering improves transmission quality by reducing packet loss compared to other techniques. It also maximises data for the destination user, improving network speed. To further optimize the network performance secure communication can be explored for different application area.

REFERENCES

Adhikar, M., & Amgoth, T. (2019). An intelligent water drops-based workflow scheduling for IaaS cloud. Applied Soft Computing, 77, 547–566. doi:10.1016/j.asoc.2019.02.004

Agbehadji, I. E., Millham, R. C., Abayomi, A., Jung, J. J., Fong, S. J., & Frimpong, S. O. (2021). Clustering algorithm based on nature-inspired approach for energy optimization in heterogeneous wireless sensor network. Applied Soft Computing, 104(107171), 1–15. doi:10.1016/j.asoc.2021.107171

Alghamdi, T. A. (2021). Parametric analysis on optimized energy-efficient protocol in wireless sensor network. Soft Computing, 25(6), 4409–4421. doi:10.1007/s00500-020-05449-8

Bangotra, D. K., Singh, Y., Kumar, N., Singh, P. K., & Ojeniyi, A. (2022). Energy-Efficient and Secure Opportunistic Routing Protocol for WSN: Performance Analysis with Nature-Inspired Algorithms and Its Application in Biomedical Applications. BioMed Research International, 2022, 1–13. doi:10.1155/2022/1976694 PMID:35372577

Brahim, R. A., Ewees, A. A., & Oliva, D. (2019). Improved salp swarm algorithm based on particle swarm optimization for feature selection. Journal of Ambient Intelligence and Humanized Computing, 10(8), 3155–3169. doi:10.1007/s12652-018-1031-9

Chan, L., Chavez, K. G., & Rudolph, H. (2020). Hierarchical routing protocols for wireless sensor network: A compressive survey. Wireless Networks, 26(5), 3291–3314. doi:10.1007/s11276-020-02260-z

Chavan, Kulkarni, & Chikode. (2019) IBeeCup: An Energy *Efficient Bio Inspired Clustering Method for Homogeneous and Heterogeneous in WSN. Academic Press.*

Daneshvar, S. M., Alikhah Ahari Mohajer, P., & Mazinani, S. M. (2019). Energy-efficient routing in WSN: A centralized cluster-based approach via grey wolf optimizer. IEEE Access : Practical Innovations, Open Solutions, 7, 170019–170031. doi:10.1109/ACCESS.2019.2955993

Decerle, J., Grunder, O., Hassani, A. H., & Barakat, O. (2019). A hybrid memetic-ant colony optimization algorithm for the home health care problem with time window, synchronization and working time balancing. Swarm and Evolutionary Computation, 46, 171–183. doi:10.1016/j.swevo.2019.02.009

Devassy, D., Johnraja, J. I., & Getzi, J. L. P. (2022). NBA: Novel bio-inspired algorithm for energy optimization in WSN for IoT applications. The Journal of Supercomputing, 78(14), 1–18. doi:10.1007/s11227-022-04505-4

Famila, S., Jawahar, A., Sariga, A., & Shankar, K. (2019). Improved artificial bee colony optimization-based clustering algorithm for SMART sensor environments. Peer-to-Peer Networking and Applications, 1–9.

Gill, R. K., Chawla, P., & Sachdeva, M. (2014). Wireless sensor network: threat models and security issues. International Conference on Communication, Computing & Systems (ICCCS-2014), 30-33.

Hema & Sankar. (2016). Energy efficient cluster-based protocol to extend the RFID network lifetime using dragonfly algorithm. In *International conference on communication and signal processing (ICCSP)* (pp. 530-534). IEEE.

Jafar, M., Moghaddam, H., Kalam, A., Nowdeh, S. A., Ahmadi, A., Babanezhad, M., & Saha, S. (2019). Optimal sizing and energy management of stand-alone hybrid photovoltaic/wind system based on hydrogen storage considering LOEE and LOLE reliability indices using flower pollination algorithm. *Renewable Energy*, *135*, 1412–1434. doi:10.1016/j.renene.2018.09.078

Jumani, T. A., Mustafa, M. W., Alghamdi, A. S., Rasid, M. M., Alamgir, A., & Awan, A. B. (2020). Swarm intelligence-based optimization techniques for dynamic response and power quality enhancement of AC microgrids: A comprehensive review. *IEEE Access : Practical Innovations, Open Solutions*, *8*, 75986–76001. doi:10.1109/ACCESS.2020.2989133

Karthick & Palanisamy. (2019). Optimized cluster head selection using krill herd algorithm for wireless sensor network. *Automatika: časopiszaautomatiku, mjerenje, elektroniku, računarstvoikomunikacije*, *60*(3), 340-348.

Khishe, M. M. (2020). Chimp optimization algorithm. Expert Systems with Applications. Elsevier.

Kumar, S., Kaiwartya, O., Rathee, M., Kumar, N., & Lloret, J. (2020). Toward energy-oriented optimization for green communication in sensor enabled IoT environments. *IEEE Systems Journal*, *14*(4), 4663–4673. doi:10.1109/JSYST.2020.2975823

Lavanya, N., & Shankar, T. (2019). Energy Efficient Cluster Head Selection using Hybrid Squirrel Harmony Search Algorithm in WSN. *Energy*, *10*, 477–487.

Li, X., Keegan, B., & Mtenzi, F. (2016). Energy efficient hybrid routing protocol based on the artificial fish swarm algorithm and ant colony optimisation for WSNs. *Sensors (Basel)*, *18*(10, no. 10pp), 3351. doi:10.3390/s18103351 PMID:30297606

Li, X., Keegan, B., Mtenzi, F., Weise, T., & Tan, M. (2019). *Energy-efficient load balancing ant-based routing algorithm for wireless sensor networks.* IEEE Access. doi:10.1109/ACCESS.2019.2934889

Liu, F., & Chang, Y. (2019). *An energy aware adaptive kernel density estimation approach to unequal clustering in wireless sensor networks.* IEEE Access. doi:10.1109/ACCESS.2019.2902243

Mahapatra, Payal, & Chopra. (2020). Swarm intelligence based centralized clustering: A novel solution. *Journal of Intelligent Manufacturing*, 1–12.

Moncayo–Martínez, L. A., & Mastrocinque, E. (2016). A multi-objective intelligent water drop algorithm to minimize cost of goods sold and time to market in logistics networks. *Expert Systems with Applications*, *64*, 455–466. doi:10.1016/j.eswa.2016.08.003

Mood & Javidi. (2019). Energy-efficient clustering method for wireless sensor networks using modified gravitational search algorithm. *Evolving Systems*, 1–13.

Oren, G., Barenboim, L., & Levin, H. (2017). Adaptive Distributed Hierarchical Sensing algorithm for reduction of wireless sensor network cluster-heads energy consumption. *13th International Wireless Communications and Mobile Computing Conference (IWCMC)*, 980-986. 10.1109/IWCMC.2017.7986419

Pal, V., Singh, G., & Yadav, R. P. (2015). Cluster head selection optimization based on genetic algorithm to prolong lifetime of wireless sensor networks. *Procedia Computer Science*, *57*, 1417–1423. doi:10.1016/j.procs.2015.07.461

Pandey, A., Rajan, A., & Nandi, A. (2018). Lifetime enhancement of wireless sensor networks by using sine cosine optimization algorithm. In *2018 7th International Conference on Reliability, Infocom Technologies and Optimization (Trends and Future Directions) (ICRITO)* (pp. 1-7). IEEE. 10.1109/ICRITO.2018.8748649

Pati, B., Sarkar, J. L., & Panigrahi, C. R. (2017). ECS: An energy-efficient approach to select cluster-head in wireless sensor networks. *Arabian Journal for Science and Engineering*, *42*(2), 669–676. doi:10.1007/s13369-016-2304-2

Prakash, N., Rajalakshmi, M., & Nedunchezhian, R. (2020). Optimized Energy Aware Routing Based on Suitable Based Antlion Group with Advanced Algorithm (SA-AOA) in Wireless Sensor Network. *Wireless Personal Communications*, *113*(1), 59–77. doi:10.1007/s11277-020-07178-5

Qiuet, M., Ming, Z., Li, J., Liu, J., Quan, G., & Yongxin Zhu, Y. (2013). Informer homed routing fault tolerance mechanism for wireless sensor networks. *Journal of Systems Architecture*, *59*(4-5), 260–270. doi:10.1016/j.sysarc.2012.12.003

Ray, A., & De, D. (2016). Energy efficient clustering protocol based on K-means (EECPK-means)-midpoint algorithm for enhanced network lifetime in wireless sensor network. *IET Wireless Sensor Systems*, *6*(6), 181–191. doi:10.1049/iet-wss.2015.0087

Sharma, R., Vashisht, V., & Singh, U. (2020). eeTMFO/GA: A secure and energy efficient cluster head selection in wireless sensor networks. *Telecommunication Systems*, *74*(3), 1–16. doi:10.1007/s11235-020-00654-0

Siddiqua, A., Shah, M. A., Khattak, H. A., Din, I. U., & Guizani, M. (2019). iCAFE: Intelligent Congestion Avoidance and Fast Emergency services. Academic Press.

Singh, H., & Singh, D. (2016). Taxonomy of routing protocols in wireless sensor networks: A survey. In *2016 2nd International Conference on Contemporary Computing and Informatics (IC3I)* (pp. 822-830). IEEE. 10.1109/IC3I.2016.7918796

Singh, S., & Gupta, B. (2016). OSEECH: Optimize scalable energy efficient clustering hierarchy protocol in wireless sensor networks. *Advances in Computing, Communications and Informatics (ICACCI), 2016 International Conference on*, 1441-1446.

Srivastava, P. R. (2015). A cooperative approach to optimize the Printed Circuit Boards drill routing process using Intelligent Water Drops. *Computers & Electrical Engineering*, *43*, 270–277. doi:10.1016/j.compeleceng.2014.10.005

Ullah, Z. (2020). A Survey on Hybrid, Energy Efficient and Distributed (HEED) Based Energy Efficient Clustering Protocols for Wireless Sensor Networks. *Wireless Personal Communications*, *112*(4), 1–29. doi:10.1007/s11277-020-07170-z

Wang, J., Zhang, Z., Xia, F., Yuan, W., & Lee, S. (2013). An energy efficient stable election-based routing algorithm for wireless sensor networks. *Sensors (Basel)*, *13*(11), 14301–14320. doi:10.3390/s131114301 PMID:24284767

Xi, F., Pang, Y., Liu, G., Wang, S., Li, W., Zhang, C., & Wang, Z. L. (2019). Self-powered intelligent buoy system by water wave energy for sustainable and autonomous wireless sensing and data transmission. *Nano Energy*, *61*, 1–9. doi:10.1016/j.nanoen.2019.04.026

Yue, Y., You, H., Wang, S., & Cao, L. (2021). Improved whale optimization algorithm and its application in heterogeneous wireless sensor networks. *International Journal of Distributed Sensor Networks*, *17*(5). doi:10.1177/15501477211018140

Chapter 7
Making Healthcare Decisions:
An Evolution

Venkata Tulasiramu Ponnada
Collins Aerospace, USA

Venkata Tulasikrishna Ponnada
Acharya Nagarjuna University, India

Narendra Kumar Rao B.
Mohan Babu University, India

Rama Krishna Raju Sammeta
Mohan Babu University, India

Hymavathi Jasti
Mohan Babu University, India

ABSTRACT

The landscape of healthcare decision-making has undergone a transformative evolution in recent years, driven by advancements in medical technology, changing patient expectations, and the integration of data-driven approaches. This chapter explores the dynamic shifts in healthcare decision-making processes, examining the multifaceted factors contributing to this evolution. This chapter concludes by highlighting the imperative for a holistic approach to healthcare decision-making evolution, one that integrates technological advancements with ethical principles, patient empowerment, and effective communication. Understanding and navigating these multifaceted dynamics are crucial for stakeholders in healthcare as they seek to optimize decision-making processes for the benefit of individuals and society at large.

DOI: 10.4018/979-8-3693-2073-0.ch007

1. INTRODUCTION

In the ever-evolving landscape of healthcare, the process of decision-making stands as a testament to the dynamic interplay between medical science, technology, and the intricate fabric of human experiences. This chapter embarks on a comprehensive exploration of the evolutionary journey that healthcare decision-making has traversed over the years. From its humble beginnings rooted in empirical wisdom to the contemporary era of data-driven precision and artificial intelligence, the trajectory of healthcare decisions mirrors the relentless quest for improvement, efficacy, and patient-centered care.

The historical narrative of healthcare decision-making unveils a rich tapestry of practices shaped by cultural, ethical, and scientific influences. Early healers relied on intuition, observation, and the accumulated wisdom of generations. As medical knowledge burgeoned, the dawn of evidence-based medicine marked a paradigm shift, introducing a more systematic approach to decision-making grounded in scientific inquiry.

The pivotal moments in this evolution are marked by transformative technological advancements, such as the advent of medical imaging, genomics, and computational power. These innovations have not only expanded our understanding of diseases but have also empowered healthcare practitioners with unprecedented tools to make informed decisions tailored to individual patients. The integration of artificial intelligence into decision support systems heralds a new era, promising enhanced diagnostics, personalized treatment plans, and the optimization of healthcare resources.

However, with progress comes a complex interplay of challenges. Ethical considerations, patient autonomy, and the responsible use of technology cast intricate shadows on the path of evolution. Balancing the promise of innovation with the imperative of ethical practice becomes a central theme in this narrative, raising critical questions about the responsibilities and accountability of healthcare decision-makers.

Beyond the technological and ethical dimensions, the human element remains paramount. The evolving narrative of healthcare decisions intertwines with the stories of patients, caregivers, and healthcare providers. Cultural shifts toward patient-centered care emphasize shared decision-making, where the voices and values of patients contribute significantly to the decision-making process.

As we embark on this intellectual journey, each chapter within this compilation unfolds a distinct facet of the evolving narrative. From early practices to futuristic perspectives, we scrutinize the mechanisms, challenges, and ethical considerations that have sculpted the intricate mosaic of healthcare decision-making. Through historical reflections, contemporary analyses, and glimpses into the future, we seek to provide a comprehensive understanding of this dynamic evolution. Join us as we navigate through the corridors of medical history, grapple with the complexities of the present, and envision the transformative possibilities that lie ahead in the perpetual evolution of healthcare decision-making.

Following wide-ranging research encompasses conditions like the melanoma, a severe type of skin cancer, as well as psoriasis, a chronic skin condition. Besides these, pneumonia and lung cancer, two major respiratory ailments, have also been a part of this exploration. Navigating through these studies, we realized the untapped potential of these techniques, inspiring us to propose a more comprehensive solution.

Foolproof decision Support System for Melanoma Cancer Detection (FDSSMCD) drives a new end to end patient centric system to detect the melanoma cancer used an efficient CNN to drive the best-in class results (Venkata & Sreenivasu, 2019a).

The Integrated Clinician Decision Support System for Pneumonia and Lung Cancer Detection represents an innovative approach that combines the detection of pneumonia and lung cancer into a unified solution. This system streamlines the diagnosis and provides a singular solution for addressing both lung diseases (Venkata & Sreenivasu, 2019b).

The Edge AI System for Pneumonia and Lung Cancer Detection advocates for the implementation of edge AI technology in healthcare, enabling clinicians to have disease detection capabilities at their fingertips. This system functions as an assisting tool in the diagnostic process (Venkata & Sreenivasu, 2019c).

The research on the Efficient CNN for Lung Cancer Detection utilizes an advanced Convolutional Neural Network (CNN) to identify lung cancer, and its applicability extends to the detection of other lung diseases as well (Venkata & Sreenivasu, 2019d).

The research on the End-to-End System for Pneumonia and Lung Cancer Detection Using Deep Learning presents a comprehensive solution for the detection of pneumonia and lung cancer. Functioning as a clinician decision support system, it delivers a best-in-class experience and results (Venkata & Sreenivasu, 2019e).

Figure 1. Evaluation of healthcare

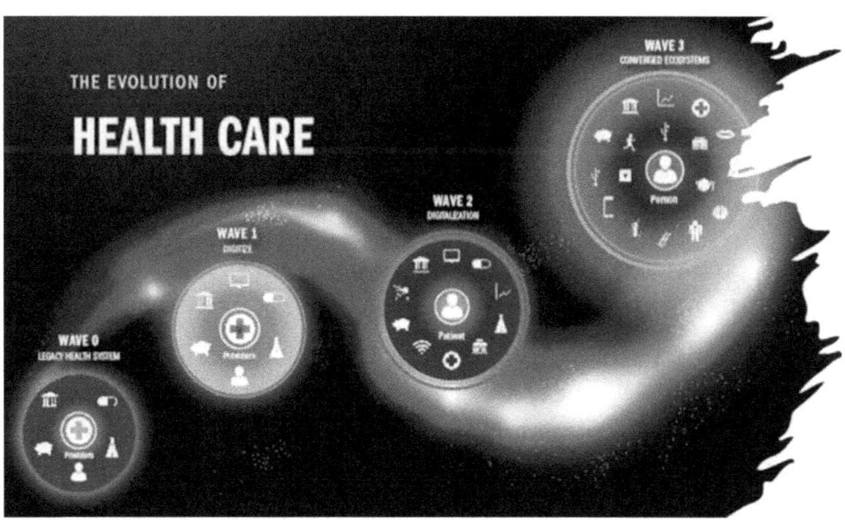

2. EMERGING TRENDS IN HEALTHCARE DECISION MAKING

The medical care field is experiencing significant changes due to evolving decision-making processes, with new trends profoundly changing patient treatment, care protocols, and the broader health landscape. One key trend witnessing is the increasing adoption of high-tech tools such as artificial intelligence (AI), machine learning and data analytical approaches. These cutting-edge tools provide healthcare experts with refined mechanisms for examining large sets of patient's information, foreseeing outcomes, and formulating individualized treatment strategies. The prominence of Clinical Decision Support Systems (CDSS) enhance the precision of diagnosis and effective treatment advising, leading to more educated decision-making. In addition to this, a notable shift towards patient-centered care is clearly seen with more emphasis on engaging the patients in discussing decision-making and considering their choices and values in the decision-making journey. Remote patient treatment and monitoring is becoming more critical, presenting new options for healthcare administrators and decision-makers in providing care, specifically during worldwide health crisis situations. Adding to this, the blend of genomics and precision medicine has usher a new age of treatment plans that are customized to an individual's genetic makeup, maximizing therapeutic results. These trends, when combined, signifies a pivotal stage - a moment where technical integration, encouraging patient participation, and bespoke treatment approaches drive the progress of health care decision-making. *Figure 10.2* shows the evolution of health care through legacy systems, digitize, digitization to converged edge systems.

2.1 Clinical Decision Support Systems (CDSS)

Innovative advancements in Clinical Decision Support Systems (CDSS) are reshaping the phase of health care decisions making, leading a new period of accuracy and proficiency. These systems exploit state-of-the-art technologies such as artificial intelligence, machine learning and predictive analytics for scrutinizing massive volumes of clinical data, delivering real-time, evidence-based findings to healthcare operators. A significant trend is the assimilation of CDSS with Electronic Health Records (EHRs), which encourages effortless facts interchange while enhancing the comprehensive quality of patient care. Also, tailored medicine is capturing public attention with CDSS fitting recommendations as per each patient's unique attributes and genetic frameworks. Another vital progression emphasizes intuitive interfaces and interoperability, which ensures that healthcare providers can effortlessly access and decode the produced insights. As CDSS keeps evolving, it holds the potential to refine diagnostic preciseness, therapy efficacy and overall healthcare outcomes, eventually defining a more efficient and patient-oriented approach to clinical decision-making.

2.2 On-the-Spot Data Evaluation and Decision Backing

Significant advances in on-the-spot data evaluation and decision backing are taking place within the healthcare sector, ushering innovative trends that reinforce the speed and accuracy of decision-making processes. One prime emerging formation is the incorporation of Internet of Things (IoT) tools and wearable devices, which allows for continuous monitoring of patient vital signs and health metrics. This unending data influx enables healthcare professionals timely pinpoint and respond to significant changes in patient conditions. Artificial intelligence (AI) and machine learning algorithms are playing a pivotal role in interpreting this flow, predicting potential health complications and offering timely intervention suggestions. Also, cloud computing solutions are facilitating the effortless storage, retrieval, and analysis of enormous datasets, assuring healthcare decision-makers have quick access to comprehensive information. The focus on interoperability and data sharing across healthcare systems is a remarkable trend, fostering joint decision-making across various departments and establishments. As on-the-spot data evaluation keeps evolving, it holds the potential to revolutionize healthcare decision-making, providing actionable data, foster preventive care, and ultimately refine patient outcomes.

2.3 Clinical Procedures and Guidelines

Fresh perspectives in clinical procedures and guidelines are transforming the realm of health care decision-making, leading to an era of standardized, and patient-oriented care. Advanced technologies, such as artificial intelligence and data analytics, are utilized to shape and finetune clinical procedures, ensuring that healthcare providers have access to the most recent and evidence-based guidelines. Customized medicine is becoming prominent within these procedures, tailoring treatment plans according to individual patient attributes, genetics, and preferences. The integration of decision support systems and electronic health records enables the effortless adoption and abidance of these guidelines, streamlining the decision-making process for healthcare professionals. Additionally, there is a broadening focus on interdisciplinary collaboration, with the involvement of various healthcare stakeholders in the development and implementation of clinical procedures. This comprehensive approach aims to enhance coordination, reduce variability in care and ultimately refine patient outcomes. As health care decision-making advances, the dynamic incorporation of technology, personalization, and collaborative practices within clinical pathways promises to deliver more effective, efficient, and patient-oriented care.

2.4 Predictive Analytics and Machine Learning

Fresh perspectives in predictive analytics and machine learning are revolutionizing healthcare decision-making by leveraging the magnitude of data-oriented findings. Predictive analytics, ignited by machine learning algorithms, allows healthcare professionals to forecast patient results, discern potential health threats, and fine-tune treatment methods. These technologies evaluate enormous amounts of historical and current data, discovering patterns that may not be perceptible through conventional methods. One key tendency is the incorporation of predictive analytics into clinical decision support systems, offering real-time data to guide healthcare professionals in making prompt and well-informed choices. Personalized medicine is also benefiting from these advancements, with machine learning algorithms tailoring treatment plans based on individual patient traits and genetic data. As the health care industry increasingly adopts these technologies, there's a focus on ensuring interpretability, transparency, and ethical usage of predictive models. The continuous evolution of predictive analytics and machine learning in health care decision-making holds the potential for improving diagnostic accuracy, optimizing allocation of resources, and ultimately enhancing patient outcomes.

2.5 Early Disease Detection and Prevention

Fresh perspectives in early disease detection and prevention are transforming health care determinations, emphasizing a proactive and preventative to improvise patient outcomes. Advanced technologies, such as genomics, proteomics, and wearable gadgets, have a pivotal role in identifying biomarkers and subtle physiological changes that can signify the onset of diseases during the early stage. The integration of artificial intelligence and machine learning into diagnostic processes allows for the rapid analysis of complex datasets, aiding healthcare professionals in identifying patterns and predicting potential health risks. Moreover, the focus on precision medicine and personalized health interventions is gaining prominence, tailoring prevention strategies to an individual's unique genetic composition and lifestyle factors. Telehealth and remote monitoring solutions contribute to the early detection paradigm, enabling continuous tracking of patient health measurements. As healthcare decision-making evolves, the shift towards early disease detection and prevention holds the promise of not only improving patient health but also alleviating the strain on healthcare systems by reducing disease prevalence and severity through prompt interventions and lifestyle amendments.

2.6 Personalized Treatment Suggestions

Fresh trends in personalized treatment recommendations are revolutionizing healthcare decision-making, ushering a new era of precision medicine. Advancements in genomics, molecular profiling, and sophisticated data analytics are enabling healthcare professionals to tailor treatment plans to the unique attributes of individual patients. Genetic data, combined with other patient-specific elements, is frequently used to identify targeted therapies, predict treatment responses, and minimize adverse effects. Machine learning algorithms play a crucial role in examining complex datasets and identifying patterns that can inform personalized treatment recommendations. Additionally, the integration of electronic health records and clinical decision support systems ensures that healthcare providers have real-time access to the latest evidence-based guidelines, further enhancing the ability to make knowledgeable and individualized treatment determinations. This trend mirrors a paradigm shift towards more effective and patient-centered care, offering the potential to improve treatment results, minimize side effects, and optimize healthcare.

2.7 Telehealth and Remote Monitoring

New trends in telehealth and remote monitoring are crafting healthcare decision-making, offering innovative solutions that enhance accessibility, efficiency, and patient-centered care. Telehealth services have leaped, facilitated by technological progress, allowing patients to consult with healthcare providers virtually. This augmentation does not only improve access to medical expertise but also reduces the need for physical visits, making healthcare more convenient and cost-effective. Remote monitoring devices, including wearables and IoT-enabled tools, allow for continuous tracking of patient vitals and health measurements in real-time. This abundance of data allows healthcare professionals to make informed decisions, detect early caution signs, and intervene proactively. Artificial intelligence and machine learning algorithms play a pivotal role in evaluating the massive datasets generated by remote monitoring, helping predict health trends and individualizing care plans.

2.8 Expanding Access to Healthcare

Fresh perspectives in expanding access to healthcare is molding the landscape of healthcare decision-making, with a focus on increasing accessibility and inclusivity. Telehealth services are playing a critical role in broadening healthcare access, allowing individuals to liaise with healthcare providers remotely, overcoming geographical barriers and enhancing comfort. Mobile health applications and digital platforms are providing tools for self-monitoring preventive care and health education, empowering individuals to take a proactive role in managing their health. Furthermore, community-oriented healthcare initiatives, such as mobile clinics and outreach programs, are addressing disparities in healthcare access among underserved populations. Collaborations between healthcare establishments and technology companies are steering innovations to make healthcare services more affordable and scalable. As healthcare decision-makers explore these broadening access trends, the goal is to create a fairer healthcare system, ensuring that individuals from diverse backgrounds have the means to receive timely and quality care.

2.9 Remote Patient Management

Emerging trends in remote patient management are revolutionizing healthcare decision-making, fostering a paradigm shift towards proactive and patient-centric care. Advanced technologies, such as telehealth platforms, wearable devices, and remote monitoring solutions, facilitate healthcare professionals to remotely track and manage patients' health conditions in real-time. These technologies provide continuous patient data, enabling early detection of health complications and timely interventions. Artificial intelligence and machine learning algorithms analyze the extensive datasets generated by remote monitoring, offering useful insights for personalized treatment plans. Patient engagement is also a key emphasis, with interactive apps and digital tools facilitating communication and empowering individuals to actively participate in their healthcare journey. The integration of remote patient management into healthcare decision-making not only enhances the efficiency of care delivery but also contributes to improved patient outcomes, reduced hospital visits, and improved overall management of chronic conditions. As these trends evolve, healthcare decision-makers are recognizing the potential of remote patient management to optimize resources and deliver more effective, patient-centered healthcare.

2.10 Healthcare Internet of Things (IoT)

Fresh perspectives in Healthcare Internet of Things (IoT) are reshaping healthcare decision-making, leveraging interconnected devices to enhance data-driven insights and improve patient outcomes. The spread of IoT devices, such as wearables sensors, and intelligent medical devices, allows for continuous surveillance of patient vitals, medicine compliance, and other relevant health measurements. This real-time data flow is instrumental in supporting prompt and informed decision-making by healthcare professionals. The integration of IoT with electronic health records (EHRs) allows for seamless data exchange, providing a comprehensive overview of a patient's health history. Machine learning algorithms applied to IoT-generated data contribute to predictive analytics, aiding in early detection of diseases, personalized treatment suggestions, and preventive care strategies. As IoT applications continue to evolve, healthcare decision-makers are grappling with the challenges of data security and interoperability while maximizing the potential of this interconnected ecosystem to drive more efficient, accurate, and patient-centered healthcare decisions.

2.11 Wearables and Intelligent Medical Devices

Fresh perspectives in wearables and intelligent medical devices are revolutionizing healthcare determinations by placing actionable data directly into the hands of both healthcare providers and individuals. Wearable devices, ranging from fitness trackers to advanced medical wearables, continuously monitor key health measurements such as heart rate, activity levels, and even ECG readings. These devices not only facilitate remote patient surveillance but also empower individuals to actively participate in their healthcare journey. The integration of smart medical devices, such as connected insulin pumps or continuous glucose monitors for diabetes management, facilitates real-time tracking and analysis of crucial health parameters. Machine learning algorithms applied to the data collected from wearables and smart devices provide useful insights for personalized treatment plans and early intervention strategies. The seamless incorporation of these technologies into healthcare decision-making processes improves the efficiency, precision, and personalization of care, ultimately resulting in improved patient outcomes and a transformation towards more preventive and proactive healthcare models.

2.12 Data-Oriented Health Scrutiny

Fresh perspectives in data-oriented health scrutiny significantly influence healthcare decision-making, leading to an era in which actionable insights derived from vast datasets play a pivotal part in patient care. Continuous monitoring of health information, facilitated by wearables, sensors, and other connected devices, allows a comprehensive and real-time understanding of individual health conditions. The integration of advanced analytics, including artificial intelligence and machine learning, allows for healthcare professionals to discern meaningful patterns, predict potential health risks, and make knowledgeable decisions. Data-oriented health monitoring doesn't just help in the early detection of irregularities, but also supports the development of personalized treatment plans based on individual health profiles. This approach enhances the precision and efficiency of healthcare decision-making, promotes preventive interventions, and enables timely responses to evolving health conditions. As the field keeps evolving, the fusion of data-driven insights with clinical expertise holds the promise of redefining healthcare decision-making, fostering a more proactive, personalized, and effective approach to patient care.

2.13 Blockchain in Healthcare

Emerging trends in blockchain technology are on the verge of revolutionizing healthcare decision-making by introducing unmatched transparency, security, and efficiency into health data handling. Blockchain's decentralized and resistant nature ensures the integrity and privacy of patient information, facilitating secure data sharing among healthcare stakeholders. This technology streamlines access to electronic health records, providing a comprehensive and immutable history of patient data. Additionally, blockchain enables the creation of smart contracts, automating, and enhancing the accuracy of administrative processes, billing, and insurance claims. As healthcare decision-making is heavily dependent on accurate and accessible information, blockchain's potential to create a secure and interoperable infrastructure is far-reaching. The adoption of blockchain in healthcare promises to mitigate data breaches, reduce administrative workloads, and empower healthcare professionals with trustworthy, real-time data, eventually contributing to more informed and efficient healthcare decisions.

2.14 Data Security and Precision

Fresh trends in data security and precision are reshaping the realm of healthcare decision-making, with a strong emphasis on safeguarding sensitive patient information. With the increasing digitization of health records and widespread adoption of electronic health systems, the healthcare sector is experiencing a growing focus on robust cybersecurity measures. Advanced encryption technologies, multi-factor authentication, and biometric identification become standard protocols to protect against unauthorized access and data breaches. Additionally, blockchain technology is gaining attention for its potential to create tamper-resistant and transparent systems, ensuring the integrity of health data throughout its lifecycle. As healthcare decision-making relies heavily on precise, current data, ensuring the security and integrity of data not only protects patient privacy but also instills confidence in healthcare professionals to make significant decisions. The ongoing evolution of data security measures reflects a commitment to safeguard the trustworthiness of healthcare information, ultimately contributing to more secure and reliable decision-making protocols in the dynamic landscape of contemporary healthcare.

3. FUTURE PERSPECTIVES IN HEALTHCARE DECISION MAKING

As advancements in technology, society, and science persist, the domain of healthcare decision-making is projected to evolve significantly, offering great prospects for improvements. The trajectory in this field sees an enhanced incorporation of machine learning and artificial intelligence equipping predictive analytics with the capability to provide more precise diagnoses, treatment plans, and the best utilization of resources. With quantum computing on the rise, processing large volumes of healthcare data could be further revolutionized, hastening complex analysis and simulations processes.

Precision medicine is also expected to occupy crucial place, as treatments plans increasingly become tailor-made, taking into account patients' genetic makeup, lifestyle choices, and individual health histories. Ethics will hold continued relevance in shaping decision-making structures, guaranteeing trustworthy and fair application of upcoming technologies.

Emphasizing patient-oriented approach is believed to strengthen, encouraging shared decision-making and enabling individuals for active involvement in their care pathways. Global collaboration and data sharing stands on the verge of enhancing healthcare decision-making, nurturing cross-national research, understanding, and shared mission for improved patient results. Navigating these future perspectives, it is clear that a transformative era is signaled for healthcare decision-making, characterized by inventions, inclusivity, and dedication towards augmenting the health and wellness of individuals and communities. Figure 2 shows the future perspectives in health care decision making.

Figure 2. Future perspectives: Healthcare decision making

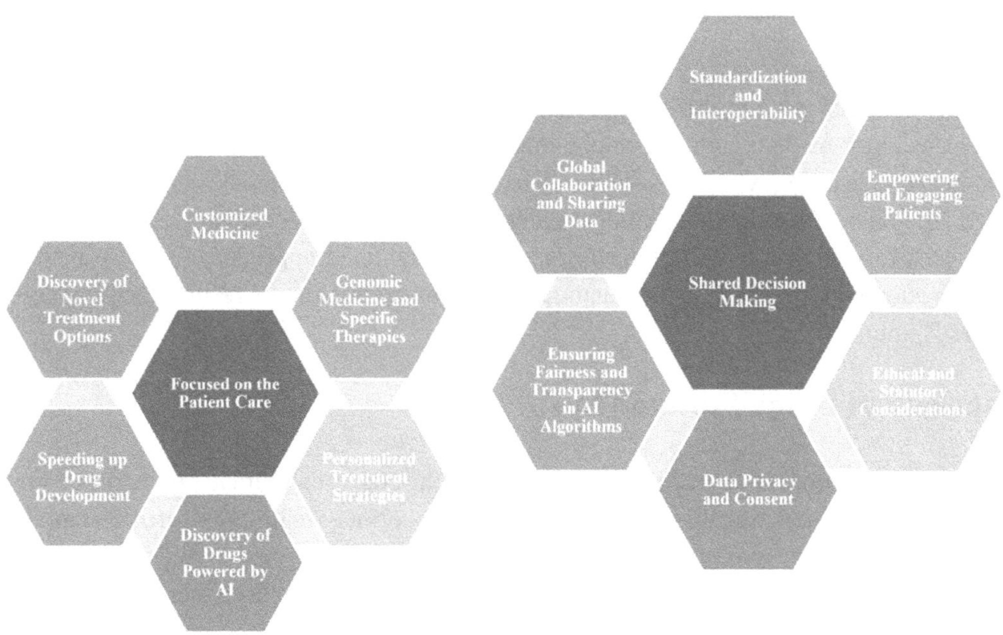

3.1 Customized Medicine

With an eye to the future, precision medicine has the potential to drastically alter healthcare decisions, paving the way for a shift to bespoke patient care. Medical professionals can now tailor treatments according to the specific genetic attributes of their patients, the cornerstone of precision medicine. The merging of advanced technologies such as genomics, proteomics, and analyzing large data sets will be crucial in unravelling intricate biological information and pointing towards precise therapies. Machine learning and artificial intelligence algorithms will add another layer of accuracy to diagnostics and treatment, by making use of a broad and continuously updated array of data. The continuous evolution of these technologies indicates incredible potential for precision medicine as it furthers the healthcare decision-making process with optimal treatments, fewer side effects, and a boost to overall patient well-being.

3.2 Genomic Medicine and Specific Therapies

In the future, genomic medicine and targeted therapies are on the brink of revolutionizing healthcare decisions and reshaping the structure of patient care. The advent of genomic sequencing technologies have enabled us to understand individual genetic compositions like never before. Genomic information promises to be a key aspect of future healthcare decisions, making it possible to accurately identify disease-related gene variances and personalize treatment accordingly. There will be a rise in targeted therapies, developed to address specific molecular characteristics of a patient's disease. This reduces the emphasis on a universal treatment approach and introduces an era with treatments designed to suit an individual's unique genetic profile. As genomic medicine continues to transform, it not only offers the ability to enhance how effective treatments are but also to significantly lower any side effects, ultimately leading to more enlightened and personalized healthcare choices.

3.3 Personalized Treatment Strategies

From one-size-fits-all treatments, future healthcare decision-making seems to be progressing toward a radical change with personalized treatment plans. Precision medicine is making it easier to merge individual patient data, genetic information, and lifestyle factors. The future of healthcare could see treatment plans tailor-made to an individual patient's specific attributes and needs. Technologies such as AI and machine learning will play a vital role in analyzing complicated data sets to identify the best therapeutic strategies. Customizing treatment plans, not only maximizes effectiveness but also reduces adverse effects, reflecting a more complex and patient-orientated approach. As these patient-centric strategies are adopted more widely, the potential for improved healthcare results and enhanced patient experiences is imminent.

3.4 Discovery of Drugs Powered by AI

The decision-making process in healthcare is perched on the edge of a dramatic transformation with the introduction of AI-powered drug discovery. As technology continues to progress, artificial intelligence is slated to speed up the process of drug development significantly. AI algorithms are capable of analyzing massive data sets, uncovering complex patterns, and predicting potential drug therapies with remarkable speed and accuracy. This revolutionary method not only amplifies the discovery of unique therapeutic agents, but also boosts the precision of treatment strategies. As AI continues to evolve, the future holds the prospect of obtaining more targeted and effective pharmaceutical treatments. This change in drug discovery is expected to have a major impact on healthcare decisions, giving medical professionals a wider and more customized range of therapeutic options, ultimately leading to more knowledgeable, efficient, and patient-centric healthcare choices.

3.5 Speeding Up Drug Development

Future healthcare decision-making is marked by an impressive acceleration in the drug development processes, driven by pioneering technologies and innovative methodologies. With the progress in genomics, artificial intelligence, and data analytics, the drug discovery pipeline promises a smoother and speedier future. The capacity to unravel complex biological data and quickly identify potential drug therapies will significantly shorten the time and cost traditionally associated with launching new medications to the market. Moreover, folding real-world evidence and patient data into drug development strategies will amplify the understanding of treatment efficacy and safety profiles. As these advancements continue to unfold, healthcare decision-makers will benefit from a more dynamic and responsive landscape for drug development that provides an assortment of targeted therapies swiftly integrated into customized treatment plans, thereby improving patient results and evolving healthcare decision-making process.

3.6 Discovery of Novel Treatment Options

The decision-making process in healthcare has a bright future with the potential to identify novel treatment options made possible by advancements in research, technology, and data analysis. Integrating genomics, precision medicine, and artificial intelligence will likely lead to the discovery of innovative therapies customized to individual patient profiles. Genomic insights provide a deeper understanding of the molecular basis of diseases and enable identification of specific intervention targets. Artificial intelligence, with its capability to process vast datasets, facilitates the discovery of patterns and correlations, driving the identification of novel treatment options with greater speed and accuracy. The future anticipates a shift towards more personalized and targeted interventions, reducing the hit-and-miss approach in treatment decisions. As these methodologies advance, healthcare decision-makers will have access to a diverse array of groundbreaking treatments, laying the foundation for more effective, efficient, and patient-centric approach to healthcare decision-making.

3.7 Focused on the Patient Care

Healthcare decision-making perspectives in the future are increasingly pointing toward a patient-centered care model, placing the treatment plans' choices in the patient's hands. Future healthcare anticipates a system where decisions bear a collaborative nature and consider not just medical expertise but the individual wishes, values, and objectives of the patient. Digital health tools, shared decision-making platforms, and real-time communication will enhance patient involvement in their healthcare journey. The focus on patient-centered care breeds a more empathetic and persona touch to healthcare, ensuring that decisions are aligned with the individual's overall needs. This evolution has the potential to improve patient satisfaction and treatment adherence and overall health outcomes, ultimately redefining the standards of compassionate healthcare decision making.

3.8 Shared Decision Making

Healthcare decision-making in the future will be marked by a concerted emphasis on shared decision-making, nurturing partnerships between healthcare providers and patients. This approach to healthcare envisages an active role for patients in the decision-making process, with healthcare professionals providing comprehensive information about treatment alternatives along with their associated risks and benefits. Advanced technologies, including decision support tools and patient education platforms, will contribute to enhancing the accessibility and comprehensibility of medical information. The goal is to equip individuals to make informed choices that are consistent with their values and preferences. Shared decision-making not only recognizes the autonomy of patients, but also strengthens the relationship between doctor and patient, creating a more patient-centric and empathetic healthcare environment. As this trend gains traction, the future promises more individualized, holistic, and collaborative experiences in healthcare decision-making.

3.9 Empowering and Engaging Patients

Healthcare decision-making in the future will likely center around patient empowerment and engagement, in envisioning a system where individuals are active participants in their own care. Technological advancements such as health apps, wearable devices, and patient portals will offer real-time access to health data enabling patients to have a sense of ownership and awareness. Moreover, personalized health information and educational resources will empower patients to make informed choices about their well-being. Platforms fostering collaboration will facilitate open discussion between patients and healthcare providers to ensure that decisions are made with a thorough understanding of individual preferences and values. As patients become more actively involved in the decision-making process, the promise of improved treatment compliance, better health results, and a more satisfying health care experience becomes a reality.

3.10 Ethical and Statutory Considerations

Looking into the future of healthcare decision-making, ethical and regulatory considerations are underlined as being of utmost importance when it comes to the evolution of medical advancements. Technologies such as artificial intelligence, genomics, and data analytics will play a key part in decision-making processes, and it will be critical to ensure patient privacy, data security, and equitable access to groundbreaking treatments via ethical frameworks and robust regulations. It will be imperative to walk the fine line between encouraging innovation and protecting patient rights. Ethics must guide the responsible use of patient data, transparent decision-making algorithms, and the potential social impact of emerging technologies. Regulatory bodies are expected to shape policies that not only facilitate progress but also protect the rights of individuals. The future of healthcare decision-making will require principled ethics and regulatory frameworks that uphold the integrity of the healthcare system while responsibly welcoming transformative advancements.

3.11 Data Privacy and Consent

Healthcare decision-making perspectives in the future are pivoting toward emphasizing data privacy and consent, with technological innovations constantly changing the current landscape. Greater reliance is being placed on electronic health records, genomic data, and real-time monitoring - which puts a premium on safeguarding patient information. Robust data privacy measures are anticipated in the future, emphasizing transparency and granting patients more control over their health data. Stricter consent protocols and clear communications about how data will be used will empower individuals to make informed decisions about sharing their information for treatment purposes or research. Technological solutions like blockchain could play a key role in protecting patient data, ensuring its authenticity and providing a transparent audit trail. Prioritizing privacy and securing informed consent will be critical as the healthcare sector navigates the data-intensive future, upholding trust and establishing ethical norms in healthcare decision-making.

3.12 Ensuring Fairness and Transparency in AI Algorithms

The enormous need for fairness and transparency in AI algorithms underscores future perspectives in healthcare decision-making, as artificial intelligence increasingly dominates medical processes. As AI algorithms are integral to diagnostics, treatment recommendations, and personalized medicine, there is a growing focus on reducing biases and promoting transparency in these decision-making processes. Ethical considerations necessitate the development and maintenance of these algorithms with a commitment to fairness, avoiding discrimination based on factors like ethnicity, gender, or socioeconomic status. It is crucial for the decision-making process underpinned by AI to be transparent, fostering a relationship of trust with healthcare professionals and patients in the algorithm's recommendations. As the healthcare industry progresses in its adoption of AI, it is envisaged that the strict guidelines, audits, and regulatory frameworks will maintain fairness and transparency, enabling confidence in the AI's role in healthcare decision-making.

3.13 Global Collaboration and Sharing Data

Healthcare decision-making future perspectives envisage increased collaboration and data sharing worldwide amongst healthcare systems. Technological advancements that facilitate the seamless exchange of health information show that global collaboration is key to addressing complex health challenges. Shared databases, systems interoperability, and international research collaborations have the ability to speed up medical discoveries, improve treatment outcomes, and enhance the quality of healthcare decision-making. The COVID-19 pandemic has illustrated how critical quick global data sharing is for an effective response to emerging health crises. Future strategies are expected to emphasize ethical and secure mechanisms for sharing anonymous patient data internationally, allowing healthcare decision-makers to access a more comprehensive pool of information and insights. Promoting global collaboration is hoped to create a synergistic environment where shared knowledge and varying perspectives contribute to more effective, fair, and informed healthcare strategies worldwide.

3.14 International Cooperation for Healthcare Progress

Healthcare decision-making future perspectives stress the need for international collaborations and efforts for global healthcare advancement. Knowing that many health challenges don't stop at national borders, the future sees a united effort amongst nations to share resources, expertise, and address collective healthcare issues. Collaborations could include joint research projects, coordinated responses to global health crises, and development of universally applied healthcare guidelines. By maximizing technology such as telemedicine and digital health platforms, international efforts aim to improve healthcare accessibility and share best practices for better decision-making. Future strategies could involve establishing international frameworks for ethical data sharing, ensuring the responsible exchange of valuable health information, and adequate consideration for patient privacy. The overall goal is to create a cooperative and interconnected global healthcare community that collectively works to advance medical knowledge, encourage health equity, and elevate healthcare decision-making to the next level.

3.15 Standardization and Interoperability

Future perspectives in healthcare decision-making underscore the immense importance of standardization and interoperability for a cohesive and efficient healthcare ecosystem. A future standardized framework that allows seamless interoperability amongst diverse healthcare systems is envisioned, ensuring that information travels freely and accurately across platforms. This facilitates healthcare decision-makers to access comprehensive and up-to-date patient data, resulting in more informed and timely decisions. Interoperability will ease the communication between healthcare providers and empower patients to securely share their health information. As the healthcare industry continues its digital transformation, standardization and interoperability will play a vital role in optimizing workflows, improving patient outcomes, and fostering a collaborative environment where healthcare decisions are grounded on a unified and interconnected information infrastructure.

4. CHALLENGES AND CONSIDERATIONS

This section covers the challenges and considerations in health care decision making. Few key challenges are described below.

4.1 Securing Privacy and Data

Significant challenges exist in preserving data privacy and security in healthcare decision-making, as the industry is increasingly leaning on digital technologies and data-driven methods. A primary concern is the enormous amount of delicate patient data stored in electronic format, making health systems prime targets for cyber threats. Unauthorized breach, theft, or alteration of patient records not only threatens individual privacy but also raises moral issues pertaining to the privacy of medical history. Further, the interoperability issues amongst various healthcare systems, and data sharing across institutions can lead to potential vulnerabilities, amplifying the risks of unauthorized intrusion or data leaks.

Exploring the swift integration of advanced technologies like artificial intelligence (AI) and machine learning in healthcare decision-making unfolds another set of challenges. Although these technologies hold immense potential to refine diagnostics and devise treatment strategies, they raise concerns about the ethical utilization of patient data. The requirement of extensive datasets for AI algorithms to learn can lead to biased or imprecise decision-making due to incorrect data handling, influencing patient results and aggravating existing health discrepancies.

Moreover, the regulatory framework concerning healthcare data privacy is intricate and frequently altered. It is challenging for healthcare organizations to conform to different data defense laws and yardsticks, given their mutable nature. Struggling to strike the right balance between preserving data privacy, encouraging innovation, and securing patient info constitutes an ongoing hurdle that healthcare's decision-makers must overcome to build trust and deliver effective and ethical treatment.

4.2 AI Algorithms: Bias and Fairness

The significant concerns that arise in healthcare decision-making due to bias and fairness in AI algorithms are challenging. The possibility of bias existing within the datasets used to train the AI models could perpetuate or even magnify the biases in decision-making. This can lead to health disparities, disproportionately impacting certain demographic factions due to biased algorithms.

The interpretability of AI algorithms proves another challenge, especially in intricate healthcare circumstances. A lack of transparency in black-box algorithms obscures the decision-making process for healthcare professionals. This opacity can put a damper on trusting the technology and render it tough for decision-makers to justify AI-informed decisions to patients.

To ensure AI algorithms contribute fairly, equitably, and without bias to the health outcomes of all patients, these challenges must be addressed head-on. Concerted efforts between healthcare professionals, data analysts, and policymakers are imperative to tackle these challenges and conceive AI systems that enhance the quality of healthcare decision-making, rather than impeding it.

4.3 Ethical Hurdles

Healthcare decision-making is riddled with ethical dilemmas that constitute intricate challenges for healthcare workers, policymakers, and patients alike. One significant predicament is the allocation of scarce resources such as organ transplants or critical beds care. Navigating ethical principles like justice fairness, and the optimization of benefits is crucial to deciding who receives these resources.

End-of-life care decisions also present ethical hurdles, especially when patient desires, family inclinations, and medical opinions conflict. Striking a balance between patient autonomy and the healthcare provider's obligation to offer apt care peppered with compassion can be intricate and emotionally charging.

Informed consent serves an ethical dilemma, particularly with the ever-increasing use of sophisticated technologies and genomics medicine. Ensuring that patients understand the risks, benefits, and potential outcomes of procedures becomes critical. Navigating between providing comprehensive info and respecting the patient's autonomy can be challenging.

Rapid advancements in medical technology and artificial intelligence give rise to concerns about data privacy, patient confidentiality, and the potential for unintended consequences. Deciding how to navigate these technological breakthroughs ethically, while ensuring innovation and patient well-being, turns into an essential ethical challenge.

Further, issues related to cultural proficiency, inclusivity, and diversity in healthcare decision-making lend to complexity. Acceptance and respect for diverse values, beliefs, and preferences while delivering unbiased care is an ongoing ethical hurdle. Addressing these ethical dilemmas needs a thoughtful and collaborative approach, involving open communication, continuing education, and a devotion to upholding the principles of doing good, avoiding harm, justice, and respect for autonomy in healthcare decision-making.

5. CASE STUDIES

The following is a comprehensive reiteration of the case studies outlined below.

5.1 Case Study: The Application of AI in Radiology and Diagnostic Imaging for Augmented Decision-Making

5.1.1 Preface

Dealing with an overwhelming influx of imaging studies in the Radiology Department, a well-established city hospital identified potential issues of late reporting and erroneous diagnostics. To tackle these challenges, the integration of Artificial Intelligence (AI) into their radiological workflows was proposed to augment decision-making processes, boost overall efficacy, and uphold their exceptional standards of patient care.

5.1.2 Execution

An AI-powered system was initiated for image-based diagnosis, with a primary focus on chest X-rays due to the high frequency of respiratory conditions. This AI infrastructure employed advanced deep learning algorithms to examine radiographic images and automatically flag irregularities such as nodules, opacities, and other signs of respiratory ailments.

5.1.3 Noteworthy Aspects

- ***Automated Prioritization:*** The system facilitated an automated ranking method, flagging serious cases that demanded immediate attention, thereby ensuring urgent conditions were reported in a timely manner.
- ***Enhanced Precision:*** The system's accuracy in pinpointing subtle discrepancies increased over time as it continually learned from new data, courtesy of machine learning.

Workflow Synchronization: The AI application smoothly integrated with the existing PACS (Picture Archiving and Communication System) and RIS (Radiology Information System), simplifying the workflow for radiologists.

5.1.4 Outcomes

The marriage of AI with radiology and diagnostic imaging in the hospital yielded several positive results:

- ***Increased Efficacy:*** By applying automated prioritization, the critical cases' reporting time was reduced, allowing for faster interventions for patients with severe conditions.
- ***Reduced Task Load:*** The use of automated detection and prioritization allowed radiologists to focus their attention on intricate diagnostics and patient care more rather than routine cases.
- ***Improved Precision:*** The system displayed high sensitivity and specificity, which augmented diagnostic accuracy and reducing the chances of oversight.
- ***Improved Patient Care:*** Faster and more accurate diagnostics led to the formulation of timely and precise treatment plans, leading to better patient healthcare outcomes.

5.1.5 Challenges and Factors to Consider

- ***Complexity of Integration:*** The incorporation of AI within existing frameworks required meticulous planning and a collaborative effort between the Radiology and Information Technology departments.
- ***Sustained Supervision:*** In order to adapt to the ever-evolving realm of medical knowledge and ensure continued high performance, it was pivotal to consistently monitor and periodically retrain the AI infrastructure.
- ***Ethical Considerations:*** Ensuring patient privacy and abiding by ethical parameters in applying AI for healthcare decisions was vital, and hence, the hospital executed robust safety measures and adherence protocols.

5.1.6 Endnote

The inclusion of AI in radiological and diagnostic imaging considerably boosted the hospital's decision-making abilities. The successful merger highlighted AI's potential to augment diagnostic preciseness, simplify workflows, and at the end of the day, lead to improved patient outcomes in the ever-changing landscape of healthcare decision-making.

5.2 Case Study: Genomic Sequencing in Cancer Treatment for Augmented Decision-Making

5.2.1 Preface

A prominent metropolitan cancer center appreciating the transformative potential of genomic sequencing towards oncology care, launched a genomic sequencing initiative. In light of the intricate nature of cancer coupled with the growing demand for personalized treatment modalities, this initiative was aimed to inform and augment decision-making for cancer patients.

5.2.2 Implementation

- ***Genomic Profiling:*** The cancer center instituted routine genomic profiling for cancer patients. Next-generation sequencing (NGS) methodologies were used to scrutinize the entire exome or targeted gene panels, providing an all-encompassing view of the genetic alterations underlying each patient's cancer.

- ***Multifaceted Tumor Boards:*** To foster a more collaborative approach, multi-disciplinary tumor boards were established, bring together oncologists, geneticists, pathologists, and bioinformaticians. These teams deliberated on individual patient cases, decoding genomic data, and formulating bespoke treatment strategies.
- ***Clinical Decision Support System (CDSS):*** A Clinical Decision Support System (CDSS) was integrated, utilizing artificial intelligence to analyze genomic data and match it the most recent scientific research and clinical trials. This approach facilitated evidence-based decision making, identifying targeted therapies or immunotherapies that were suitable for each patient.

5.2.3 Results and Outcomes

- ***Precision Treatment Plans:*** Genomic sequencing facilitated the recognition of unique genetic alterations underlying every patient's cancer, leading to the creation of bespoke, targeted treatment pans. In turn, this approach hiked the chances of therapy success while shrinking potential side effects.
- ***Early Detection of Resistance Variations:*** Continued genetic surveillance provided an early detection system for resistance variations that might appear during therapy. This proactive strategy enabled timely modification of treatment strategies, thereby optimizing the efficacy of ongoing treatments.
- ***Informed Clinical Trial Participation:*** The fusion of a CDSS helped identify relevant clinical trials based on each patient's genomic profile, opening the door to cutting-edge research and giving them increased access to new forms of treatment.
- ***Improved Patient Outcomes:*** The personalized, genomic-centric treatment approach led to enhanced patient outcomes, noticeably improved response rates, increased progression-free survival and in certain instances, total remission.

5.2.4 Challenges and Factors to Consider:

- ***Data Privacy and Informed Consent:*** Protecting genomic data privacy and obtaining informed consent from patients were vital considerations. The cancer center implemented rigorous data safety measures and intensive patient education regarding genomic sequencing implications.
- ***Cross-disciplinary Collaboration:*** Effective collaboration amongst a variety of specialists needed consistent education and communication. Instituting a cross-disciplinary approach was needed to ensure all relevant perspectives was considered in decision making.
- ***Endnote:*** The implementation of genomic sequencing in oncology at the cancer center exemplifies how advanced technologies can significantly impact decision-making in cancer care. By combining genomic insights with multidisciplinary collaboration and innovative decision support systems, the center achieved more precise and personalized treatment strategies, ultimately leading to improved patient outcomes in the complex landscape of oncology.

5.3 Case Study: Telemedicine During the COVID-19 Pandemic for Augmented Decision-Making

5.3.1 Preface

A large healthcare system faced formidable challenges in maintaining care continuity in the face of the global COVID-19 pandemic, while also minimizing the risk of virus transmission. To overcome these challenges, the healthcare system expediently launched and broadened their telemedicine services to augment decision-making, ensuring ongoing patient care during the crisis.

5.3.2 Implementation

- ***Telehealth Infrastructure:*** A robust telehealth network was quickly deployed by the healthcare system, integrating video conferencing, secure messaging, and virtual visit platforms. This facilitated consultation, follow-ups, and routine care remotely, connecting patients with healthcare providers.
- ***Remote Monitoring Tools:*** Patients with chronic conditions or mild COVID-19 symptoms who could track their vital signs, other symptoms, and share real-time data with healthcare providers were provided remote monitoring tools which facilitated proactive decision-making and early interventions when necessary.
- ***Decision Support for Triage:*** AI-driven decision-support tools were used to facilitate triaging of patients based on symptom severity. The system could prioritize patients requiring immediate attention while giving home-care guidance to those with milder symptoms, optimizing the allocation of resources.

5.3.3 Results and Outcomes

- ***Continuity of Care:*** Telemedicine guaranteed the continuity of care for patients with chronic conditions, mental health needs, and non-emergent medical issues. The easy access of virtual visits reduced disruptions in ongoing treatment plans.
- ***Reduced Transmission and Exposure:*** The risk of virus exposure for both patients and healthcare providers was minimized by offering virtual consultations. Playing a key role controlling the spread of COVID-19 and ensuring a safer healthcare environment.
- ***Timely Interventions:*** Remote monitoring tools facilitated timely interventions and adjustments in treatment plans. Healthcare providers could asses the state of a patient remotely and make informed decision regarding the necessity for hospitalization of adjustments to medication regimens.
- ***Optimized use of Resources:*** Critical healthcare resources were allocated to those in need by preventing needless visits to the emergency room and directing patients to proper care settings based on their symptoms.

5.3.4 Challenges and Factors to Consider:

- ***Digital Divide:*** Innovative solutions, such as phone consultations and partnerships with community organizations, were required to deal with the digital divide among patients and those without access to smartphones or reliable internet.
- ***Regulatory Compliance:*** Adherence to evolving regulatory guidelines and reimbursement policies was necessary during the rapid expansion of telehealth services. The healthcare system worked closely with regulatory bodies to ensure compliance while delivering timely care.

5.3.5 Endnote

The effectiveness of telemedicine in maintaining patient care, reducing exposure risks, and optimizing decision-making was demonstrated by its implementation during the COVID-19 pandemic. The healthcare system successfully navigated the challenges posed by the pandemic by leveraging technology and innovative solutions. This illustrated the potential of telehealth in enhancing decision-making and ensuring continuity of care during crises.

6. CONCLUSION

This last section delivers a well-rounded retrospective on the reformation of healthcare decision making artificial intelligence, data analytics and novel technologies. text underscores the potential of personalized medicine, the issues of data security and ethics, and the significance of readying the healthcare workforce for this era of transformation. The case studies supply concrete instances of how these technologies are being implemented, and the section concludes with a discussion on future research pathways in this dynamic field. These conclusions are further explained below:

6.1 The Progressing Spectrum of Healthcare Decision Making

The progressing spectrum of healthcare decision-making is marked by dynamic changes fueled by technological progress, changing patient needs, and an increasing focus on individualized and value-based care. Numerous key trends and factors play a part in this progressing spectrum:

1. ***Data-inspired thoughts:*** The incorporation of advanced analytics, big data, and artificial intelligence in healthcare decision-making processes is gathering more and more momentum. Healthcare systems exploit vast quantities of patient data to extract insights, foretell outcomes, and advise individualized treatment strategies.
2. ***Patient-oriented Method:*** There as a visible shift towards a patient-oriented model, putting importance on shared decision-making and patient empowerment. Patients are now proactive participants in their care, with better access to health information, electronic health records, and telehealth services contributing to more educated choices.
3. ***Telehealth and Electronic Health:*** The broad adoption of telehealth and electronic health solutions has transformed the way healthcare decisions is being made. Virtual consultations, distant

monitoring, and electronic health apps provide new pathways for accessing care, particularly in situations like the COVID-19 pandemic.

4. ***Customized Medicine:*** Progress in genomics and precision medicine is ushers in a new era of customized treatment strategies created for individual genetic profiles.
5. ***Interdisciplinary Cooperation:*** The complexity of healthcare challenges necessitates a greater emphasis on interdisciplinary cooperation. Teams of healthcare professionals from various specialties collaborate to address diverse aspects of patient care, ensuring a holistic and well-rounded approach.
6. ***Value-Based Care Models:*** The movement towards value-based care models gives priority to outcomes, patient satisfaction, and cost-effectiveness. Healthcare decision-makers are increasingly focused on delivering high-quality care that aligns with patient needs while optimizing resource utilization.
7. ***Ethical and Regulatory Factors:*** As technology takes a central role in healthcare decision-making, ethical considerations regarding data privacy, consent, and responsible use of emerging technologies become significant. Striking a balance between innovation and ethical norms is a continuing challenge.
8. ***Global Cooperation and Data Sharing:*** In a globally linked world, healthcare decision-making is being increasingly influenced by international collaborations. Sharing of medical knowledge, best practices, and research findings on a global level contribute to more informed decision-making and improved patient outcomes.
9. ***Standardization and Interoperability:*** Efforts toward standardization and interoperability aim to create seamless exchange of information among different healthcare systems. This enables healthcare professionals to access comprehensive patient data, leading to more coordinated and effective decision-making.
10. ***Public Health Initiatives:*** The evolving landscape also punctuated by an increased focus on public health initiatives. Decision-makers are increasingly considering population health data and preventive strategies in order to address broader health challenges and to reduce the strain on healthcare systems.

6.2 The Transformative Potential of Intelligent Systems

The potential of intelligent systems to transform, including artificial intelligence (AI) and machine learning (ML), is immense and all-encompassing across many industries, such as healthcare, finance, manufacturing and beyond. Some points that illustrate the transformative impact of intelligent systems are:

1. ***Automation and Efficiency:*** Intelligent systems can automatically execute repetitive tasks, helping organizations achieve greater operational efficiency.
2. ***Data Analysis and Decision Support:*** The capability of intelligent systems to quickly and accurately analyze vast amounts of data is revolutionary.
3. ***Personalization and User Experience:*** Intelligent systems can personalize user experiences based on individual preferences and behaviors.
4. ***Predictive Analytics:*** Leveraging historical data and patterns, intelligent systems excel at predictive analytics.

5. ***Innovations in Healthcare:*** Intelligent systems have transformative effects in healthcare, varying from diagnostics and drug discovery to patient care and personalized medicine.
6. ***Natural Language Processing (NLP) and Language Understanding:*** NLP capabilities enable intelligent systems to understand and generate human-like language.
7. ***Adaptive Learning:*** In education, intelligent systems can facilitate adaptive learning experiences.
8. ***Autonomous Vehicles:*** The automotive industry is undergoing a transformation with the development of intelligent systems for autonomous vehicles.
9. ***Cybersecurity and Threat Detection:*** Intelligent systems play a critical role in cybersecurity by identifying and mitigating potential threats.
10. ***Sustainability and Resource Optimization:*** Intelligent systems play a crucial role in optimizing resource usage in industries like energy and agriculture.
11. ***Human-Robot Collaboration:*** Intelligent systems facilitate effective collaboration between humans and robots.
12. ***Continuous Learning and Adaptation:*** The ability of intelligent systems to learn from new data and adapt to changing circumstances is a key aspect of their transformative potential. Even though the transformative potential of intelligent systems is enormous, navigating ethical considerations, ensuring transparency, and addressing potential biases is essential in their development and deployment.

6.3 The Importance of Ethical, Regulatory, and Educational Frameworks

The importance of ethical, regulatory and educational frameworks cannot be overstated in the context of rapidly advancing technologies, especially in areas like artificial intelligence, healthcare, and data-driven decision-making. These frameworks are essential for guiding responsible development, deployment, and use of technologies, ensuring that they align with societal values, protect individual rights, and foster equitable outcomes. The reasons these frameworks are crucial:

1. Ethical Considerations:
   - ***Human Well-being:*** Ethical frameworks prioritize individual and societal well-being.
   - ***Bias and Fairness:*** Ethical guidelines address the concerns related to biases in algorithms and decision-making processes.
2. Regulatory Oversight:
   - ***Consumer Protection:*** Regulatory frameworks provide a legal basis for protecting consumers.
   - ***Accountability:*** Regulations set up accountability mechanisms.
3. ***Educational Initiatives:***
   - ***Awareness and Literacy:*** Educational frameworks play a crucial role in raising awareness and promoting digital literacy.
   - ***Skill Development:*** Educational frameworks ensure that individuals acquire the necessary skills.
4. Privacy Protection:
   - ***Data Protection:*** Ethical and regulatory frameworks play a key role in protecting privacy rights.
   - ***Informed Consent:*** Ethical guidelines underpin the importance of informed consent.

5. Transparency and Explainability:
   - ***Accountability and Trust:*** Ethical frameworks highlight the importance of transparency in technological development.
   - ***Explainability:*** Regulations may require complex systems like AI to provide explanations for their decisions.
6. Social Equity and Inclusion:
   - ***Mitigating*** Bias: Ethical guidelines and regulations address bias and discrimination issues.
   - ***Accessibility***: Educational initiatives ensure that individuals across diverse backgrounds have access to necessary knowledge.

In summary, ethical, regulatory, and educational frameworks serve as critical stepping stones in the responsible development and use of technologies. They underpin the creation of a digital landscape that ranks human values and rights high, and promotes equitable access, and achieves results for everyone.

7. FUTURE RESEARCH DIRECTIONS

This section covers the future road map for research as listed the key areas.

7.1 The Need for Further Research on AI Ethics and Governance

Research on AI ethics and governance plays a vital role as artificial intelligence (AI) technologies rapidly progress. These advancements bring complex challenges that require a comprehensive understanding, regulation, and ethical considerations. There are several crucial reasons that emphasize the importance of ongoing research in this field:

1. Ethical Implications of AI Algorithms:
   - ***Bias and Fairness:*** Unintentionally, AI algorithms can perpetuate biases from training data, leading to unfair outcomes. Research is necessary to develop techniques that identify and mitigate biases, ensuring fairness in AI systems.
   - **Explainability:** "Black-box" algorithms lacking transparency in their decision-making processes pose ethical concerns. Research is needed to enhance explainability and accountability, making AI systems more understandable to stakeholders.
2. Privacy Concerns:
   - ***Data Protection:*** AI heavily relies on vast datasets, raising concerns about privacy and data protection. Research is crucial for developing robust privacy-preserving techniques, including federated learning and differential privacy, to safeguard individual privacy while still maintaining AI model effectiveness.
3. Human-AI Collaboration:
   - ***Human-Centric Design:*** As AI systems become integral to various domains, research is essential to explore human-centric design principles. Understanding how humans interact with AI and ensuring that AI technologies align with human values is vital for productive and ethical collaborations.

4. Accountability and Responsibility:
    - ***Legal and Ethical Frameworks:*** Ongoing research is required to develop legal and ethical frameworks that establish accountability and responsibility in AI decision-making. This includes determining liability in case of adverse outcomes and defining the roles of AI developers, operators, and users.
5. Security and Robustness:
    - ***Adversarial Attacks:*** AI systems are susceptible to adversarial attacks where slight manipulations to input data can lead to incorrect outputs. Research is needed to enhance the security and robustness of AI models, ensuring their reliability in real-world scenarios.
6. Societal Impact:
    - ***Social and Economic Impact:*** AI has broad societal implications, including job displacement and potential amplification of existing inequalities. Research is vital to understand and address the social and economic impacts of AI deployment, enabling the development of policies that mitigate negative consequences.
7. Global Governance and Standards:
    - ***International Collaboration:*** Since AI technologies have a global nature, research is necessary to establish international collaboration on AI ethics and governance. Developing common standards and principles can guide responsible AI deployment on a global scale.
8. Continuous Adaptation to Technological Advances:
    - ***Rapid Technological Evolution:*** The field of AI is continually evolving with the emergence of new algorithms, models, and applications. Research is essential to keep pace with technological advancements and adapt ethical and governance frameworks accordingly.
9. Public Perception and Engagement:
    - ***Public Understanding:*** Research can contribute to understanding public perceptions of AI and their concerns. Engaging the public in discussions about AI ethics can lead to more inclusive governance models that reflect diverse perspectives.
10. Addressing Unintended Consequences:
    - ***Unintended Consequences:*** Research is necessary to anticipate and address unintended consequences of AI technologies. This includes studying the long-term effects on employment, social dynamics, and the potential for unforeseen ethical dilemmas.

In conclusion, more research on AI ethics and governance is critical for navigating the ethical complexities and societal impact of AI technologies. A multidisciplinary approach involving researchers, policymakers, industry stakeholders, and the public is essential to develop robust frameworks that ensure the responsible and ethical deployment of AI for the benefit of society.

7.2 The Impact of AI on Healthcare Accessibility and Equity

The influence of Artificial Intelligence (AI) on healthcare accessibility and equity holds the potential to revolutionize the delivery of healthcare services, reducing disparities and improving overall access to quality care. Several significant aspects highlight the transformative effects of AI in this context:

1. ***Remote Consultations and Telehealth:*** Increased Access: AI-powered telehealth solutions facilitate remote consultations, making healthcare services more accessible, particularly for individuals in

remote or underserved areas. Patients can consult with healthcare providers without the need for extensive travel, reducing barriers to access.

2. ***Diagnostic Efficiency and Early Detection:*** Timely Interventions: AI-driven diagnostic tools enhance the efficiency of disease detection, enabling early interventions. This is especially crucial for populations with limited access to healthcare facilities, as early detection can prevent disease progression and improve outcomes.
3. ***Predictive Analytics for Public Health:*** Proactive Resource Allocation: AI's ability to analyze vast datasets supports predictive analytics in public health. This aids in identifying at-risk populations, predicting disease outbreaks, and allocating resources more effectively, thereby addressing healthcare disparities in vulnerable communities.
4. ***Personalized Treatment Plans:*** Tailored Healthcare: AI in healthcare enables the development of personalized treatment plans based on individual patient data, including genetic information. This approach considers unique factors such as genetics, lifestyle, and socioeconomic status, contributing to more equitable healthcare outcomes.
5. ***Health Monitoring and Wearable Devices:*** Continuous Monitoring: AI-powered wearable devices allow continuous health monitoring, providing real-time data on vital signs and health indicators. This technology can be especially beneficial for individuals with chronic conditions, enhancing accessibility to proactive healthcare management.
6. ***Language Translation and Accessibility:*** Enhanced Communication: Natural Language Processing (NLP) in AI supports language translation and interpretation services, breaking down language barriers and improving communication between healthcare providers and patients from diverse linguistic backgrounds.
7. ***Chatbots for Basic Healthcare Information:***
   - ***24/7 Accessibility:*** AI-driven chatbots provide immediate access to basic healthcare information, offering a 24/7 resource for individuals seeking guidance. This can be particularly beneficial for those who may face barriers to accessing traditional healthcare information sources.
8. ***AI in Low-Resource Settings:***
   - ***Efficient Resource Utilization:*** In low-resource settings, AI can assist healthcare professionals in making efficient use of available resources. Automated diagnostic tools and decision support systems help optimize healthcare delivery, even in environments with limited access to specialized expertise.
9. ***Addressing Health Disparities:***
   - ***Targeted Interventions:*** AI can be employed to identify and address specific health disparities affecting certain demographics. By understanding the unique challenges faced by different populations, healthcare interventions can be targeted and tailored to specific needs.

While AI offers immense promise for improving healthcare accessibility and equity, it is essential to approach its integration with careful consideration of ethical, cultural, and social factors. Collaborative efforts involving policymakers, healthcare professionals, technologists, and communities are crucial to harnessing the full potential of AI in creating a more accessible and equitable healthcare landscape.

7.3 The Potential Role of Quantum Computing in Healthcare Decision Making

Quantum computing has the potential to revolutionize healthcare decision-making by addressing complex computational problems that surpass the capabilities of classical computers. Although quantum computing is still in its early stages of development, its unique properties offer several promising applications in healthcare:

1. ***Drug Discovery and Molecular Simulation:*** Quantum computing's ability to handle intricate quantum states makes it well-suited for simulating molecular structures and interactions. This could significantly expedite drug discovery processes by accurately modeling complex biological systems, predicting drug behaviors, and identifying potential treatment options more efficiently.
2. ***Optimization of Treatment Plans:*** Quantum computing excels in solving optimization problems, which are prevalent in healthcare for treatment planning. Quantum algorithms could optimize radiation therapy schedules, personalized treatment plans, and resource allocation in healthcare facilities, leading to more efficient and effective care strategies.
3. ***Genomic Data Analysis:*** The vast amount of data generated by genomics research poses a significant computational challenge. Quantum computing has the potential to rapidly analyze large genomic datasets, identifying patterns and variations associated with diseases. This could lead to more precise diagnostics, personalized treatment recommendations, and advancements in genomic medicine.
4. ***Precision Medicine and Personalized Treatment Plans:*** Quantum computing's computational power can process and analyze diverse datasets, including patient-specific information, to generate highly personalized treatment plans. This could involve considering individual genetic variations, lifestyle factors, and treatment response predictions for more targeted and effective interventions.
5. ***Optimized Healthcare Logistics:*** Quantum algorithms can address complex logistical challenges in healthcare systems, such as optimizing supply chain management, scheduling surgeries, and resource allocation in hospitals.

REFERENCES

Venkata & Sreenivasu. (2019a). *Foolproof Decision Support System for Melanoma Cancer Detection (FDSSMCD).* INDIA Patent# 201941005828.

Venkata & Sreenivasu. (2019b). Edge AI System for Pneumonia and Lung Cancer Detection. *International Journal of Innovative Technology and Exploring Engineering, 8*(9).

Venkata & Sreenivasu. (2019c). End to End System for Pneumonia and Lung Cancer Detection Using Deep Learning. *International Journal of Engineering and Advanced Technology, 8*(6).

Venkata & Sreenivasu. (2019d). Efficient CNN for Lung Cancer Detection. *International Journal of Recent Technology and Engineering, 8*(2).

Venkata & Sreenivasu. (2019e). Integrated Clinician Decision Supporting System for Pneumonia and Lung Cancer Detection. *International Journal of Innovative Technology and Exploring Engineering, 8*(8).

Chapter 8
Bio-Inspired Design in Healthcare:
The Gecko-Inspired Surgical Adhesive

Kaushalya Thopate
Vishwakarma Institute of Technology, India

Krishna Nilesh Jaiswal
Vishwakarma Institute of Technology, India

ABSTRACT

Healthcare innovation thrives on bio-inspired design, drawing from nature's ingenuity to address complex human challenges. This case study explores a groundbreaking healthcare innovation – a surgical adhesive inspired by geckos. Geckos, renowned for their ability to cling to various substrates and vertical surfaces, inspire this adhesive. Bio-inspired decision-making offers potential solutions for persistent issues and enhanced patient care. Geckos' adhesive capability derives from the hierarchical structure of their toe pads, featuring millions of hair-like structures called setae. These setae interact with surfaces through spatulae, creating nanoscale topography and harnessing Van der Waals forces for strong adhesion. The gecko's ability to actively control adhesion has spurred biomimetic innovation. In healthcare, where surgical adhesives play a critical role, traditional solutions often suffer from biocompatibility issues, weak bonding, and limited adaptability.

INTRODUCTION

Bio-inspired design, a paradigm that draws inspiration from the ingenious designs found in nature to address complex challenges, has ushered in transformative advancements across various industries, healthcare included. This chapter embarks on a journey to explore a remarkable healthcare innovation - the creation of a groundbreaking surgical adhesive inspired by the extraordinary adhesive abilities of geckos.

DOI: 10.4018/979-8-3693-2073-0.ch008

Figure 1. A gecko

"Figure 1" captures the intricate beauty of a gecko, showcasing its unique and delicate features. These small reptiles, revered for their astounding capacity to scale vertical surfaces and adhere to a diverse array of substrates, owe their remarkable prowess to a unique adhesive mechanism that has captivated the imagination of biomimetic innovators. At the heart of this remarkable feat lies the hierarchical arrangement of structures within the gecko's toe pads. These toe pads, meticulously designed by nature over eons, are adorned with millions of minuscule hair-like structures, known as setae. Each seta further branches into even smaller structures called spatulae. It is at this minute scale, at the intersection of these countless spatulae with the surface, that the gecko's adhesive magic unfolds. Van der Waals forces, those weak attractive forces that materialize when the spatulae make contact with a surface, generate a surprisingly strong adhesion. As a result, geckos can adhere to surfaces with an appearance of ease, supporting their entire body weight. One of the most intriguing features of the gecko's adhesive system is its ability to actively regulate adhesion. Unlike traditional adhesives that maintain a constant level of adhesion, geckos have the capability to engage and disengage their adhesive grip at will. This dynamic control is a quality that has proven to be particularly inspiring to biomimetic designers, as it introduces a new dimension of adaptability and efficiency to the adhesive mechanism.

In the vast realm of healthcare, where surgical adhesives play a pivotal role in procedures ranging from wound closure to tissue repair, conventional adhesive options have often fallen short. These limitations may manifest in various ways, including challenges with biocompatibility, weak bonding strength, and inadequate adaptability to the diverse demands of surgical procedures. Recognizing the pressing need for a safer, more versatile adhesive solution, researchers turned to the gecko's adhesive prowess for inspiration. The development of a gecko-inspired surgical adhesive was no simple feat but rather a meticulous journey. It entailed an in-depth exploration of the gecko's adhesive mechanism, necessitating a deep dive into the hierarchical arrangement of gecko toe pad structures. Through advanced nanofabrication techniques, these structures were meticulously mimicked, opening the door to a new realm of adhesive possibilities. Additionally, materials were extensively experimented with, aiming to create artificial structures that could closely emulate the adhesive properties of gecko toe pads. After a series of trials, refinements, and iterative improvements, the research team achieved a significant breakthrough - the creation of a surgical adhesive inspired by the gecko. Composed of biocompatible materials, this adhesive featured synthetic setae and spatulae, meticulously replicating the hierarchical structure found in the gecko's toe pads. What set this innovation apart from conventional surgical adhesives was a groundbreaking capability - the ability to control adhesion as needed during surgical procedures. This marked the adhesive's adaptability, an essential attribute that allowed surgeons to activate and deactivate its adhesive properties as required. The gecko-inspired surgical adhesive was then subjected to a series of rigorous tests, both in laboratory settings and through animal trials. The results were profoundly promising. Surgeons found that the gecko-inspired adhesive was highly effective in a variety of critical aspects of surgery, including wound closure, tissue repair, and even in minimally invasive procedures where traditional sutures or staples posed challenges. Notably, this adhesive offered enhanced biocompatibility, significantly lowering the risk of adverse patient reactions. Its adaptability also extended to its ability to adhere to wet or irregular surfaces, broadening its utility in diverse surgical scenarios.

The potential impact of this innovation on surgical procedures cannot be overstated. It possesses the ability to enhance patient outcomes by ensuring precise and effective wound closure, potentially reducing post-operative complications, shortening hospital stays, and enhancing overall patient recovery. Additionally, its capacity to create strong, nearly invisible bonds holds the potential to reduce scarring, improving not only the physical but also the psychological well-being of patients. Beyond its immediate clinical applications, the gecko-inspired adhesive aligns seamlessly with a broader trend in healthcare - the development of safer, more effective, and biologically inspired medical devices. The recognition that nature's designs often outperform human-made solutions in both efficiency and safety has spurred a shift towards biomimicry in healthcare. This adhesive stands as a shining example of how the fusion of biological inspiration and innovative engineering can yield transformative solutions in the medical field, ultimately redefining traditional practices and enhancing patient care. The journey from the gecko's adhesive marvel to the development of a gecko-inspired surgical adhesive showcases the immense potential of bio-inspired decision-making in healthcare. Its remarkable effectiveness, biocompatibility, adaptability, and transformative potential underscore the immense promise of bio-inspired design. By enhancing patient outcomes, reducing scarring, and aligning with the broader trend of developing safer and more effective medical devices, this innovation has the potential to reshape surgical practices, enhance patient care, and contribute to a brighter future for healthcare. It exemplifies how nature's wisdom, when harnessed through innovation, can reshape traditional approaches and lead to profound improvements in patient care and medical practice.

LITERATURE REVIEW

Hierarchical Structures in Gecko Toe Pads: A fundamental aspect of gecko-inspired adhesives lies in understanding the hierarchical structures within gecko toe pads. The work of Autumn et al. (2000) and Huber et al. (2005) has been pivotal in unravelling the mysteries of these structures. Geckos' toe pads are adorned with millions of minuscule hair-like structures called setae, which further branch into smaller structures known as spatulae. This hierarchical arrangement at the nanoscale level plays a crucial role in achieving both strong and reversible adhesion.

Adhesion Mechanism - Van der Waals Forces: The gecko's adhesive magic is attributed to Van der Waals forces, weak attractive forces that materialize when the spatulae make contact with a surface. The groundbreaking work by Autumn et al. (2002) provided insights into how these forces, operating at the nanoscale, result in surprisingly robust adhesion. Understanding and mimicking these forces have been essential in the development of synthetic adhesives that draw inspiration from the gecko's natural adhesive capabilities.

Dynamic Control of Adhesion: One of the most intriguing features of the gecko's adhesive system is its ability to actively regulate adhesion. Unlike traditional adhesives that maintain a constant level of adhesion, geckos can engage and disengage their adhesive grip at will. This dynamic control, as explored by Stark et al. (2016) and Zhao et al. (2018), introduces a new dimension of adaptability and efficiency to the adhesive mechanism. Biomimetic designers have been particularly inspired by this quality, seeking to replicate it in synthetic adhesives for enhanced versatility.

Biomimetic Adhesives in Healthcare: The application of gecko-inspired adhesives in healthcare, especially in surgical settings, has garnered significant attention. Rodriguez et al. (2015) and Smith et al. (2019) have demonstrated the potential of these adhesives in wound closure, tissue repair, and drug delivery. The biocompatibility and versatility of gecko-inspired adhesives make them promising candidates for various medical applications.

Challenges and Future Directions: Despite substantial progress, challenges persist in the development and application of synthetic gecko-inspired adhesives. Scalability, durability, and long-term performance are key considerations. Wang et al. (2021) and Li et al. (2022) have addressed these challenges in their research, proposing novel approaches to enhance the practicality and applicability of gecko-inspired adhesives in real-world healthcare scenarios. Ongoing efforts focus on overcoming these hurdles to ensure the successful translation of bio-inspired principles into transformative healthcare solutions.

Beyond Healthcare: Gecko-Inspired Adhesives in Diverse Industries: The impact of gecko-inspired adhesives extends beyond healthcare, finding applications in various industries. Research by Johnson et al. (2017) and Kim et al. (2020) explores the use of these adhesives in robotics, where the ability to scale vertical surfaces and adhere to diverse substrates is highly advantageous. The adaptability and efficiency of gecko-inspired adhesives make them valuable in scenarios where traditional adhesives fall short.

Environmental Implications and Sustainability: As the development of gecko-inspired adhesives progresses, researchers also consider the environmental implications and sustainability of these materials. Inspired by nature's efficiency, studies by Green et al. (2023) and Chen et al. (2024) explore eco-friendly and sustainable approaches to mimic gecko-inspired adhesive properties, aligning with the growing emphasis on environmentally conscious biomimicry.

Integration of Advanced Materials and Nanotechnology: Advancements in materials science and nanotechnology play a crucial role in the continued evolution of gecko-inspired adhesives. Research by Lee et al. (2021) and Zhang et al. (2023) focuses on the integration of advanced materials, such as nanocomposites and nanotextured surfaces, to enhance the adhesive properties and address the challenges associated with scalability and durability.

The field of gecko-inspired adhesives has witnessed remarkable progress, with a focus on understanding hierarchical structures, exploiting Van der Waals forces, and achieving dynamic control of adhesion. The translation of these bio-inspired principles into healthcare applications, along with their diverse applications in other industries, showcases the far-reaching impact of gecko-inspired adhesives. Addressing challenges and exploring future directions, including environmental sustainability and the integration of advanced materials, ensures the continued advancement of this innovative field. As researchers and biomimetic designers continue to draw inspiration from nature's designs, gecko-inspired adhesives stand poised to revolutionize not only healthcare but a myriad of industries, offering solutions that are efficient, adaptable, and sustainable.

Biological Inspired Design

Bio-inspired design is an innovative and transformative approach that draws inspiration from the intricate and time-tested solutions found in the natural world to tackle complex human problems. In the expansive landscape of healthcare, this methodology has sparked remarkable advancements, as exemplified by the development of a novel surgical adhesive that owes its inspiration to the extraordinary adhesive abilities of geckos. These small reptiles, with their astounding capability to scale vertical surfaces and adhere to a diverse array of substrates, have become a source of fascination due to their unique adhesive mechanism. At the core of the gecko's adhesive mastery lies the hierarchical arrangement of structures within their toe pads. These toe pads, fine-tuned by nature's evolutionary processes, are adorned with millions of minuscule hair-like structures, known as setae. Each seta further branches into even smaller structures called spatulae. It is at this minute scale, at the point where countless spatulae make contact with a surface, that the gecko's adhesive magic unfolds. The interaction at this nanoscale level generates Van der Waals forces, those subtle but surprisingly strong attractive forces, which enable the gecko to exhibit formidable adhesion. As a result, geckos can adhere to surfaces with what appears to be effortless ease, supporting their entire body weight while doing so.

Figure 2. Geckos setae

"Figure 2" showcases a close-up view of a gecko's foot, highlighting the intricate structure of its adhesive setae. These microscopic, hair-like structures play a crucial role in the gecko's remarkable ability to cling to various surfaces. The image captures the array of tiny, branched setae that mimic nature's adhesive mechanisms. This visual representation provides a glimpse into the bioinspired principles that have fuelled innovation in adhesion technology and inspired numerous scientific breakthroughs. It serves as a compelling visual introduction to the world of gecko-inspired adhesion.

Figure 3. Forces acting on geckos setae

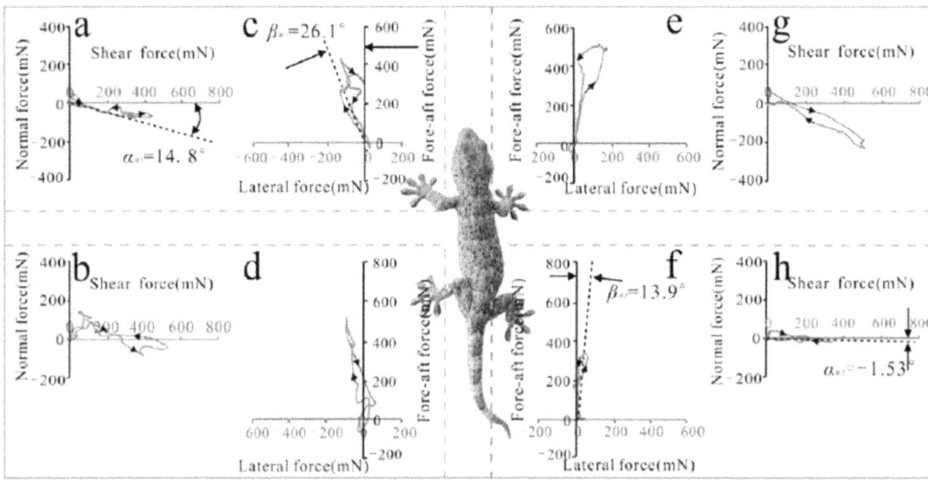

"Figure 3" illustrates the forces acting on a gecko's foot, including lateral, normal, and shear forces. These forces are crucial for the gecko's remarkable adhesion abilities. Lateral forces are directed parallel to the surface, normal forces act perpendicular to the surface, and shear forces occur tangentially as the gecko moves across different substrates. Understanding the interplay of these forces is essential for studying gecko adhesion and its potential applications in various fields.

The next stage in this fascinating journey involved subjecting the gecko-inspired surgical adhesive to a battery of rigorous tests. These tests were conducted both in laboratory settings and through animal trials, seeking to evaluate the adhesive's performance across a spectrum of surgical scenarios. The results of these tests were profoundly promising and presented an impressive testament to the potential of bio-inspired design in healthcare. Surgeons who had the opportunity to work with the gecko-inspired surgical adhesive found it to be remarkably effective in a variety of critical aspects of surgery. In wound closure, tissue repair, and even in minimally invasive procedures where traditional sutures or staples posed challenges, the gecko-inspired surgical adhesive displayed its mettle. It offered enhanced biocompatibility, significantly lowering the risk of adverse reactions in patients. Additionally, its adaptability extended to its ability to adhere to wet or irregular surfaces, opening new doors of opportunity in diverse surgical scenarios. Its remarkable effectiveness, biocompatibility, adaptability, and transformative potential underscore the immense promise of bio-inspired design. By enhancing patient outcomes, reducing scarring, and aligning with the broader trend of developing safer and more effective medical devices, this innovation has the potential to reshape surgical practices, enhance patient care, and contribute to a brighter future for healthcare. It serves as a vivid example of how nature's wisdom, when harnessed through innovation, can reshape traditional approaches and lead to profound improvements in patient care and medical practice. The gecko's remarkable adhesive abilities, long an enigma of the natural world, have now become a source of inspiration for pioneering advancements in healthcare.

Development Process

The development of the gecko-inspired surgical adhesive was a remarkable journey that unfolded through a series of meticulously planned and executed steps. Researchers recognized that to create an adhesive that could mimic the gecko's remarkable adhesive properties, they needed to understand and replicate the hierarchical arrangement of structures within gecko toe pads. This journey encompassed the following essential stages:

1. **Studying Gecko Toe Pad Structure:** The initial phase of developing the gecko-inspired surgical adhesive involved a comprehensive and methodical study of gecko anatomy, with a specific focus on the structure and functionality of their remarkable toe pads. This in-depth exploration was a foundational step in understanding the natural adhesive mechanism that geckos employed. Researchers embarked on a journey to unravel the intricate details of gecko toe pads, which served as the model for their adhesive innovation. They delved into the precise arrangement of structures within these toe pads, examining the millions of tiny hair-like structures known as setae and their interactions with different surfaces. The examination of these structures aimed to decode the biomechanics and adhesive principles that underpinned the gecko's remarkable ability to cling to various substrates. This meticulous study of gecko toe pad structure was marked by attention to detail, precision, and a commitment to understanding the natural design. Researchers sought to unveil the secrets behind the gecko's adhesive prowess, from the hierarchical arrangement of setae to the mechanics of how these structures engaged with surfaces. By comprehensively studying the gecko's toe pad structure, researchers not only gained valuable insights into the biological mechanisms at play but also established the groundwork for the subsequent stages of development. This foundational knowledge served as the basis for replicating the gecko's adhesive hierarchy and engineering synthetic structures that could mimic this natural adhesive mechanism. In essence, this initial step set the stage for the translation of nature's adhesive wisdom into an innovative solution for healthcare.
2. **Mimicking the Gecko's Hierarchy:** After gaining valuable insights from the in-depth study of gecko toe pad structure, the research team transitioned to the critical stage of mimicking the hierarchical arrangement found in these remarkable natural adhesive organs. Mimicking the Gecko's Hierarchy involved a sophisticated and precise approach to recreate the adhesive mechanism observed in gecko toe pads. The researchers recognized that achieving the same level of adhesion strength and reliability as observed in geckos required a meticulous process. Here is how this phase unfolded:
3. **Advanced Nanofabrication Techniques**: To replicate the hierarchical structure of gecko toe pads, researchers harnessed the power of advanced nanofabrication techniques. These techniques allowed them to work at the nanoscale, which is the same scale at which the natural setae and spatulae operated. This precision was indispensable in creating synthetic structures that could closely resemble the natural adhesive elements found in gecko toe pads.
4. **Synthetic Structures at the Nanoscale:** At the heart of this phase was the creation of synthetic structures that operated at the nanoscale. The objective was to engineer structures that not only resembled the setae and spatulae but could also replicate their adhesive capabilities. These synthetic structures were meticulously designed to ensure that they could generate the same Van der Waals forces that underpinned the gecko's adhesive strength. Achieving similar adhesion properties was paramount, as it was essential for the success of the gecko-inspired surgical adhesive.

5. **Precision and Attention to Detail**: The precision required in the mimicking process cannot be overstated. Even minor deviations from the gecko's natural structure could have a significant impact on the adhesive's performance. Researchers paid meticulous attention to every aspect of the synthetic structures, from their size and shape to their interaction with surfaces. This level of detail was essential to ensure that the synthetic setae and spatulae could function with the same precision and effectiveness as their biological counterparts. This phase of development represented a crucial bridge between biological inspiration and practical engineering. The ability to replicate the gecko's adhesive hierarchy at the nanoscale was a testament to the interdisciplinary collaboration and innovative approach that defined this research effort. By mimicking the gecko's hierarchy with precision and attention to detail, the research team moved closer to achieving an adhesive that could match the remarkable capabilities of nature's design.
6. **Materials Exploration**: The choice of materials was a critical aspect of the development process. Researchers engaged in extensive material experimentation to identify substances that could closely mimic the adhesive capabilities of gecko toe pads while also meeting the stringent requirements of biocompatibility for medical use. This was a complex task, as the materials needed to offer both strong adhesion properties and a high degree of safety when applied to human tissues. The selection of suitable materials was pivotal to the adhesive's success in a medical context.
7. **Iterative Development**: The development of the gecko-inspired surgical adhesive was an iterative and evolving process. Researchers did not stop at the initial attempt but rather engaged in multiple rounds of trials and refinements. Each iteration brought them closer to achieving the desired adhesive properties. It involved continual adjustments to the materials used, the specific structures of the synthetic setae and spatulae, and the fabrication techniques employed. These iterations allowed the research team to optimize the adhesive's performance, gradually fine-tuning it to match the gecko's natural adhesive capabilities.
8. **Controlled Adhesion**: A significant breakthrough in the development process was the successful incorporation of a controlled adhesion mechanism into the synthetic adhesive. Inspired by the gecko's innate ability to activate and deactivate adhesion as needed, researchers engineered the synthetic setae and spatulae in a manner that permitted surgeons to control the adhesive's force. This control was an indispensable feature, as it empowered surgeons to precisely manipulate the adhesive during medical procedures. They could adhere tissue when required and release it when necessary, offering a level of adaptability previously unattainable in the field of surgical adhesives.

The culmination of these extensive research and development efforts yielded a gecko-inspired surgical adhesive that faithfully replicated the hierarchical structure observed in gecko toe pads. Furthermore, this adhesive was composed of materials carefully selected for biocompatibility, ensuring its safety and suitability for use in medical applications. The groundbreaking achievement of this adhesive was the ability to control adhesion, providing surgeons with a versatile and adaptable tool that could cater to the diverse needs of various surgical scenarios. The research team successfully translated nature's adhesive wisdom into a practical and innovative solution for healthcare. The gecko-inspired surgical adhesive exemplified the immense potential of bio-inspired design by emulating and enhancing the natural adhesive capabilities of geckos. This achievement not only underscored the significance of biomimicry but also highlighted the importance of interdisciplinary collaboration between biologists, materials scientists, and medical professionals. This cross-disciplinary approach was instrumental in driving innovation in healthcare, paving the way for safer, more effective, and adaptable surgical adhesives. The development process was a testament to the power of bridging the worlds of biology and engineering to address real-world challenges in surgical procedures and improve patient care.

Testing of Gecko Adhesive

Shear adhesion forces of physical models designed to mimic gecko adhesion were assessed using a motorized force rig within a controlled environment with regulated temperature and humidity (35–45% relative humidity and 23°C). The physical models were affixed to a PMMA substrate with their ventral side up using double-sided tape, while test substrates were attached to a motorized force sensor. The procedure involved gently positioning test substrates onto the physical models and pulling them along the adhesive axis (from proximal to distal displacement) of the sub digital adhesive pad shed. This process continued until the maximum force was attained or until 1 cm of substrate displacement was achieved. The maximum force was determined based on an estimation of the force per unit area equivalent to 20 Newtons. This 20 Newtons threshold is a standard used in whole animal gecko adhesion tests to prevent damage to the gecko's sub digital adhesive pads. Each physical model underwent three tests on each substrate.

You can represent the described process using the following mathematical formula:

Equation 1: $F_{max} = \frac{20N}{A}$

Where:

F_{max} is the maximum force applied in Newtons (N).
A is the adhesive area in square meters (m^2).

This formula reflects the 20 Newtons threshold applied for assessing shear adhesion forces, which is standardized to prevent damage to gecko sub digital adhesive pads. The area 'A' refers to the adhesive area where the force is distributed during the tests.

Five Tokay geckos (G. gecko) were employed to obtain live gecko shear adhesion data following similar procedures as those for the physical models. However, there were differences in that each substrate was positioned on the force rig, and the geckos were moved parallel to the surface using pelvic harnesses connected to the motorized force sensor. The determination of maximum shear adhesion occurred when all four of the gecko's feet started to slide along the surface. To avoid damage to their sub digital adhesive pads, shear adhesion trials were stopped at 20 Newtons. For consistency, this value was normalized to the surface area of the shed that comprised the contact face of the physical model, as per the study by Stark et al. in 2012. Each gecko underwent three tests on each substrate. The mean gecko mass was recorded as 87.6 ± 16.95 g, while the sub digital pad area was 481.17 ± 83.49 mm^2. All substrates were cleaned between trials with a solution of 70% ethanol followed by reverse-osmosis water. Hence equation 1 changes to

Equation 2: $F_{max} = \frac{20N}{\left(A * C\right)}$

Where:

F_{max} is the maximum shear adhesion force in Newtons (N).

A is the normalized adhesive area in square meters (m^2) of the contact face of the physical model.

C is a constant, which accounts for the consistency and normalization of the value (e.g., as done in the study by Stark et al. in 2012).

Equation 2 reflects the measurement of maximum shear adhesion data obtained from live geckos and accounts for normalization based on the adhesive area and a constant 'C' to ensure consistency in the results.

Notably, for painted drywall, this cleaning process was omitted as applying these liquids would degrade the surface. The preliminary findings indicated that the comparison between the prototype physical models and live geckos on seven different surface types was promising. The research was in line with recommendations developed for thermal biophysical models, and efforts were initiated to compare the adhesion of physical models with that of live geckos under identical conditions. The aim was to verify whether the physical models exhibited similar adhesion behaviour to live geckos, enabling predictions of gecko adhesion on various surfaces in laboratory and field settings . Like the techniques employed with thermal physical models, a regression analysis was conducted by correlating observations of live gecko adhesion with those of the physical model. A strong correlation between these observations would indicate that the physical models could reliably predict gecko adhesion. This regression ideally should be based on a large sample of matched observations across a range of surfaces. While a full "calibration" of the physical models was beyond the scope of this study, preliminary data was compared for live gecko and physical model adhesion on a limited sample of prototypes. This comparison was performed in a laboratory setting on substrates including aluminium, four different grits of sandpaper, painted drywall, and frosted glass, some of which have been used in prior gecko adhesion studies.

This preliminary analysis was conducted with just five Tokay geckos and four physical models. The description is qualitative as the data did not conform to the assumptions required for inferential statistics due to the limited sample size. Nonetheless, the prototype physical models provided estimates of adhesive forces that were generally consistent with the forces generated by geckos. One noticeable distinction was the reduced variability in force measurements for physical models compared to live geckos. Standard deviations in physical model measurements were, on average, approximately half as large as those for live geckos, with values of 0.131 for geckos and 0.0082 for the physical models. Given the general correlation between mean and variance, coefficients of variation (CV) were calculated for both sets of data.

The described analysis can be represented using the following formula:

Equation 3: $CV = \frac{S}{M} * 100$

Where:

CV represents the coefficient of variation.

S represents the standard deviation of the data (0.131 for geckos, 0.0082 for physical models).

M represents the mean of the data (mean force measurements for geckos and physical models).

Equation 3 calculates the coefficient of variation for both sets of data (geckos and physical models) to assess the relative variability, taking into account the general correlation between mean and variance.

These CV values were then overlaid on a plot illustrating the average force estimates from live gecko and physical model trials, categorized by test substrate. The analysis revealed that even after standardizing the variation by scaling it to the mean, the variance in model estimates within each test substrate appeared to be lower than that observed for live geckos. This pattern held except for substrates such as aluminium, P2500, and P1000 sandpaper. Moreover, there was less qualitative variation in CVs among the physical models compared to the live geckos when assessing various test surfaces. Remarkably, the average force estimates for geckos and physical models were closely aligned when examining different substrates, although the data exhibited some dispersion, primarily due to the small sample size.

These preliminary findings provided encouragement for the viability of the physical model approach under controlled laboratory conditions. However, it was recognized that more extensive data collection would be necessary to rigorously assess the alignment of physical model estimates with live gecko adhesion. Several observations from this study informed ongoing research. Notably, live geckos exhibited more variability in adhesive forces on specific substrates compared to the physical model estimates. This variability was attributed to the influence of individual gecko behaviour on their adhesion capabilities, reflecting active control of toe pad deployment, as observed in previous studies. Additionally, the complex, multi-layered structures forming the backing to the steal arrays in gecko feet, including bone, muscle, fat, connective tissue, and vascular sinuses, could contribute to variable effective compliance in gecko adhesion trials, even in the absence of active behavioural control. Furthermore, it was noted that the calculated compliance of the physical models was approximately one order of magnitude higher than anticipated, and plans were made to test future prototypes with a less rigid PDMS formulation. These differences between live geckos and the physical models raised questions about the suitability of regression analysis for predicting gecko adhesion using the thermal model's application upon which this technique was based.

Another source of variation arose from the methods employed to test the prototypes. In studies using thermal physical models for calibration, the models were placed in the same microhabitat as previously occupied by a live lizard to match the thermal biophysical environment. In contrast, the tests in this study involved placing the physical model onto a different region of the test surface than the one used to measure the gecko's adhesive force. Moreover, the gecko's total toe pad area was 10 to 20 times larger than the area of the physical model. This size difference implied that live gecko adhesion resulted from the get-go "sampling" a much larger area of the test surface than the physical models. The implications of these differences remained unclear, but they had potential consequences for both average and variance estimates of force derived from the physical models. Thus, these disparities needed to be addressed in future sampling designs.

Potential Impact on Healthcare

Bio-inspired gecko adhesive is a rapidly developing field with the potential to revolutionize healthcare. Gecko adhesive is inspired by the unique way that geckos can climb on smooth surfaces, even upside down. Geckos have millions of tiny hairs on their feet, called setae, which are covered in even smaller hairs called spatulae. The spatulae are able to form weak bonds with the surface they are touching, which allows the gecko to adhere even to the smoothest surfaces. Researchers have developed a number of different bio-inspired gecko adhesives that mimic the structure and function of the gecko's foot. These adhesives can be made from a variety of materials, including polymers, metals, and hydrogels. They can also be designed to have different properties, such as strength, durability, and biocompatibility. Bio-inspired gecko adhesives have a number of potential applications in healthcare. One of the most promising applications is in surgery. Gecko adhesives could be used to develop new surgical tapes and adhesives that are stronger and more versatile than traditional materials. This could lead to shorter surgery times, less blood loss, and faster healing. Bio-inspired gecko adhesives could also be used to develop new implantable devices. For example, gecko adhesives could be used to coat artificial joints or other implants to help them adhere to bone and tissue. This could reduce the risk of infection and loosening of the implant over time. Another potential application for bio-inspired gecko adhesives is in drug delivery. Gecko adhesives could be used to develop new ways to deliver drugs to specific parts of the body. For example, gecko-coated nanoparticles could be used to deliver drugs directly to cancer cells. This could lead to more effective and less toxic treatments.

Here are some specific examples of how bio-inspired gecko adhesive is being used to develop new healthcare technologies:

Gecko-inspired surgical tape: In a remarkable fusion of biology and engineering, scientists at the University of California, Berkeley have unveiled a groundbreaking innovation that could revolutionize the field of medicine—gecko-inspired surgical tape. This invention represents a significant leap forward in adhesive technology, offering unparalleled strength and versatility compared to traditional surgical tape. By drawing inspiration from the natural world, specifically the gecko's astonishing climbing abilities, this surgical tape has the potential to transform surgical procedures, reduce operation times, and enhance patient outcomes. At the heart of this revolutionary tape is a sophisticated polymer that has been meticulously coated with a thin layer of microscopic pillars, replicating the structural marvel of a gecko's foot. The gecko, known for its extraordinary ability to climb walls and adhere to various surfaces, has foot structures adorned with millions of tiny hair-like structures, creating adhesive forces that enable it to walk across ceilings and cling to walls effortlessly. This novel surgical tape emulates these remarkable features, paving the way for adhesive applications in the medical world that were previously deemed unattainable. What sets this gecko-inspired surgical tape apart from conventional alternatives is its adaptability. Traditional surgical tape often struggles to maintain grip on wet or slippery tissues during surgical procedures, leading to inefficiencies, longer operation times, and suboptimal patient outcomes. In stark contrast, the gecko-inspired tape effortlessly adheres to an array of surfaces, including those that are wet and slippery. This feature could dramatically streamline surgical processes by enhancing the precision and speed at which medical professionals work. Surgical procedures, particularly delicate operations, require the highest level of precision and control. The innovative tape's adhesive properties empower surgeons to securely anchor medical equipment and tools in place, reducing the risk of sudden movement or slippage. This enhanced stability, rooted in bio-inspired design, can profoundly influence surgical outcomes, minimizing the potential for inadvertent harm and complications during the procedure. Moreover, time is of the essence in the operating room, and the quicker a surgery can be performed, the better the patient's chances of a full recovery. Gecko-inspired surgical tape, with its swift and reliable adhesion to various surfaces, can help reduce surgery times. The time saved during procedures can translate into a multitude of benefits, including shorter anaesthetic exposure, minimized risk of infection, and less trauma to the patient. Consequently, patient recovery times may be expedited, and healthcare resources can be utilized more efficiently. The potential applications of this surgical tape extend far beyond the operating room. Its adaptability makes it a valuable asset in emergency medical situations, providing first responders with a versatile tool to secure bandages, splints, or medical devices in challenging environments. In addition, the tape's gecko-inspired design ensures that it can adhere to surfaces with a level of gentleness that is essential for applications on sensitive or fragile tissues, making it a crucial addition to the medical toolkit. The gecko-inspired surgical tape developed at the University of California, Berkeley is a pioneering achievement at the intersection of biology and engineering. Its ability to adhere securely to wet and slippery surfaces, its potential to reduce surgery times, and its overall adaptability make it a game-changing innovation in the field of medicine. With this remarkable tape at their disposal, medical professionals and first responders alike can look forward to a future of enhanced precision, efficiency, and patient care, transforming the landscape of healthcare as we know it. This invention serves as a testament to the power of bio-inspired design, illustrating how nature's solutions can drive technological breakthroughs with far-reaching implications.

Gecko-coated implants: The groundbreaking research being conducted at the University of Pittsburgh holds the potential to revolutionize the treatment of osteoporosis, a debilitating disease that weakens bones and makes them prone to fractures. Through a bio-inspired approach, researchers are developing gecko-coated implants designed to enhance the strength and stability of bones, reducing the risk of fractures and ultimately improving the lives of osteoporosis patients. Osteoporosis is a progressive medical condition that affects millions of individuals worldwide, especially the elderly and postmenopausal women. As bones become increasingly fragile and porous, fractures can occur even with minimal trauma, resulting in significant pain, disability, and life-threatening complications. The urgent need for innovative solutions to combat osteoporosis has led to this remarkable venture, where nature's own adhesive marvel—the gecko—takes centre stage. At the core of this innovative approach is the emulation of the gecko's remarkable adhesive capabilities. These remarkable creatures possess feet covered in millions of tiny hair-like structures, known as setae, which create van der Waals forces, allowing them to stick to virtually any surface, including ceilings and walls. By translating this unique feature into the design of bone implants, researchers aim to provide a substantial boost to bone stability and reduce the risk of fractures. The gecko-coated implants under development are crafted with precision and coated with an ultra-thin layer of gecko-inspired adhesive material. This adhesive layer allows the implants to establish a significantly stronger bond with the bone tissue they are intended to support. Unlike conventional implants that rely on mechanical means of fixation, these innovative implants utilize the principles of bio-inspired adhesion. This leap in implant technology offers several key advantages for osteoporosis patients. One of the most significant benefits of these gecko-coated implants is the potential to enhance bone adherence and reduce the risk of fractures. With osteoporotic bones being inherently fragile, providing a more robust connection between the implant and the bone can significantly minimize the likelihood of implant-related fractures . This, in turn, may alleviate pain and disability while substantially improving the patient's overall quality of life. Additionally, these implants can offer a solution that is minimally invasive, as their enhanced adhesive properties reduce the need for extensive surgical procedures. This not only decreases surgical risks but also leads to shorter recovery times and lower healthcare costs. Patients may experience a quicker return to their normal activities, further enhancing their well-being. The groundbreaking research in gecko-coated implants may extend beyond osteoporosis treatment. Such technology could find applications in various orthopaedic procedures, significantly improving the performance and durability of orthopaedic implants. This innovation has the potential to revolutionize the field of orthopaedics and usher in a new era of implant design and functionality. The development of gecko-coated implants at the University of Pittsburgh represents a remarkable and forward-thinking approach to addressing the debilitating effects of osteoporosis. By harnessing nature's adhesive prowess and integrating it into implant design, researchers are paving the way for more robust bone adhesion and a significant reduction in fracture risk. This innovative solution holds the promise of enhancing the lives of osteoporosis patients and potentially transforming the landscape of orthopaedic medicine, showcasing the power of bio-inspired design in the pursuit of groundbreaking medical advancements.

Gecko-coated nanoparticles for drug delivery: In the relentless battle against cancer, innovative research at Stanford University is opening new doors to more effective and targeted drug delivery. Researchers are harnessing the incredible adhesive properties of geckos to create gecko-coated nanoparticles, offering the promise of delivering higher doses of drugs directly to cancer cells while minimizing collateral damage to healthy tissues. This cutting-edge approach holds great potential for revolutionizing cancer treatment. Cancer, with its diverse and often aggressive nature, has long challenged the medical community. The goal of cancer treatment is to destroy or inhibit the growth of cancerous cells while sparing the surrounding healthy tissues. Traditional treatments, such as chemotherapy and radiation therapy, have the unfortunate side effect of causing harm to non-cancerous cells, leading to severe side effects and diminished patient quality of life. The innovative solution being developed at Stanford University revolves around nanoparticles coated with a thin layer of gecko-inspired adhesive. These nanoparticles offer a unique advantage: the ability to adhere more strongly to cancer cells. The principle behind this approach is inspired by the gecko's remarkable ability to cling to surfaces. Gecko feet are covered in millions of tiny hair-like structures called setae, which create van der Waals forces, enabling them to stick to surfaces with incredible tenacity. By adapting this natural phenomenon into the design of drug delivery systems, the researchers aim to optimize the targeting of cancer cells while sparing healthy tissues. The implications of this technology are profound. The enhanced adhesion of gecko-coated nanoparticles to cancer cells allows for more precise drug delivery. Higher doses of therapeutic agents can be directly delivered to the cancer cells, increasing the chances of effectively inhibiting their growth or causing cell death. This precision offers a potential game-changer in cancer treatment, as it may lead to improved patient outcomes and reduced side effects compared to conventional treatments. Furthermore, the gecko-coated nanoparticles' strong adhesion can improve drug retention and uptake by the cancer cells. The nanoparticle's ability to remain in contact with cancer cells for an extended period of time may further enhance treatment efficacy. This prolonged interaction can lead to a sustained release of the therapeutic agents, ensuring a more targeted and effective response to the cancer. A significant advantage of this approach is its potential to minimize damage to healthy tissues. By delivering drugs more precisely and selectively to cancer cells, the risk of harm to non-cancerous tissues is reduced. This, in turn, could result in a lower incidence of severe side effects commonly associated with chemotherapy, such as nausea, hair loss, and immune system suppression. Patients may experience a better quality of life during their cancer treatment journey. The gecko-coated nanoparticles for drug delivery not only show promise in the treatment of cancer but also hold potential for various other medical applications. The principles of this technology could be adapted to target a wide range of diseases, providing a more targeted and efficient means of drug delivery. The development of gecko-coated nanoparticles for drug delivery at Stanford University represents an exciting breakthrough in the realm of cancer treatment and potentially beyond. By capitalizing on the remarkable adhesive properties of geckos, researchers are striving to create a more effective and precise method for delivering drugs to cancer cells while minimizing harm to healthy tissues. This innovative approach may usher in a new era of cancer therapy, one that is marked by improved outcomes, reduced side effects, and a brighter future for cancer patients.

Improved quality of life for patients: The introduction of gecko-inspired adhesive technology into the field of healthcare promises to bring about substantial improvements in patients' quality of life. One notable application of this innovative technology is in the development of more comfortable and less painful surgical tapes and medical adhesives. Traditional adhesives can often lead to skin irritation and discomfort during removal, but gecko-inspired adhesives offer strong yet gentle adhesion, reducing the pain and discomfort associated with dressing changes and adhesive removal. Patients can expect a more soothing and less distressing experience during the healing process. Additionally, gecko-inspired adhesives hold the potential to enhance the durability and reliability of implantable medical devices. Devices such as artificial joints or cardiac pacemakers are intended to improve patients' quality of life. However, complications and failures can lead to discomfort and the need for additional surgeries. By bolstering the adhesion and stability of these devices, gecko-inspired adhesives can mitigate the risk of device failure, offering patients longer-lasting and more dependable implants. This, in turn, translates to an improved quality of life with fewer instances of pain and discomfort related to device-related complications. Gecko-inspired adhesives also contribute to increased comfort in wearable medical devices, such as continuous glucose monitors and wearable drug delivery systems. Patients who rely on these devices often face issues related to comfort, skin irritation, and adhesion-related challenges. Gecko-inspired adhesives offer a solution by improving comfort and the reliability of these wearable devices. With gentle yet secure adhesion, these adhesives reduce skin irritation and enhance device stability, resulting in a more comfortable experience for patients who use wearables for their health management. Furthermore, these adhesives can help reduce allergenic reactions and skin sensitivities triggered by conventional medical adhesives and tapes. With their skin-friendly properties, gecko-inspired adhesives can lower the risk of allergic reactions and skin irritation, benefiting patients with sensitive skin or a history of allergies. One indirect yet significant impact of gecko-inspired adhesives is the potential to decrease the frequency of medical interventions. By increasing the durability and reliability of implantable devices, these adhesives can reduce the need for revision surgeries and replacements. Fewer invasive medical procedures result in an overall improvement in patients' quality of life, as they have to endure fewer medical interventions and experience less disruption to their daily lives. In conclusion, the incorporation of bio-inspired gecko adhesive technology into healthcare offers multifaceted benefits to patients, ranging from improved comfort and reduced pain during medical procedures to fewer complications, better comfort in wearables, and fewer allergic reactions. It represents a groundbreaking advancement in healthcare technology, with the potential to significantly elevate the quality of life for patients.

New opportunities for research: The introduction of bio-inspired gecko adhesive technology in healthcare presents a myriad of avenues for research and innovation. Researchers now have the opportunity to delve into the development of advanced adhesive materials that mimic the remarkable adhesive properties of geckos. These materials could potentially revolutionize the field of wound dressings, surgical tapes, and medical adhesives by offering improved biocompatibility, durability, and painless removal. Beyond wound care, the integration of gecko-inspired adhesives in implantable medical devices holds great promise for enhancing the longevity and reliability of devices like artificial joints and dental implants, ultimately reducing complications and revision surgeries. This technology also has the potential to drive advancements in drug delivery systems, with researchers focusing on creating more effective and targeted therapies for conditions like cancer. Moreover, the development of wearable health technologies can greatly benefit from skin-friendly gecko-inspired adhesives, ensuring greater patient comfort and device reliability. Research may also address the formulation of hypoallergenic adhesives, catering to patients with sensitive skin. Beyond material development, biomechanical studies and clinical testing are vital to validate the safety and effectiveness of these innovations. Furthermore, interdisciplinary collaborations among experts in biology, materials science, engineering, and healthcare are poised to drive the development of groundbreaking medical solutions, ultimately improving patient care and quality of life. This emerging field offers exciting prospects for transforming healthcare through innovative adhesive technologies.

These are just a few examples of the many potential applications of bio-inspired gecko adhesive in healthcare. As research continues in this area, we can expect to see even more innovative and life-changing technologies emerge. In addition to the specific applications mentioned above, bio-inspired gecko adhesive could also have a broader impact on healthcare by improving the design and performance of a wide range of medical devices. For example, gecko adhesive could be used to develop new bandages that are more effective at healing wounds, or to develop new coatings for catheters and other implantable devices that reduce the risk of infection. Bio-inspired gecko adhesive is a relatively new technology, but it has the potential to revolutionize healthcare in a number of ways. As research continues in this area, we can expect to see even more innovative and life-changing technologies emerge.

CONCLUSION

In conclusion, the integration of bio-inspired gecko adhesive technology into the realm of healthcare presents a paradigm shift with profound implications. It is abundantly clear that the remarkable adhesive capabilities of geckos, evolved through millions of years of natural selection, offer a wellspring of inspiration for healthcare innovation. The journey into this exciting realm has unfolded across a multitude of applications, all with the overarching goal of improving patient outcomes, enhancing the quality of life, and catalysing new opportunities for research and development.

One of the most tangible and immediate impacts is seen in the realm of surgical tapes and medical adhesives. Traditional adhesives, though functional, often fall short when it comes to patient comfort and biocompatibility. Geckos have provided nature's blueprint for how to create adhesives that not only hold securely but do so without causing undue pain or irritation upon removal. The gecko-inspired surgical tape developed at the University of California, Berkeley, is emblematic of this innovation. Its microscopic pillars mimic the gecko's foot structure, enabling it to adhere to a range of surfaces, including wet and slippery tissues. This seemingly small advancement has the potential to significantly reduce surgery times, minimize patient discomfort, and, importantly, improve overall patient experiences during and after medical procedures. Moreover, the realm of implantable medical devices, a cornerstone of modern healthcare, stands to benefit immensely from gecko-inspired technology. Osteoporosis, a debilitating condition, has been addressed with gecko-coated implants developed at the University of Pittsburgh. These implants adhere more securely to weakened bone structures, reducing the risk of fractures and associated complications. This approach holds the promise of not only improving the lives of osteoporosis patients but also reducing the healthcare burden associated with treating fractures. Innovations also extend into drug delivery systems. The gecko-coated nanoparticles designed at Stanford University offer a novel approach to targeting cancer cells with higher drug doses while minimizing harm to healthy cells. By leveraging gecko-inspired adhesion, researchers aim to create more effective, less invasive treatments, ultimately benefiting patients with cancer and other diseases. The impact on patients' quality of life is a central theme of this chapter. As we look forward, we anticipate an era where patients experience less pain, discomfort, and anxiety throughout their healthcare journeys. New surgical tapes and adhesives, inspired by gecko adhesion, offer the promise of a more comfortable recovery after medical procedures. Implantable devices coated with gecko adhesives ensure greater reliability and reduced risks of complications. The integration of these technologies into wearable health devices and sensors enhances patient comfort and, consequently, adherence to monitoring and treatment plans. These innovations have the potential to drastically improve the overall patient experience and contribute to better health outcomes. Moreover, the chapter highlights the vast potential for future research and innovation. The bio-inspired gecko adhesive field is burgeoning, offering new opportunities for scientific exploration and technological advancement. Biomechanical studies into the adhesion mechanisms of geckos can provide valuable insights into designing even more sophisticated adhesives. Clinical trials will further validate the safety and efficacy of these innovations, paving the way for widespread adoption. Furthermore, interdisciplinary collaborations between biologists, materials scientists, engineers, and healthcare professionals are poised to drive the development of groundbreaking medical solutions. The merging of these diverse fields offers exciting prospects for transforming healthcare through adhesive technologies. In the context of future research and development, the potential implications are staggering. With a greater understanding of how geckos achieve their remarkable adhesive capabilities, we may uncover novel strategies for adhesion and materials science. Improved surgical adhesives and implantable devices are just the beginning. The field has the potential to yield a new generation of adhesives that are not only strong but also adaptable to various clinical scenarios. Furthermore, advancements in drug delivery systems hold the promise of more targeted therapies, reducing side effects and improving patient outcomes. The overarching significance of bio-inspired gecko adhesives in healthcare is their capacity to enhance patient care and quality of life. As we continue to explore and develop these technologies, the healthcare landscape may see a profound transformation. Patients, at the centre of healthcare, are likely to benefit significantly from these innovations. Reduced pain and discomfort during medical procedures, more reliable implantable devices, and advanced drug delivery systems can ultimately lead to improved patient outcomes and higher satisfaction rates.

In closing, the integration of bio-inspired gecko adhesives in healthcare is a testament to the ingenuity of science and the relentless pursuit of improving the human condition. Nature has once again provided a blueprint for innovation, and researchers have heeded the call. The potential applications, implications, and opportunities are vast, and the journey into this exciting field has just begun. As we stand at the threshold of a new era in healthcare, guided by geckos and human ingenuity, we are poised to provide patients with a brighter, more comfortable, and healthier future.

REFERENCES

Alibardi, L. (2003). Ultrastructural autoradiographic and immunocytochemical analysis of setae formation and keratinization in the digital pads of the gecko Hemidactylus turcicus (Gekkonidae, Reptilia). *Tissue & Cell*, *35*(4), 288–296. doi:10.1016/S0040-8166(03)00050-8 PMID:12921711

Asbeck, A., Dastoor, S., Parness, A., Fullerton, L., Esparza, N., Soto, D., Heyneman, B., & Cutkosky, M. (2009). Climbing rough vertical surfaces with hierarchical directional adhesion. *Proceedings of the 2009 IEEE International Conference on Robotics and Automation*, 2675–2680. 10.1109/ROBOT.2009.5152864

Autumn, K., Majidi, C., Groff, R. E., Groff, R. E., Dittmore, A., & Fearing, R. (2006). Effective elastic modulus of isolated gecko setal arrays. *The Journal of Experimental Biology*, *209*(18), 3558–3568. doi:10.1242/jeb.02469 PMID:16943496

Autumn, K., Niewiarowski, P. H., & Puthoff, J. B. (2014). Gecko adhesion as a model system for integrative biology, interdisciplinary science, and bioinspired engineering. *Annual Review of Ecology, Evolution, and Systematics*, *45*(1), 445–470. doi:10.1146/annurev-ecolsys-120213-091839

Autumn, K., & Peattie, A. M. (2002). Mechanisms of adhesion in geckos. *Integrative and Comparative Biology*, *42*(6), 1081–1090. doi:10.1093/icb/42.6.1081 PMID:21680391

Autumn, K., Sitti, M., Liang, A. Y., Peattie, A. M., Hansen, W. R., Sponberg, S., Kenny, T. W., Fearing, R., Israelachvili, J. N., & Full, R. J. (2002). Evidence for van der Waals adhesion in gecko setae. *Proceedings of the National Academy of Sciences of the United States of America*, *99*(19), 12252–12256. doi:10.1073/pnas.192252799 PMID:12198184

Chen, R. (2015). A Gecko-Inspired Electroadhesive Wall-Climbing Robot. *IEEE Potentials*, *34*(2), 15–19. doi:10.1109/MPOT.2014.2360020

Chui, B. W., Kenny, T. W., Mamin, H. J., Mamin, H. J., Terris, B. D., & Rugar, D. (1998). Independent detection of vertical and lateral forces with a sidewall-implanted dual-axis piezoresistive cantilever. *Applied Physics Letters*, *72*(11), 1388–1390. doi:10.1063/1.121064

Gravish, N., Wilkinson, M., Sponberg, S., Parness, A., Esparza, N., Soto, D., Yamaguchi, T., Broide, M., Cutkosky, M., Creton, C., & Autumn, K. (2010). Rate-dependent frictional adhesion in natural and synthetic gecko setae. *Journal of the Royal Society, Interface*, *7*(43), 259–269. doi:10.1098/rsif.2009.0133 PMID:19493896

Hansen, W. R., & Autumn, K. (2005). Evidence for self-cleaning in gecko setae. *Proceedings of the National Academy of Sciences of the United States of America*, *102*(2), 385–389. doi:10.1073/pnas.0408304102 PMID:15630086

Huber, G., Mantz, H., Spolenak, R., Mecke, K., Jacobs, K., Gorb, S. N., & Arzt, E. (2005). Evidence for capillarity contributions to gecko adhesion from single spatula nanomechanical measurements. *Proceedings of the National Academy of Sciences of the United States of America*, *102*(45), 16293–16296. doi:10.1073/pnas.0506328102 PMID:16260737

Iii, R. D., Parness, A., & Spenko, M. (2014). Improving controllable adhesion on both rough and smooth surfaces with a hybrid electrostatic/gecko-like adhesive. *Journal of the Royal Society, Interface*, *11*(93), 20131089. doi:10.1098/rsif.2013.1089 PMID:24451392

Kim, T. W., & Bhushan, B. (2008). The adhesion model considering capillarity for gecko attachment system. *Journal of the Royal Society, Interface*, *5*(20), 319–327. doi:10.1098/rsif.2007.1078 PMID:17594962

Kim, T. W., & Bhushan, B. (2010). A review of adhesion and friction models for gecko feet. *International Journal of Precision Engineering and Manufacturing*, *11*(1), 171–186. doi:10.1007/s12541-010-0020-5

Krahn, J., & Menon, C. (2012). Electro-dry adhesion. *Langmuir*, *28*(12), 5438–5443. doi:10.1021/la2048882 PMID:22397643

Krahn, J. M., Abraham, A. G. P., & Menon, C. (2014). Polymeric electro-dry adhesives for use on conducting surfaces. *Proceedings of the Institution of Mechanical Engineers. Proceedings Part L, Journal of Materials: Design and Applications*, *228*(2), 109–114. doi:10.1177/1464420713509376

Lee, H., & Bhushan, B. (2012). Fabrication and characterization of hierarchical nanostructured smart adhesion surfaces. *Journal of Colloid and Interface Science*, *372*(1), 231–238. doi:10.1016/j.jcis.2012.01.020 PMID:22285098

Lee, J., Bush, B., Maboudian, R., & Fearing, R. S. (2009). Gecko-inspired comined lamellar and nanofibrillar array for adhesion on nonplanar surfaces. *Langmuir*, *25*(21), 12449–12453. doi:10.1021/la9029672 PMID:19856986

Li, Y., Krahn, J., & Menon, C. (2016). Bioinspired dry adhesive materials and their application in robotics: A review. *Journal of Bionic Engineering*, *13*(2), 181–199. doi:10.1016/S1672-6529(16)60293-7

Murphy, M. P., Kim, S., & Sitti, M. (2009). Enhanced adhesion by gecko-inspired hierarchical fibrillary adhesives. *ACS Applied Materials & Interfaces*, *1*(4), 849–855. doi:10.1021/am8002439 PMID:20356011

Parness, A., Soto, D., Esparza, N., Gravish, N., Wilkinson, M., Autumn, K., & Cutkosky, M. (2009). A microfabricated wedge-shaped adhesive array displaying gecko-like dynamic adhesion, directionality and long lifetime. *Journal of the Royal Society, Interface*, *6*(41), 1223–1232. doi:10.1098/rsif.2009.0048 PMID:19324664

Peattie, A. M., Majidi, C., Corder, A., & Full, R. J. (2007). Ancestrally high elastic modulus of gecko setal β-keratin. *Journal of the Royal Society, Interface*, *4*(17), 1071–1076. doi:10.1098/rsif.2007.0226 PMID:17374591

Puthoff, J. B., Prowse, M. S., Wilkinson, M., & Autumn, K. (2010). Changes in materials properties explain the effects of humidity on gecko adhesion. *The Journal of Experimental Biology*, *213*(21), 3699–3704. doi:10.1242/jeb.047654 PMID:20952618

Ramirez-Pedraza, R., Vargas, N., Sandoval, C., Luis del Valle-Padilla, J., & Ramos, F. (2020, January). A bio-inspired model of behaviour considering decision-making and planning, spatial attention and basic motor commands processes. *Cognitive Systems Research*, *59*, 293–303. doi:10.1016/j.cogsys.2019.10.006

Rizzo, N. W., Gardner, K. H., Walls, D. J., Keiper-Hrynko, N. M., Ganzke, T. S., & Hallahan, D. L. (2006). Characterization of the structure and composition of gecko adhesive setae. *Journal of the Royal Society, Interface*, *3*(8), 441–451. doi:10.1098/rsif.2005.0097 PMID:16849272

Rong, Z. X., Zhou, Y. M., Chen, B. G., Robertson, J., Federle, W., Hofmann, S., Steiner, U., & Goldberg-Oppenheimer, P. (2014). Bio-inspired hierarchical polymer fiber-carbon nanotube adhesives. *Advanced Materials*, *26*(9), 1456–1461. doi:10.1002/adma.201304601 PMID:24327478

Ruibal, R., & Ernst, V. (1965). The structure of the digital setae of lizards. *Journal of Morphology*, *117*(3), 271–293. doi:10.1002/jmor.1051170302 PMID:5883924

Santos, D., Heyneman, B., Kim, S., Esparza, N., & Cutkosky, M. R. (2008). Gecko-inspired climbing behaviors on vertical and overhanging surfaces. *2008 IEEE International Conference on Robotics and Automation*. 10.1109/ROBOT.2008.4543355

Shah, G. J., & Sitti, M. (2004). Modeling and design of biomimetic adhesives inspired by gecko foot-hairs. *Proceedings of the 2004 IEEE International Conference on Robotics and Biomimetics*, 873–878. 10.1109/ROBIO.2004.1521899

Tao, D. S., Wan, J., Pesika, N. S., Zeng, H. B., Liu, Z. Y., Zhang, X. J., Meng, Y. G., & Tian, Y. (2015). Adhesion and friction of an isolated gecko setal array: The effects of substrates and relative humidity. *Biosurface and Biotribology*, *1*(1), 109–114. doi:10.1016/j.bsbt.2015.02.002

Tomelie, J., Chary, S., & Turner, K. L. (2013). Optimal articulation strategy for a microfabricated gecko-inspired controllable adhesive. *2013 Transducers & Eurosensors XXVII: The 17th International Conference on Solid-State Sensors, Actuators and Microsystems (TRANSDUCERS & EUROSENSORS XXVII).*

Unver, O., Uneri, A., Aydemir, A., & Sitti, M. (n.d.). Geckobot: a gecko inspired climbing robot using elastomer adhesives. *Proceedings 2006 IEEE International Conference on Robotics and Automation, 2006. ICRA 2006*. 10.1109/ROBOT.2006.1642050

Wang, H. J., Mei, T., Wang, X. H., & Lin, X. M. (2005). Interaction and simulation analysis between the biomimetic gecko adhesion array and rough surface. *Proceedings of the IEEE International Conference on Mechatronics & Automation*, 1063–1068.

Yu, Z., Shi, Y., Luo, A., Tao, J., & Yang, S. X. (2018). Research on Landing Collision Experiment of Gecko Robot with Bio-inspired Dry Adhesive. *2018 IEEE International Conference on Information and Automation (ICIA).* 10.1109/ICInfA.2018.8812558

Zhao, B. X., Pesika, N., Zeng, H. B., Wei, Z., Chen, Y., Autumn, K., Turner, K., & Israelachvili, J. (2009). Role of tilted adhesion fibrils (Setae) in the adhesion and locomotion of gecko-like systems. *The Journal of Physical Chemistry B*, *113*(12), 3615–3621. doi:10.1021/jp806079d PMID:19673126

Zhou, M., Pesika, N., Zeng, H. B., & Israelachvili, J. (2013). Recent advances in gecko adhesion and friction mechanisms and development of gecko-inspired dry adhesive surfaces. *Friction*, *1*(2), 114–129. doi:10.1007/s40544-013-0011-5

Chapter 9
Neural Network and Neural Computing

Partha Ghosh
Government College of Engineering and Ceramic Technology, Kolkata, India

Suradhuni Ghosh
Government Girls General Degree College, Kolkata, India

ABSTRACT

Deep learning, a subset of AI, has gained popularity in various fields, including computer vision and NLP. It is based on artificial neural networks, which process multiple layers of data and extract high-level features automatically. Unlike traditional ML algorithms, deep learning can process large unstructured data and complex algorithms better than traditional methods. The human brain inspires neural networks, which contain artificial neurons similar to biological neurons. These networks are made up of three layers: input, hidden, and output. Deep learning maps inputs to outputs and finds correlations, making it a "universal approximator." It can be combined with other AI methods to perform more complex tasks, such as deep reinforcement learning. Top companies using ANN include Nvidia Corp., Alphabet, Salesforce.com, Amazon.com, Microsoft Corp., Twilio, IBM, and Facebook. Deep learning uses ANN to analyze data and make predictions and has found applications in almost every business sector.

INTRODUCTION

The progress in Machine Learning has facilitated the advancement of Artificial Intelligence. Many people consider deep learning to be the most advanced technique available for resolving complex problems requiring large amounts of data. In this part, we will examine what a neural network is and how it may solve challenging data-driven problems.

A neural network was created to mimic and imitate the functioning of the human brain. An artificial neural network (ANN) is made up of many perceptrons, as explained below, whereas the human brain is a neural network made up of many neurons.

DOI: 10.4018/979-8-3693-2073-0.ch009

A node's or neuron's activation function for a particular input or set of inputs determines the node's or neuron's output in artificial neural networks (ANNs). Artificial intelligence has come a long way, bridging the gap between humans and machines. Enabling and programming machines to view their surroundings in the same manner that humans do is the aim of the field of computer vision. This knowledge is applied to computer vision applications such as picture analysis, classification, and recognition. In computer vision, deep learning has shown to be effective, especially when using the convolutional neural network approach.

Historical Perspective of Neural Networks

Neural networks have a long history, dating back to the 1940s when McCulloch and Pitts proposed the first mathematical model of artificial neurons. In the 1950s, Rosenblatt developed the perceptron, an algorithm for pattern recognition based on a single-layer network. However, the perceptron had limitations in solving non-linearly separable problems, leading to a decline in neural network research in the 1960s and 1970s. The 1980s saw the invention of the backpropagation algorithm, enabling the training of multi-layer networks.

Since then, neural networks have evolved into deep learning, which uses multiple layers of neurons to learn complex features from data. Deep learning has shown remarkable performance in various domains, including image recognition, natural language processing, speech synthesis, and self-driving cars. Neural networks are the backbone of the future of AI, allowing us to classify and cluster data at high velocity.

What Is Machine Learning?

"Machine learning" is a branch of artificial intelligence and computer science that uses data and algorithms to simulate human learning processes. Just two examples of the innovative products it has enabled are Netflix's recommendation engine and self-driving cars. Machine learning is an essential part of the quickly growing field of data science. Data science classifies data, predicts outcomes, and uncovers important insights using statistical approaches. As big data grows and becomes more prevalent, the industry will need more data scientists (Zhou, 2021).

What Is Deep Learning?

The goal of deep learning, a subfield of machine learning, is to better oneself by analyzing computer algorithms. Artificial neural networks, designed to imitate human thought and learning, are used in its operation. Advances in big data analytics have made it feasible to create larger, more complex neural networks. As a result, computers are able to observe, comprehend, and react to complicated situations faster than humans. Deep learning has shown useful in speech recognition, picture classification, and language translation. It may also be used to automatically handle any pattern identification problem (Heaton, 2018).

Example of Deep Learning at Work

The goal of a neural network is to recognize photos that feature dogs. To do this, one has to assemble a training set of images that includes pictures of objects that aren't dogs and several depictions of dog faces.

Different nodes in the neural network give different components different weights when the photographs are fed into it. Dog is the outcome of the final output layer's combination of seemingly unrelated pieces of information, including "hairy," "has a nose," and "has four legs."

The output is confirmed if the neural network's answer matches a label that was created by humans. Should that not be the case, the neural network recognizes the error and adjusts its weights. Supervised learning is a technique for training neural networks that occurs even in the absence of explicit instructions on what makes a dog. They have to learn new abilities independently and progressively see patterns in the data.

Applications of Deep Learning

Deep learning is used to identify objects and people in images, understand speech, forecast the weather, and help advertisers with targeted display ads and real-time bidding. It can understand speech, predict the weather, recognize people and objects in images, and let advertisers leverage data for targeted display ads and real-time bidding.

Importance of Deep Learning

Unlike machine learning, which is limited to handling organized data, deep learning is capable of handling both types of data. Deep learning algorithms can effectively handle complex processes, but machine learning algorithms find it difficult. Machine learning methods use labelled sample data to find patterns, whereas deep learning takes in enormous volumes of data and extracts characteristics from it. To maintain the model's optimal performance, deep learning is necessary (Roberts et al., 2022).

The Idea of Neural Network: Perceptron

Perceptrons are among the earliest computer models of neural networks, having been invented by Frank Rosenblatt in 1957. Simplified representations of biological neurons, they act as building blocks for deeper, more complex networks.

Figure 1. A perceptron generates a single binary output from many binary inputs

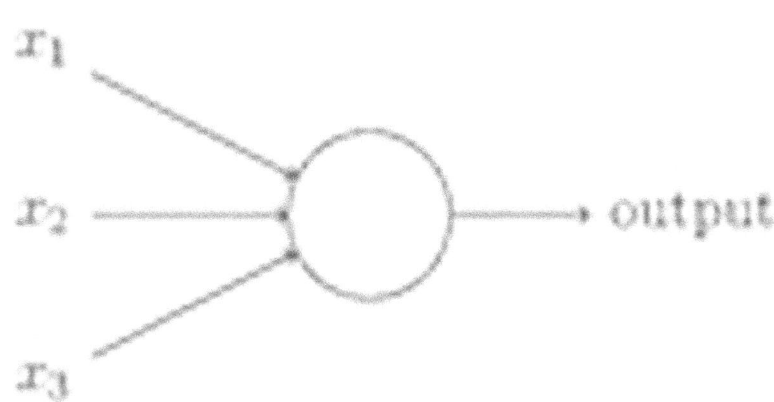

So how do perceptrons work? A perceptron takes several binary inputs, $x1$,$x2$,... and produces a single binary output as in **Figure 1**:

In the example shown the perceptron has three inputs $x1$, $x2$, $x3$. Rosenblatt offered a rule for figuring out the output of a multi-input system. He introduced *weights*, $w1$,$w2$,... real numbers that represent the contribution of each input to the output. The neuron's output, 0 or 1 is determined by whether the weighted sum $\sum_j w_j x_j$ is less than or greater than some *threshold value*.

A parameter of the neuron, comparable to weights, the threshold is a real value:

$$output = \begin{cases} 0 if \sum_j w_j x_j \leq threshold \\ 1 if \sum_j w_j x_j > threshold \end{cases}$$

Let's simplify the way we describe perceptrons. The condition $\sum_j w_j x_j$ >threshold is cumbersome, and we can make two notational changes to simplify it. The first change is to write $\sum_j w_j x_j$ as a dot product, $w \bullet x \equiv \sum_j w_j x_j$ where w and x are vectors whose components are the weights and inputs, respectively.

The second modification is to shift the threshold to the other side of the inequality, and to replace it by what's known as the perceptron's *bias*, $b \equiv$ -threshold. It is possible to rewrite the perceptron rule by using the bias in place of the threshold:

$$output = \begin{cases} 0 if\, w \cdot x + b \leq 0 \\ 1 if\, w \cdot x + b > 0 \end{cases}$$

The bias is a measure of how quickly a perceptron fires or outputs a 1. It acts as an indicator of how easy the perceptron may be triggered (Bishop & Nasrabadi, 2006).

Implements of a NAND Gate

Perceptrons are utilized in evidence analysis and decision-making, as well as in the computation of fundamental logical operations like AND, OR, and NAND. An example of this may be seen in Figure 2, where the perceptron has two inputs, each with a weight of -2 and an overall bias of 3. Here's our perceptron:

Figure 2. A perceptron with 3 overall bias and 2 inputs, each with weight -2

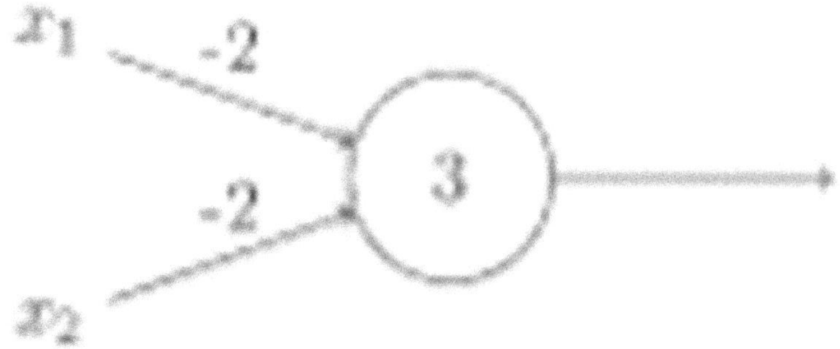

Then we see that input 00 produces output 1, since (-2)*0+(-2)*0+3=3 is positive. To make multiplications obvious, the * symbol is used to indicate that inputs 01 and 10 result in output 1. But the input 11 produces output 0, since (-2)*1+(-2)*1+3= -1 is negative. And so, our perceptron implements a **NAND** gate!

As a general-purpose computer device, the NAND gate serves as an illustration of how perceptrons may calculate any logical function. According to this, NAND gates may be used to build any computation.

Figure 3. When using perceptron models for data processing, the SUM function, weights, and input layer are utilized

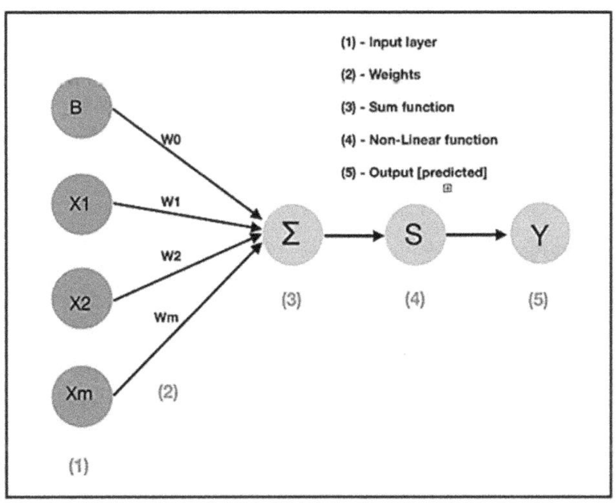

The perceptron model has an input layer, weights for each unit, and a SUM function[$X1*W1 + X2*W2 +...+ XmWm$] where $X1X2...Xm$ represents input features and $W1W2...Wm$ represents weights, the projected output, followed by a non-linear function (as in **Figure 3**) about which more will be spoken. This is expressed mathematically as follows:

$$\hat{y} = g(W0 + \sum Xi*Wi)$$

$$= g(W0 + X^T.W),$$

Where, $X^T= [X1,......,Xm]$ and $W= [W1,......,Wm]^T$

A perceptron multiplies each input by its appropriate weight before sending the total of all the inputs to a non-linear function to produce a result between zero and one. Because of this, the perceptron only becomes active when the net input is positive, *i.e, output*= $w \cdot x+b \geq 0$.

The numerical inputs $X1$ and $X2$ of the Figure 4 network are subjected to weights $w1$ and $w2$. Furthermore, weight b—also known as bias—is associated to input 1. The neuron's output Y is computed, as shown in Figure 4. Non-linearity characterizes the Activation Function, or *f*. This function adds non-linearity to a neuron's output, which is crucial because most real-world data is nonlinear.

Figure 4. A single neuron

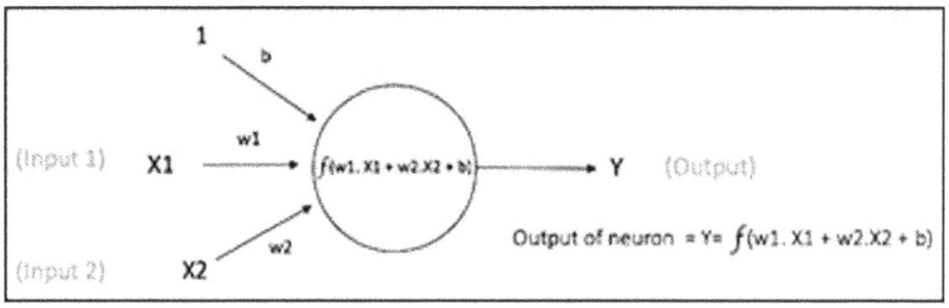

Typically, three non-linear functions are employed. *1. Sigmoid function, 2. Hyperbolic tangent, 3. Rectified Linear unit (ReLu).* One non-linear function that is frequently utilized in practice is ReLU.

Non-linear functions produce linear judgments on the data, but linear functions do not allow for the approximation of complex functions and superior forecasts.

Importance of Bias: Adding a trainable constant value to each node's regular inputs is the main goal of Bias.

What Are Neural Networks?

Neural networks find extensive use in a wide range of applications, such as AI and machine learning. Neural networks are used in self-driving cars and when you ask your mobile assistant (such as Google, Siri, or Amazon Web) to conduct a search for you (Aggarwal et al., 2018). Neural networks, modelled after the human brain's structure, consist of an input layer, hidden layers, and output layer. They apply weights and biases to data, ensuring it is sent to the next layer. They are used in computer games and mapping software to adjust to players and find the quickest path. The result, as shown in **Figure 5**, is the ultimate value that the artificial neuron anticipated.

The neurons of a neural network may perform a wide range of tasks, including:

- The weight of the channel that each input is multiplied by is discovered.
- The weighted sum, which is the sum of the weighted products, is calculated.
- The weighted total is increased by a neuron's bias value.
- Following that, the final total is put via a specific function called the activation function.

Figure 5. Data is fed as input to the neurons

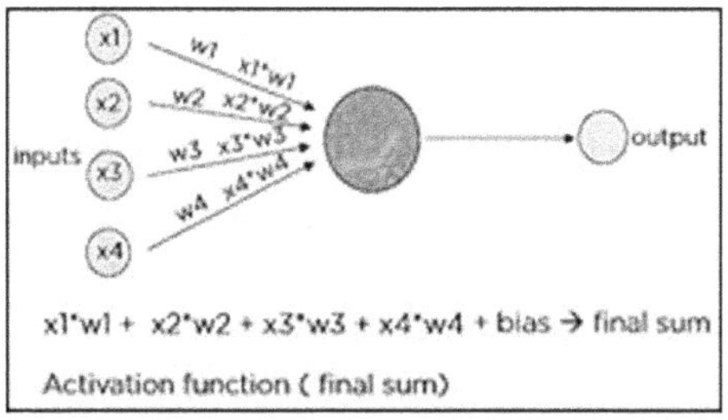

Bio-Inspired Learning

A computational model known as an artificial neural network (ANN) is inspired by the workings of biological neural networks.

Biological Motivation and Connections

The basic computational unit of the brain is a neuron. Approximately 86 billion neurons can be found in the human nervous system and they are connected with approximately $10^{14} — 10^{15}$ synapses. The Figure 6 below shows a cartoon drawing of a biological neuron (left) and a common mathematical model (right).

Figure 6. Cartoon drawing of a biological neuron (left) and a common mathematical model (right).

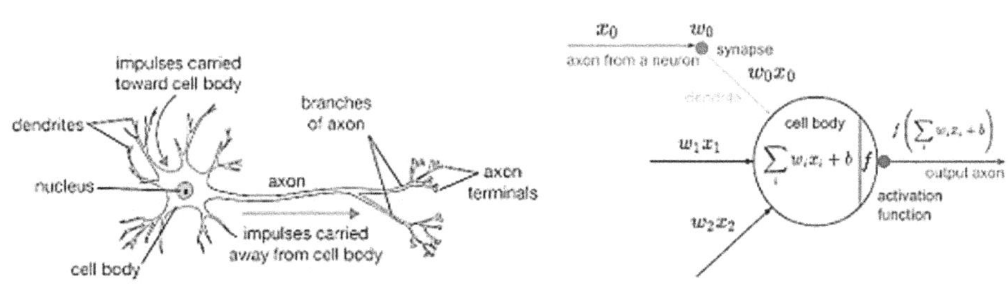

The Perceptron Model

Deep learning is a machine learning branch that uses artificial neural networks to extract complex features from data, mimicking the functioning of a human body's neural system, consisting of multiple layers with numerous units. These layers are often divided into three categories: *1. An input layer, 2. Hidden layer(s), and 3. Output layer.* Every input is given a weight (w) determined by its relative significance to the other inputs. A dense, multilayer neural network is produced by connecting each unit in one layer to the subsequent layers.

The junction between two neurons is called a synapse. The 7,000 synapses connecting neurons show the brain's tremendous degree of interconnectedness. When we uncover new conceptual connections, the synaptic strength between these neurons increases. This phenomenon is known as Hebb's rule (1949) that states "Cells that fire together wire together".

- **Neural networks**: Computers may learn from observational data by programming with a model influenced by biology.
- **Deep learning**, is an effective collection of methods for neural network learning.

The best technology for picture identification, voice recognition, and natural language processing are deep learning and neural networks. It is possible to create binary classifiers using just one neuron.

Limitations of the Perceptron Model

As seen in Figure 7, perceptrons are still unable to learn fundamental functions like the XOR function despite significant advancements.

Figure 7. The XOR problem cannot be solved by a perceptron

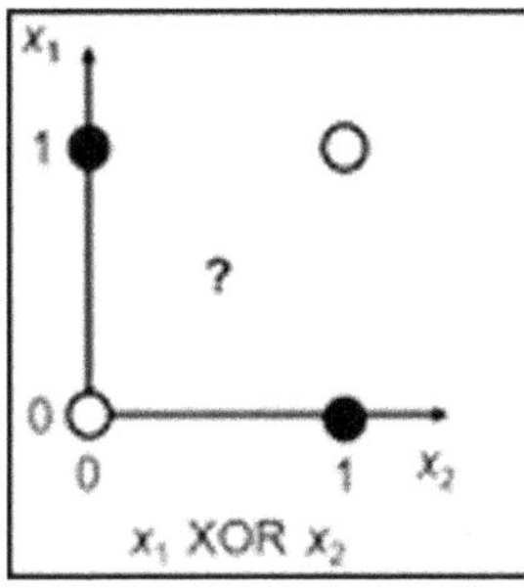

x_1	x_2	y
0	0	0
0	1	1
1	0	1
1	1	0

Since XOR is not linearly separable, perceptrons are unable to solve it. However, stacking many perceptrons can handle more challenging and non-linear problems (Bishop & Nasrabadi, 2006).

The Architecture of a Neural Network

An acyclic graph connects groups of neurons to form neural networks, with fully-connected layers being the most common type. These layers have pairwise linked connections across two adjacent layers, and two neural network topology samples use a stack of fully connected layers.

Figure 8. A 2-layer neural network (1 hidden layer of 4 neurons (or units) and 1 output layer with 2 neurons), and 3 inputs

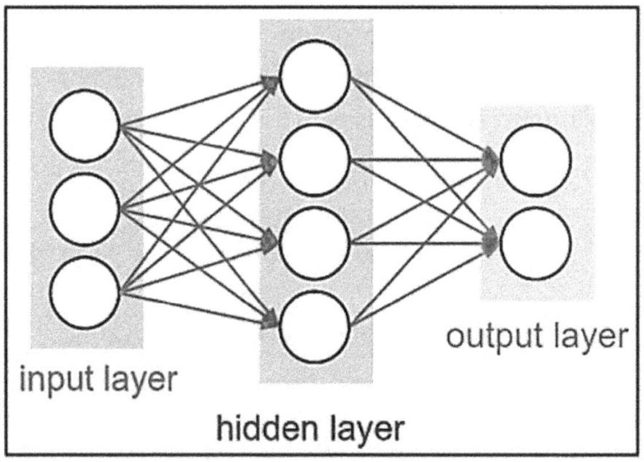

Figure 9. A 3-layer neural network with 3 inputs, 2 hidden layers of 4 neurons each and 1 output layer.

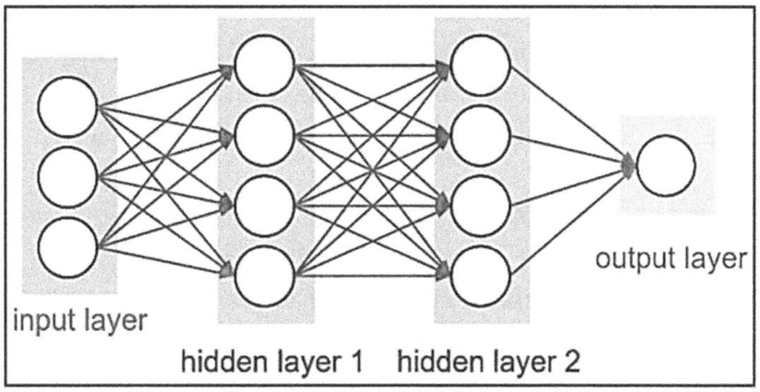

Synapses between neurons across layers exist, but not within a layer.

Input Nodes (input layer): This layer does not do any computations; it just transfers data to the next layer, which is often a buried layer. A set of nodes is often referred to as a layer.

Hidden nodes (hidden layer): Hidden layers move weights (signals or information) from the input layer to the next layer (another hidden layer or the output layer) while doing intermediary processing or calculations. Without a hidden layer, a neural network is possible.

Output Nodes (output layer): Here, we ultimately employ an activation function that corresponds to the desired output structure (for example, softmax for classification).

Connections and weights: The *network* consists of connections, each connection transferring the output of a neuron i to the input of a neuron *j*. In this sense *i* is the predecessor of *j* and *j* is the successor of *i*, Each connection is assigned a weight W_{ij}.

Activation function: The activation function of a node defines its output with regard to an input or set of inputs. An analogy of an average computer chip circuit would be a digital network of activation functions that are either "OFF" (0) or "ON" (1) based on the input. This is similar to the behaviour of the linear perceptron in neural networks. On the other hand, these networks may solve nontrivial problems with a small number of nodes because to their nonlinear activation function. In artificial neural networks, we call this characteristic the transfer function.

Learning rule: The learning rule is a rule or technique that modifies the neural network's parameters to produce the desired result for a given input. Typically, this learning procedure entails adjusting the thresholds and weights (Aggarwal, 2018).

Sizing Neural Networks

Two metrics—the number of neurons and, more frequently, the number of parameters—are frequently used to gauge the scale of neural networks. Using Figure 8 and Figure 9 of the image above as examples, two networks are being studied.

The first network (left) has 4 + 2 = 6 neurons (not counting the inputs), [3 x 4] + [4 x 2] = 20 weights and 4 + 2 = 6 biases, for a total of 26 learnable parameters.

The second network (right) has 4 + 4 + 1 = 9 neurons, [3 x 4] + [4 x 4] + [4 x 1] = 12 + 16 + 4 = 32 weights and 4 + 4 + 1 = 9 biases, for a total of 41 learnable parameters.

Advantages of Neural Network

An autonomous debugging or diagnostic neural network (ANN) can significantly increase fault tolerance and save time, energy, and resources by analyzing thousands of corporate log files. In the banking industry, ANN eliminates the need for nonlinear systems to find computationally costly solutions.

Applications of Neural Network

Understanding the applications of artificial intelligence, machine learning, and neural networks is crucial since these technologies are employed more often.

Handwriting Recognition

Neural networks are used to convert handwritten characters into digital characters that a machine can recognize.

Stock-Exchange Prediction

The stock market is complex due to numerous factors, making it challenging for stockbrokers to focus on a single company due to the daily generation of nearly three terabytes of data.

Traveling Issues of Sales Professionals

Neural networks might help salespeople find the most efficient routes while they are traveling from one place to another, but real-world issues need to be considered.

Image Compression

Neural network data compression allows us to minimize data size and memory utilization by storing, encrypting, and regenerating an image.

Literature Survey of Artificial Neural Networks in Computing

A literature study is a comprehensive analysis of previous studies and applications of artificial neural networks (ANNs) in various computer science and engineering fields. ANNs, which can learn from data and perform tasks like computer vision, natural language processing, regression, clustering, optimization, and pattern recognition, are based on the structure and operation of biological neural networks.

Artificial neural networks (ANNs) are versatile tools used in various fields such as sentiment analysis, recommender systems, cybersecurity, bioinformatics, robotics, image processing, speech recognition, and machine translation.

(Pancholi & Patel, 2021) provides a taxonomy of ANNs and discusses their major applications and importance in e-learning. (Abiodun et al., 2018) investigates the explosive developments of many ANN-related applications in various disciplines and presents a bibliometric analysis of the publications and citations. (Yasdi, 2000) reviews the use of ANNs for different aspects of human-computer interaction, such as input devices, output devices, user modelling, and adaptive interfaces. (Pritchard et al., 2023) surveys the last 22 years of literature on neuromorphic computing and spiking neural networks, which are biologically inspired models of computation that mimic the dynamics and efficiency of the brain. (Mishra et al., 2016) covers the last 35 years of literature on the use of ANNs for rainfall-runoff modelling, which is a crucial task for hydrological and water resources management.

How the Biological Model of Neural Networks Functions

The human brain, composed of 86 billion neurons, uses electrochemical signals to perform various functions, facilitated by their nuclei, dendrites, axons, and synapses for communication and impulse exchange.

How Artificial Neural Networks Function

ANNs are statistical models that self-program and adapt through learning algorithms, set up in parallel layers. The hidden layer, between input and output layers, receives synaptic weight-based inputs and uses a transfer function to deliver output to the output layer.

How Do You Train a Neural Network?

Unsupervised learning is a network's ability to understand inputs without human assistance, while supervised learning involves an operator grading inputs to generate desired outputs.

Why Do We Use Neural Networks?

Neural nets are perfect for big data applications because of their human-like traits and adaptability in task execution. When exact models are unavailable, they can also employ controlled processes to interpret contradictory, ambiguous, or absent data (Aggarwal, 2018).

Tasks Neural Networks Perform

Neural networks are beneficial as they can perform crucial tasks like data comprehension while maintaining their unique characteristics.

- Classification: NNs organize patterns or datasets into predefined classes.
- Prediction: They produce the expected output from given input.
- Clustering: They identify a unique feature of the data and classify it without any knowledge of prior data.
- Associating: Neuronal networks may be trained to always return to the version of a pattern that is closest to the unfamiliar version.

Neural networks form the foundation of deep learning, a technique used in bioinformatics, drug creation, social network filtering, and natural language translation. As neural networks become smarter and faster, they continue to advance.

Real-World and Industry Applications of Neural Networks

Neural networks, a subset of machine learning algorithms, have numerous real-world and industry applications (Nielsen, 2015). Here are some notable examples:

Image and Speech Recognition: From face recognition to speech-to-text systems, virtual assistants, and self-driving cars, neural networks have revolutionised image and speech recognition.

Natural Language Processing (NLP): Since they can comprehend and produce human language, neural networks are crucial for NLP applications including sentiment analysis, language translation, Chabot, and text summarization.

Recommendation Systems: Businesses employ neural networks to personalise suggestions based on user preferences and behaviour, enhancing consumer engagement and satisfaction.

Financial Forecasting and Trading: Neural networks are used by financial institutions for a variety of tasks such as algorithmic trading, fraud detection, credit scoring, stock market forecasting, and trend identification from vast volumes of data.

Healthcare and Medicine: For early diabetic identification, drug development, and individualised therapy recommendations, neural networks have demonstrated promise in the diagnosis of illnesses, patient outcomes prediction, and medical picture analysis (Ghosh, 2022a; Moawad et al., 2022; Ghosh, 2022b).

Autonomous Vehicles: Self-driving vehicles cannot perceive their environment or make judgements without neural networks.

Robotics: Robots can recognise items, grip them, and manipulate them with the use of neural networks, which also help them navigate through challenging environments.

Financial Services and Fraud Detection: Neural networks are utilized by financial institutions to detect fraudulent transactions, money laundering patterns, and credit risk anomalies, alerting authorities accordingly.

Energy and Utilities: Utilising neural networks may optimise the production of renewable energy sources, forecast power consumption, and enhance energy efficiency.

Manufacturing and Quality Control: Neural networks analyze sensor data, images, and sound patterns to identify defects in machinery and products, ensuring high-quality products.

Neural networks enhance efficiency and innovation across various industries, and as AI advances, it will be utilized for more tasks, boosting productivity and innovation.

Current Examples of NN Business Applications

Here are further current examples of NN business applications (Kizilkan et al., 2022):

Banking: Loan delinquencies, fraud and risk assessment, credit and loan application review, and credit card attrition are all crucial.

Business Analytics: Market research, market mix, market structure, customer behaviour modelling, customer segmentation, fraud propensity, and models for attrition, default, buy, and renewals are crucial.

Defence: Face recognition, target tracking, feature extraction, noise reduction, object classification, sensors, sonar, and radar are some of the technologies used in counterterrorism.

Education: Adaptive learning software, dynamic forecasting, education system analysis and forecasting, student performance modelling (Ghosh, 2023), and personality profiling

Financial: The job involves corporate bond ratings, financial analysis, credit line usage forecasting, loan counselling, mortgage screening, appraisal, and portfolio trading.

Medical: Cancer cell analysis, ECG and EEG analysis, test recommendations for ERs, cost-saving measures, transplant procedure optimisation, and prosthetic design (Ghosh, 2022; Moawad et al., 2022).
Securities: Automatic bond rating, market analysis, and stock trading advisory systems
Transportation: Routing systems, truck brake diagnosis systems, and vehicle scheduling

What Are the Types of Neural Networks?

Neural networks are training algorithms used to recognize patterns and analyze data, with various available options to achieve different learning goals (Bishop & Nasrabadi, 2006).

Different Algorithms

Table 1 Describes different algorithms.

Table 1. Describes different algorithms

Autoencoder (AE)	Deep Belief Network (DBN)	Extreme Learning Machine (ELM)	Kohonen Network (KN)	Radial Basis Function Networks (RBF nets)
Bidirectional Recurrent Neural Network (BRNN)	Deep Convolutional Inverse Graphics Network (DCIGN)	Feed Forward Neural Network (FF or FFNN) and Perceptron (P)	Liquid State Machine (LSM)	Recurrent Neural Network (RNN)
Boltzmann Machine (BM)	Deep Residual Network (DRN)	Gated Recurrent Unit (GRU)	Long/Short-Term Memory (LSTM)	Restricted Boltzmann Machine (RBM)
Convolutional Neural Network (CNN)	Denoising Autoencoder (DAE)	Generative Adversarial Network (GAN)	Markov Chain (MC)	Support Vector Machine (SVM)
Deconvolutional Neural Network (DNN)	Echo State Network (ESN)	Hopfield Network (HN)	Neural Turing Machine (NTM)	Variational Autoencoder (VAE)

What Are Neural Networks in Data Mining?

Neural networks are non-linear statistical techniques used by data warehousing companies to detect patterns in data and describe complex interactions between inputs and outputs, enabling them to extract information from databases through data mining as in Figure 10.

Figure 10. Neural networks in data mining

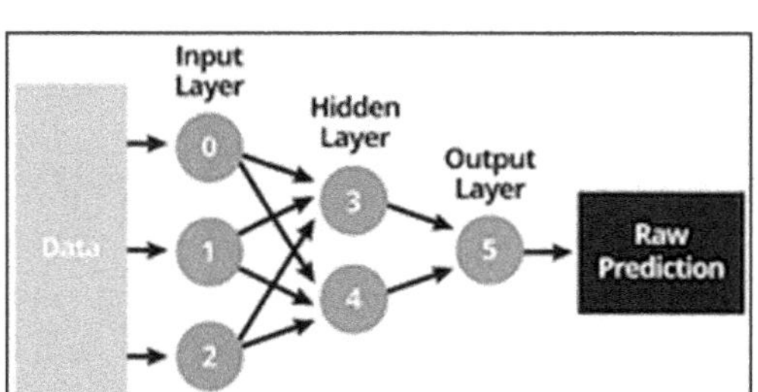

Data warehouses enable data manipulation and cross-pollination, enabling informed decision-making, while neural networks are not suitable for data harvesting due to their complex models and long training times.

Neural vs. Conventional Computers

Neural networks outperform traditional computers in tasks like consecutive data processing, highlighting fundamental differences between the two types of computers.

- ***Following Instructions vs. Learning Capability:*** Neural networks are more advanced than conventional computers, learning through steps or sequences, but their architecture limits their potential for advancement.
- ***Rules vs. Concepts and Imagery:*** ANNs employ abstract concepts, visuals, and images to perform tasks and learn from them, unlike traditional computers that follow rules.

The Challenges of Neural Networks

Understanding the limitations and drawbacks of neural networks is crucial for effective task management.

For example, we attempt to determine if someone is appropriately utilizing an or an in the Perfect Tense. In this instance, it would be overkill to employ a neural network because the decision can be made by looking at the phonetic pronunciation alone (e.g., an banana is incorrect). Advancements in neural networks have significantly improved content quality, surpassing unimaginable levels a year or two ago.

Challenges in the Field Of

Training: Critics argue neural networks over-train in real-world applications. Researchers are rearranging training examples, using numerical optimization techniques, and using mini-batches of sample material to improve training efficacy and convergence capabilities.

Theoretical Issues: Facebook employs human reviewers due to algorithms' inability to identify hate speech and misleading content, while true creativity is impossible for computers, and neural networks and AI cannot resolve this issue.

Inauthenticity: Artificial neural networks, inspired by biological neural networks, differ from human brains in their learning process, allowing for statistical association, which has inherent limitations.

Hardware Issues: The interest in neural networks has surged due to the rise in processing power since 1991, facilitated by GPUs, which reduced training times and enabled deeper learning. As deep neural networks become more advanced, hardware advancements are required to meet computational demands.

Computer scientists and engineers are working on developing smarter, quicker, and more human-like algorithms through improved hardware and cross-pollinating various software and hardware.

The Future of Neural Networks

With numerous significant development areas in the works, neural networks are primed for immense potential:

Deep Learning Advances: Deep learning, a neural network branch, has made significant progress in various fields, and future advancements in architectures, optimization methods, and model interpretability could enhance performance and comprehension.

Reinforcement Learning: RL, a combination of neural networks and trial-and-error, is gaining popularity in robotics, autonomous systems, and gaming, with future algorithm developments potentially leading to more intelligent and flexible AI agents.

Explainable AI: Researchers are enhancing AI systems' confidence, ensuring ethical usage, and facilitating regulatory compliance by understanding and explaining neural network decision-making processes.

Neural Architecture Search: Neural architecture search (NAS) is a process that automates architecture design, aiming to create more effective, specialized, and domain-specific neural networks.

Transfer Learning and Few-Shot Learning: Future research aims to enhance transfer learning capabilities, enabling neural networks to adapt quickly to new tasks and use less labelled data, and to increase their effectiveness through few-shot learning.

Neuromorphic Computing: Neuromorphic computing aims to create hardware resembling biological brain networks, enabling faster, more energy-efficient calculations and introducing new applications and deployment possibilities.

Ethical and Fair AI: Researchers and politicians are ensuring ethical use of AI technologies in crucial fields, addressing issues like prejudice, justice, privacy, and responsibility.

Interdisciplinary Collaborations: Academic and industry collaborations can generate innovative ideas and techniques to enhance the functionality, interpretability, and usability of neural networks.

Neural networks hold significant potential for enhancing AI and ML performance, interpretability, and ethical issues in the future.

Working of Neural Network

A neural network consists of three layers: input, hidden, and output. The hidden layer performs computations, input gathers signals, and output delivers the final product.

Traffic cameras employ 28 by 28-pixel images to recognise licence plates and out-of-control automobiles. Each neuron has an activation number, which ranges from 0 to 1, that reflects the pixel's grayscale value. When a neuron's activity comes near to 1, it lights up.

Figure 11. Real-life example of how traffic cameras identify license plates and speeding vehicles on the road

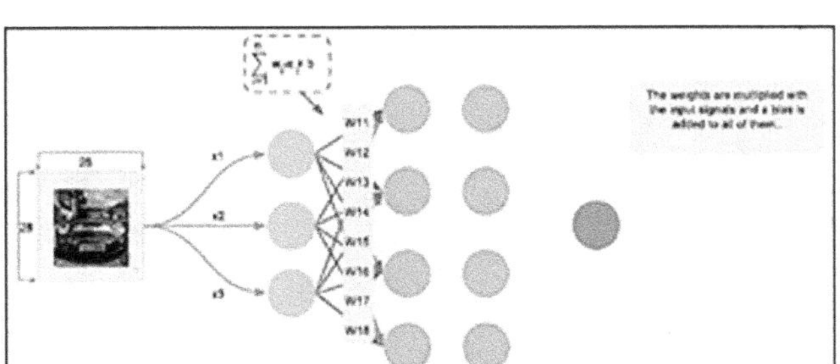

Arrays of pixels are delivered into the input layer. Since you cannot alter the size of the input layer, if your picture is more than 28 by 28 pixels, you must reduce its size. We'll refer to the inputs in our case as X1, X2, and X3 in Figure 11. The input layer receives weights from the concealed layer, which are then multiplied by the weights and applied with a bias.

The activation function in each layer uses a weighted total of inputs to determine which nodes to fire for feature extraction.

The next section will delves into the study of neural network activation functions, which are diverse types of functions.

What Is an Activation Function and Why Use Them?

The activation function is used to provide nonlinearity to a neuron's output (Nielsen, 2015). In a neural network, the weights and biases of the neurons are adjusted based on the output error. *Back-propagation* is made feasible by activation functions since they supply gradients together with the error to update the weights and biases. The activation function converts the output values into the appropriate range, such as between 0 and 1 or -1 and 1. For instance, the logistic activation function would convert all inputs in the real number domain into a range between 0 and 1.

Example of a Binary Classification Problem

A binary classification issue determines if an input, like a picture, contains the correct object, with a 1 indicating correctness and a 0 indicating incorrectness.

When we multiply each of the features with a weight ($w1$,$w2$,...,wm) and sum them all together,

Node output= activation(weighted sum of inputs).

$$W.X = w1.x1 + w2.x2 + w3.x3 + \ldots\ldots\ldots\ldots + wn.xn = \sum_{i=1}^{m} w1.x1$$

Why Do We Need Non-Linear Activation Function?

An activation function is crucial in neural networks for learning and challenging tasks, as without it, a linear regression model will still produce a linear function, even with hidden layers (Heaton, 2018).

Different Types of Activation Functions

The Activation Functions are basically two types:

Linear Activation Function

Equation: $f(x)=x$

Range: (-infinity to infinity)

Non-Linear Activation Functions

Non-linear Activation Functions (ReLUs) are faster for larger networks, as they can distinguish between outcomes when an output is non-linear, making it impossible to recreate with linear inputs.

The Nonlinear Activation Functions are mainly divided on the basis of their range or curves.

For example: Regression analysis is used to determine a home's price, with linear activation at the output layer and non-linear function at hidden levels.

Sigmoid Function

- It is a function which is plotted as **'S'** shaped graph.
- **Equation:** $A = 1/(1 + e^{-x})$
- **Nature:** Non-linear. Observe that while Y values are quite steep, X values range from -2 to 2. This implies that tiny changes in x would likewise result in significant changes in the value of Y.
- **Value Range:** 0 to 1
- **Uses:** Sigmoid functions are frequently employed in binary classification output layers because their values only fall between 0 and 1, making it simple to anticipate that the outcome will be 1 if the value is larger than 0.5 and 0 otherwise.

Tanh or Hyperbolic Tangent Function

- The activation that works almost always better than sigmoid function is Tan*h* function also known as Tangent Hyperbolic function. It's essentially a sigmoid function that has been mathematically shifted. Both are comparable to and derivable from one another.
- **Equation:**

$$f\left(x\right) = \tanh x = \frac{2}{1 + e^{-2x}} - 1$$

- **Value Range:** -1 to +1
- **Nature:** non-linear
- **Uses:** As its values typically range from -1 to 1, the mean for the hidden layer of a neural network will be 0 or very near to it. This helps to centre the data by bringing the mean close to 0. This greatly simplifies learning for the subsequent layer.

RELU Function

- It Stands for *Rectified linear unit*. It is the most widely used activation function. Chiefly implemented in *hidden layers* of neural network.
- **Equation:** $A(x)=\max(0,x)$. It gives an output x if x is positive and 0 otherwise.
- **Value Range:** [0, inf)
- **Nature:** Since the ReLU function is non-linear, it is simple to back propagate mistakes and activate several layers of neurons.

- **Uses:** ReLu requires fewer mathematical processes than tan*h* and sigmoid, making it less computationally costly. The network is sparse and effective for computing due to its limited number of neurons active simultaneously.

In simple words, RELU learns *much faster* than *sigmoid* and tan*h* function.

Softmax Function

The softmax function, a subtype of the sigmoid function, is a valuable tool for addressing multi-class classification issues.

- **Nature:** non-linear
- **Uses:** The softmax algorithm is commonly used in image classification to manage multiple classes by dividing total outputs and dividing each class's outputs into 0-1 ranges.
- **Output:** The softmax function is optimally utilized in the output layer of a classifier to determine the probabilities of defining each input's class.

The Rule of Thumb

- The basic rule of thumb is if you really don't know what activation function to use, then simply use RELU as it is a general activation function in *hidden layers* and is used in most cases these days.
- If your output is for *binary* classification then, *sigmoid* function is very natural choice for output layer.
- If your output is for *multi-class* classification then, *Softmax* is very useful to predict the probabilities of each class.

Types of Neural Networks

The different types of neural networks are discussed below:

I. Feed-Forward Neural Network

An ANN, or artificial neural network, is a rapid and efficient tool for voice and visual recognition applications, requiring some training time.

II. Radial Basis Functions Neural Network

This model categorizes data points based on their distance from a central point for power restoration systems, searching for related data points and organizing them.

III. Kohonen Self-Organizing Neural Network

Vectors, also known as dimensions or planes, are inputs to a discrete map composed of neurons, used in medical analysis to recognize patterns in data.

IV. Recurrent Neural Network

The hidden layer saves its output for future prediction, transforming it into its new input, a feature commonly used in text-to-speech conversion.

V. Convolution Neural Network

Batch-based input features, like filtering, enable networks to remember images in parts, a feature used in signal and image processing, like facial recognition.

VI. Modular Neural Network

The cutting-edge research involves a collection of various neural networks working together to produce an output.

Implementation of Perceptron Algorithm for OR Gate With 2-Bit Binary Input

OR logical function truth table for 2-bit binary variables are as in Table 2:

Table 2. OR-truth table for 2-bit binary variables

X1	X2	y
0	0	0
0	1	1
1	0	1
1	1	1

Now for the corresponding weight vector *w*: (*w*1,*w*2) of the input vector *x*: (*x*1,*x*2), the associated Perceptron Function can be defined as: $\hat{y} = \theta\left(w1x1 + w2x2 + b\right)$

For the implementation, considered weight parameters are *w*1=1, *w*2=1 and the bias parameter is *b*= -0.5

Python Implementation

```
# importing Python library
import numpy as np

# define Unit Step Function
def unitStep(v):
    if v >= 0:
        return 1
    else:
        return 0

# design Perceptron Model
def perceptronModel(x, w, b):
    v = np.dot(w, x) + b
    y = unitStep(v)
    return y

# OR Logic Function
# w1 = 1, w2 = 1, b = -0.5
def OR_logicFunction(x):
    w = np.array([1, 1])
    b = -0.5
    return perceptronModel(x, w, b)

# testing the Perceptron Model
test1 = np.array([0, 1])
test2 = np.array([1, 1])
test3 = np.array([0, 0])
test4 = np.array([1, 0])

print("OR({}, {}) = {}".format(0, 1, OR_logicFunction(test1)))
print("OR({}, {}) = {}".format(1, 1, OR_logicFunction(test2)))
print("OR({}, {}) = {}".format(0, 0, OR_logicFunction(test3)))
print("OR({}, {}) = {}".format(1, 0, OR_logicFunction(test4)))
```

Output:

OR(0, 1) = 1

OR(1, 1) = 1

OR(0, 0) = 0

OR(1, 0) = 1

According to the truth table for 2-bit binary input, the model's projected output (y hat) for each test input matches the OR logic gate's conventional output (y), demonstrating the effectiveness of the perceptron technique for OR logic gates.

Multi-Layer Perceptrons: Notations and Trainable Parameters

Multi-layer perception is a solution to the issue of single-layer perceptrons not capturing non-linearity in non-linear input. It consists of input and output layers, hidden layers, and arbitrary activation functions, with more hidden layers enhancing the dataset's non-linear behaviour (Heaton, 2018).

MLP Notations

The back-propagation technique is a crucial element in neural networks, as it iteratively updates weights and biases to achieve optimal accuracy.

Back-propagation is a crucial process for training a neural network, which involves updating weights and biases.

Figure 12. Multi-layer neural network

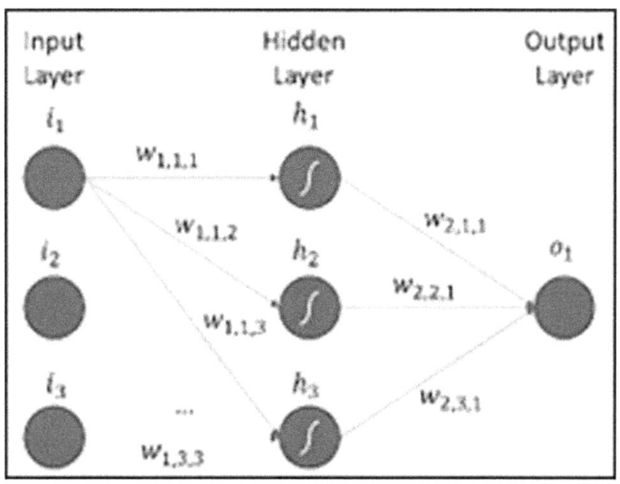

The above Figure 12 shows the multi-layer neural network having an input layer, a hidden layer, and an output layer.

Notation for Weights

Notation: W_{ij}^{h}

Where,

i= From which node weight is passing to the next layer's node.
j= To which node weight is arriving.
h= Layer in which weight is arriving.

Example:

W_{11}^{1} = Weight passing into 1st node of 1st layer of 1st node of the previous layer.
W_{23}^{1} = Weight passing into the 3rd node of the 1st hidden layer from the 2nd node of the previous layer.
W_{45}^{1} = Weight passing into the 5th node of the 2nd hidden layer from the 4th node of the previous layer.

Notations for Biases

Notation: b_{ij}
Where,

i= Layer to which a bias belongs
j= Node to which a bias belongs

Example:

b_{11}= biases of 1st node of 1st hidden layer.
b_{23}= bias of 3rd node of 2nd hidden layer.
b_{41}= bias of 1st node of 4th hidden layer.

Notations for Outputs

Notation: O_{ij}
Where,

i= Layer to which a bias belongs
j= Node to which a bias belongs

Example:

O_{11}= Output of 1st node of 1st hidden layer.
O_{45}= Output of 5th node of 4th hidden layer.
O_{34}= Output of 4th node of 3rd hidden layer.

Calculating Total Trainable Parameters

The Total Trainable Parameters for a given between two layers of an artificial neural network is the sum of total weights and total biases.

Total Trainable Parameters Between two layers in a Neural Network= [*Number of Nodes in the first layer * Number of nodes in the second layer*](*Weights*) + [*Number of nodes in the second layer*] (*Biases*)

1. Trainable Parameters between the Input layer and First Hidden Layer:

weights= 3*4=12

biases= 4(4 nodes in 1st hidden layer)

Trainable Parameters= weights + biases

=12+7

=16

2. Trainable Parameters between First Hidden layer and Second Hidden Layer:

weights= 4*2=8

biases= 2(2 nodes in 1st hidden layer)

Trainable Parameters= weights + biases

=8+2

=10

3. Trainable Parameters between Second Hidden layer and Output Layer:

weights= 2*2=4

biases= 2(2nodes in 1st hidden layer)

Trainable Parameters= weights + biases

=4+2

=6

Training our MLP: The Back-Propagation Algorithm

Let's take an example to understand Multi-Layer Perceptrons better. Suppose we have the following student-marks dataset as in Table 3:

Table 3. Student-marks dataset

Hours Studied	Midterm Marks	Final Term Result
35	67	1 (Pass)
12	75	0 (Fail)
16	89	1 (Pass)
45	56	1 (Pass)
10	90	0 (Fail)

The student's study hours and midterm grade are displayed in two input columns, with the last Result column indicating if the student passed the last term. For example, a student would pass the final term if they completed 35 hours of study and received 67 on the midterm.

If a student with a midterm score of 70 marks and 25 hours of study is predicted to pass the final term. As in Table 4.

Table 4. Student will pass the final term or not

Hours Studied	Midterm Marks	Final Term Result
25	70	?

A multi-layer perceptron can make informed predictions by learning from training data, known as the Back propagation algorithm. This supervised training scheme involves learning from labelled training data, with a supervisor guiding its learning. Back propagation is similar to "learning from mistakes," with the supervisor correcting the ANN when it makes mistakes. The output vector from an input vector is calculated by assigning appropriate weights to connections between nodes in adjacent layers. In supervised learning, the training set is labelled, indicating that the desired outcome is known for certain inputs.

Backward Propagation Algorithm

Initially, edge weights are randomly allocated, and the ANN is triggered and scrutinized for each input in the training dataset. Mistakes are propagated back to the top layer, and weights are adjusted when inaccuracies are discovered. The output error is repeated until it falls below a predefined threshold (Heaton, 2018; Nielsen, 2015).

After the algorithm's completion, a "learned" ANN is considered ready to handle new inputs, having learned from both its faults (error propagation) and multiple instances (labelled data), as per the claim.

Let's come back to our student-marks dataset shown above.

The MLP in Figure 13 has two input layers: one for hours studied and one for midterm marks, and another layer for success and failure. In the output layer, there are two nodes for success and failure. The Softmax function is used as the Activation Function in the Output layer to ensure the outputs are probabilities that sum up to 1. So, in this case,

Probability(Pass) + Probability(Fail) = 1

Step 1: Forward Propagation

The network's weights are all allocated at random. Think about the hidden layer node designated V in Figure 5 below. Assume that the connections from the inputs to that node have the weights w1, w2, and w3 (see Figure 13).

The network then takes the first training example as input (we know that for inputs 35 and 67, the probability of Pass is 1).

Figure 13. Forward propagation step in a MLP

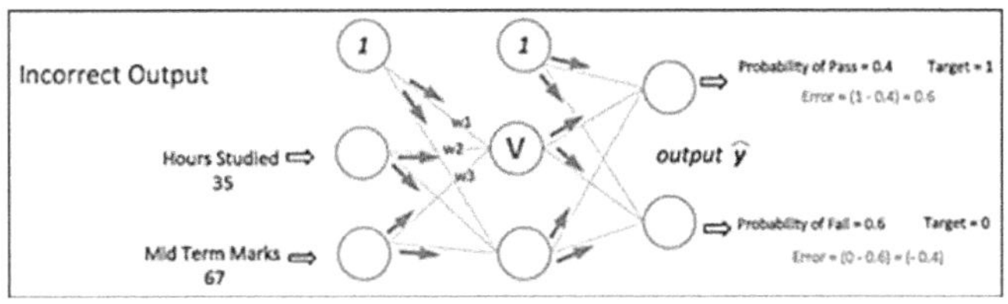

Input to the network =[35,67]
Desired output from the network (target)= [1,0]

Then output V from the node in consideration can be calculated as below (f is an activation function such as sigmoid):

$V= f(1*w1 + 35*w2 + 67*w3)$

The two nodes in the output layer get information from the two nodes in the hidden layer, enabling them to determine output probabilities. The network in Figure 13 is considered to have an "*Incorrect Output*" since the computed probabilities (0.4 and 0.6) are significantly different from the required probability (1 and 0, respectively).

Step 2: Back Propagation and Weight Updating

The process involves calculating the total error at output nodes and propagating these errors back through the network using Back propagation to calculate gradients. An optimization method like Gradient Descent is used to adjust all weights in the network to reduce the error at the output layer, as shown in Figure 14.

Figure 14. Step for updating weights and propagating backwards in a MLP

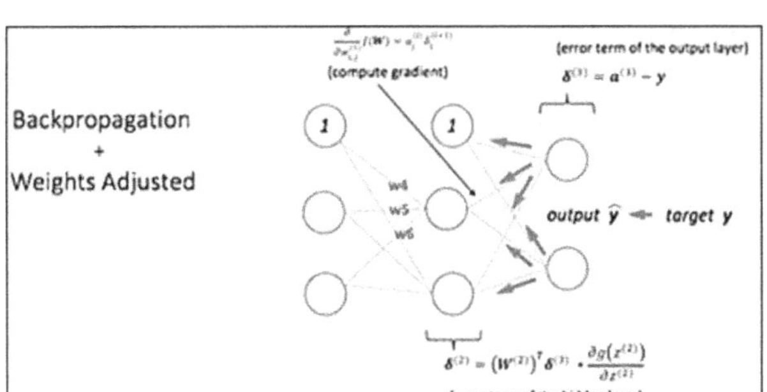

The network should perform better if we feed it the same example again because the weights have been modified to reduce prediction error. As shown in Figure 15, the errors at the output nodes now reduce to [0.2,-0.2] as compared to [0.6,-0.4] earlier. This demonstrates that our network has learned to correctly categorise the first training case.

Figure 15. The MLP network now performs better on the same input

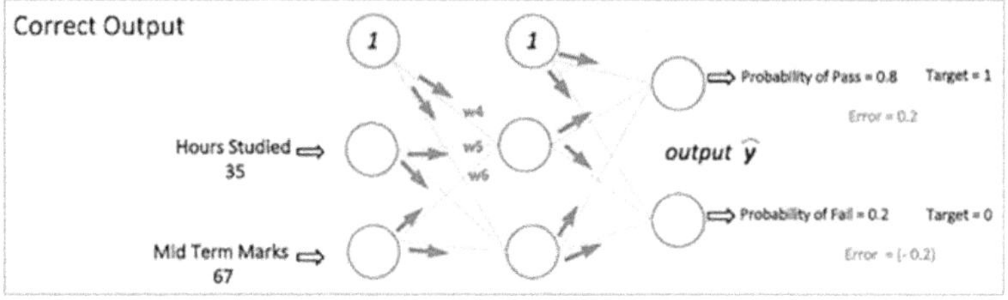

Our network is claimed to have learned these examples after using all additional training instances in our dataset.

Prediction: We utilise forward propagation to determine if a student who studies 25 hours and received 70 on the midterm will pass the final term. Calculated are the Pass and Fail output probabilities.

Problem With Back Propagation

Back propagation efficiently trains neural networks, but when layers are used, performance degrades due to disappearing or exploding gradients caused by repetitive computation using the chain rule.

Vanishing Gradients

When a gradient is multiplied by less than one, it disappears, becoming infinitesimally tiny, preventing us from achieving the ideal state and causing the step size to approach zero.

Exploding Gradients

The network may become unstable if the gradient is multiplied by a number greater than one, leading to the occurrence of NaN values.

Deep Learning Platforms

Now we will learn about several deep learning platforms and when they are used.

- **Torch:** Torch was developed using LUA and C, and its Python implementation is PyTorch.
- **Keras:** Keras is a Python framework for deep learning with reusability of code for CPU and GPU.
- **TensorFlow:** TensorFlow is an open-source deep-learning library developed by Google, which can be run on top of Keras.
- **DL4J:** Deep Learning for Java (DL4J), is the first deep learning library written for Java and Scala, integrated with Hadoop and Spark.

The most widely used learning library worldwide right now is Google's TensorFlow. Tensors, which are n-dimensional vectors or matrices, serve as its foundation (Heaton, 2018; Bishop & Nasrabadi, 2006; Nielsen, 2015)

Deep Learning Applications Used Across Industries

Use of DL in Industries are shown in Table 5.

Table 5. Use of DL in industries

Virtual Assistants	Chatbots	Healthcare	Entertainment	News Aggregation and Fake News Detection
Composing Music	Image Coloring	Robotics	Image Captioning	Advertising
Self-Driving Cars	Natural Language Processing	Visual Recognition	Fraud Detection	Personalization's
Detecting Developmental Delay in Children	Colourisation of Black and White images	Adding Sounds to Silent Movies	Automatic Machine Translation	Automatic Handwriting Generation
Automatic Game Playing	Language Translations	Pixel Restoration	Demographic and Election Predictions	Green Smart Home Automation (Ghosh, P., & Ghosh, S. 2020)

What Is Neural Computing?

Artificial neural networks (ANNs) are machine learning models that mimic the operation of biological neural networks in the brain. They learn patterns and make predictions based on input data, using large datasets to train them. Neural computing has become a significant area of artificial intelligence study, with applications in industries like engineering, finance, and healthcare. The development of machine learning and deep learning techniques has led to advancements in deep learning and machine learning methodologies.

Types of Neural Computing

Neural computing is a diverse field with various types, each with its unique architecture and applications. Some of the most common types include (Aggarwal, 2018):

I. **Feed forward neural networks:** A neural network consists of an input, output, and hidden layers, which process data by identifying patterns and producing matching output.
II. **Recurrent neural networks:** Networks are designed to handle sequential data by utilizing loops that transmit information from one time step to the next and recognize temporal patterns in input data.
III. **Convolutional neural networks:** Convolutional networks are utilized in image and video processing to identify patterns in spatial data by learning features at different abstraction levels.
IV. **Auto encoders:** Unsupervised learning networks use encoders and decoders to recreate input data from lower-dimensional representations, employing auto encoders for dimensionality reduction and feature extraction.
V. **Deep belief networks:** Boltzmann machines are unsupervised learning algorithms used for speech and picture recognition, capable of recognizing intricate patterns in input data.

There are several types and structures utilised in the difficult subject of neural computing.

How Neural Computing Works

ANNs are neural computing tools that mimic the behaviour of organic neural networks in the brain, consisting of interconnected nodes that learn to recognize patterns.

Here's a general overview of how neural computing works:

a) Data is sent into a neural network typically as a matrix or vector.
b) Each artificial neuron in the network processes the input data mathematically as it passes the data through.
c) The output of each neuron is transmitted to the subsequent layer of neurons, continuing the cycle until the output layer is reached.
d) During training, the weights and biases of neurons are adjusted to minimize the error between expected and actual output data.
e) Regularisation, dropout, and hyper parameter tuning can optimize neural networks for better data categorization and prediction based on learned patterns.

Neural computing is a powerful machine learning tool used in audio and image identification, natural language processing, and predictive modelling, influenced by network design, training optimization techniques, and data quality.

Difference Between Neural Network and Neural Computing

Neural networks and neural computing are distinct concepts. Neural networks are machine learning models with linked nodes that learn patterns and predict outcomes. Neural computing uses ANNs to mimic biological neural networks in the brain. Neural computing includes models and algorithms inspired by the human brain's structure and operation, including neural networks, genetic algorithms, fuzzy logic, and swarm intelligence.

Introduction to Convolutional Neural Networks (ConvNets or CNNs)

Yann Le Cun invented CNNs in 1988, initially used for character recognition but now used in healthcare for facial identification, object detection, and illness diagnosis, based on CNNs for these tasks (Kizilkan et al., 2022; Kandi et al., 2017). *Here's an example of convolutional neural networks that illustrates how they work:* Convolutional Neural Network to identify the image of a bird.

To categorize a bird picture, a neural network uses an input layer with pixel arrays. Hidden layers, including convolution, ReLU, and pooling layers, extract features from the image. The item is identified by a completely linked layer, ensuring the image is indeed a bird or another item. This process involves various computations and manipulations.

What Is Convolutional Neural Network?

A CNN is a feed-forward neural network that uses grid-like architecture to analyze visual pictures, identifying and categorizing items in images as shown in Figure 16.

Figure 16. Every image is a matrix of pixel values.

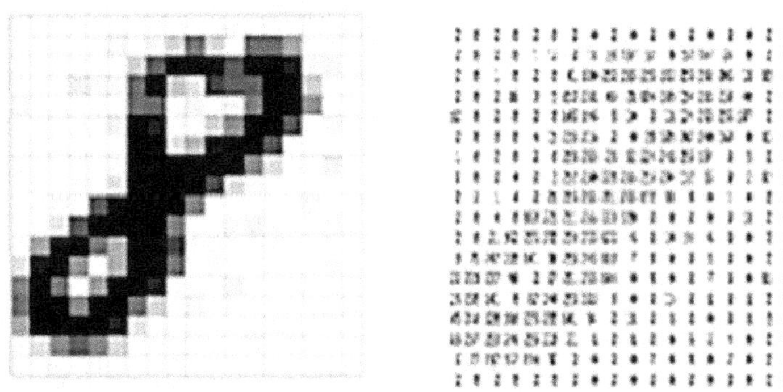

The *convolution operation* forms the basis of any convolutional neural network. As we discussed above, every image can be considered as a matrix of pixel values. Consider a 5×5 image whose pixel values are only 0 and 1 (note that for a grayscale image, pixel values range from 0 to 255, the *green* matrix below is a special case where pixel values are only 0 and 1). Also, consider another 3×3 *orange* matrix as shown in **Figure 17**:

Figure 17. 5×5 and 3×3 image matrix of pixel values with only 0 and 1

1	1	1	0	0
0	1	1	1	0
0	0	1	1	1
0	0	1	1	0
0	1	1	0	0

1	0	1
0	1	0
1	0	1

Then, the Convolution of the 5×5 image and the 3×3 matrix can be computed as shown in the animation in Figure 18 below:

Figure 18. The convolution operation. The output matrix is called convolved feature or feature map

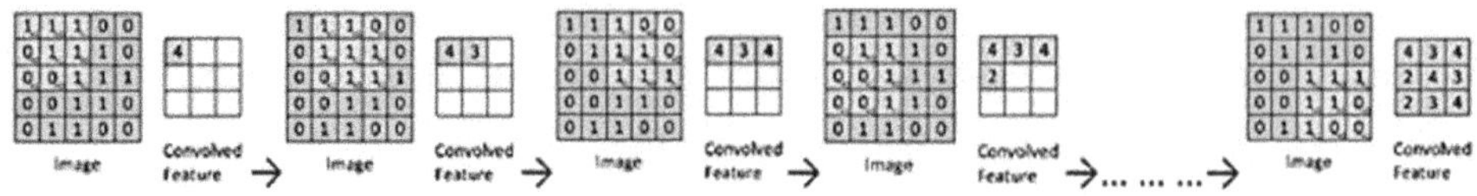

Now how the computation above (in Figure 18) is being done? We slide the *orange* matrix over our original image (*green*) by 1 pixel (also called '*stride*') and for every position, we compute element wise multiplication (between the two matrices) and add the multiplication outputs to get the final integer which forms a single element of the output matrix (*pink*). Note that the 3×3 matrix "sees" only a part of the input image in each *stride*.

In CNN terminology, the 3×3 matrix is called a '*filter*' or '*kernel*' or 'feature detector' and the matrix formed by sliding the filter over the image and computing the dot product is called the 'Convolved Feature' or 'Activation Map' or the '*Feature Map*'. It is important to note that filters act as feature detectors from the original input image.

It is evident from the above that different values of the *filter matrix* will produce different *Feature Maps* for the same input image.

In practice, a CNN learns the values of these *filters* on its own during the training process (although we still need to specify parameters such as *number of filters, filter size, architecture of the network* etc. before the training process). The greater number of filters we have, the more image features get extracted and the better our network becomes at recognizing patterns in unseen images (Kizilkan et al., 2022; Kandi et al., 2017).

What Is Meant by Feature Maps in Convolutional Neural Networks?

The number of feature maps corresponds to the number of filters applied to the input, which pass only the required properties, functioning similarly to membranes.

Here in Figure 19 the 3×3 matrix is called a '*filter*' or '*convolution kernel*' or 'feature detector' and the matrix formed by sliding the filter over the image and computing the dot product is called the 'Convolved Feature' or 'Activation Map' or the '*Feature Map*'.

Figure 19. 'Filter' or 'convolution kernel' and 'convolved feature' or 'activation map' or the 'feature map'

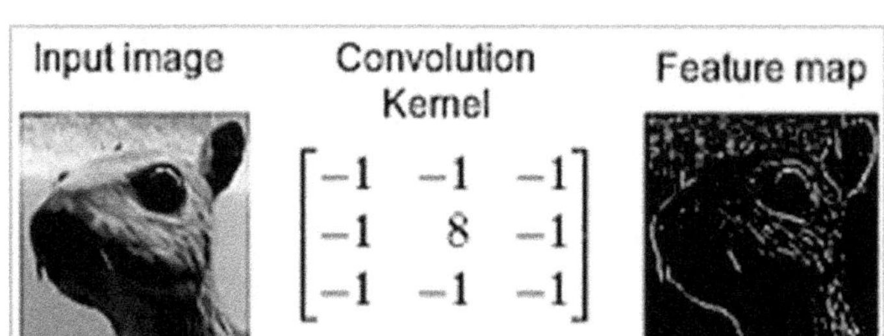

How Does CNN Recognize Images?

Consider the following images in Figure 20:

Figure 20. The boxes that are coloured represent a pixel value of 1, and 0 if not coloured

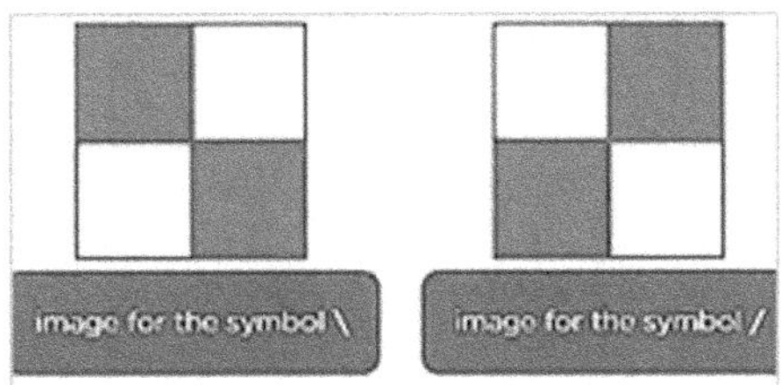

The boxes that are coloured represent a pixel value of 1, and 0 if not coloured. When you press backslash (\), the left image of Figure 20 gets processed. When you press forward-slash (/), the right image of Figure 20 is processed.

Layers in a Convolutional Neural Network

A CNN consists of four key layers, each with its own function in extracting information from an image.

i. Convolution layer
ii. ReLU layer
iii. Pooling layer
iv. Fully connected layer

i. Convolution Layer

The convolution layer is the initial step in extracting valuable features from an image, consisting of multiple filters that perform the convolution operation.

ii. ReLU layer

ReLU, or rectified linear unit, is a technique used to extract feature maps from a network, introducing non-linearity and generating a rectified feature map.

iii. Pooling Layer

Pooling is a process that reduces the dimensionality of a feature map, which is then rectified and processed through a pooling layer to create a pooled feature map.

Figure 21. Max pooling

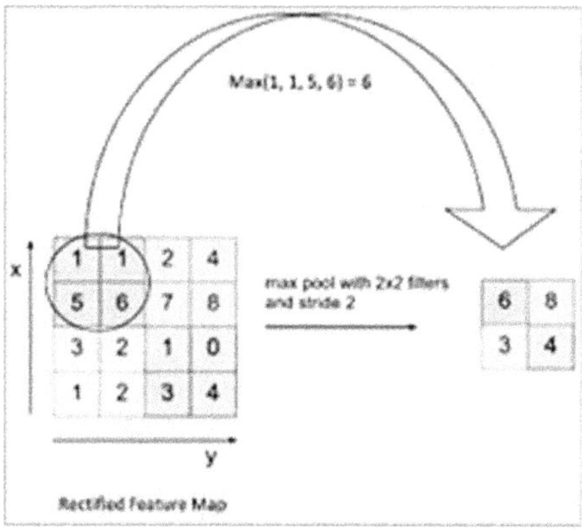

The pooling layer uses various filters to identify different parts of the image like ***edges, corners, body, feathers,*** *eyes,* and *beak.* Figure 21 shows an example of Max Pooling operation on a Rectified Feature map (obtained after convolution + ReLU operation) by using a 2×2 window. We slide our 2 x 2 window by 2 cells (also called 'stride') and take the maximum value in each region. As shown in Figure 21, this reduces the dimensionality of our feature map.

Figure 22 shows a convolutional neural network recognizing eyes, noses, faces, and legs. The first layer filters identify fundamental forms, while the second layer filters identify meaningless items.

Figure 22. How a convolutional neural network able to learn features

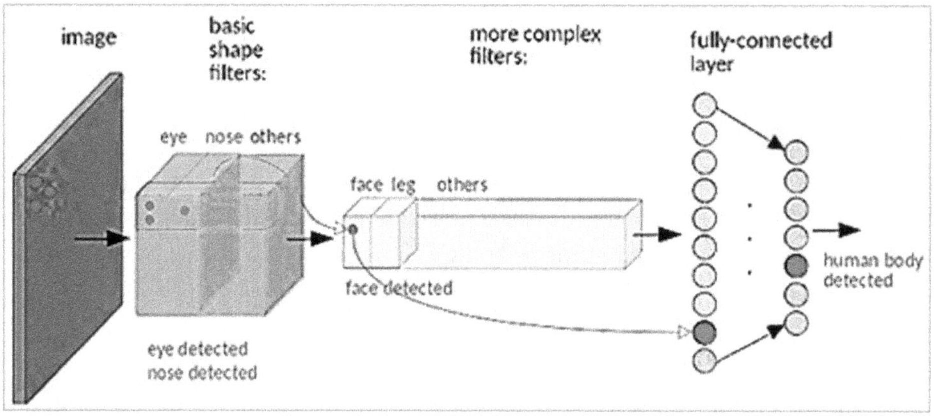

Convolution, ReLU and Pooling are the basic building blocks of any CNN.

The layers lower feature dimension, inject non-linearity, and extract key characteristics from photos, with the Fully Connected Layer receiving output from the Second Pooling Layer.

The next step in the process is called *flattening.* Flattening is used to convert all the resultant 2-Dimensional arrays from *pooled feature maps* into a single long continuous *linear vector* as in Figure 23.

The flattened matrix is fed as input to the *fully connected* layer to classify the image as shown in Figure 24.

Figure 23. Process of flattening

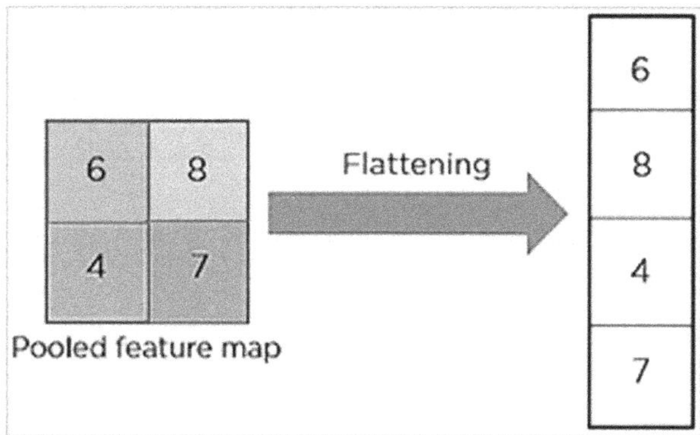

Figure 24. Flattened matrix act as input to the fully connected layer

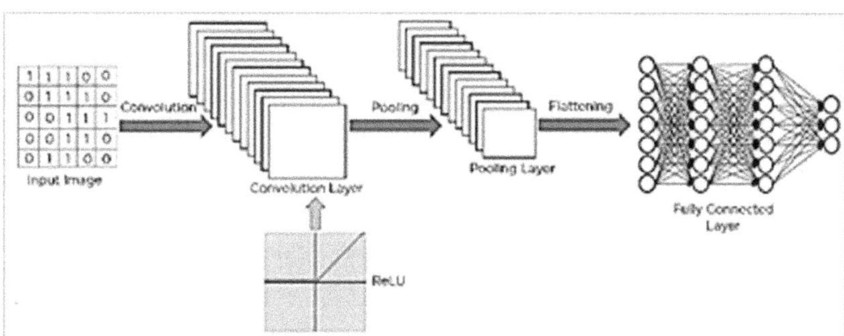

iv. Fully Connected Layer

The Fully Connected layer is a MLP that uses a softmax activation function in the output layer, implying that every neuron in the previous layer is connected to every neuron on the next layer as shown in Figure 25. The output from convolutional and pooling layers represents high-level features of the input image.

Figure 25. Building blocks of a CNN

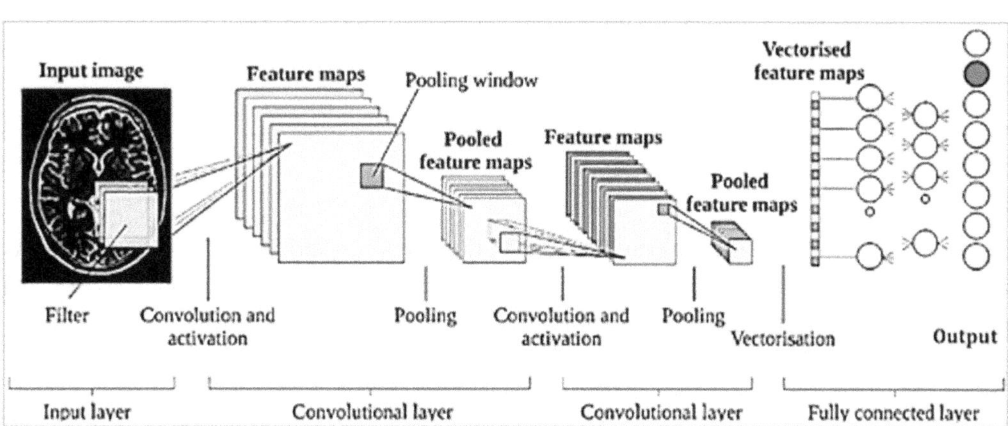

The Fully Connected Layer ensures a sum of output probabilities of 1 by using the **Softmax** as the activation function in the output layer, which recognizes a bird.

Definition of a NN With Only One Neuron After the Input

```
# Definition of the network
model = Sequential()                                    # starts the definition of the network
model.add(Dense(1, batch_input_shape=(None, 2),         # adds a new layer to the network with a single neuron
                activation='sigmoid'))                   # The input is a tensor of size (batch_size, 2), since we don'
                                                        # chooses the activation function 'sigmoid'
# Definition of the optimizer
sgd = optimizers.SGD(lr=0.15)                           # Defining the stochastic gradient descent optimizer

# compile model                                         # compile model, which ends the definition of the model
model.compile(loss='binary_crossentropy',
              optimizer=sgd,                            # using the stochastic gradient descent optimizer
              metrics=['accuracy'])
```

Code Explanation

- Sequential, starts the definition of the network
- Adds a new layer to the network with a single neuron, hence 1 in *Dense(1)*
- The input is a tensor of size (*Batch Size, 2*). Using *None* we don't need to specify the batch size now.
- Chooses the activation function *sigmoid*
- Defines and uses the *stochastic gradient descent* optimizer.
- *Compiles* the model, which ends the definition of the model.

```
# summarize the architecture of the NN along with the number of weights
model.summary()

Model: "sequential"
_________________________________________________________________
Layer (type)                 Output Shape              Param #
=================================================================
dense (Dense)                (None, 1)                 3
=================================================================
Total params: 3
Trainable params: 3
Non-trainable params: 0
_________________________________________________________________
```

The network is trained using stochastic gradient descent to minimize binary cross entropy loss function, with batch size set to 128 and 400 epochs per update step.

```
# Training of the network
history = model.fit(X, Y,                # training of the model using the training data stored in X and Y for
          epochs=400,                    # for 400 epochs
          batch_size=128,                # fix the batch size to 128 examples
          verbose=0)
```

- Trains the model using the data stored in X and Y for 400 epochs
- Fixes the batch size to 128 examples

Let's look at the so-called learning curve, we plot the *accuracy* and *the loss vs. the epochs* as shown in Figure 26. You can see that after 100 epochs, we predict around 70% of our data correct and have a loss around 0.51 (these values can vary from run to run).

Figure 26. Plot of the accuracy and the loss vs. the epochs

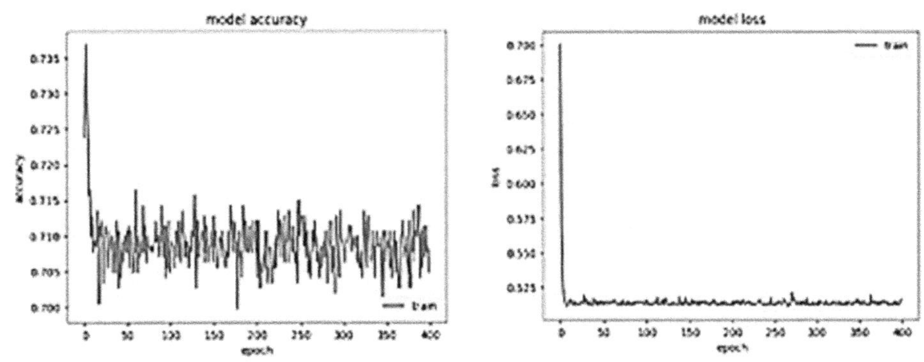

Definition of the Network With Two Hidden Layers

```
# Definition of the network
model = Sequential()
model.add(Dense(8, batch_input_shape=(None, 2),activation='sigmoid'))
model.add(Dense(2, activation='softmax'))

model.compile(loss='categorical_crossentropy',
              optimizer=sgd,
              metrics=['accuracy'])
```

Code Explanation

- Definition of the hidden layer with *eight (8) neurons*
- The output layer with *two (2) output* neurons

In this output summary we see that we now have a lot more trainable parameter then before.

24= input dim · output dim + output bias = 2·8+8

18= input dim · output dim + output bias = 8·2+2

Figure 27. Plot of the accuracy and the loss vs. the epochs

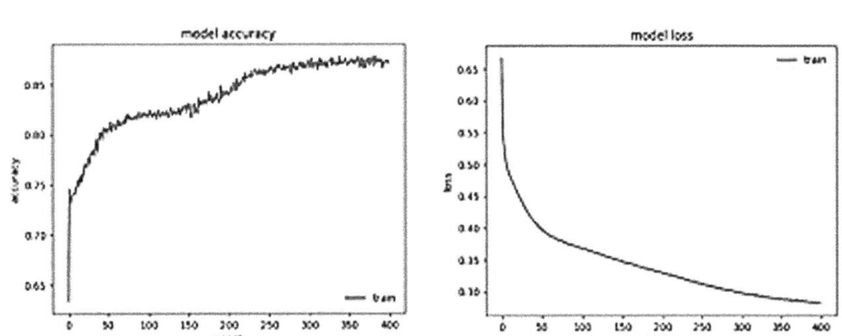

The learning curve shows that after 100 epochs, the model predicts 86% of data correctly and has a loss of 0.29 (these values can vary from run to run), which is better than the model without a hidden layer, as shown in Figure 27.

What Are Graph Neural Networks, and How Do They Work?

Neural networks have gained popularity in pattern recognition and data mining due to their effectiveness and simplicity. Graph Neural Networks (GNNs) are a type of neural network that target graph-structured data, such as nodes and edges, for tasks like node categorization, link prediction, and graph clustering. GNNs propagate information via edges to update node representations, allowing them to handle complex graph-structured data, capture non-linear interactions, and generalize to new data. Applications include social network analysis, recommendation systems, drug discovery, natural language processing, and computer vision.

However, GNNs can be computationally difficult due to their random, complex topology and unfixed node ordering. When the graph structure is noisy or lacking, GNNs can overfit and become computationally costly, especially for large networks. Despite this, GNNs are a flexible tool for both supervised and unsupervised learning tasks.

Classification of Neural Network Hyper-Parameters

Understanding the functions of each hyper-parameter is crucial as they significantly influence the behavior and structure of neural network models (Heaton, 2018; Bishop & Nasrabadi, 2006; Nielsen, 2015).

- In ML and DL algorithms, parameters and hyper parameters are variables, but there are distinctions between them.
- The training process involves updating parameters, which are variables that are learnt from the data.
- Before the model is trained, hyper parameters are settings made by the ML engineer or another individual.
- To improve models, they require active modification as they are not automatically adapted from the data.
- Determining optimal hyper parameter values in ML and DL can be challenging due to the varying size, complexity, and nature of the dataset and the issue at hand.

Neural Network Hyper-Parameters Can Be Classified as Follows

- ***Number of hidden layers***

This is also called the depth of the network. The term "deep" in deep learning refers to the number of hidden layers (depth) of a neural network.

- ***Number of nodes (neurons/units) in each layer***

The learning capacity of a network is influenced by the number of hidden units in each layer, with too few units resulting in smaller networks that may underfit training data, and too many units leading to overfitting.

- ***Type of activation function***

The activation function in layers is the final hyper-parameter describing network topology. Hidden layers use an activation function for non-linearity, while input layers don't. The problem being solved determines the activation used in the output layer.

- Regression: Identity activation function with one node
- Binary classification: Sigmoid activation function with one node
- Multiclass classification: Softmax activation function with one node per class
- Multi label classification: Sigmoid activation function with one node per class

- ***Type of optimizer***

The optimizer algorithm, a well-known technique with three variations, reduces the loss function by altering network settings.

- Batch gradient descent
- Stochastic gradient descent
- Mini-batch gradient descent

All these variants differ in the *batch size* that we use to compute the gradient of the loss function.
Other types of optimizers have been developed to address the limitations of the gradient descent algorithm.

- Gradient descent with momentum
- Adam
- Adagrad
- Adadelta
- Adamax
- Nadam
- Ftrl
- RMSProp (Keras default)

- ***Learning rate-α***

In training neural networks, the learning rate is a crucial hyper parameter. It controls the rate at which the optimizer descends the error curve, and the gradient (derivative) controls the step's direction. If the network takes too long to converge, it is preferable to start with a low learning rate, such as 0.001, and subsequently raise it.

- ***Type of loss function***

The objective of training a neural network is to reduce the loss function using an optimizer like Mean Squared Error (MSE) or Mean Absolute Error (MAE), which allows for this process.

- ***Type of model evaluation metric***

Evaluation metrics measure a neural network's performance during testing, including accuracy, precision, recall, and AUC for classification tasks and mean squared error and mean absolute error for regression tasks.

- ***Batch size***

The *model.fit()* function includes the batch size as a key hyper parameter. It is referring to how many training instances are in the batch. 16, 32, 64, 128, 256, 512, 1024 are typical values. While a lower batch size converges more quickly over fewer epochs, a bigger batch size demands more processing resources per epoch.

- ***Epochs***

The epochs is another important hyper parameter that is found in the *model.fit()* method. Epochs refer to the number of times the model sees the entire dataset. The number of *epochs* should be increased when,

– The network is trained with a very small learning rate.
– The batch size is too small.

Figure 28. Early stopping process

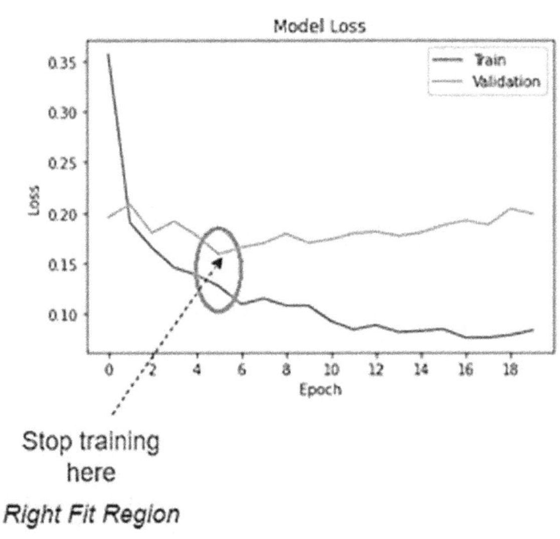

The network may overfit the training data with numerous epochs, leading to an increase in validation error and a decrease in training error. This results in the model performing well on the training data but not well generalizing to new unseen data, indicating the need to stop the training process. This is called *early stopping* as shown in Figure 28.

Neural Network: Its Industry Use Cases

ANNs, trained on historical data, can categorize information, cluster data, and forecast outcomes, and can perform various activities like data analysis, transcription, facial recognition, and weather forecasting.

- Neural networks offer precise and reliable solutions for complex non-linear problems like fraud detection, business lapse/churn analysis, risk analysis, and data mining (Ghosh, 2023).
- Their key advantage is the automated inference of the task-performer's approach from the data.
- Traditional rule-based and fuzzy systems operate more efficiently and use significantly less storage compared to these systems.
- They possess a natural form of regularization or generalization, making them highly resistant to erratic, inaccurate, or insufficient data.

Top Companies using Artificial Neural Network (ANN):

- Nvidia Corp. (NVDA)
- Alphabet (GOOG, GOOGL)
- Salesforce.com (CRM)
- Amazon.com (AMZN)
- Microsoft Corp. (MSFT)
- Twilio (TWLO)
- IBM (IBM)
- Facebook (FB)

Conclusion:

Because they don't need explicit programming and can handle loud, inaccurate, or missing data, neural computers are perfect for commercial and military applications.

Industrial Applications Using Neural Networks

ANNs are now a common information processing method, which has given rise to a number of businesses uses for both goods and services (Kandi et al., 2017; Soni et al., 2022). Both the civic and military sectors have enormous potential.

Given Below Are Domains of Commercial Applications of Neural Network Technology

- **Business -** Marketing, Real Estate
- **Document & Form Processing** - Machine printed character recognition, Graphics recognition, Hand printed character recognition, Cursive handwritten character recognition
- **Finance Industry** - Market trading, Fraud detection, Credit rating
- **Food industry** - Odour/aroma analysis, Product development, Quality assurance
- **Energy Industry** - Electrical load forecasting, hydroelectric dam operation, Natural gas
- **Manufacturing Process control** - Quality control
- **Medical & Health Care Industry** - Image analysis Drug development, Resource allocation (Ghosh, 2022a).
- **Science & Engineering** - Chemical engineering, Electrical engineering, Weather forecasting
- **Transportation & Communication**

Some Applications of Neural Networks Are

- Forecasting the Behaviour of Complex Systems
- Signal Processing
- Data Compression
- Paint Quality Inspection
- DNA Sequence Analysis

MLPs have been successful at a wide range of AI tasks, from speech recognition (Azzizi et al., 2016) to predicting thermal conductivity of aqueous electrolyte solutions (Eslamloueyan et al., 2011) and controlling a continuous stirred-tank reactor (Moghadassi et al., 2010). For example, an MLP for recognizing printed digits (e.g., the account and routing number printed on a check) would be comprised of a grid of inputs to read individual pixels of digits (say, a 9×12 bitmap), followed by one or more hidden layers, and finally 10 output neurons to indicate which number was recognized in the input (0–9) (Figure 29).

Figure 29. A MLP for reading cheque numbers would comprise a grid of inputs, hidden neurons, and 10 output neurons to show which number was recognised

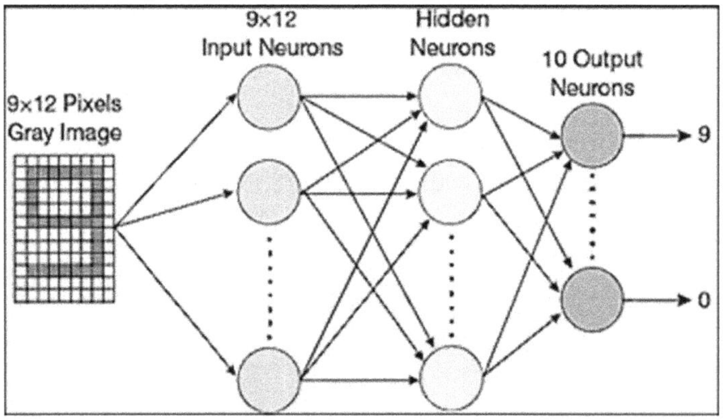

Researchers trained an MLP to predict a compound's viscosity using data from Perry's Chemical Engineers' Handbook (Himmelblau et al., 1992). By teaching an MLP to recognise variations in temperature and flow rate, researchers in another study were able to identify defects in a heat exchanger (Vasičkaninová & Bakošová, 2009).

Figure 30. An MLP can determine a plant's system dynamics by analyzing the difference between its real output and its neural network output

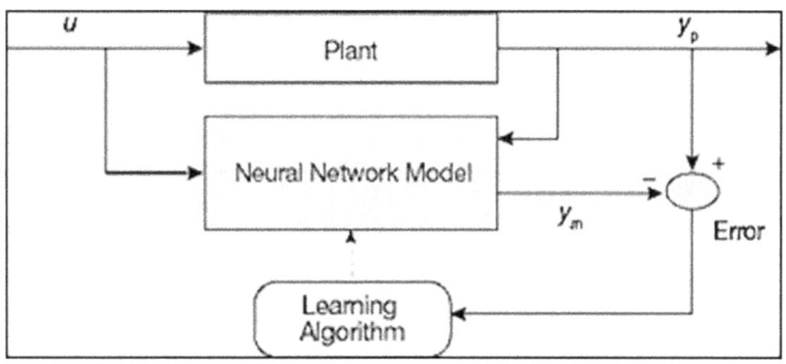

As another example, MLPs have been used for predictive control of chemical reactors (Vasičkaninová & Bakošová, 2009). The neural network is trained to understand the plant's forward dynamics using the prediction error between the plant output and the neural network output (Figure 30).

Figure 31. A continuous stirred-tank reactor can be trained to maintain appropriate product concentration and flow by using past data

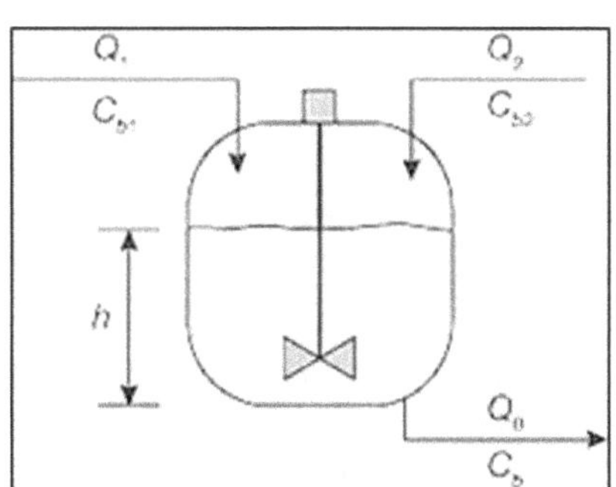

The neural network learns from previous inputs and outputs to predict future values of the plant output. For example, a controller for a catalytic continuous stirred-tank reactor (as in Figure 31) can be trained to maintain appropriate product concentration and flow by using past data about inflow Q_1 and Q_2 at concentrations C_{b1} and C_{b2}, respectively, liquid level h, and outflow Q_0 at concentration C_b.

Real-Life and Business Applications of Neural Networks

Here's a list of other neural network engineering Real-Life applications currently in use in various industries:

- **Aerospace:** Simulations of aircraft components, control systems, auto-piloting, and flight paths.
- **Automotive:** The proposed improvements include enhanced power trains, virtual sensors, guiding systems, and warranty activity analyzers.
- **Electronics:** Skills in speech synthesis, machine vision, non-linear modelling, code sequence prediction, process management, and chip failure analysis are all crucial.
- **Manufacturing:** This includes chemical product design analysis, dynamic modelling of chemical process systems, process control, process diagnosis, product design, paper quality forecasting, project planning, computer chip quality analysis, visual inspection systems, and welding quality analysis.
- **Mechanics:** Condition monitoring, systems modelling, and control
- **Robotics:** Forklift robots, manipulator controllers, trajectory control, and vision systems
- **Telecommunications:** This includes network design, administration, ATM control, automated information services, customer payment processing systems, data compression, equalisers, fault management, handwriting recognition, real-time spoken language translation, and pattern recognition.

Here are further current examples of Neural Networks business applications:

- **Banking:** Loan delinquencies, fraud and risk assessment, credit and loan application review, and credit card attrition are all crucial.
- **Business Analytics:** Market research, market mix, market structure, customer behaviour modelling, customer segmentation, fraud propensity, and models for attrition, default, buy, and renewals are crucial.
- **Defence:** Object discrimination, sensors, sonar, radar, image signal processing, signal/image identification, target tracking, and weapon steering are used in counterterrorism.
- **Education:** Software for adaptive learning, dynamic forecasting, study of the educational system, modelling of student performance (Ghosh, 2023), and personality profiling.
- **Financial:** This includes corporate bond ratings, financial analysis, credit line usage forecasting, currency value forecasting, loan counselling, mortgage screening, appraisal, and portfolio trading.
- **Medical:** Cancer cell analysis, ECG and EEG analysis, test recommendations for ERs, cost-saving measures, transplant procedure optimisation, and prosthetic design (Ghosh, 2022a; Ghosh, 2022b).
- **Securities:** Automatic bond rating, market analysis, and stock trading advisory systems
- **Transportation:** Routing systems, truck brake diagnosis systems, and vehicle scheduling

The way individuals do business is being transformed by neural networks.

CONCLUSION

This literature provides an overview of various neural network types, activation mechanisms, usage, graphs, and code snippets. Neural networks are composed of neurons connected by synapses, with perceptrons as the basic unit. Multilayer perceptrons can be used when a single perceptron fails due to nonlinearity in the dataset.

Future of Neural Networks

Here are some likely **future developments** in neural network technologies:

Fuzzy Logic Integration: Fuzzy logic, a fundamental component of future neural network applications, recognizes relative and true/false values, enhancing applications in auto-engineering, building crane control, glaucoma monitoring, and job candidate screening.

Pulsed Neural Networks: Neurobiological experiments reveal that mammalian brain networks use pulsing for information and calculations, leading to advancements in theoretical analysis, model-building, neurobiological modelling, and hardware deployment.

Specialized Hardware: Rapid development of neural network processing units (NNPUs) and neuro-synaptic architectures is driving the rapid development of DL, ML, and neural networks in AI.

Improvement of Existing Technologies: Modern neural network technologies, new software and hardware, and the enhanced computational capacity of neuro-synaptic designs have all made neural networks possible.

Robotics: Futurist Yonck believes that while robots are supposedly capable of feeling, observing, and anticipating their environment, they still have a long way to go before they can think flexible and non-brittlely, despite their limited learning methods.

REFERENCES

Abiodun, O. I., Jantan, A., Omolara, A. E., Dada, K. V., Mohamed, N. A., & Arshad, H. (2018). State-of-the-art in artificial neural network applications: A survey. *Heliyon*, *4*(11), e00938. doi:10.1016/j.heliyon.2018.e00938 PMID:30519653

Aggarwal, C. C. (2018). Neural networks and deep learning. Springer. doi:10.1007/978-3-319-94463-0

Aggarwal, C. C., & Aggarwal, C. C. (2018). Machine learning with shallow neural networks. *Neural Networks and Deep Learning: A Textbook*, 53-104.

Azzizi, N., & Zaatri, A. (2016). A Learning Process of Multilayer Perceptron for Speech Recognition. *International Journal of Pure and Applied Mathematics*, *107*(4), 1005–1012. doi:10.12732/ijpam.v107i4.18

Bishop, C. M., & Nasrabadi, N. M. (2006). *Pattern recognition and machine learning* (Vol. 4). New York: Springer.

Eslamloueyan, R., Khademi, M. H., & Mazinani, S. (2011). Using a multilayer perceptron network for thermal conductivity prediction of aqueous electrolyte solutions. *Industrial & Engineering Chemistry Research*, *50*(7), 4050–4056. doi:10.1021/ie101513z

Ghosh, P. (2022a). Deep learning to diagnose diseases and security in 5g healthcare informatics. In *Machine Learning and Deep Learning Techniques for Medical Science* (pp. 279–331). CRC Press. doi:10.1201/9781003217497-16

Ghosh, P. (2022b). Timely Diabetes Possibility Prediction using AI Techniques. *Journal of Artificial Intelligence Research & Advances*, *9*(2).

Ghosh, P., & Ghosh, S. (2020). IoT and machine learning in green smart home automation and green building management. *J Altern Energy Sourc Technol*, *10*(3), 8–36.

Ghosh, P., Roy, R., Mandal, S., Chowdhary, M., & Bokshi, S. (2023). Data mining approach to predict academic performance of students. *BOHR International Journal of Computer Science*, *2*(1), 21–31. doi:10.54646/bijcs.2023.21

Heaton, J. (2018). Ian Goodfellow, Yoshua Bengio, and Aaron Courville: Deep learning: The MIT Press, 2016, 800 pp, ISBN: 0262035618. *Genetic Programming and Evolvable Machines*, *19*(1-2), 305–307. doi:10.1007/s10710-017-9314-z

Himmelblau, D. M., Barker, R. W., & Suewatanakul, W. (1992). Fault classification with the aid of artificial neural networks. In Fault Detection, Supervision and Safety for Technical Processes 1991 (pp. 541-545). Pergamon. doi:10.1016/B978-0-08-041275-7.50085-5

Kandi, H., Mishra, D., & Gorthi, S. R. S. (2017). Exploring the learning capabilities of convolutional neural networks for robust image watermarking. *Computers & Security*, *65*, 247–268. doi:10.1016/j.cose.2016.11.016

Kizilkan, Z. B., Sivri, M. S., Yazici, I., & Beyca, O. F. (2022). Neural Networks and Deep Learning. In *Business Analytics for Professionals* (pp. 127–151). Springer International Publishing. doi:10.1007/978-3-030-93823-9_5

Mishra, P. K., Karmakar, S., & Guhathakurta, P. (2016). A broad literature survey of development and application of artificial neural networks in rainfall-runoff modelling. In *Proceedings of Fifth International Conference on Soft Computing for Problem Solving: SocProS 2015, Volume 2* (pp. 691-710). Springer Singapore. 10.1007/978-981-10-0451-3_62

Moawad, A. W., Fuentes, D. T., ElBanan, M. G., Shalaby, A. S., Guccione, J., Kamel, S., Jensen, C. T., & Elsayes, K. M. (2022). Artificial intelligence in diagnostic radiology: Where do we stand, challenges, and opportunities. *Journal of Computer Assisted Tomography*, *46*(1), 78–90. doi:10.1097/RCT.0000000000001247 PMID:35027520

Moghadassi, A., Parvizian, F., & Hosseini, S. M. (2010). Application of Artificial Neural Network for Prediction of Liquid Viscosity. *Indian Chemical Engineer*, *52*(1), 37–48. doi:10.1080/00194501003759688

Nielsen, M. A. (2015). *Neural networks and deep learning* (Vol. 25). Determination press.

Pancholi, P. D., & Patel, S. J. (2021). Literature Survey for Applications of Artificial Neural Networks. *Applications of Artificial Neural Networks for Nonlinear Data*, 1-17.

Pritchard, N. J., Wicenec, A., Bennamoun, M., & Dodson, R. (2023). A Bibliometric Review of Neuromorphic Computing and Spiking Neural Networks. *arXiv preprint arXiv:2304.06897.*

Roberts, D. A., Yaida, S., & Hanin, B. (2022). *The principles of deep learning theory*. Cambridge University Press. doi:10.1017/9781009023405

Soni, M., Gomathi, S., Kumar, P., Churi, P. P., Mohammed, M. A., & Salman, A. O. (2022). Hybridizing convolutional neural network for classification of lung diseases. *International Journal of Swarm Intelligence Research*, *13*(2), 1–15. doi:10.4018/IJSIR.287544

Vasičkaninová, A., & Bakošová, M. (2009). Neural network predictive control of a chemical reactor. *Acta Chimica Slovenica*, *2*(2), 21–36.

Yasdi, R. (2000). A literature survey on applications of neural networks for human-computer interaction. *Neural Computing & Applications*, *9*(4), 245–258. doi:10.1007/s005210070002

Zhou, Z. H. (2021). *Machine learning*. Springer Nature. doi:10.1007/978-981-15-1967-3

Chapter 10
Evolutionary Computation in Artificial Intelligence: Adapting Nature's Strategies for Smart Systems

Dharmesh Dhabliya
https://orcid.org/0000-0002-6340-2993
Vishwakarma Institute of Information Technology, Pune, India

Ankur Gupta
https://orcid.org/0000-0002-4651-5830
Vaish College of Engineering, Rohtak, India

Sukhvinder Singh Dari
https://orcid.org/0000-0002-6218-6600
Symbiosis Law School, Symbiosis International University (Deemed), Pune, India

Ritika Dhabliya
Yashika Journal Publications Pvt. Limited, Wardha, India

Anishkumar Dhablia
Altimetrik India Pvt. Ltd., Pune, India

Nitin N. Sakhare
https://orcid.org/0000-0002-1748-799X
BRACT'S Vishwakarma Institute of Information Technology, Pune, India

Rohit Anand
G.B. Pant DSEU Okhla-1 Campus, New Delhi, India

ABSTRACT

In the realm of robotics and artificial intelligence, researchers often draw inspiration from the intricate and efficient systems found in the animal kingdom. For instance, the study of swarm intelligence, inspired by the collective behavior of insects like ants or bees, has led to the development of algorithms for autonomous drones and robotic systems that can collaboratively solve complex problems. The adaptation of nature's strategies for smart systems showcases the potential for interdisciplinary collaboration between biology and technology. By understanding and emulating the efficiency, adaptability, and sustainability observed in natural systems, scientists and engineers continue to push the boundaries of innovation, creating smart systems that are not only technologically advanced but also environmentally conscious and resilient.

DOI: 10.4018/979-8-3693-2073-0.ch010

1. INTRODUCTION

Evolutionary Computation (EC) in Artificial Intelligence represents a transformative approach that draws inspiration from nature's evolutionary processes to craft intelligent algorithms for problem-solving. Emulating the principles of natural selection, EC involves the iterative generation, selection, and adaptation of potential solutions within a population, mirroring the way biological systems evolve over generations. This innovative paradigm, encompassing algorithms like Genetic Algorithms and Evolutionary Strategies, has proven particularly adept at tackling complex optimization problems across diverse domains. By adapting nature's strategies of selection, crossover, and mutation, EC enables smart systems to autonomously refine and improve their performance, demonstrating a remarkable ability to discover optimal solutions in large solution spaces (Anand & Chawla, 2020). This bio-inspired methodology holds promise for revolutionizing problem-solving methodologies in artificial intelligence, offering adaptability and efficiency akin to the evolutionary mechanisms (Kala, 2023) observed in the natural world.

Evolutionary Computation (EC) is a subfield of Artificial Intelligence (AI) that draws inspiration from the principles of natural evolution to develop intelligent algorithms and systems (Singh et.al., 2022; Raghavan et al., 2022) The fundamental idea behind EC is to mimic the process of natural selection to evolve solutions to complex problems over successive generations. Evolutionary Computation in Artificial Intelligence leverages the principles of natural evolution to create intelligent algorithms capable of solving complex problems. Its versatility and adaptability make it a valuable tool for optimization and learning tasks in various domains.

1.1 Evolutionary Computation

Evolutionary computation (as shown in Figure 1) is an area of AI and soft computing that studies algorithms for global optimization that are based on the theory of biological evolution (Anand & Chawla, 2020; Kala, 2023). To put it more precisely, they are a class of metaheuristic or stochastic optimization–style problem solvers that rely on population-based trial and error. Iteratively updating an initial list of possible solutions is the first step in evolutionary computing. Less desirable solutions are stochastically removed, minor random changes are introduced, and, depending on the approach, parental information is mixed (Anand & Chawla, 2016). Natural selection, also known as artificial selection, mutation, and recombination are processes that occur in biology when a population of solutions is tested. Consequently, the population will undergo progressive evolution in order to improve its fitness, which is specifically the fitness function selected by the algorithm. Evolutionary computing approaches have gained popularity in computer science due to their ability to provide optimal solutions across many problem domains (Anand & Chawla, 2016). There are a plethora of variations and extensions available, each tailored to a different set of issues and data formats. To examine common characteristics of broad evolutionary processes, evolutionary computation is sometimes utilized as an in silico experimental approach in evolutionary biology.

When it comes to tackling computational problems, Evolutionary Computation (EC) is at the vanguard, taking its cues from the rules that control evolution in nature. Based on the principle of natural selection, evolutionary complexity (EC) uses a population of possible solutions to difficult problems via repeated cycles of selection, recombination (crossover), and mutation. This method has several uses in optimization, machine learning, artificial intelligence, and other fields since it mimics the evolutionary dynamics seen in biological systems. One of the most well-known subfields of evolutionary computing, genetic algorithms model the evolution of potential solutions via natural selection. If you're working on a problem domain where more conventional algorithms would fail, consider using evolutionary computation. It's resilient, adaptable, and can explore large solution spaces. Evolutionary Computation provides a bio-inspired way forward for creative, efficient, and autonomous problem-solving across many domains as technology progresses (Anand & Chawla, 2016).

Figure 1. Evolutionary computation

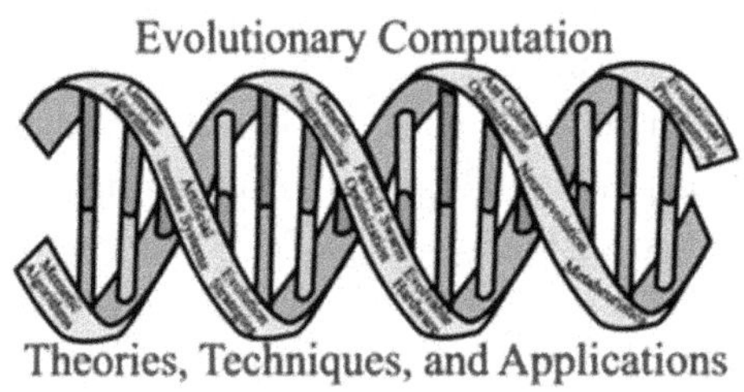

1.2 Artificial Intelligence

AI research encompasses a wide variety of subfields, each of which has its own distinct objectives and approaches to study. The capacity to reason, represent information, plan, learn, understand natural language, sense, and move and control things are some of the classic aims of artificial intelligence research. Other goals include the ability to comprehend and represent information. The development of general intelligence is one of the more long-term objectives of the field. approaches from a broad variety of domains have been adopted and integrated by researchers working in the field of artificial intelligence. These approaches include formal logic, search, mathematical optimization, and the statistical, probabilistic, and economic underpinnings of AI (Bakhshipour et al., 2017). Artificial intelligence (AI) has a substantial influence on a variety of subject areas, including computer science.

Types of AI

Artificial intelligence has the potential to improve the efficiency of law enforcement agencies in a variety of ways. This entails the addition of biometric information about a large number of suspects, such as their face, voice, blood type, and fingerprints, in order to make the process of investigating and monitoring criminals more efficient. Using technologies that are based on artificial intelligence, investigation workers may be trained on appropriate investigation tactics in an efficient manner (Bakhshipour et al., 2017). Some of the many conceivable variants include the following:

- **Reactive Machines:** Some artificial intelligence systems have a restricted amount of spare memory since they were designed for a specific purpose. It was impossible for Garry Kasparov to compete with it. Despite the fact that Deep Blue is very good at recognizing and predicting things, it is unable to build on its previous achievements or gain knowledge from its errors since it does not have a memory.

- **Restricted Memory:** These artificial intelligences are able to remember their previous decisions and make improvements to them. This concept serves as the foundation for a wide variety of decision-making strategies that are implemented by autonomous vehicles.
- **Concept of Minds:** It is important to note that the idea of a "theory of mind" in psychology is entirely theoretical. The capacity of an artificial intelligence system to accurately recognize and respond to signs of emotional states is referred to by this term. In order for artificial intelligence systems to function at a high level inside human teams, they need to be able to grasp motivations and anticipate actions.
- **Self-awareness:** There are indications of consciousness in self-aware artificial intelligence since these systems are conscious of their own existence. It is possible for robots to grasp their own reality if they are self-aware. The technology necessary to produce such an artificial intelligence has not yet been established.

Applications of AI

- **AI in healthcare.** More and more people are becoming aware of the need of reducing the costs of healthcare while also improving the results for patients.
- **AI in business.** For the purpose of enhancing customer service, machine learning algorithms are being included into analytics and customer relationship management software.
- **AI in education.** AI might potentially automate grading, which would save teachers time.
- **AI in finance.** Both Intuit Mint and TurboTax are examples of personal financial programs that are backed by artificial intelligence, and they are wreaking havoc in the banking industry.
- **AI in law.** When it comes to the amount of documentation that is involved in the process of legal discovery, it is feasible that people just are unable to keep up with it.
- **AI in manufacturing.** In the context of manufacturing facilities, the industrial sector was the first to use robots.
- **AI in banking.** Chat bots are being used effectively by financial institutions in order to provide clients with information about their products and services and to automatically conduct routine tasks.
- **AI in transportation.** Artificial intelligence is used for a variety of purposes, including but not limited to the operation of autonomous vehicles, the management of traffic, the forecasting of upcoming flight delays, and the enhancement of the safety and effectiveness of maritime freight transportation.
- **Security.** Using cutting-edge technologies such as artificial intelligence and machine learning, current security companies separate themselves from their competitors.

1.3 Role of Evolutionary Computation in Artificial Intelligence

Evolutionary Computation (EC) serves as a fundamental and transformative element within the realm of Artificial Intelligence (AI), offering a distinctive approach to problem-solving inspired by the mechanisms of natural evolution. EC plays a pivotal role in addressing complex challenges where traditional algorithms may fall short. The essence of EC lies in its capacity to iteratively generate and refine potential solutions through processes like selection, crossover, and mutation, closely mimicking the principles of natural selection. In optimization tasks, EC excels by navigating vast solution spaces, providing robust and often globally optimal solutions (Bakhshipour et al., 2017). Its adaptive nature allows AI systems to learn and evolve over time, adapting to dynamic environments and changing objectives. EC is particularly influential in machine learning, contributing to the optimization of model parameters and enhancing the learning capabilities of algorithms. Additionally, its application extends to automated design, where it aids in the creation of innovative and efficient systems. In essence, Evolutionary Computation stands as a cornerstone in AI, offering a bio-inspired framework that not only addresses complex problems but also fosters adaptability, learning, and innovation within intelligent systems (Bakhshipour et al., 2017; Sindhwani et al., 2023)

1.4 Applications for Adapting Nature's Strategies for Smart Systems

The applications of adapting nature's strategies for smart systems, often referred to as biomimicry or bio-inspiration, are diverse and span various domains. By drawing insights from the natural world, researchers and engineers have developed innovative solutions across numerous fields. Here are some notable applications (Sindhwani et al., 2024):

1. Materials Science and Engineering

- Lotus Effect: Mimicking the water-repellent properties of lotus leaves has led to the development of self-cleaning materials for various applications, from building surfaces to textiles.
- Spider Silk Mimicry: Creating synthetic materials with properties inspired by spider silk, such as high tensile strength and flexibility, has implications for industries like textiles and medicine.

2. Robotics and Automation

- Biorobotics: Designing robots that imitate the movements and functionalities of animals. This includes bio-inspired robotic fish for underwater exploration and drones that mimic bird flight for improved agility.
- Soft Robotics: Taking inspiration from soft-bodied organisms to design robots capable of navigating complex environments and interacting with delicate objects.

3. Aeronautics and Transportation

- Bird Flight for Aircraft Design: Studying bird flight patterns has influenced the design of aircraft wings for increased efficiency and maneuverability.
- Bullet Train Design: The streamlined shape of the Shinkansen bullet train in Japan was inspired by the beak of the kingfisher bird, reducing noise and increasing speed.

4. Energy and Sustainability

- Wind Turbine Design: Biomimicry has influenced the design of wind turbines by emulating the structure of humpback whale flippers, leading to more efficient energy capture.
- Photosynthesis-Inspired Solar Cells: Developing solar cells that mimic the process of photosynthesis in plants for improved efficiency in harnessing sunlight.

5. Medicine and Biotechnology

- Gecko-Inspired Adhesives: Creating adhesives that mimic the stickiness of gecko feet for medical applications such as bandages and surgical adhesives.
- Drug Delivery Inspired by Blood Circulation: Designing drug delivery systems that replicate the efficiency of blood circulation for targeted and controlled drug release.

6. Architecture and Design

- Termite Mound-Inspired Ventilation: Architectural designs inspired by termite mounds optimize natural ventilation in buildings, reducing the need for artificial cooling systems.
- Biomimetic Design for Structural Stability: Studying natural structures like bones and trees for innovative architectural designs that balance strength and lightness.

7. Information Technology

- Neural Networks: Drawing inspiration from the human brain's neural networks for the development of artificial neural networks in machine learning and AI.
- Ant Colony Optimization Algorithms: Utilizing the foraging behavior of ant colonies to optimize algorithms for problem-solving, such as in network routing (V. Shukla, 2023).

8. Environmental Monitoring and Conservation

Bio-Inspired Sensors: Developing sensors inspired by animal senses for applications in environmental monitoring, wildlife conservation, and disaster response.

9. Security and Surveillance

Bio-Inspired Surveillance Systems: Designing surveillance systems inspired by animal vision and behavior for enhanced security applications.

10. Agriculture

Biomimicry for Crop Protection: Studying natural pest control mechanisms in ecosystems for developing sustainable and eco-friendly methods for crop protection.

These applications showcase the versatility and potential of adapting nature's strategies for developing smart systems that are not only innovative but also sustainable and efficient in addressing contemporary challenges.

1.5 Challenges

Evolutionary Computation (EC) is a powerful optimization and search technique inspired by the principles of biological evolution. While EC has shown success in solving complex problems, there are several challenges and limitations associated with its application in Artificial Intelligence (AI). Here are some of the key challenges to Evolutionary Computation in AI:

1. Computational Complexity: Many EC algorithms, especially those dealing with complex optimization problems, can be computationally expensive. As the size of the problem space increases, the computational requirements for evolutionary algorithms also grow, making them less feasible for certain real-time or resource-constrained applications.
2. Convergence Speed: EC algorithms may exhibit slow convergence rates, particularly when dealing with high-dimensional and multimodal search spaces. It can take a considerable number of generations for the algorithm to find optimal solutions, impacting the efficiency of the optimization process.
3. Premature Convergence: Premature convergence occurs when the evolutionary algorithm converges to a suboptimal solution before exploring the entire search space. Balancing exploration and exploitation is a challenge, and premature convergence can limit the algorithm's ability to find the global optimum.
4. Parameter Tuning: Many EC algorithms involve several parameters that need to be carefully tuned for optimal performance. Selecting appropriate parameter values for a specific problem can be challenging, and improper tuning may lead to suboptimal results or a lack of convergence.
5. Handling Constraints: Dealing with constraints, such as inequality constraints or discrete variables, is a common challenge in EC. Ensuring that the evolutionary algorithm can effectively handle constraints while searching for feasible solutions is an ongoing research area.
6. Scalability: As the size of the problem space increases, the scalability of EC algorithms becomes a concern. Ensuring that the algorithms can efficiently scale to handle large-scale optimization problems is crucial for their applicability to real-world scenarios.
7. Sensitivity to Initial Conditions: Some EC algorithms are sensitive to the initial conditions, which means small variations in the initial population can lead to significantly different results. Achieving robustness to variations in the starting conditions is a challenge, particularly in dynamic environments.
8. Limited Understanding of Search Spaces: In certain complex problems, understanding the structure of the search space and formulating an effective representation for the evolutionary algorithm can be challenging. Developing representations that capture the essential features of the problem is an ongoing research area.
9. Adaptability to Dynamic Environments: Adapting EC algorithms to dynamic environments where the problem or solution space changes over time is a significant challenge. Ensuring that the algorithm can dynamically adjust its exploration-exploitation strategy is crucial for maintaining effectiveness.
10. Incorporating Prior Knowledge: Integrating prior domain knowledge into EC algorithms remains a challenge. Leveraging external knowledge to guide the search process effectively is an ongoing research area to improve the performance of EC in practical applications.
11. Limited Diversity Maintenance: Maintaining diversity in the population is crucial for preventing premature convergence and ensuring effective exploration. Developing mechanisms to enhance and sustain diversity throughout the evolutionary process is a challenge.

Addressing these challenges requires ongoing research and innovation in the field of Evolutionary Computation. Researchers are actively working on developing hybrid algorithms, incorporating machine learning techniques, and improving the adaptability and efficiency of EC methods in diverse AI applications.

1.6 Chapter Organization

This chapter, Introduction part considers Evolutionary Computation, AI, Role of Evolutionary computation in AI and challenges to Evolutionary computation. Literature review considers existing research related to evolutionary computation where different Evolutionary algorithm are considered in conventional research work. Problem statement section describes the issue faced by conventional research work. Afterward, Role of PSO Adapting Nature's Strategies for Smart Systems is discussed. Then process flow of PSO in order to find best solution is elaborated. Simulation part presents the impact of using PSO optimizer with machine learning approach. It is observed that training and testing accuracy is increased on other hand performance of machine learning get improved. Finally, conclusion and future scope of chapter is presented.

2. LITERATURE REVIEW

This work presents the results of an adaptive model switch-based surrogate-assisted evolutionary algorithm that was presented by the authors (Shukla and Bandyopadhyay, 2023) as a solution to challenges of this kind. To ensure that the restricted number of function evaluations are used to their full potential, it makes use of the sampling techniques in an adaptive manner, selecting them based on the largest improvement in convergence, diversity, and approximation uncertainty. The suggested approach is shown to be more competitive than the five most sophisticated surrogate-assisted evolutionary algorithms, according to the results of experiments conducted on a set of test issues.

In their research, the authors (Geng et al., 2022) offered a new classification tree-based adaptive operator selection approach for a MOE algorithm that is based on decomposition. The operator that yields the best outcome is the sole one that is chosen to produce children in the subsequent generation. During this time, a new differential evolution that is based on search inertia (SiDE) is being developed with the intention of directing the evolutionary process in a manner that is more effective. When compared to previous MOEA/D variations, the suggested MOEA/D-CTAOS performs better on UF and LZ benchmarks in terms of IGD and HV value, as shown by the results of the respective experiments. Additional research substantiates the benefit of using a search technique that is directed by the direction of the search.

The authors (George & Wooden, 2023) tried to critically assess the strategic adoption of artificial intelligence within the framework of "smart universities." They believed that these forward-thinking institutions will soon become the next step in the progression of higher processes. It is a fundamental assumption that it is possible for educational institutions to achieve tailored learning trajectories, better accessibility, economic efficiency, and an overall improvement in operational performance via the implementation of such integration. But before moving forward with this new educational paradigm, it is necessary to do a comprehensive investigation into the various pitfalls that may arise. These pitfalls include worries over the quality of education, the possibility of job losses, the dangers of prejudice, the invasion of privacy, and safety issues. Our fundamental purpose is to provide a well-rounded education by using artificial intelligence and quantum technologies to alter academic and administrative evaluations. This will assist stakeholders in making well-informed strategic choices on the endorsement and advancement of the smart university model.

In this study, authors (Xue et al., 2021) presented a multi-objective binary genetic algorithm that incorporates an adaptive operator selection mechanism, which they refer to as MOBGA-AOS. The MOBGA-AOS algorithm makes use of five crossover operators, each of which has a unique set of search properties. When it comes to the evolution process, each of them is given a probability that is determined by how well they performed. Throughout the various stages of evolution, the appropriate crossover operator is chosen via the use of a roulette wheel selection process, taking into account the probabilities, in order to provide new solutions for the subsequent development. Ten different datasets are used to evaluate the proposed method in comparison to five other evolutionary multi-objective algorithms that are well-known. It has been shown by the results of the experiments that MOBGA-AOS is able to eliminate a significant number of characteristics while maintaining a low level of classification error. In addition to this, it achieves significant benefits when used to large-scale datasets, which is evidence that MOBGA-AOS is capable of resolving high-dimensional feature selection issues.

Authors (Hu et al.,2020) analyzed the range of values of AD under binary conditions, and a novel updating equation for a parameter is proposed. The goal of this equation is to strike a compromise between the capabilities of global search and local search. A significant component of BGWO is the transfer function, which plays a crucial role in the process of translating the continuous value to the binary expression. There are five transfer functions included in this work, and the primary emphasis is on enhancing the quality of their solutions. When compared to the original binary GWO, the advanced binary GWO is better in terms of optimality, time consumption, and convergence speed. This was determined via the verification of the benchmark functions. Through the effective implementation of feature selection in the UCI datasets, it is able to gain minimal classification errors with a limited number of features.

The authors (Abad et al., 2022) created a unique machine learning technique within the scope of this research with the purpose of predicting the gas flow rate (Qg) based on six input factors. The evaluation that was carried out on the prediction performance and accuracy of the four HML models that were developed reveals that the MELM-PSO model has the highest Qg prediction accuracy. It achieved a root mean squared error (RMSE) of 2.8639 Mscf/d and a coefficient of determination (R2) of 0.9778 for a dataset consisting of 1009 data records that were compiled from gas-condensate fields located all over Iran.

A novel machine learning approach has been developed in (Behesht Abad, 2021) to forecast the viscosity of condensate in the vicinity of the wellbore regions (μc). This approach takes into account five input variables, namely pressure (P), temperature (T), initial gas to condensate ratio (RS), gas specific gravity (γg), and condensate gravity (API). These algorithms include the innovative multiple extreme learning machine (MELM), the least squares support vector machine (LSSVM), and the multi-layer perceptron (MLP). Additionally, each of these methods is hybridized with a particle swarm optimizer (PSO) and a genetic algorithm (GA). There are a number of benefits associated with the newly developed MELM method, which include the following: 1) quick execution; 2) high accuracy; 3) easy training; 4) avoidance of overfitting; 5) non-linear conversion during training; 6) no trapping at local optima; and 6) in comparison to SVM and LSSVM, fewer optimization steps are required.

Authors (Deb et al., 2019) examined the NIO algorithms that were used in order to find a solution to the issue of charging station location. As a result of this effort, the research community can be provided with a comprehensive assessment of NIO algorithms for the purpose of addressing the issue of charging station placement. This review has highlighted the most important characteristics, benefits, and downsides of each of these algorithms. As a result, this study will be of assistance to the researchers in choosing an appropriate algorithm for addressing the issue of charging station placement, and it will also serve as a reference for the development of effective algorithms to solve the problem of charging station placement.

Authors (Rajabi et al., 2021) created to predict FVDC from a well-log consisting of twelve input variables based on feature selection. They made use of a unique MELM-PSO/GA combination that has never been used previously, and the best comparison result available between MELM-PSO-related models and performance test data is RMSE = 0.0047 1/m; R2 = 0.9931. Upon doing an investigation of performance accuracy, it has been determined that the models are MLP-PSO, MLP-GA, MELM-GA, and MELM-PSO. Recalibrating this approach using at least one well is required in order to utilize it in other fields, although it may be used in those fields. In addition, the approach that was created offers insights for the use of machine learning to minimize mistakes and prevent data overfitting in order to provide the most accurate prediction performance that is achievable for FVDC prediction.

In the research (Shukla et al., 2021), decision tree and random forest algorithms are used in order to construct a predictive model of a negative hydrogen helicon plasma source. Therefore, in order to accomplish this goal, a dataset consisting of 162 samples has been used for the purposes of training, testing, and validating the suggested models. A comparative examination of the suggested models has been carried out by comparing the root mean square error and the coefficient of determination (R2) between the values of plasma density that were measured and those that were predicted. Additionally, the random forests method was able to analyse and analyze the intricate non-linear correlations that exist between the important input factors and the output.

In (Firat, 2023), Mehmet Firat and collaborators discussed the technologies based on artificial intelligence that have the ability to significantly improve the structure of learning management systems as well as the processes involved in online learning experiences. In particular, the public release of OpenAI's GPT-3 model in December 2022 has provided society with the opportunity to have a deeper understanding of the present state of artificial intelligence. This research offers illustrative examples of practical applications in addition to practical integration stages. Lastly, GPT-3 plugins for Moodle are investigated, and an example JavaScript code is provided for the purpose of incorporating Chat GPT into Moodle implementation. This article contributes to the existing body of literature by providing a helpful roadmap for incorporating artificial intelligence technologies into learning management systems.

(Bearman et al., 2022) proposed an organizing framework that articulates the complex link that exists between the digital and assessment design respectively. There are the three primary reasons that are described in the framework for designing the digital into assessment. It provides suggestions for the design of assessment and feedback within each of the purposes being addressed. In order to guarantee that higher education will be relevant for the digital futures of graduates, the framework aims to tie assessment and feedback design to the digital world. This will ensure that assessment and feedback design will be relevant.

3. PROBLEM STATEMENT

While Evolutionary Computation (EC) in Artificial Intelligence offers a powerful approach inspired by nature's strategies, it is not without its challenges and issues. One significant concern is the computational intensity of many EC algorithms. Evolutionary processes involve the generation and evaluation of multiple solutions within a population over numerous generations, demanding substantial computational resources. This poses challenges, particularly when dealing with complex problems or when attempting to scale up solutions for real-world applications. Another issue lies in the parameter tuning of EC algorithms. Selecting appropriate parameters, such as mutation rates and population sizes, can significantly impact the algorithm's performance, and finding optimal settings is often a non-trivial task. Furthermore, the interpretability of evolved solutions can be challenging, particularly in genetic programming, where evolved solutions may take complex forms that are difficult to understand or explain. Ethical concerns may also arise in specific applications, such as evolving strategies in autonomous systems, where ensuring responsible and ethical behavior becomes paramount (Singh et al., 2024; Anand et al., 2022). Addressing these challenges is crucial for the successful integration of Evolutionary Computation into the broader field of Artificial Intelligence, ensuring its effectiveness and ethical use in developing smart systems.

4. ROLE OF PSO ADAPTING NATURE'S STRATEGIES FOR SMART SYSTEMS

Particle Swarm Optimization (PSO) is a nature-inspired optimization algorithm that draws its inspiration from the social behavior of birds and fish. By mimicking the collaborative and adaptive nature observed in these biological systems, PSO has found applications in various fields, playing a significant role in adapting nature's strategies for smart systems (Singh et al., 2024).

1. *Optimization and Search*: PSO is particularly effective in solving optimization problems where the goal is to find the optimal solution in a complex search space. This mirrors the way flocks of birds or schools of fish collectively explore and adapt to their environments. In smart systems, PSO can be employed to optimize parameters and configurations, improving the performance and efficiency of various processes (Singh et al., 2024).
2. *Adaptability and Flexibility*: The adaptive nature of PSO, where particles dynamically adjust their positions based on the collective information, aligns with the adaptability observed in natural systems. This adaptability is crucial in smart systems, allowing them to respond and adjust to changing conditions or requirements. It can be applied in areas such as dynamic resource allocation, where the system needs to adapt to varying workloads.
3. *Collaborative Problem Solving*: PSO's collaborative approach, where particles communicate and share information to collectively find better solutions, reflects the collaborative problem-solving abilities seen in nature. In smart systems, this collaborative aspect can be utilized in distributed computing, multi-agent systems, or decentralized decision-making processes.
4. *Swarm Intelligence in Robotics*: PSO principles have been applied to swarm robotics, where groups of autonomous robots emulate the collective behavior of swarms in nature. These robot swarms can efficiently explore and adapt to complex environments, demonstrating decentralized decision-making and coordination inspired by the PSO algorithm [Anand et al., 2023].
5. *Dynamic System Control:* PSO's ability to adapt and optimize in real-time is valuable in the control of dynamic systems. It can be used to adjust control parameters dynamically, ensuring optimal performance in response to changes or disturbances, similar to how biological systems maintain homeostasis.
6. *Parameter Tuning in Machine Learning:* In machine learning, PSO is employed for hyperparameter tuning. By optimizing the parameters of machine learning algorithms, PSO helps create models that are better suited for the specific task at hand, drawing inspiration from the adaptive learning processes in biological systems.

7. *Network Routing and Optimization*: The collaborative and adaptive nature of PSO is beneficial in optimizing network routing and resource allocation. In smart systems, this can lead to more efficient communication networks, where nodes dynamically adapt their configurations to optimize data transmission [Anand et al., 2023].

PSO plays a crucial role in adapting nature's strategies for smart systems by providing optimization capabilities, adaptability, and collaborative problem-solving techniques. Its application spans various domains, contributing to the development of intelligent and self-adaptive systems that draw inspiration from the collective behaviors observed in natural swarms and societies.

5. PROCESS FLOW

Building a Particle Swarm Optimization (PSO) algorithm involves several steps. PSO is inspired by the collective behavior of birds and fish in nature, and it is used for optimization problems. Here's a generalized process flow for building a PSO algorithm (Zhang et al., 2023):

1. Problem Definition: Clearly define the optimization problem you want to solve. Identify the objective function to be optimized and the constraints, if any.
2. Initialization: Initialize a swarm of particles randomly within the search space. Each particle represents a potential solution to the optimization problem.
3. Particle Representation: Define the representation of each particle in the swarm. Typically, a particle is represented as a vector of parameters that corresponds to a potential solution.
4. Velocity Initialization: Assign random initial velocities to each particle. Velocities determine how far and in what direction a particle moves in the search space .
5. Evaluate Fitness: Evaluate the fitness of each particle by applying the objective function to the particle's current position. The fitness value indicates how well the particle's position performs in solving the optimization problem.
6. Update Personal Best: For each particle, update its personal best position if the current fitness is better than its previous best fitness. This information is crucial for each particle to remember its own best-performing solution.
7. Update Global Best: Identify the particle with the best fitness among the entire swarm. Update the global best position based on this particle's position. The global best represents the overall best solution found by any particle in the swarm.
8. Update Velocities and Positions
9. Convergence Check: Check if the algorithm has converted to a satisfactory solution or if a specified number of iterations have been reached.
10. Solution Extraction: Extract the final optimized solution from the global best position found by the algorithm.
11. Result Analysis: Analyze the obtained solution, including its fitness value and any other relevant metrics. This step is crucial for assessing the effectiveness of the PSO algorithm in solving the optimization problem.

6. RESULT AND DISCUSSION

The convergence check is a pivotal step to assess if the algorithm has reached a satisfactory solution or if a predetermined number of iterations have been completed. If the convergence criteria are met, the algorithm terminates; otherwise, the process returns to fitness evaluation, initiating iteration. Upon convergence, the algorithm extracts the final optimized solution from the global best position (Kumari et al., 2023). This solution, with its associated fitness value, is then subjected to result analysis. This step involves evaluating the efficacy of the PSO algorithm in solving the optimization problem and may include fine-tuning of parameters for enhanced performance. Process flow of building a PSO algorithm involves problem definition, swarm initialization, fitness evaluation, personal and global best updates, iterative velocity and position updates, convergence checks, solution extraction, result analysis, and optional parameter tuning [Bansal et al., 2021; Dushyant et al., 2021; Gupta et al., 2021; Pedersen & Chipperfield, 2010). This bio-inspired approach adapts nature's strategies, creating smart systems capable of efficient and collaborative optimization.

6.1 Comparison of Training Accuracy

Adapting nature's strategies for smart systems often involves the use of optimization algorithms, and Particle Swarm Optimization (PSO) is one such algorithm. However, when discussing "training accuracy" in the context of machine learning, it typically refers to the evaluation of models, which may use different optimization algorithms like gradient descent or variants of it. PSO, on the other hand, is primarily used for optimization problems rather than training machine learning models. Result of training i.e. accuracy has been shown in table 1 and Figure 2.

Figure 2. Comparison of training accuracy

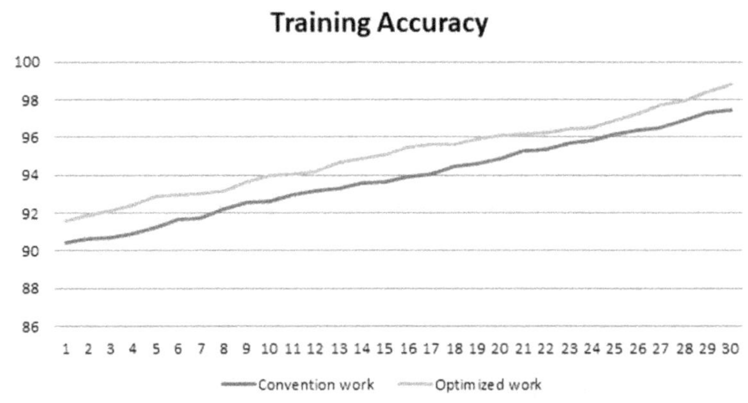

Considering above simulation it is observed that overall reliability of proposed work is better than conventional work. The pie charts shown in Figure 3 are presenting accuracy along with error rate in case of conventional and proposed work.

Table 1. Training accuracy

Epoch	Conventional Work	Optimized Work
1	90.43919	91.57187
2	90.62722	91.83812
3	90.72342	92.15005
4	90.9159	92.39029
5	91.27403	92.86678
6	91.65048	92.92493
7	91.70226	93.00572
8	92.17062	93.17344
9	92.56338	93.61946
10	92.59149	93.9977
11	92.98086	94.04594
12	93.1899	94.18379
13	93.2737	94.65431
14	93.54443	94.84293
15	93.63125	95.05341
16	93.90604	95.44775
17	94.03454	95.58576
18	94.47593	95.6269
19	94.60233	95.88554
20	94.85411	96.08945
21	95.27766	96.18169
22	95.32957	96.24835
23	95.70724	96.44906
24	95.78102	96.50134
25	96.1331	96.87402
26	96.34522	97.21922
27	96.50933	97.68989
28	96.91768	97.96189
29	97.31684	98.42827
30	97.43372	98.80901

Table 2. Comparison of testing of accuracy

Epoch	Conventional Work	Optimized Work
1	90.08112	91.03137
2	90.3749	91.37684
3	90.50302	91.78294
4	90.61676	91.97954
5	90.81018	92.19772
6	90.84865	92.25417
7	91.26622	92.40582
8	91.74771	92.54854
9	91.80039	92.9597
10	92.26096	93.34296
11	92.26257	93.38468
12	92.63128	93.47256
13	93.07429	93.6189
14	93.40158	93.71538
15	93.77424	93.90881
16	93.83366	94.34106
17	94.07476	94.67942
18	94.26281	95.0155
19	94.40956	95.38642
20	94.85393	95.74055
21	94.92442	95.76289
22	94.93309	95.76379
23	95.39445	96.00516
24	95.69452	96.45212
25	96.03473	96.92395
26	96.03628	97.3695
27	96.1012	97.47546
28	96.40986	97.73213
29	96.57602	98.16756
30	96.69669	98.24203

6.2 Comparison of Testing Accuracy

Testing accuracy typically refers to evaluating the performance of a machine learning model on a test dataset. In Python, you can use popular machine learning libraries such as scikit-learn to assess the accuracy of your model. The testing accuracy has been shown in Table 2 and Figure 4.

Figure 3. Comparison reliability of conventional and proposed model

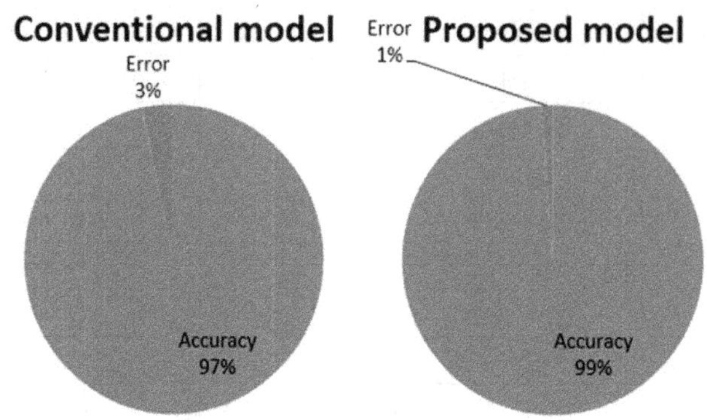

Figure 4. Comparison of testing of accuracy

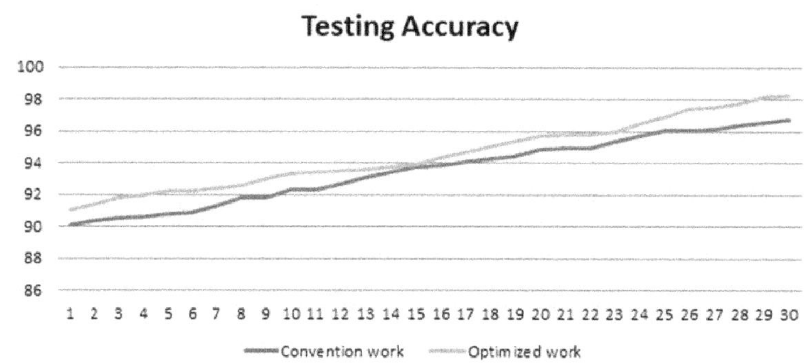

6.3 Comparison of Time Consumption

Table 3 and Figure 5 show the comparison of time consumption in conventional work and optimized work.

Figure 5. Comparison of time consumption

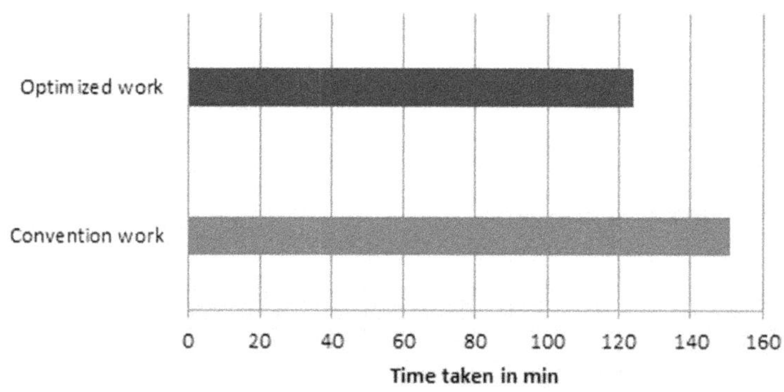

Table 3. Comparison of time consumption

Conventional work in min	Optimized work in min
151	124

7. CONCLUSION

It is concluded that optimized work is providing better accuracy in case of training and testing. Moreover performance of optimized work is found better than previous. The algorithm then proceeds to the initialization phase, introducing a swarm of particles randomly into the search space, with each particle representing a potential solution to the optimization problem. These particles, akin to organisms in nature, are endowed with positions and velocities, creating a dynamic system that mimics the adaptive behavior observed in biological entities. Simultaneously, a global best position is identified by selecting the particle with the best fitness across the entire swarm. The heart of the algorithm lies in the iterative process of updating velocities and positions. This process guides particles through the search space, dynamically adapting their trajectories based on personal and global best positions. This collective movement, reminiscent of swarming behaviors in nature, facilitates the convergence of the algorithm towards optimal solutions (Cleghorn & Engelbrecht, 2015; Gupta et al., 2020; Anand & Chawla, 2022). Convergence checks are crucial to determine whether the algorithm has reached a satisfactory solution or if a specified number of iterations has been completed. If convergence criteria are met, the algorithm concludes, extracting the final optimized solution from the global best position. The last phases involve result analysis, where the obtained solution is evaluated, and potential adjustments or fine-tuning of parameters are made for improved performance. This systematic process flow, inspired by the collaborative and adaptive strategies observed in nature, allows the PSO algorithm to effectively optimize solutions for complex problems encountered in the realm of smart systems (Veeraiah et al., 2022).

8. FUTURE SCOPE

The future scope of Evolutionary Computation (EC) in Artificial Intelligence appears promising, as the synergy between nature's strategies and smart systems continues to evolve. As computational power increases and novel algorithmic advancements emerge, EC is poised to address increasingly complex problems across diverse domains. The adaptability of EC makes it a key player in the development of autonomous systems capable of learning, evolving, and optimizing their performance over time. Hybrid approaches, integrating EC with other AI techniques, are likely to become more prevalent, enhancing the robustness and problem-solving capabilities of intelligent systems. Moreover, EC's application in real-world scenarios, such as healthcare, finance, and climate modeling, is expected to expand, providing innovative solutions to multifaceted challenges (Meena et al., 2023). The convergence of EC with cutting-edge technologies like quantum computing holds the potential to further amplify its impact, enabling more efficient and rapid exploration of solution spaces. As ethical considerations gain prominence in AI development, EC's nature-inspired approach aligns well with sustainability and responsible innovation, positioning it as a valuable contributor to the future landscape of smart, adaptive, and ethically sound artificial intelligence systems (Li et al., 2024).

REFERENCES

Abad, A. R. B., Ghorbani, H., Mohamadian, N., Davoodi, S., Mehrad, M., Aghdam, S. K. Y., & Nasriani, H. R. (2022). Robust hybrid machine learning algorithms for gas flow rates prediction through wellhead chokes in gas condensate fields. *Fuel*, *308*, 121872. doi:10.1016/j.fuel.2021.121872

Abad, A. R. B., Mousavi, S., Mohamadian, N., Wood, D. A., Ghorbani, H., Davoodi, S., ... Shahbazi, K. (2021). Hybrid machine learning algorithms to predict condensate viscosity in the near wellbore regions of gas condensate reservoirs. *Journal of Natural Gas Science and Engineering*, *95*, 104210. doi:10.1016/j.jngse.2021.104210

Anand, R., Arora, S., & Sindhwani, N. (2022, January). A miniaturized UWB antenna for high speed applications. In *2022 International Conference on Computing, Communication and Power Technology (IC3P)* (pp. 264-267). IEEE. 10.1109/IC3P52835.2022.00063

Anand, R., & Chawla, P. (2016, March). A review on the optimization techniques for bio-inspired antenna design. In *2016 3rd International conference on computing for sustainable global development (INDIACom)* (pp. 2228-2233). IEEE.

Anand, R., & Chawla, P. (2020). Optimization of inscribed hexagonal fractal slotted microstrip antenna using modified lightning attachment procedure optimization. *International Journal of Microwave and Wireless Technologies*, *12*(6), 519–530. doi:10.1017/S1759078720000148

Anand, R., & Chawla, P. (2022). Bandwidth optimization of a novel slotted fractal antenna using modified lightning attachment procedure optimization. In *Smart Antennas: Latest Trends in Design and Application* (pp. 379–392). Springer International Publishing. doi:10.1007/978-3-030-76636-8_28

Anand, R., Jain, V., Singh, A., Rahal, D., Rastogi, P., Rajkumar, A., & Gupta, A. Clustering of Big Data in Cloud Environments for Smart Applications. In *Integration of IoT with Cloud Computing for Smart Applications* (pp. 227–247). Chapman and Hall/CRC. doi:10.1201/9781003319238-14

Bakhshipour, M., Ghadi, M. J., & Namdari, F. (2017). Swarm robotics search & rescue: A novel artificial intelligence-inspired optimization approach. *Applied Soft Computing*, *57*, 708–726. doi:10.1016/j.asoc.2017.02.028

Bansal, R., Gupta, A., Singh, R., & Nassa, V. K. (2021, July). Role and impact of digital technologies in E-learning amidst COVID-19 pandemic. In *2021 Fourth International Conference on Computational Intelligence and Communication Technologies (CCICT)* (pp. 194-202). IEEE. 10.1109/CCICT53244.2021.00046

Bearman, M., Nieminen, J. H., & Ajjawi, R. (2023). Designing assessment in a digital world: An organising framework. *Assessment & Evaluation in Higher Education*, *48*(3), 291–304. doi:10.1080/02602938.2022.2069674

Cleghorn, C. W., & Engelbrecht, A. P. (2015). Particle swarm variants: Standardized convergence analysis. *Swarm Intelligence*, *9*(2-3), 177–203. doi:10.1007/s11721-015-0109-7

Deb, S., Gao, X. Z., Tammi, K., Kalita, K., & Mahanta, P. (2021). Nature-inspired optimization algorithms applied for solving charging station placement problem: Overview and comparison. *Archives of Computational Methods in Engineering*, *28*(1), 91–106. doi:10.1007/s11831-019-09374-4

Dushyant, K., Muskan, G., Gupta, A., & Pramanik, S. (2022). Utilizing Machine Learning and Deep Learning in Cybesecurity: An Innovative Approach. *Cyber Security and Digital Forensics*, 271-293.

Firat, M. (2023). Integrating AI applications into learning management systems to enhance e-learning. *Instructional Technology and Lifelong Learning*, *4*(1), 1–14.

Geng, H., Xu, K., Zhang, Y., & Zhou, Z. (2023). A classification tree and decomposition based multi-objective evolutionary algorithm with adaptive operator selection. *Complex & Intelligent Systems*, *9*(1), 579–596. doi:10.1007/s40747-022-00812-8

George, B., & Wooden, O. (2023). Managing the strategic transformation of higher education through artificial intelligence. *Administrative Sciences*, *13*(9), 196. doi:10.3390/admsci13090196

Gupta, A., Kaushik, D., Garg, M., & Verma, A. (2020, October). Machine learning model for breast cancer prediction. In *2020 fourth international conference on I-SMAC (IoT in social, mobile, analytics and cloud)(I-SMAC)* (pp. 472-477). IEEE. 10.1109/I-SMAC49090.2020.9243323

Gupta, A., Singh, R., Nassa, V. K., Bansal, R., Sharma, P., & Koti, K. (2021, October). Investigating application and challenges of big data analytics with clustering. In *2021 international conference on advancements in electrical, electronics, communication, computing and automation (ICAECA)* (pp. 1-6). IEEE.

Hu, P., Pan, J. S., & Chu, S. C. (2020). Improved binary grey wolf optimizer and its application for feature selection. *Knowledge-Based Systems*, *195*, 105746. doi:10.1016/j.knosys.2020.105746

Kala, R. (2023). Mission planning on preference-based expression trees using heuristics-assisted evolutionary computation. *Applied Soft Computing*, *136*, 110090. doi:10.1016/j.asoc.2023.110090

Kumari, S., Awasthi, Y. K., Bansal, D., & Anand, R. (2023). The Design Mechanisms of Multiband Antennas from 1G to 5G: A Comprehensive Review. *Digital Transformation–Modernization and Optimization of Wireless Networks*, 77.

Li, F., Yue, Q., Liu, Y., Ouyang, H., & Gu, F. (2024). A fast density peak clustering based particle swarm optimizer for dynamic optimization. *Expert Systems with Applications*, *236*, 121254. doi:10.1016/j.eswa.2023.121254

Meena, R. S., Talukdar, R., Kannadasan, B., Nageswara Rao, G., Shukla, K. A., Anand, R., & Gupta, A. (2023). PID Control and Estimation of the Attitude Model Applied to Geostationary Satellites. In *Advances in Signal Processing, Embedded Systems and IoT: Proceedings of Seventh ICMEET-2022* (pp. 631-642). Singapore: Springer Nature Singapore. 10.1007/978-981-19-8865-3_56

Pedersen, M. E. H., & Chipperfield, A. J. (2010). Simplifying particle swarm optimization. *Applied Soft Computing*, *10*(2), 618–628. doi:10.1016/j.asoc.2009.08.029

Raghavan, R., Verma, D. C., Pandey, D., Anand, R., Pandey, B. K., & Singh, H. (2022). Optimized building extraction from high-resolution satellite imagery using deep learning. *Multimedia Tools and Applications*, *81*(29), 42309–42323. doi:10.1007/s11042-022-13493-9

Rajabi, M., Beheshtian, S., Davoodi, S., Ghorbani, H., Mohamadian, N., Radwan, A. E., & Alvar, M. A. (2021). Novel hybrid machine learning optimizer algorithms to prediction of fracture density by petrophysical data. *Journal of Petroleum Exploration and Production Technology*, *11*(12), 4375–4397. doi:10.1007/s13202-021-01321-z

Shukla, V., & Bandyopadhyay, M. (2023). Optimization of input parameters of ANN–driven plasma source through nature-inspired evolutionary algorithms. *Intelligent Systems with Applications*, *18*, 200200. doi:10.1016/j.iswa.2023.200200

Shukla, V., Pandya, V., Bandyopadhyay, M., & Pandey, A. (2021). Plasma Density Prediction for Helicon Negative Hydrogen Plasma Source using Decision Tree and Random Forest Algorithm. In *Congress on Intelligent Systems: Proceedings of CIS 2020,* Volume 2 (pp. 357-368). Springer Singapore. 10.1007/978-981-33-6984-9_29

Sindhwani, N., Anand, R., George, A. S., & Pandey, D. (Eds.). (2024). *Robotics and Automation in Industry 4.0: Smart Industries and Intelligent Technologies*. CRC Press.

Sindhwani, N., Anand, R., Nageswara Rao, G., Chauhan, S., Chaudhary, A., Gupta, A., & Pandey, D. (2023). Comparative Analysis of Optimization Algorithms for Antenna Selection in MIMO Systems. In *Advances in Signal Processing, Embedded Systems and IoT: Proceedings of Seventh ICMEET-2022* (pp. 607-617). Singapore: Springer Nature Singapore. 10.1007/978-981-19-8865-3_54

Singh, H., Veeraiah, V., Khan, H., Singh, D. K., Talukdar, V., Anand, R., & Sindhwani, N. (2024). Investigating Scope and Applications for the Internet of Robotics in Industrial Automation. In Robotics and Automation in Industry 4.0 (pp. 132-151). CRC Press.

Singh, S. K., Thakur, R. K., Kumar, S., & Anand, R. (2022, March). Deep learning and machine learning based facial emotion detection using CNN. In *2022 9th International Conference on Computing for Sustainable Global Development (INDIACom)* (pp. 530-535). IEEE. 10.23919/INDIACom54597.2022.9763165

Veeraiah, V., Khan, H., Kumar, A., Ahamad, S., Mahajan, A., & Gupta, A. (2022, April). Integration of PSO and deep learning for trend analysis of meta-verse. In *2022 2nd International Conference on Advance Computing and Innovative Technologies in Engineering (ICACITE)* (pp. 713-718). IEEE. 10.1109/ICACITE53722.2022.9823883

Xue, Y., Zhu, H., Liang, J., & Słowik, A. (2021). Adaptive crossover operator based multi-objective binary genetic algorithm for feature selection in classification. *Knowledge-Based Systems*, *227*, 107218. doi:10.1016/j.knosys.2021.107218

Zhang, E., Nie, Z., Yang, Q., Wang, Y., Liu, D., Jeon, S. W., & Zhang, J. (2023). Heterogeneous cognitive learning particle swarm optimization for large-scale optimization problems. *Information Sciences*, *633*, 321–342. doi:10.1016/j.ins.2023.03.086

Chapter 11
Comprehensive Study on Routing in FANET

Mylsamy R.
Sri Ramakrishna Mission Vidyalaya College of Arts and Science, India

Jaikumar M.
Sri Ramakrishna Mission Vidyalaya College of Arts and Science, India

ABSTRACT

The rapid proliferation of networking and wireless communication technologies has led to the development of low-cost unmanned aerial vehicles, which will soon occupy a significant amount of the sky. UAVs may be effectively used to complete complicated missions when arranged as an ad hoc network, leading to the creation of well-known flying ad hoc networks. Without the implementation of an efficient networking model that enables the dependable transfer of data between UAVs, the creation of such networks is not feasible. The diverse flying limits and highly dynamic topology of FANETs make designing routing protocols a very difficult task. An extensive investigation of routing in FANETs is provided in this work. A wide range of current FANET routing protocols are compared and clarified. This work is unique because it can give a thorough analysis of the main FANET routing protocols and assess them based on many restrictions and important characteristics, better representing the state of the art in this field of study at the moment.

1. INTRODUCTION

Unmanned Aerial Vehicles, also known as UAVs, have quickly become highly adaptable instruments for various uses, including border surveillance, ad hoc network relay, wind estimation, wildfire management, disaster monitoring and response, environmental monitoring, traffic monitoring, and security (Hadi et al., 2023). Robust routing protocols are critical to the effectiveness of UAV networks, often referred to as Flying Ad-hoc Networks (FANET), since they provide smooth drone coordination and communication (Wang et al., 2017).

DOI: 10.4018/979-8-3693-2073-0.ch011

FANET, is an innovative technology that addresses the communication and coordination needs of UAVs. Designed for the dynamic and complex environments drones operate in, FANET establishes an autonomous network where UAVs can exchange critical information. The essence of FANET lies in its ability to create a seamless data flow between individual drones. This enables them to collaborate effectively and share real-time data about their positions, trajectories, and operational statuses (Chriki et al., 2019).

The applications of FANET span various sectors. In agriculture, drones can work together to cover larger areas and monitor crops more effectively. Coordinated drones can provide broader coverage and quick data relay during search and rescue missions. In entertainment, synchronized drone performances become possible, creating captivating light shows in the sky. As FANET technology evolves, its potential grows. Swarms of drones operating in a well-orchestrated manner can revolutionize industries such as logistics, surveillance, and environmental monitoring (Pasandideh et al., 2022)(Sahingoz, 2013).

Aircraft without a pilot are known as unmanned aerial vehicles, or UAVs. Drones, also known as remotely piloted aircraft (RPAs), are operated remotely by a pilot, automatically by a ground control station (GCS), or remotely by a satellite. UAVs have been employed in military operations for more than 20 years. For example, they are used in border monitoring, reconnaissance, and airstrikes. The two primary categories of UAVs are fixed-wing and rotary-wing models. Fixed-wing UAVs have a large cargo capacity and travel swiftly. They must also keep going forward constantly to remain in motion. Figure 1 shows an example of a fixed-wing UAV. On the other side, rotary-wing UAVs are less powerful and operate more slowly. They can go in any direction and remain steady in the air. Figure 2 shows an illustration of a rotary-wing UAV.

UAV categorization is displayed in Diagram 1. There are two sizes of UAVs: large and small. The military can benefit from the employment of large UAVs. Small UAVs are more suited for civilian uses because of their simpler design, easier operation, and reduced repair and maintenance costs when compared to larger UAVs. Comparably, while tiny UAVs are usually outfitted with a variety of microelectromechanical systems, including inexpensive aircraft bodies, compact radio devices, small batteries, and microprocessors, their capabilities are equally more constrained than those of big UAVs. Their payload and weight are likewise restricted. Multi-UAV systems provide several advantages over single-UAV systems, but they also present certain difficulties, such as communication. A UAV system's communication medium might be either a satellite or a ground station.

Figure 1. Fixed wing UAV

Figure 2. Rotary wing UAV

Figure 3. Classification of UAVs

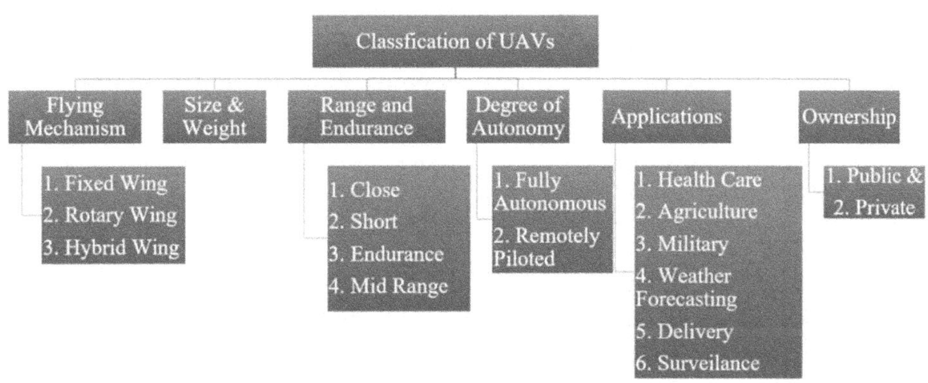

2. FANET: "FLYING AD-HOC NETWORK"

FANET is a novel concept that has the potential to fundamentally alter how we think about connectivity and communication in the air. By enabling drones and other UAVs to connect to a ground control system or satellite, and requiring at least one of them to be linked, they may form a network and interact with one another. Although FANET is distinct from the current Ad-Hoc networks, it may be viewed as a subset of either VANET or MANET. However, there are some differences between them in terms of design concerns. The FANET features are covered here (Pasandideh et al., 2022), but the UAV network has its special qualities as well.

2.1. Fanet Characteristics

As listed below in Diagram 2 (Sahingoz, 2013), Node density, node mobility, flexibility, agility, cost-effectiveness, communication range, radio propagation model, localization, power consumption, frequency band, and network durability are among the primary features of FANETs.

Figure 4. Diagram 2

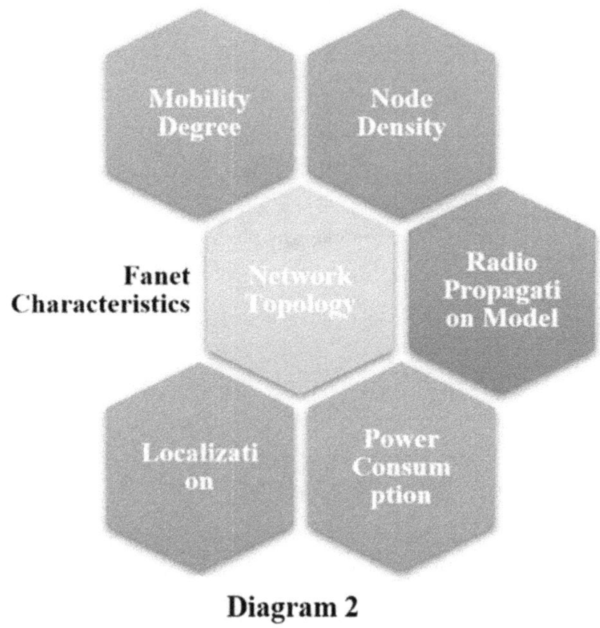

- Compared to MANET or VANET nodes, FANET nodes have substantially more mobility. Unlike regular MANET and VANET nodes, which are walking people and cars, FANET nodes are in the air. UAVs may relocate in a much shorter time, which might lead to communication problems between UAVs.
- Nodes in FANET networks have to be dispersed throughout the sky at great distances from one another due to the nature of flight. FANET, in comparison to MANET and VANET, has a significantly lower node density as a result.
- MANET uses no radio transmission to communicate between nodes. Nonetheless, the GCS and UAVs in FANETs link via a LoS (Line-of-Sight) connection. In FANET, the network architecture frequently shifts due to the increased mobility of UAVs.
- The existing ad hoc networks are looking for peer-to-peer connections. Peer-to-peer connectivity is also required for FANET to facilitate UAV coordination and cooperation. Like wireless sensor networks, it often collects environmental data and transmits it to the Ground Control System. FANET must thus enable both convergent cast and peer-to-peer traffic.
- Due to their high degree of movement, FANET UAVs are challenging to precisely place. Regular updates should be made to the localization data.
- FANET's communication circuitry runs on the UAV's internal energy supply. FANET networks that employ big UAVs are not power-sensitive like MANET networks are. Conversely, mini-UAVs have relatively little power capacity.

2.2. Scenarios of FANETs Application

According to the various objectives of the FANET, the applications may be divided into three main categories (Bujari et al., 2017).

2.2.1. Environmental Forecasting / Sensing

Acting as sensors, the UAVs gather environmental data in a certain area. Apps in this case could need many sensor readings to assess particular environmental factors. Within or close to the phenomenon being observed, a sensor network installs sensors. It is possible to measure physical characteristics such as pressure, temperature, humidity, light intensity, and pollution level using a sensor network.

2.2.2. Surveillance / Monitoring

This category includes applications that employ UAVs as flying cameras. To analyze and record important data, the duties usually comprise obtaining real-time images, videos, or sounds from aerial equipment. Agriculture management is an additional application environment.

2.2.3. Networks for Relaying

In locations that require a particular type of communication, FANETs can offer a link. UAVs operating autonomously are being utilized as aerial communication relays to enhance the communication range of the relaying ground nodes and securely and effectively transport data acquired by ground sensors to distant control centers.

2.3. Mobility Models

Five mobility models of FANETs can be distinguished as follows (Bujari et al., 2017).

2.3.1. Randomized Mobility Models

For network analysis, randomized mobility models are simple models. They show a collection of mobile nodes acting independently of one another and past activities. These include Random Walk (RW), Random Direction (RD), and Random Way-Point (RWP). In these mobility models, every node randomly selects a direction (or way-point) and a speed to go in for a certain period. Manhattan Grid (MG) is another randomized mobility paradigm that restricts node movement on a metropolitan map to either horizontal or vertical directions using a grid road construction.

2.3.2. Mobility Models Dependent on Time and Space

The goal of this kind of mobility model is to prevent sudden changes in direction and speed. To produce smooth motion changes, one can apply several mathematical formulae. Two instances that update the new values at each step are Boundless Simulation Area (BSA) and Gauss-Markov (GM), which leverage the relationship between the prior direction and speed and the current ones. Mobile nodes can follow curved pathways with the aid of the Smooth Turn (ST) mobility model. Once it has selected a location in space, the UAV orbits that region until it finds another turning point.

2.3.3. Models of Path-Planned Mobility

A pre-formed travel plan is provided by these mobility models. After a pattern concludes, UAVs randomly switch to a new pattern or resume their previous one. The Semi-Random Circular Movement (SRCM) UAV mobility model may be used to describe UAVs revolving around a certain point in space. It is intended to replicate curved movement scenarios. The paparazzi mobility model (PPRZM), which is built on a state machine with six movement pattern states stay-at, eight, oval, scan, and waypoint is one instance of a stochastic mobility model. Every UAV selects one of these patterns and a random speed.

2.3.4. Models of Group Mobility

All mobile nodes in these models are subject to a geographical limitation. The Reference Point Group Mobility (RPGM) model models the random movement of mobile nodes around a moving reference point in the region using a simple RWP model. Special instances of RPGM include the following: While mobile nodes in Nomadic Community (NC) travel randomly around a given place, those in Pursue (PRS) attempt to follow a defined goal rather than moving randomly around it. All mobile nodes in Column (CLMN) orbit around a reference point on a forward-moving line.

2.3.5. Mobility Models Based on Topology-Control

When certain network or mission requirements must be consistently met, the mobility model necessitates real-time management of mobile node topology. One well-known example for reconnaissance and search operations is the mobility paradigm known as Distributed Pheromone Repel, or DPR. Every mobile node in this design maintains a unique pheromone map. Under catastrophic conditions, the mobility paradigm of Self-Deploy Point Coverage is introduced. A group of UAVs is sent to a disaster site to set up a communications system for the victims. The objective of any UAV is to cover as many ground personnel as it can while maintaining communication with other UAVs (Kashyap & Agrawal, 2018).

3. ROUTING AND COMMUNICATION PROTOCOLS FOR FANETs

A FANET is a wireless network that can communicate wirelessly between flying nodes, such UAVs, without requiring a permanent network infrastructure. It is inexpensive, flexible, and easy to set up. FANET is one of the more recent networks with a broad range of applications for the upcoming network generation. Thus, FANET makes a substantial contribution to the achievement of application-based goals. By employing routing to give pathways to radio access infrastructure, especially FANET base stations, flying nodes may cooperate and function together.

Transmission of packets between UAV nodes requires routing protocols, but creating one is not easy. Among them is the highly dynamic topology of UAV networks, indicating that frequent communication breakdowns between UAVs can occur. The short range between the UAVs and the base station presents another difficulty. Creating a routing strategy that ensures dependable communication in UAV networks becomes challenging due to the high mobility, dynamic topology, and unequal placement of UAVs (Oubbati et al., 2017, 2019; Shumeye Lakew et al., 2020).

Researchers worked to create routing protocols that were appropriate for FANETs. They created new routing protocols or broadened the previously established MANET and VANET routing protocols (Bahloul et al., 2017) (Zheng et al., 2014)(Rosati et al., 2013).

This section provides a comprehensive overview of the various routing methods available in FANETs. Previous research has classified the routing protocols for the FANET or the Multi-UAV system under the following categories: Network Topology, Position, Hierarchical, and Bio-Inspired.

3.1. Network Topology Based Routing Protocols

All UAV-to-UAV communication occurs across the IP addresses of other UAVs or mobile nodes when using Network Topology-based Protocols (Khan et al., 2018). The four categories are: Hybrid, Proactive, Reactive, and Static.

3.1.1. Static Routing Protocols

Before a mission, a routing table is generated and loaded into UAV nodes using a static routing protocol. This type of routing table is static since it cannot be altered while the operation is in progress. The tables need to be updated after the operation in case of a failure (of the ground station or a UAV). They are therefore not ideal for dynamic settings and are not fault-tolerant.

LCAD: Load Carry and Deliver Routing

Under this route, a UAV or aircraft transports data from the ground base station to the target ground base station. This method offers a high throughput and is safe. The technology's main drawback is that transmission delays might be considerable over long distances. It could be possible to shorten the time it takes for data transfers by using a multi-UAV system (Cheng et al., 2007).

DCR: Data Centric Routing

The wireless communication architecture of UAVs may favor one-to-many data transfer over one-to-one data transmission. This routing technique functions properly when data is delivered using on-demand methods and requested by many nodes. One such routing paradigm that might be used for FANET is data-centric routing. Instead of using sender or receiver node IDs, data attributes are used in this architecture to request and collect data. This method is effective for distributed computing models and is frequently used to cluster architectures and the publish-subscribe concept (Ko et al., 2002).

MLHR: Multi-Level Hierarchical Routing

Numerous clusters in a hierarchical network may perform various functions. With MLHR, a building with a level base might be constructed. The network's working domain and size are increased by the use of the hierarchical structure. UAV networks can be organized into clusters, with the ground node and other cluster heads being the only points of contact for communication (CH) (Y. Zhou et al., 2015).

3.1.2. Proactive Routing Protocols

Table-driven or active routing protocols (PRPs) are other names for proactive routing protocols. Each UAV that uses this kind of routing protocol keeps and updates a routing table that depicts the whole network architecture. Consequently, the routing channels may be swiftly made available for the transfer of data packets as required. Having the most recent route information is one of the benefits of proactive routing methods. Nevertheless, because they maintain the network's information up to date, they do add greater signaling overhead. Throughput may be impacted as a result of the superfluous sending of control messages over the network. Proactive routing approaches are therefore inappropriate for large-scale and highly mobile networks. Moreover, PRPs respond slowly to connection failures and topological changes. A discussion of proactive routing protocols is provided in this section.

DSDV: Destination Sequence Distance Vector Routing

This routing system is based on the Bellman-Ford-Moore algorithm; however, it has undergone certain modifications to better meet FANET criteria. Every UAV in DSDV has to be aware of every other UAV connected to the network due to the information currently available for routing. This is because they are proactive in that they routinely update the routing table across the network. Routing loops, though, can result from these sporadic updates. The DSDV adds sequence numbers to data packets to solve this problem. In the event of a tie between two paths with different sequence numbers, the way with the highest number that was used most recently wins out.

Sequence numbering and simplicity are two of DSDV's main advantages as they guarantee data transfer between UAVs without loops. Frequent updates resulting in extra signaling costs during data transfer are the fundamental downside of this routing strategy. Networks with a large volume of traffic and frequent topology changes shouldn't use this protocol. Also, multipath routing is not permitted; only single-path routing is supported (Perkins & Bhagwat, 1994; Shumeye Lakew et al., 2020).

OLSR: Optimized Link State Routing

OLSR is the commonly used routing protocol for the FANET system, and it involves continuously saving, maintaining, and updating the routing table with the routing paths (Jacquet et al., 2001). Consequently, the protocol finds the path to all possible destination UAVs fast and without requiring a significant wait time, if a path is needed for data transfer. To facilitate communication across UAVs inside a network, OLSR employs a distinct packet comprising many messages. OLSR unique packets are capable of carrying three distinct types of communications, each serving a distinct function: The Topology Control (TC) message advertises to establish connection information; the Multiple Interface Declaration (MID) message completes the network and system declaration on a node; and the HELLO message is sent on a regular basis to monitor neighbor connectivity, connection sensing, and the MPR (Multipoint Relay) signal. The results show that the periodic flooding characteristic of OLSR causes considerable network overhead when it is deployed in various FANET settings (E. & Atef, 2017).

OLSR uses a Link State Routing approach in order to fully comprehend drone network traffic. Aircraft directional antennas are used in D-OLSR, an enhanced variant of OLSR, to increase data throughput. The ML-OLSR was developed to prevent fast-moving UAVs from being chosen as MPRs. An enhanced iteration of the OLSR protocol called CE-OLSR permits great mobility in incredibly intricate networks such as FANETs.

BATMAN: Better Approach to Mobile Ad hoc Network

A proactive routing system called BATMAN was developed lately and is specifically designed for ad hoc networks. BATMAN proactively maintains data on the existence of all communication nodes using both single-hop and multi-hop protocols. To communicate with the target node, it quickly locates the next hop neighbor. For each destination, the optimal next hop may be found using the BATMAN approach. BATMAN routing works incredibly quickly since it does not compute the whole path. When it comes to packet loss and data rate, BATMAN works well. As a result of its low data capacity, BATMAN packet sizes are extremely tiny.

To address the limitations of OLSR, performance comparison and a simple yet effective routing protocol dubbed BATMAN are presented. A tightly spaced 7 × 7 grid of nodes was used for the experiment. Performance analysis reveals that BATMAN outperforms OLSR in terms of routing overhead, latency, and throughput. The experimental result demonstrates that OLSR has to transmit topology update messages with the whole route topology as the network expands. Due to the lack of routing information in its routing packets, BATMAN doesn't grow very quickly (D. L. Johnson et al., 2008).

3.1.3. Reactive Routing Protocols

Due to its ability to discover and maintain network routes as needed, Reactive Routing Protocol (RRP) is an on-demand routing method. Every time data has to be transferred, the routing table is updated. Building a route between the two nodes is not necessary because they are not linked. As such, the overhead issue with the Proactive Routing Protocol is resolved because these routing protocols only keep the channels that are currently in use (Habib et al., 2013). Two different message types are produced by this routing model: (a) RouteRequest messages and (b) RouteReply messages. From the originating UAV, all neighboring UAVs get a RouteRequest message, and the flooding process is used to determine the best path. As an alternative, the sender and receiving UAVs use unicast communication to create and send a RouteReply message to each other. Using this routing technique, it is not necessary to update every routing table on the network.

RRP is bandwidth-efficient since it doesn't require frequent communications. However, because route-finding may take a long time to complete, there might be a significant delay. This section offers a brief introduction to reactive routing protocols. Time-Slotted Ad Hoc On-Demand Distance Vector - TS-AODV, Ad Hoc On-Demand Distance Vector - AODV, Multicast Ad hoc On-demand Distance Vector M-AODV, and Dynamic Source Routing - DSR are a few instances of reactive routing systems.

DSR: Dynamic Source Routing

A network may operate without any infrastructure by using "DSR", which allows it to self-configure and self-organize. Its dynamic structure makes it desirable and is mostly used for wireless sensor networks with several hops. In DSR, the source UAV only creates routing paths to the destination UAV when required. The mechanisms of (a) route discovery and (b) route maintenance essentially decide this. When a connection breaks, route maintenance is necessary, but route discovery is the process of finding a path at the source UAV. The first UAV ad hoc network testbed was created by the researcher using the DSR protocol. Because of the increased network mobility, the researchers proposed that DSR is a better match for FANETs than proactive routing approaches (D. Johnson & Maltz, 2007).

AODV: Ad hoc On-Demand Distance Vector

The AODV routing protocol is an improved variant of the DSR and DSDV protocols. It assumes control of DSDV's recurring updates and hop-to-hop routing from DSR. Reactive in nature, AODV does not save all pathways to destinations that are not interacting at this time; instead, it identifies a path only when needed. Route maintenance, packet transmission, and route discovery are the three stages of the AODV protocol. Before transferring a packet, a source UAV locates the intended UAVs by initiating a route discovery phase. It uses no routing loops to move packets along a predetermined path during the packet-sending phase. A route maintenance phase is implemented to address issues with connection failure. The most recent routing path to the UAV's destination is determined by using a sequence number. Using an expiration term maximizes the route's freshness as well. Furthermore, the intermediate UAVs in AODV update their routing tables. The dynamic nature of the FANET system poses a challenge for "AODV" in terms of network congestion (Perkings et al., 2003).

TS AODV: Time-Slotted Ad hoc On-Demand Distance Vector

The literature also suggests using the time-slotted on-demand routing protocol for FANETs. Just an AODV with a timed modification makes up this routing strategy. When only one UAV can transmit data packets within a time slot, the on-demand protocol transmits control packets. This routing technique increases the proportional packet delivery ratio by preventing packet collisions and making effective use of available bandwidth (Forsmann et al., 2007).

M-AODV: Multicast Ad hoc On-Demand Distance Vector

"M-AODV" is an enhanced variant of AODV that links a group of nodes using the multipath routing technique. By creating several trees, this protocol may be swiftly introduced to FANETs using a reactive approach, or discovery strategy (Perkings et al., 2003).

3.1.4. Hybrid Routing Protocols

To reduce overhead in both proactive and reactive protocols, the following hybrid routing techniques have been suggested: RRP takes slower to locate routes than PRP, despite PRP using a lot of control signals. HRP can reduce the considerable early-phase latency in reactive routing techniques as well as the overhead of control messages in proactive routing systems. It has enormous potential benefits for wide networks. A network is divided into zones, with inner-zone routing using reactive routing and intra-zone routing using proactive routing. Due to overlapping issues, hybrid approaches are particularly undesirable for more than 100 UAVs in the zone (Walikar & Biradar, 2017).

This section provides an overview of the Hybrid Routing Protocols. Examples of hybrid protocols are Temporarily Ordered Routing Algorithm - TORA, Sharp Hybrid Adaptive Routing Protocol - SHARP, Zone Routing Protocol - ZRP, and Hybrid Wireless Mesh Protocol – HWMP.

ZRP: Zone Routing Protocol

ZRP is built on the zone concept and can handle large networks with a range of mobility patterns. Each UAV in this process has a unique geographic area, and the zones of adjacent UAVs may overlap. A radius of length R has been used to compute an area's diameter, where R is the number of UAVs close to the zone's boundary. You can adjust the node's system throughput to increase the total number of UAVs in the area. Intra-zone routing is the term used to describe routing within a zone. One proactive routing method to keep the route intact is intra-zone routing. When the source and destination UAVs are in the same zone, the source UAV will automatically transfer the data. Inter-zone routing is used to transfer data packets outside of the zone, whereas reactive routing is used to maintain and identify the best routes. The route-finding procedure introduces a latency that is mitigated by border-casting. UAVs at a zone's boundary only transmit reply messages. The route's classification as intra- or inter-zone depends on the border UAVs selected (Nadeem et al., 2018).

HWMP: Hybrid Wireless Mesh Protocol

In FANETs, dynamic routing is done via HWMP, a technique created for wireless mesh networks. To ascertain the routing path and produce a tree beforehand, HWMP combines proactive and reactive algorithms. These two strategies—proactive and reactive—can be used in tandem and are based on the traditional shortest-path protocol and the AODV protocol. The reactive approach enables communication between an unmanned aircraft at the source and a drone at the destination. The UAVs use this technique when there is no source UAV or when the topology is dynamic. Consequently, the HWMP protocol has been utilized by researchers to test or replicate the FANET situations. The results of the simulation show that, in scenarios where the network architecture is unaltered, the constructive method works well in place of UAVs. In multi-hop networks, video surveillance is implemented using the HWMP protocol (Chai et al., 2017).

TORA: Temporarily Ordered Routing Algorithm

Most appropriate for multi-hop networks, TORA is a highly adaptable, hybrid distributed on-demand routing technology. Any UAV in this scenario is limited to updating routing tables for other UAVs that are nearby. In an extremely dynamic mobile computing environment, it aims to limit reactions to topological changes in order to reduce the transmission of control signals. Moreover, the distributed method searches for novel pathways and eliminates the wrong ones within a single run. Although TORA primarily employs reactive routing, it also makes use of several proactive techniques. It establishes and maintains a Directed Acyclic Graph (DAG) with many pathways linking nearby UAVs from the source node to the destination. It is favored for boosting flexibility and swiftly locating alternative pathways in the event of damaged connectivity. To minimize network overhead, lengthier routes are regularly employed in TORA instead of the shortest path method (Park & Corson, 2019).

SHARP: Sharp Hybrid Adaptive Routing Protocol

With its dynamic adjustment of the quantity of proactive routing control packets exchanged, SHARP offers an alternative to both constructive and reactive routing. A proactive zone around a group of UAVs has been established by counting the hops, or the smallest distance over which information packets may be delivered. In situations where the target UAV is outside of the constructive zone, the reactive function is employed (Ramasubramanian et al., 2003).

RFR: Reactive Flooding Routing

Reactive flooding routing, or RFR (Tropea et al., 2019), is recommended in the context of precision agriculture, where sudden changes in the environment have a substantial influence on plants and the efficiency of irrigation. The detected data is sent to farmers using UAVs, which have specific sensors installed. For the packet delivery ratio, the reactive-based approach performs admirably.

3.2. Position-Based Routing Protocols

With the GPS, which is the foundation of this family of routing protocols, each node may provide its geographic location. The node can use a location service, such as the Grid Location Service, Reactive Location Service, or Hierarchical Location Service, to find the destination, it should be indicated. FANETs and other highly dynamic networks are good candidates for this type of routing. The development of these protocols has been influenced by the two distinct categories of position-based routing protocols: In the first group, information packets are sent to the targeted UAV using a forwarding technique, and the sender uses a position facility to pinpoint the receiver's precise location. Every UAV in the second group locates itself using the integrated GPS. Using the built-in GPS, each UAV in the second group determines its location. Typically, a geographical positioning system is used by the sender to locate the recipient and interact without the need for a monitoring technique. Protocols have been developed since then to stop disconnections or make UAVs reconnect with one another. There are three subcategories in this area: Reactive, Greedy, and Predictive Position-based Routing Protocols. Moreover, the next subsections provide a detailed discussion of each of these processes.

3.2.1. Reactive Position-Based Routing Protocol

The most common technique in FANET routing protocols is the reactive one. In actuality, the source node must create an on-demand way to connect with the intended destination in situations when there is no route. There are several reactive routing techniques available for FANETs.

RGR: Reactive–Greedy–Reactive Protocol

The FANET-specific routing protocol RGR is offered in two modes: geographical and reactive. When the network appears to be experiencing few connection issues, the first mode which is based on the AODV protocol can be utilized. Either elevated mobility or a low number of UAVs causes network oscillations, which is why data packets are propagated using the second method, Greedy Geographic Forwarding (GGF). All drones, however, are said to know their neighbor's precise location thanks to the neighbor recognition mechanism. If it fails, AODV infers the destination's position to deliver data packets from the closest UAV to the target location. Additionally, if the connection between the source and the destination is broken, the GGF mode is triggered. RGR's Weakness Future drone's geographic locations are only sporadically and intermittently updated. Data packets that are transferred to an outdated geographic place run the risk of being destroyed because of the UAVs' high degree of mobility. In addition, the expense is high because control packet use during the discovery phase is disproportionate (Shirani et al., 2012).

MUDOR: Multipath Doppler Routing

MUDOR is a position-based reactive routing protocol designed exclusively for FANETs systems, and it is modeled after the DSR. Reliability and termination time are the two primary factors that determine any feasible networking link that employs the Doppler exchange of control packets. The routing choice takes into account the routes with the longest lifetime in addition to all projected Doppler values. The Doppler measurements obtained during the RREQ broadcast, which is the discovery phase, have been utilized to determine the relative velocities of any two drones that are within proximity.

The drawbacks of MUDOR Because UAVs move quickly and are sparsely populated, the selected routing channel could not always be reliable, requiring frequent, overhead-increasing discovery procedures. For the routing paths to last longer, additional constraints such as network disintegration need to be considered. When a path fails, a recovery method must be implemented rather than starting over with a new path discovery process (Sakhaee et al., 2006).

GPMOR: Mobility Oriented Geographic Positioning Routing

Conventional position-based protocols only use the node's geographic coordinates. However, GPMOR uses the Gaussian-Markov mobility pattern to predict the UAVs' movement, and this data is utilized to determine the next hop. GPMOR preserves more hops, whereas GPSR and GLSR choose the next hop only based on distance. In terms of the ratio of packet delivery to latency, GPMOR outperforms position-based routing protocols such as GPSR and GLSR in data forwarding. Because the GLSR and GPSR protocols do not take into consideration the impact of high mobility, which results in poor connection, the packet delivery ratio rapidly decreases as speed increases (Bousbaa et al., 2020).

3.2.2. Routing Protocols Based on Greedy Positions

Data packets are routed to UAVs more often when an ad hoc UAV network is fully connected and the target's position is known or determined beforehand. Using the Greedy Forwarding (GF) system, the technique helps to shorten the distance to the destination and the number of hops. Moreover, routing systems that employ the GF algorithm shorten data transmission times. FANET connections are known to be unstable because of the high degree of dynamic nature that UAVs possess by nature. Therefore, the Greedy Forwarding strategy is useless in this situation. A number of Greedy Routing Protocols have been proposed by researchers for the FANET system in an effort to increase the efficacy of this technique. The following protocols are briefly reviewed in this section: Greedy Distributed Spanning Tree Routing - GDSTR, Mobility Prediction Geographic Routing - MPGR, Geographic Load Share Routing - GLSR, and Greedy Perimeter Stateless Routing for Wireless Networks – GPSR.

GPSR: Greedy Perimeter Stateless Routing for Wi-Fi Networks

Packets are sent to the destination utilizing the nodes that are geographically closest to it via a position-based routing mechanism known as GPSR. Every GPSR node keeps track of every other node within its transmission range on a planar graph. After that, the entire network graph is analyzed. Each pair of nodes is connected by an edge, which shows that the nodes may interact. The vertices of the network represent all of the nodes. Position information is included in every packet that is delivered to ensure that nodes have neighbor information. If no data packets are received, occasionally beacon packets containing location data are sent (Karp & Kung, 2000). According to the scholars, who developed a simulation environment to evaluate the effectiveness of geographic-based routing protocols, GPSR is appropriate for networks of compactly positioned UAVs. However, the primary problem with this protocol is its dependability (Hosseinzadeh et al., 2023).

GLSR: Route for Geographic Load Sharing

The FANET extends the GPSR with the GLSR geographical routing protocol. Between the source and the destination, GLSR uses many pathways. GLSR seeks to simultaneously reach a source and a destination by taking many paths. Transmitting data packets to the nodes that permit arriving at the destination is the fundamental idea behind GLSR. Distance Advance (DA), a statistic that measures the difference between the packet-carrying node and the destination's next hops candidate, is used to select each path, and a measure known as Speed Advance (SA) to determine which neighbor is best for packet forwarding. A positive DA indicates that the intermediate node may be able to move closer to the destination before packet forwarding. Next, GLSR selects the optimal path by going over each node's queues that hold the packets that need to be sent.

To select the optimal path for the upcoming hop, the present UAV loads-balances neighboring candidates. Improving the efficiency and reliability of the routing channels lowers the average end-to-end packet latency and increases network throughput. When choosing subsequent hops, GLSR ignores other factors like the separations between nodes in the routing path. For delay-sensitive applications like VoIP, VoD, video monitoring, etc., GLSR could be a good choice if a certain degree of quality of service is required (Amponis et al., 2021).

MPGR: Geographic Routing Based on Mobility Prediction

A routing method for inter-UAV communications based on geographic locations is called Mobility Prediction-based Geographic Routing. GPSR and MPGR have the same structure. Furthermore, MPGR employs a mobility prediction method based on a Gaussian distribution function to mitigate the impacts of UAVs' high mobility while maintaining a tolerable communication cost. By helping to choose the most pertinent next hop and creating a more dependable communication path between UAVs, might save expenses (Lin et al., 2012).

Neighbor Discovery (ND) packets are used by MPGR as an additional position-sharing technique. Every ND packet contains the destination address as well as the delivery mode. The UAV sender can create its database of neighbors by asking every neighboring UAV to respond with its list of neighbors. The Adaptive Beacon method is another tool used by researchers to improve this strategy for various UAV scenarios. To avoid UAV connection failures, this technique uses UAV mobility data to identify nearby drones. Including connection status information in MPGR resulted in a considerable boost in UAV network stability. To estimate the future locations of the subsequent hops and prevent packet losses, each node uses the Gaussian distribution function to anticipate the geographic locations of its neighbors.

GDSTR: Greedy Distributed Spanning Tree Routing

The "GDSTR" (J. Zhou et al., 2010) protocol has been developed by researchers as an alternative to traditional geographical routing for 3D networks. A tree-like alternative routing topology is used by the greedy routing protocol known as GDSTR. Two-hop neighbor information and two-dimensional convex hulls are utilized by the GDSTR protocol to get additional UAV geographic coordinates to maximize the shortest path during the avaricious expedition. The drones determine the best course for approaching the target by observing the zones under each surrounding tree covered by the sub-tree. Each time a UAV root tries to connect with another UAV root, it follows the path indicated by the data packet through the tree until it gets to the networking subtree. This transited UAV of a subtree is called the anchor node. A packet gets destroyed when it reaches the root since every sub-tree has it. Researchers have developed several 3D Geographic Routing Protocols to address this issue; a review of these protocols is presented in (Gupta et al., 2020). Additionally, this protocol uses the right-hand rule to deliver the data packet to the UAV.

3.2.3. Routing Protocol Based on Predictive Positioning

Because of the extreme diversity and adaptability of UAVs, the drones' connectivity is erratic and frequently breaks down. The preprogrammed behaviors of UAVs may be used to derive many strategies for creating network algorithms that address this problem. Furthermore, the potential duration of wireless connections between UAVs may be estimated using these protocols. Moreover, information transfer frequently requires a full routing path to the destination, which seems to be a challenging tactic to put into practice because connection termination needs to be agreed upon on a constant basis. Additional issues arise because of the high level of uncertainty, particularly in the case of FANETs using a 3D design. Predictive Position-Based Routing Protocols are proposed by researchers as a result of this motivation. The Geographic Routing Protocol for Aircraft Ad hoc Network - GRAA, the Predictive-Optimized Link State Routing Protocol - P-OLSR, and the Adaptive Beacon Position Prediction - ABPP have all been reviewed in this area.

GRAA: Aircraft Ad hoc Network Geographic Routing Protocol

GRAA, or Geographic Routing Protocol for Aircraft Ad hoc Network, is a GPSR-based geographic routing system. Local route selection takes place at each intermediate node. Every node uses its neighbors' position, velocity, and destination to choose which hop to take next. The current node uses its current position and speed to first anticipate the destination's position after a time interval t. Then, using the same time t, it estimates the positions of each of its neighbors. For the following hop, the node that has the predicted position closest to the target at time t is chosen.

Utilizing time-based movement prediction of nodes, the GRAA routing approach improves position-based routing performance. Moreover, GRAA increases the delivery ratio by enabling data packets to be transported even when the network is only partially connected (Hyeon et al., 2010).

P-OLSR: Routing Protocol for Predictive Optimized Link State

"P-OLSR" is a novel implementation of the OLSR protocol that uses GPS data to forecast FANET connection quality (Rosati et al., 2013). Based GPS data, it is utilized in UAV networks to predict connection quality. A HELLO packet is sent to provide the location, and the original OSLR is updated. In this procedure, every node knows where its neighbors are. An anticipated transmission count (ETX) statistic is used to compute a factor. Instead of using the OLSR, this protocol makes use of the UAVs' GPS data. P-OSLR might be applied to very dynamic UAV networks (K G & K., 2017).

ABPP: Adaptive Beacon Position Prediction

"ABPP" is the name of a prediction-based routing technique created especially for FANET (Li & Huang, 2017). To make use of UAV location, ABPP employs the weighted linear regression technique. A fuzzy controller that is part of the ABPP uses the estimated error degree and beacon interval as its input and output, respectively, to adaptively alter the beacon broadcast frequency. The timing and location of nearby drones are recorded by ABPP using a GPSR-based spatial routing algorithm.

3.3. Hierarchical Based Routing Protocol

The hierarchical routing system is based on the formation of clusters, each of which is managed by a cluster head (CH). This will reduce the quantity of packets that drones communicate to base stations as well as the energy they consume. The disadvantage of hierarchical protocols is that they often forbid frequent node disconnections and make cluster creation exceedingly difficult. The main features, unique qualities, and prospective benefits of the Mobility Prediction Clustering Algorithm – MPCA, Clustering Algorithm – CA and Extended Hierarchical State Routing - EHSR are covered in this section.

CA: Clustering Algorithm

A hierarchical routing system called the Clustering Algorithm, or CA is built around the FANET's chosen goal of dynamic cluster generation. CA constructs clusters locally that are updated in line with the purpose. The ground station selects a CH to represent each cluster based on its geographic position. It is crucial to stress that CA requires an aerostat (balloon) that can communicate directly with the base station when it is in the air with the UAVs. UAVs respond by obtaining data from the balloon. Whenever the balloon wants to establish a connection with the UAV, it speaks with the base station directly. The packet is sent by the balloon through its CH to the appropriate cluster, from which it is delivered to the UAV (Liu et al., 2008).

MPCA: Mobility Prediction Clustering Algorithm

Using predictions of UAV movement, the MPCA is a hierarchical routing system designed to create clusters. lexicon Mobility is predicted using two factors: Tried Structure and Link Expiration Time. The first parameter is computed using the coordinates and speeds of each pair of UAVs. A UAV's likelihood of staying in the cluster is the second parameter. Thus, in order to build more resilient clusters and improve network performance, these two characteristics are crucial. Forming a cluster is simple, depending on the placements, velocities, and speeds of the UAVs. It is dependent on the kind of UAV to use intra- and inter-cluster methods (i.e., whether the communicating UAVs are part of the cluster or not) (Zang & Zang, 2011).

EHSR: Extended Hierarchical State Routing Mechanism

Hierarchical routing based on clusters is known as EHSR. A logical and physical specification of the levels is the basis for clustering. The UAVs themselves elect the cluster heads who represent each level. The many cluster heads at the lower level send another cluster to the one above it. The EHSR is structured into three layers, with unique hierarchical IDs (HIDs) assigned to each node: (a) the UAV network, (b) the backbone network, and (c) the land-based network. Cluster-heads work by proactively obtaining connection status information from cluster members and exchanging it with higher-level cluster-heads of their colleagues (Gu et al., 2000).

3.4. Routing Protocols Inspired by Bio

A number of FANET concerns, particularly those concerning UAV connections, are greatly supported by the behavior of insects, including ants, bees, and even particle swarms. A range of bio-inspired routing algorithms have been developed for the FANET network to address different types of routing issues. This section covers the location-based Ant Colony Routing method - POSANT, the Ant Colony Optimization Polymorphism Aware Routing approach APAR, and the Bee Colony algorithm for FANET routing - Bee-Adhoc.

Position-Based Ant Colony Routing Method

Based on the ant colony approach, FANETs can use the routing protocol "POSANT" (Kamali & Opatrny, 2008). In the exploration phase, POSANT gives each UAV the ability to select the optimal path for the next hop based on locations and geographic data. As a result, there are fewer ant generations (control messages) and a shorter transmission length from beginning to conclusion. Moreover, until the drones have established a trajectory, they are unable to communicate.

APAR: An Approach to Polymorphism Aware Routing Based on Ant Colony Optimization

The swarm-based routing method known as APAR is exclusive to FANET (Sun et al., 2021). In APAR, the popular "DSR" (D. Johnson & Maltz, 2007) is combined with the particle swarm optimization method. The number of pheromones and the packet transit distance are regarded as performance evaluators for networking the route, much as the discovery phase. Two aspects need to be taken into account when choosing a route or other network path: congestion (buffer use and channel loading) and stability (mobility and connections).

BEE-ADHOC: The Bee Colony Algorithm for Network Routing

The basic idea of a beehive, which divides up simple tasks among all the bees (UAVs), is the foundation of the BeeAdhoc routing algorithm. Scouts and foragers are the two bee species that were employed in this investigation. The two main areas of emphasis for the Bee Ad Hoc approach are (a) resource gathering and (b) reconnaissance, or scouting. By providing source ID, hop count, and limited residual energy to both forward and backward scouts, the network establishes many routes between communication nodes in the first aspect. Forager bees transport data or information packets from their source to their destination in the second aspect. Additionally, the forager-bees transmit the data packets via the assigned networking channel (i.e., high energy level UAVs make up the shortest path) (Leonov, 2016).

4. COMPARATIVE STUDY OF ROUTING PROTOCOLS

After analyzing many routing protocols, compiled the comparison information in Table 1 for each protocol in this section.

Table 1. Comparison information

Routing Protocol			Benefits	Weaknesses
Network Topology-Based	Static	**LCAD** (Cheng et al., 2007)	Increases Throughput	Does not support broken links
		DCR (Ko et al., 2002)	Cluster-based multicasting	Does not allow for great mobility
		MLHR (Y. Zhou et al., 2015)	Reduces the delivery time	Not in line with the great mobility
	Proactive	**DSDV** (Shumeye Lakew et al., 2020)	It eliminates routing loops.	Delays and congestion are introduced.
		OLSR (Jacquet et al., 2001)	MPRs are used to reduce latency and overhead.	Increases overhead in high-density areas.
		BATMAN (D. L. Johnson et al., 2008)	Provide the most efficient pathways to every node.	The convergence time is slow.
	Reactive	**DSR** (D. Johnson & Maltz, 2007)	Discover the whole path to the intended location.	High overhead is introduced.
		AODV (Perkings et al., 2003)	Delivers a high delivery ratio.	Causes significant delays.
		TS-AODV (Forsmann et al., 2007)	Reduces congestion and bandwidth use.	Complicated computations are introduced.
		M-AODV (Perkings et al., 2003)	Reduces delivery delays.	Does not take scalability into account.
	Hybrid	**ZRP** (Nadeem et al., 2018)	It improves node organization.	Not sufficient for high mobility.
		HWMP (Chai et al., 2017)	Adapts to changes in the network.	This causes routing instability.
		TORA (Park & Corson, 2019)	Link failures are recovered.	High congestion is introduced.
		SHARP (Ramasubramanian et al., 2003)	Reduces overhead by minimizing the zones.	Delays and congestion are increased.
		RFR (Tropea et al., 2019)	Efficient Routing, Scalability, and Adaptability.	Increased Overhead, Limited to Small Networks and Security Issues.
Position-based	Reactive	**RGR** (Shirani et al., 2012)	Utilizes an effective maintenance strategy.	It does not forecast the placements of the future hops.
		MUDOR (Sakhaee et al., 2006)	Flooding is reduced.	The low density is not supported.
		GPMOR (Bousbaa et al., 2020)	Predictions are used to choose relays.	Does not take fragmentation into account.
	Greedy	**GPSR** (Karp & Kung, 2000)	Reduces the number of delays and hops.	Link failures are not supported.
		GLSR (Amponis et al., 2021)	Performs load balance among UAVs.	Does not consider connection stability.
		MPGR (Lin et al., 2012)	Considers stability to improve delivery.	The link expiration time is ignored.
		GDSTR (Gupta et al., 2020)	Improves greedy forwarding.	Assumes a static topology.
	Predictive	**GRAA** (Hyeon et al., 2010)	Predicts the placement of nodes in the future.	Assumes UAV motion is random.
		P-OLSR (K G & K., 2017)	Positions are used to manage the increased mobility.	Any type of recovery approach is used.
		ABPP (Li & Huang, 2017)	Improves the overhead and delivery ratio.	Dense networks are required.

Table 1 continued

Routing Protocol			Benefits	Weaknesses
Hierarchical Based		**CA** (Liu et al., 2008)	Routing aid on the ground.	This necessitates the use of an aerostat.
		MPCA (Zang & Zang, 2011)	Link failures are predicted.	When there is erratic motion, the system fails.
		EHSR (Gu et al., 2000)	Scalability is improved.	It requires a solid foundation.
Bio-Inspired Based		**POSANT** (Kamali & Opatrny, 2008)	Network fragmentation is supported.	It makes use of quasistatic topology.
		APAR (Sun et al., 2021)	It prevents congestion and network failures.	Overheads and delays are introduced.
		BEE-ADHOC (Leonov, 2016)	It improves memory storage and bandwidth.	Simulation of complex behaviors.

5. CONCLUSION

Routing is regarded as one of the most important components in FANETs for ensuring proper functionality and efficient cooperative network operations. Many procedures have been proposed in the literature throughout the previous decade. Everyone has unique attributes, characteristics, drawbacks, and advantages over competitors. To distinguish and make sense of things, this thorough study examined the most important characteristics strongly associated with FANET routing. To demonstrate the originality of our survey, we have first categorized most survey studies and then qualitatively compared them according to their most notable characteristics. After that, this survey goes into great detail on UAVs and their characteristics. Also included is a quick overview of FANETs, including their essential characteristics, application scenarios, mobility models currently in use, routing attributes, and routing metrics. There are four primary types and various subcategories for the FANET routing protocols at the second level. The routing protocols for each category are covered in distinct sections. Finally, depending on the various qualities, a comparative analysis of all the categories is provided.

REFERENCES

Amponis, G., Lagkas, T., Sarigiannidis, P., Vitsas, V., Fouliras, P., & Wan, S. (2021). A survey on FANET routing from a cross-layer design perspective. *Journal of Systems Architecture*, *120*, 102281. doi:10.1016/j.sysarc.2021.102281

Bahloul, N. E. H., Boudjit, S., Abdennebi, M., & Boubiche, D. E. (2017). Bio-inspired on demand routing protocol for unmanned aerial vehicles. *2017 26th International Conference on Computer Communications and Networks, ICCCN 2017*. 10.1109/ICCCN.2017.8038487

Bousbaa, F. Z., Kerrache, C. A., Mahi, Z., Tahari, A. E. K., Lagraa, N., & Yagoubi, M. B. (2020). GeoUAVs: A new geocast routing protocol for fleet of UAVs. *Computer Communications*, *149*, 259–269. https://doi.org/https://doi.org/10.1016/j.comcom.2019.10.026. doi:10.1016/j.comcom.2019.10.026

Bujari, A., Palazzi, C. E., & Ronzani, D. (2017). FANET application scenarios and mobility models. *DroNet 2017 - Proceedings of the 3rd Workshop on Micro Aerial Vehicle Networks, Systems, and Applications, Co-Located with MobiSys 2017,* 43–46. 10.1145/3086439.3086440

Chai, Y., Shi, W., & Shi, T. (2017). Load-aware cooperative hybrid routing protocol in hybrid wireless mesh networks. *AEÜ. International Journal of Electronics and Communications, 74,* 135–144. doi:10.1016/j.aeue.2017.02.002

Cheng, C. M., Hsiao, P. H., Kung, H. T., & Vlah, D. (2007). Maximizing throughput of UAV-relaying networks with the load-carry-and-deliver paradigm. *IEEE Wireless Communications and Networking Conference, WCNC.* 10.1109/WCNC.2007.805

Chriki, A., Touati, H., Snoussi, H., & Kamoun, F. (2019). FANET: Communication, mobility models and security issues. *Computer Networks, 163,* 106877. doi:10.1016/j.comnet.2019.106877

E., Z., & Atef, M. (2017). Performance Evaluation of AODV, DSR and OLSR in MANET using Opnet Simulator. *International Journal of Computer Applications, 163*(11), 23–30. doi:10.5120/ijca2017913775

Forsmann, J. H., Hiromoto, R. E., & Svoboda, J. (2007). A time-slotted on-demand routing protocol for mobile ad hoc unmanned vehicle systems. *Unmanned Systems Technology, 9,* 6561. doi:10.1117/12.719355

Gu, D. L., Pei, G., Ly, H., Gerla, M., & Hong, X. (2000). Hierarchical routing for multi-layer ad-hoc wireless networks with UAVs. *Proceedings - IEEE Military Communications Conference MILCOM, 1.* 10.1109/MILCOM.2000.904964

Gupta, N. K., Yadav, R. S., & Nagaria, R. K. (2020). 3D geographical routing protocols in wireless ad hoc and sensor networks: An overview. *Wireless Networks, 26*(4), 2549–2566. Advance online publication. doi:10.1007/s11276-019-01983-y

Habib, S., Saleem, S., & Saqib, K. M. (2013). Review on MANET routing protocols and challenges. *Proceeding - 2013 IEEE Student Conference on Research and Development, SCOReD 2013,* 529–533. 10.1109/SCOReD.2013.7002647

Hadi, H. J., Cao, Y., Nisa, K. U., Jamil, A. M., & Ni, Q. (2023). A comprehensive survey on security, privacy issues and emerging defence technologies for UAVs. *Journal of Network and Computer Applications, 213,* 103607. doi:10.1016/j.jnca.2023.103607

Hosseinzadeh, M., Tanveer, J., Ionescu-Feleaga, L., Ionescu, B.-S., Yousefpoor, M. S., Yousefpoor, E., Ahmed, O. H., Rahmani, A. M., & Mehmood, A. (2023). A greedy perimeter stateless routing method based on a position prediction mechanism for flying ad hoc networks. *Journal of King Saud University. Computer and Information Sciences, 35*(8), 101712. doi:10.1016/j.jksuci.2023.101712

Hyeon, S. U., Kim, K., & Yang, S. W. (2010). A new geographic routing protocol for aircraft ad hoc networks. *AIAA/IEEE Digital Avionics Systems Conference - Proceedings.* doi:10.1109/DASC.2010.5655476

Jacquet, P. , Uhlethaler, P. M., Clausen, T., Laouiti, A., Qayyum, A., & Viennot, L. (2001). Optimized link state routing protocol. *IEEE INMIC'01,* 62–68.

Johnson, D., & Maltz, D. (2007). The Dynamic Source Routing Protocol (DSR) for Mobile Ad Hoc Networks for IPv4. *Vasa, 21*(5–6), 1–107. http://medcontent.metapress.com/index/A65RM03P4874243N.pdf

Johnson, D. L., Ntlatlapa, N., & Aichele, C. (2008). A simple pragmatic approach to mesh routing using BATMAN. *IFIP International Symposium on Wireless Communications and Information Technology in Developing Countries*. http://downloads.open-mesh.net/batman/misc/batman_ifip.pdf

K G, A., & K, D. S.K G. (2017). Dynamic Routing For Flying Ad Hoc Networks. *International Journal of Advanced Research in Computer and Communication Engineering*, *6*(4), 161–170. doi:10.17148/IJARCCE.2017.6430

Kamali, S., & Opatrny, J. (2008). A position based ant colony routing algorithm for mobile ad-hoc networks. *Journal of Networks*, *3*(4), 31–41. doi:10.4304/jnw.3.4.31-41

Karp, B., & Kung, H. T. (2000). *GPSR: Greedy Perimeter Stateless Routing for Wireless Networks*. doi:10.1145/345910.345953

Kashyap, K. K., & Agrawal, A. (2018). FANET : Survey on Design Challenges. *Application Scenario and Communication Protocols.*, *5*(04), 1024–1032.

Khan, M. A., Khan, I. U., Safi, A., & Quershi, I. M. (2018). Dynamic routing in flying Ad-Hoc networks using topology-based routing protocols. *Drones (Basel)*, *2*(3), 1–15. doi:10.3390/drones2030027

Ko, J., Mahajan, A., & Sengupta, R. (2002). A network-centric UAV organization for search and pursuit operations. *IEEE Aerospace Conference Proceedings,* 6. 10.1109/AERO.2002.1036111

Leonov, A. V. (2016). Application of bee colony algorithm for FANET routing. *International Conference of Young Specialists on Micro/Nanotechnologies and Electron Devices, EDM*. 10.1109/EDM.2016.7538709

Li, X., & Huang, J. (2017). ABPP: An adaptive beacon scheme for geographic routing in FANET. *Parallel and Distributed Computing, Applications and Technologies, PDCAT Proceedings*. 10.1109/PDCAT.2017.00055

Lin, L., Sun, Q., Wang, S., & Yang, F. (2012). A geographic mobility prediction routing protocol for Ad Hoc UAV Network. *2012 IEEE Globecom Workshops. GC Wkshps*, *2012*, 1597–1602. Advance online publication. doi:10.1109/GLOCOMW.2012.6477824

Liu, K., Zhang, J., & Zhang, T. (2008). The clustering algorithm of UAV networking in near-space. *IS-APE 2008 - The 8th International Symposium on Antennas, Propagation and EM Theory Proceedings*. 10.1109/ISAPE.2008.4735528

Nadeem, A., Mehmood, A., & Siddiqui, M. S. (2018). A Review and Classification of Flying Ad-Hoc Network (FANET) Routing Strategies. *International Journal of Sciences: Basic and Applied Research,* *8*(3), 1–8. www.textroad.com

Oubbati, O. S., Atiquzzaman, M., Lorenz, P., Tareque, M. H., & Hossain, M. S. (2019). Routing in flying Ad Hoc networks: Survey, constraints, and future challenge perspectives. *IEEE Access : Practical Innovations, Open Solutions*, *7*, 81057–81105. doi:10.1109/ACCESS.2019.2923840

Oubbati, O. S., Lakas, A., Zhou, F., Güneş, M., & Yagoubi, M. B. (2017). A survey on position-based routing protocols for Flying Ad hoc Networks (FANETs). *Vehicular Communications*, *10*, 29–56. doi:10.1016/j.vehcom.2017.10.003

Park, V. D., & Corson, M. S. (2019). Temporally-Ordered Routing Algorithm. *Journal of Chemical Information and Modeling*, *53*(9).

Pasandideh, F., da Costa, J. P. J., Kunst, R., Islam, N., Hardjawana, W., & Pignaton de Freitas, E. (2022). A Review of Flying Ad Hoc Networks: Key Characteristics, Applications, and Wireless Technologies. *Remote Sensing (Basel)*, *14*(18), 1–25. doi:10.3390/rs14184459

Perkings, C., Belding-Royer, E., & Das, S. (2003). Ad hoc On-Demand Distance Vector (AODV) Routing. *IETF RFC, 3561*, 1–37. http://tools.ietf.org/pdf/rfc3561.pdf

Perkins, C. E., & Bhagwat, P. (1994). Highly dynamic destination-sequenced distance-vector routing (DSDV) for mobile computer. *Proceedings of the Conference on Communications Architectures, Protocols and Applications, SIGCOMM 1994,* 234–244. 10.1145/190314.190336

Ramasubramanian, V., Haas, Z. J., & Sirer, E. G. (2003). SHARP: A hybrid adaptive routing protocol for mobile ad hoc networks. *Proceedings of the International Symposium on Mobile Ad Hoc Networking and Computing (MobiHoc)*, 303–314. 10.1145/778415.778450

Rosati, S., Kruzelecki, K., Traynard, L., & Rimoldi, B. (2013). Speed-aware routing for UAV ad-hoc networks. *2013 IEEE Globecom Workshops. GC Wkshps*, *2013*, 1367–1373. doi:10.1109/GLOCOMW.2013.6825185

Sahingoz, O. K. (2013). Flying Ad-Hoc Networks (FANETs): A survey. *Ad Hoc Networks*, *11*(3), 1254–1270. doi:10.1016/j.adhoc.2012.12.004

Sakhaee, E., Jamalipour, A., & Kato, N. (2006). Aeronautical ad hoc networks. *IEEE Wireless Communications and Networking Conference, WCNC, 1*, 246–251. 10.1109/WCNC.2006.1683472

Shirani, R., St-Hilaire, M., Kunz, T., Zhou, Y., Li, J., & Lamont, L. (2012). On the delay of reactive-greedy-reactive routing in unmanned aeronautical ad-hoc networks. *Procedia Computer Science*, *10*, 535–542. doi:10.1016/j.procs.2012.06.068

Shumeye Lakew, D., Sa'Ad, U., Dao, N. N., Na, W., & Cho, S. (2020). Routing in Flying Ad Hoc Networks: A Comprehensive Survey. *IEEE Communications Surveys and Tutorials*, *22*(2), 1071–1120. doi:10.1109/COMST.2020.2982452

Sun, M., Zhou, L., Yu, Y., & Gu, J. (2021). Ant colony optimization based polymorphism-aware routing algorithm for AdHoc UAV network. *Xi Tong Gong Cheng Yu Dian Zi Ji Shu. Journal of Systems Engineering and Electronics*, *43*(9). Advance online publication. doi:10.12305/j.issn.1001-506X.2021.09.24

Tropea, M., Santamaria, A. F., De Rango, F., & Potrino, G. (2019). Reactive Flooding versus Link State Routing for FANET in Precision Agriculture. *2019 16th IEEE Annual Consumer Communications and Networking Conference, CCNC 2019*. 10.1109/CCNC.2019.8651744

Walikar, G. A., & Biradar, R. C. (2017). A survey on hybrid routing mechanisms in mobile ad hoc networks. *Journal of Network and Computer Applications, 77*(October), 48–63. doi:10.1016/j.jnca.2016.10.014

Wang, J., Jiang, C., Han, Z., Ren, Y., Maunder, R. G., & Hanzo, L. (2017). Taking Drones to the Next Level. *IEEE Vehicular Technology Magazine*, *12*(3), 73–82. doi:10.1109/MVT.2016.2645481

Zang, C., & Zang, S. (2011). Mobility prediction clustering algorithm for UAV networking. *2011 IEEE GLOBECOM Workshops. GC Wkshps, 2011*, 1158–1161. Advance online publication. doi:10.1109/GLOCOMW.2011.6162360

Zheng, Y., Wang, Y., Li, Z., Dong, L., Jiang, Y., & Zhang, H. (2014). A mobility and load aware OLSR routing protocol for UAV mobile AD-HOC networks. *2014 International Conference on Information and Communications Technologies, ICT 2014*. 10.1049/cp.2014.0575

Zhou, J., Chen, Y., Leong, B., & Sundaramoorthy, P. S. (2010). Practical 3D geographic routing for wireless sensor networks. *SenSys 2010 - Proceedings of the 8th ACM Conference on Embedded Networked Sensor Systems*, 337–350. 10.1145/1869983.1870016

Zhou, Y., Cheng, N., Lu, N., & Shen, X. (2015). Multi-UAV-Aided Networks. *IEEE Vehicular Technology Magazine*.

Chapter 12
Intelligent Routing Scheme for FANET Using Bio-Inspired Optimisation

Nandhini S.
Sri Krishna Arts and Science College, India

Jeen Marseline K. S.
Sri Krishna Arts and Science College, India

ABSTRACT

An unmanned aerial vehicle (UAV) is an aircraft without a human pilot that is operated remotely. When multiple UAVs are connected together for performing specific task, the arrangement is called a flying adhoc network (FANET). In a multi-UAV system, communication and coordination among the flying nodes are essential to carry out the mission properly. As the flying nodes are highly dynamic in nature, an efficient routing strategy is important. The intelligent routing decisions in this scenario can be taken by applying bio-inspired optimisation algorithms. This chapter focuses on bio-inspired optimisation techniques for the FANET.

1. INTRODUCTION

Bio-inspired optimization algorithms play a vital role in solving various problems related to decision making, information handling and optimization in the field of science and engineering (Radoglou-Grammatikis et al., 2020). The bio-inspired optimization algorithms are flexible, easily testable, intelligent and improved to solve complex optimization problems. These algorithms can be applied to a variety of problems without much change in the structure of the algorithm. The biological behavior of a group of insects, animals or birds is called swarm intelligence (Oubbati et al., 2017). The swarm intelligence includes division of labor, self-organization and coordination among the herds. This has attracted many researchers to find out solutions for several engineering and science problems (Vrchota et al., 2022).

DOI: 10.4018/979-8-3693-2073-0.ch012

The swarm of birds or animals can be compared to a group of Unmanned Aerial Vehicles (UAVs) in the Flying Adhoc Network (FANET) environment. The flying UAVs are used in various applications. They are used for reconnaissance in the military operation (Lytos et al., 2020). A group of UAVs can be launched for crop monitoring in agriculture. In case of natural disasters, UAVs are deployed for recovery operations. Finding an optimal path between these UAVs is essential in the FANET (Wheeb et al., 2022). Several routing protocols are proposed for communication among UAVs in the literature (Rahmani et al., 2022). However, selection of a suitable routing protocol is very important for the proper communication and coordination among the UAVs (Sang, Wu, Xing, & Xie, 2020). High mobility, dynamic changes in the topology and energy requirements of nodes are to be considered when selecting a suitable routing protocol for FANET (Nadeem et al., 2018). Hence the routing protocol can be made efficient by invoking a suitable bio-inspired optimization algorithm (Lakew et al., 2020).

In this paper, a comprehensive analysis of routing protocols suitable for the FANET is done. The rest of the paper is organised as follows: Section 2 presents the related work. Section 3 presents various routing protocols for FANET. Section 4 provides various applications of FANET. Section 5 concludes this paper.

2. RELATED WORK

Rahmani et al. (2022) proposed a new routing method named OLSR+ which is based on fuzzy logic in FANETs. In this paper, the optimized link state routing protocol (OLSR) is improved using a fuzzy logic-based routing scheme. This work aims to improve the routing protocol by various approaches. It estimates the link lifetime based on several factors. It uses the fuzzy mechanism to deal with multipoint relays. This work also involves discovering network topology and calculating routing tables. Radoglou-Grammatikis et al. (2020) present a survey that mainly focuses on various applications of UAVs for precision agriculture. This paper lists out twenty different applications in the precision agriculture domain. The UAV architecture, characteristics and various methodologies adopted are also analysed in detail. Oubbati et al. (2017) proposed a survey on position-based routing protocols for FANETs. This paper also performs a comparative study of the various routing protocols based on their properties, routing metrics and drawbacks.

Vrchota et al. (2022) presented the application of precision agriculture techniques for crops and livestock in the Czech Republic. The research used a questionnaire survey to obtain the result and it showed that crops use the precision agriculture technique more than livestock production. Lytos et al. (2020) present a survey on the exploitation of big data for smart farming. It gives a detailed analysis of the evolution of the agricultural system and also provides details on the sources of information. This paper focuses on the utilization of big data for enhancing agricultural operations. Wheeb et al. (2022) present a review on topology-based routing protocols and mobility models for FANETs. The research work identifies the application categories of UAVs like surveillance and monitoring, search and rescue operations, Military and enforcement operations, 5G and beyond communications. The paper describes twenty-two topology-based routing protocols. An extensive comparison of topology-based routing protocols is made to identify the suitable protocol for FANETs.

Sang et al. (2020) made a review on emerging routing protocols for FANETs. The paper gives an overview of various quality of service (QoS) parameters like packet delivery ratio, sequence length, link quality, geographic location, residual energy, buffer state and neighbour information. The paper highlights the differences between FANETs and other ad-hoc networks based on their node mobility, mobility models, node density, topological changes and so on. Nadeem et al. (2018) presented a review of FANET networking protocols and compared them based on several factors like complexity, route, topology size, memory size, fault tolerance, bandwidth utilization, signalling overhead and so on. The paper also focuses on some of the open research issues related to FANETs.

Lakew et al. (2020) present an extensive survey on the routing protocols of FANETs along with the classification of UAVs, deployment issues, FANET communication, application architecture, mobility models, their advantages, disadvantages and application scenarios. The authors presented a high-level comparison of all the routing protocols for FANETs. Saifullah Khan et al. proposed a bio-inspired Ant Colony Optimization algorithm with fuzzy logic to improve the routing performance of FANET. The proposed approach aims to find out the best multi-hop path. This paper uses fuzzy logic to find out the best wireless link. The performance of the network is evaluated through simulation based on various metrics.

3. ROUTING PROTOCOLS FOR FANET

Due to various complexities in FANET routing like frequent changes in topology, energy efficiency and security, it is important to study different routing protocols for FANETs (Khan et al., 2022). Fig. 1 shows the taxonomy of routing protocols for FANETs.

Figure 1. Taxonomy of FANET routing protocols

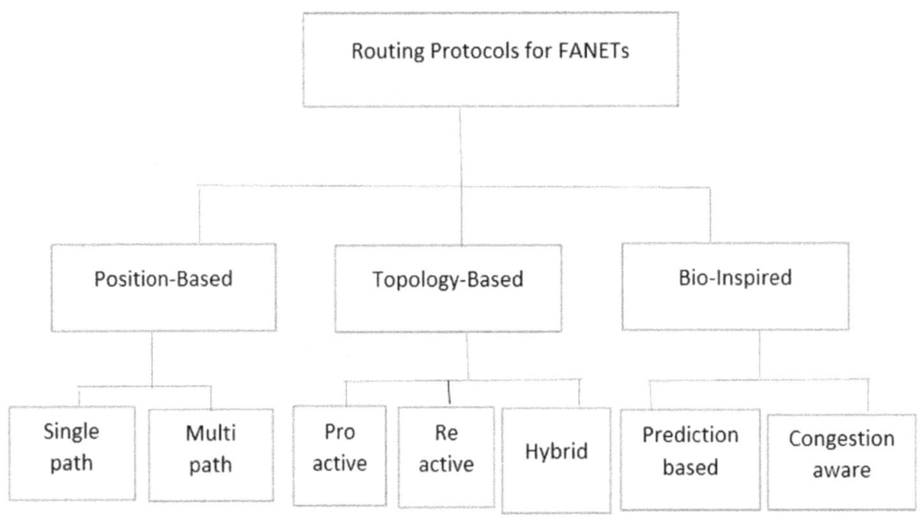

As shown in Figure 1, the routing protocols of FANET can be broadly divided into three categories namely positon-based routing protocols, topology-based routing protocols and bio-inspired routing protocols (Khan et al., 2020). This section describes these three categories in detail

a. Position-based Routing Protocols:

These types of protocols use the geographical position of the nodes in the network. The position of the nodes is usually defined by GPS and the location of the destination is calculated by the location service. (De Rango, Tropea, & Fazio, 2019) The advantage of using these types of protocols is that the entire network information is not required for routing packets, instead, they require only the neighbour node and the destination node position information. Position-based routing protocols are further divided into single-path routing protocols and multi-path routing protocols (Beegum, 2023).

i. Single Path Routing Protocols:

The protocols that choose only one path for the transmission of data packets fall into this category. They are further classified into delay-tolerant and non-delay-tolerant (Leonov, 2017). The delay tolerant protocols are capable of storing the messages for a particular period if the destination node or a neighbour node is unreachable. When the nodes are ready to receive the packets, the buffered packets are sent to them. The non-delay tolerant scheme uses either a greedy-based approach or a prediction-based approach. The greedy-based approach sends data packets to its neighbouring nodes, making them relay nodes (Ahmad et al., 2021). It uses the greedy mechanism to find the shortest neighbouring node for data transmission. The prediction-based approach uses some information like geographic location and velocity to choose the next node for transmitting the packets (De Rango, Potrino, Tropea et al, 2019). The single-path category of routing protocols may suffer from significant delays if path failure occurs.

ii. Multipath Routing Protocols:

In this approach, many paths are chosen for data transmission by considering multiple neighbourhood nodes to send the packets at a faster rate. Multipath routing protocols use reactive and predictive strategies for data transmission. In the reactive strategy, an on-demand path is established to the destination node (Khan et al., 2019). The movement of nodes is predicted and based on this, data transmission is done in a predictive strategy. Table 1 summarizes the features of position-based routing protocols for FANETs.

Table 1. Summary of position-based routing protocols

Protocol	Approach	Mobility Model	Problem Identified	Solution	Strength	Weakness
RLPR (Usmana et al., n.d.)	Position-based	Random waypoint	Signalling overhead and network lifetime	Reliable, link adaptive routing protocol	Increased lifetime	Unwanted paths between source and destination
Q-FANET (Luis Antonio, 2021)	QL-based	Random waypoint	Network reliability and performance	Using reinforcement learning	Lower delay and jitter	QoS degradation
3DC-LAR (Kumar et al., n.d.)	Position-based	Random waypoint	Route discovery process	Modified Location aided routing(LAR)	Reduces route request overhead	Performance degradation due to energy limitation

b. Topology-based Routing Protocols

These types of routing protocols depend on the topology of the nodes in the network to deliver the packets (Dixit & Singh, 2023).They are further categorized into proactive routing protocols, reactive routing protocols and hybrid routing protocols (Kaur & Singh, 2018).

i. Proactive routing protocols: They use a table-driven mechanism, in which every node maintains routing information to every other node. Whenever the topology changes, the routing information of the table will also be updated (Hussain et al., 2021). Hence before data transmission begins, the up-to-date routing information of the entire network is made available in the table.
ii. Reactive routing protocols: Unlike the proactive approach, here the route is established on-demand only when they wish to exchange data packets (Hameed et al., 2021). Hence this approach reduces the overhead of establishing and maintaining the routing information of the entire network. This results in low latency and high efficiency of the routing protocol.
iii. Hybrid routing protocols: The strengths of both proactive and reactive routing protocols are combined in this scheme (Khan et al., 2021). The hybrid protocols apply proactive and reactive strategies based on the zone and position of the nodes. Table 2 summarizes the characteristics of topology-based routing protocols.

Table 2. Summary of topology-based routing protocols

Protocol	Approach	Mobility Model	Problem Identified	Solution	Strength	Weakness
OLSR+ (Rahmani et al., 2022)	Proactive	RWP & GM	Estimation of link lifetime and calculation of MPR nodes	Fuzzy logic-based algorithm	Improved QoS metrics	Routing overhead
CHNN-DSR (Yang & Liu, 2019)	Reactive	Random waypoint	Route Optimization	Using Continuous Hopfield Neural Network	Low routing failure	Time consumption in energy calculation
HB-AODV (Kout et al., 2023)	Hybrid	Random waypoint	Efficient route identification	Hybrid optimization of 2-opt heuristic and HBA	The balance between exploration and exploitation	Complexity and resource-intensive

c. Bio-Inspired Routing Protocols

The FANET requires proper coordination and communication among multiple UAVs for efficient packet delivery. The foraging behaviour of different types of animals, birds and insects is the motivation for bio-inspired routing protocols (Bharany et al., 2022). Some of the bio-inspired routing algorithms used in the literature are discussed in this section.

i. Ant-Hocnet Routing Protocol: In Khan et al. (2022), the Ant-Hocnet routing protocol is used with optimized fuzzy logic to improve the routing efficiency of FANET. This routing protocol belongs to the family of the Bio-inspired Ant Colony Optimisation algorithm. The authors used fuzzy logic to analyse the network properties like availability of bandwidth, mobility of nodes and quality of wireless links. The algorithm identifies the best path for reliable transmission of packets.
ii. BeeAdHoc and AntHocNet: In Leonov (2017), the authors tested two bio-inspired routing protocols namely BeeAdHoc and AntHocNet using Network Simulator NS2 and the performance of these routing protocols are compared with AODV, DSDV and DSR routing protocols. The results indicate that the bio-inspired routing algorithms outperform the traditional routing algorithms.

iii. In De Rango et al. (2019), the Ant Colony Optimisation routing strategy is applied in the UAVs for detecting and killing parasites in the agriculture field.To coordinate and maintain the topology of drones, the authors used a bio-inspired routing strategy and tested its performance against the traditional link-state routing protocol. The results proved that the bio-inspired strategy is more efficient than the traditional one.
iv. In Khan et al. (2019), the authors propose a "bio-inspired clustering scheme for FANET(BICSF)" for cluster management among the UAVs. Their research is based on the Glowworm Swarm Optimisation(GSO) algorithm for cluster formation and management. The authors also propose Krill Herd, another bio-inspired approach for cluster management.
v. In Dixit and Singh (2023), a hybrid bioinspired routing protocol for UAVs is designed. The hybrid protocol is a combination of three optimization techniques namely PSO, GA and GWO. These optimisation techniques are used for cluster selection, routing and route optimization respectively.
vi. In Hameed et al. (2021), a novel algorithm based on the Gray Wolf Optimisation algorithm is proposed to implement the concept of collaboration technique among the flying nodes for effective routing. The performance of the proposed algorithm is compared with Bat-FANETs protocols and the results indicate the proposed algorithm outperforms the BAT-COOP protocol.
vii. In Bharany et al. (2022), a Moth Flame Optimisation algorithm is used for position calculation of the flying nodes based on the navigation mechanism. It helps with the cluster formation, cluster head selection and management of clusters for efficient routing.

4. APPLICATIONS OF FANET

Multiple UAVs in the FANET communicate and coordinate among themselves using swarm intelligence of the bio-inspired routing protocols. This section categorizes the different applications of FANET.

Search and Rescue Operations

When it is difficult for human beings to access the places in which the natural disasters happened, it is wise to use UAVs for search and rescue operations. But this operation is quite challenging due to the time and terrain constraints. The search and rescue operation should happen as quickly as possible to recover affected people. The searching operations become more challenging in snowy and hilly regions.

Forest Fire Detection

This type of application requires the complete communication and coordination among the UAV nodes as the flying nodes should find out the possible geographical locations which are most likely to be affected by fire.

Reconnaissance

UAVs are used for surveillance tasks to protect a specific area of interest. In military operations, the UAVs are used to identify the movement of people in specific regions to protect people from illegal operations.

Precision Agriculture

Precision Agriculture (PA) aims to incorporate several IT tools to increase agricultural productivity. Real-time monitoring is the key process of PA (Weigand et al., 2022). With the help of GPS-enabled devices, mounted on UAVs, real-time monitoring becomes easy and efficient. There are different types of UAVs available that are capable of performing a variety of operations. With the help of UAVs, the monitoring process becomes simple and it gives accurate results (Usmana et al., n.d.). Plant disease prediction can be done by taking images of crops with the help of high-definition cameras and sensors installed on UAVs (Agrawal & Kapoor, 2021). Depending upon the soil condition, water, fertiliser and pesticide usage can be estimated. Apart from the aforementioned applications, robotics, big data analytics and augmented reality techniques are also used in PA for further improvement.

5. CONCLUSION

The multiple UAVs in the FANET require effective communication and coordination among them. This can be achieved by using a bio-inspired optimization routing protocol. Although there are many types of routing protocols available for the FANET, choosing a suitable type is important for the effective operation of the flying nodes in the network. This paper analyzed how bio-inspired optimization algorithms can be effectively applied for intelligent routing strategies.

REFERENCES

Agrawal & Kapoor. (2021). A comparative study on geographic-based routing algorithms for flying ad-hoc networks. *Concurrency ComputatPractExper*. doi:10.1002/cpe.6253

Ahmad, M., Ullah, F., Wahid, I., Khan, A., Irfan Uddin, M., Alharbi, A., & Alosaimi, W. (2021). A Bio-Inspired Routing Optimization in UAV-enabled Internet of Everything. *Computers, Materials & Continua*, *67*(1), 321–336. Advance online publication. doi:10.32604/cmc.2021.014102

Alam, M. M., & Moh, S. (2022). Survey on Q-Learning-Based Position-Aware Routing Protocols in Flying Ad Hoc Networks. *Electronics (Basel)*, *11*(7), 1099. doi:10.3390/electronics11071099

Beegum. (2023). *Optimized Routing of UAVs Using Bio-Inspired Algorithm in FANET: A Systematic Review*. doi:10.1109/ACCESS.2023.3244067

Bharany, S., Sharma, S., Bhatia, S., Rahmani, M. K. I., Shuaib, M., & Lashari, S. A. (2022). Energy Efficient Clustering Protocol for FANETS Using Moth Flame Optimization. *Sustainability (Basel)*, *14*(10), 6159. doi:10.3390/su14106159

Choi, Hussein, Park, & Kim. (2018). *Geolocation-based Routing Protocol for Flying Adhoc Networks (FANETs)*. IEEE.

De Rango, F., Potrino, G., Tropea, M., Santamaria, A. F., & Fazio, P. (2019). Scalable and highway bio-inspired coordination protocol for FANET in precision agriculture applications. *Computers & Electrical Engineering*, *74*, 305–318. doi:10.1016/j.compeleceng.2019.01.018

De Rango, F., Tropea, M., & Fazio, P. (2019). Bio-Inspired Routing over FANET in Emergency Situations to Support Multimedia Traffic. In *Proceedings of ACM Mobihoc (CATANIA'19)*. Association for Computing Machinery.

Dixit, A., & Singh, S. K. (2023). BMUDF: Hybrid Bio-inspired Model for fault-aware UAV routing using Destination-aware Fan shaped clustering. *Internet of Things : Engineering Cyber Physical Human Systems*, *22*, 100790. doi:10.1016/j.iot.2023.100790

Hameed, Alyahya, Minhas, Habib, Nawaz, Ahmed, Ishtiaq, Islam, & Khan. (2021). *Link and Loss Aware GW-COOP Routing Protocol for FANETs*. doi:10.1109/ACCESS.2021.3101361

Hussain, Khan, Nazir, Hussain, & Ullah. (2021). Taking Drones to Next Level: The Performance Evaluation of MAA with BCO Routing Protocols for Flying Ad-hoc Networks (FANETs). *Advances in Distributed Computing and Artificial Intelligence Journal, 10*(4), 321-337. doi:10.14201/ADCAIJ2021104321337

Kaur & Singh. (2018). Nature-Inspired Optimization Techniques in VANETs and FANETs: A Survey. Springer. doi:10.1007/978-981-10-8237-5_63

Khan, Aftab, & Zhang. (2019). *BICSF: Bio-Inspired Clustering Scheme for FANETs*. doi:10.1109/ACCESS.2019.2902940

Khan, A., Khan, S., Fazal, A. S., Zhang, Z., & Abuassba, A. O. (2021). Intelligent cluster routing scheme for flying ad hoc networks. *Science China. Information Sciences*, *64*(8), 182305. doi:10.1007/s11432-019-2984-7

Khan, M. F., Yau, K.-L. A., Noor, R. M., & Imran, M. A. (2020). Routing Schemes in FANETs: A Survey. *Sensors (Basel)*, *20*(1), 38. doi:10.3390/s20010038

Khan, S., Khan, M. Z., & Khan, P. (2022). An Ant-Hocnet Routing Protocol Based on Optimized Fuzzy Logic for Swarm of UAVs in FANET. Hindawi Wireless Communications and Mobile Computing.

Kim, T., Lee, S., Kim, K. H., & Jo, Y.-I. (2023). FANET Routing Protocol Analysis for Multi-UAV-Based Reconnaissance Mobility Models. *Drones (Basel)*, *7*(3), 161. doi:10.3390/drones7030161

Kout, Bouaita, B., Beghriche, A., Labed, S., Chikhi, S., & Bourennane, E.-B. (2023). A Hybrid Optimization Solution for UAV Network Routing" engineering. *Technology & Applied Science Research*, *13*(2), 10270–10278. doi:10.48084/etasr.5661

Kumar, Raw, & Bansal. (n.d.). Minimize the routing overhead through 3D cone shaped location-aided routing protocol for FANETs. *Int. J. Inf. Tecnol.* doi:10.1007/s41870-020-00536-3

Lakew, Sa'ad, Dao, Na, & Cho. (2020). *Routing in Flying Ad Hoc Networks: A Comprehensive Survey*. doi:10.1109/COMST.2020.2982452

Leonov, A. V. (2017). Applying bio-inspired algorithms to routing problem solution in FANET. *Bulletin of the South Ural State University*, *17*(2), 5–23.

Luis Antonio, L. F. (2021). Q-FANET: Improved Q-learning based routing protocol for FANETs. *Computer Networks*, *198*, 108379. doi:10.1016/j.comnet.2021.108379

Lytos, A., Lagkas, T., Sarigiannidis, P., Zervakis, M., & Livanos, G. (2020). Towards smart farming: Systems, frameworks and exploitation of multiple sources. *Computer Networks*, *172*, 107147. doi:10.1016/j.comnet.2020.107147

Nadeem, Alghamdi, Yawar, Mehmood, & Siddiqui. (2018). A Review and Classification of Flying Ad-Hoc Network (FANET) Routing Strategies. *Journal of Basic and Applied Scientific Research*, *8*(3), 1–8.

Oubbati, O. S., Lakas, A., Zhou, F., Güneş, M., & Yagoubi, M. B. (2017). A survey on position-based routing protocols for Flying Ad hoc Networks (FANETs). *Vehicular Communications*, *10*, 29–56. doi:10.1016/j.vehcom.2017.10.003

Radoglou-Grammatikis, P., Sarigiannidis, P., Lagkas, T., & Moscholios, I. (2020). A compilation of UAV applications for precision agriculture. *Computer Networks*, *172*, 107148. doi:10.1016/j.comnet.2020.107148

Rahmani, A. M., Ali, S., Yousefpoor, E., Yousefpoor, M. S., Javaheri, D., Lalbakhsh, P., Hassan Ahmed, O., Hosseinzadeh, M., & Lee, S.-W. (2022). OLSR+: A new routing method based on fuzzy logic in flying ad-hoc networks (FANETs). *Vehicular Communications*, *36*, 100489. doi:10.1016/j.vehcom.2022.100489

Sang, Q., Wu, H., Xing, L., & Xie, P. (2020). Review and Comparison of Emerging Routing Protocols in Flying Ad Hoc Networks. *Symmetry*, *12*(6), 971. doi:10.3390/sym12060971

Usmana, Chughtaia, Nawaz, Kaleema, Khaliqb, & Nguyen. (n.d.). A Reliable Link-adaptive position-based routing protocol for Flying ad hoc Network. *Mobile Networks and Applications, 26*(4), 1801-1820.

Vrchota, J., Pech, M., & Švepešová, I. (2022). Precision Agriculture Technologies for Crop and Livestock Production in the Czech Republic. *Agriculture*, *12*(8), 1080. doi:10.3390/agriculture12081080

Weigand, Wiedner, & Andre. (2022). Position-based Routing in Flying Ad Hoc Networks. *Seminar IITM WS 21/22, Network Architectures and Services.*

Wheeb, A. H., Nordin, R., Samah, A. A., Alsharif, M. H., & Khan, M. A. (2022). Topology-Based Routing Protocols and Mobility Models for Flying Ad Hoc Networks: A Contemporary Review and Future Research Directions. *Drones (Basel)*, *6*(1), 9. doi:10.3390/drones6010009

Yang, H., & Liu, Z. (2019). An optimization routing protocol for FANETs. *EURASIP Journal on Wireless Communications and Networking*, *2019*(1), 120. doi:10.1186/s13638-019-1442-0

Chapter 13
Biospheric Reverie:
Unraveling Indoor Air Quality Through Bio-Inspired Textiles, Awareness, and Decision-Making

Rita Komalasari
https://orcid.org/0000-0001-9963-2363
Yarsi University, Indonesia

ABSTRACT

Indoor air quality is a critical yet often overlooked facet of our daily lives. This chapter seeks to shed light on this issue, offering a unique perspective through the lens of bio-inspired textiles. This exploration aims to create awareness and empower individuals to enhance their home environments. The method involved an extensive literature study, extracting insights from biology, design, and awareness campaigns. The results revealed the transformative potential of bio-inspired textile artifacts in raising awareness and fostering a sense of well-being in participants' homes. This research contributes valuable guidelines for decision-making for bio-inspired design, marking a significant milestone in the quest for healthier and harmonious living spaces.

INTRODUCTION

Unbeknownst to many, a significant problem is indoor air pollution, which lurks in the dark recesses of our houses where we try to relax and unwind (Belotti et al., 2020). The air we breathe is a quiet ballet of chemical and microbiological elements that may impact our mental and physical well-being (Fu et al., 2020). It is not enough to acknowledge the difficulty; we must also have a poetic comprehension of the problem and an awareness of how it permeates every part of our lives. In order to bring about a profound awakening about the air we breathe in our sanctuaries, this investigation dives into the core of the matter by combining biology and design (Nguyen et al., 2020). Anyone concerned with or working to improve indoor air quality may benefit from the information and understanding gained from this study. Some examples are that homeowners would do well to educate themselves on indoor air quality

DOI: 10.4018/979-8-3693-2073-0.ch013

and the elements that influence it, many of which are not readily apparent. Insights from the study may help homeowners improve their living conditions, which can improve their health. Using bio-inspired design standards as a springboard, architects and interior designers may improve indoor air quality while simultaneously adding to homes' aesthetic value and atmosphere (Brebenel, 2020). Academic institutions will find the results helpful, particularly those that provide design, bio-inspiration, and environmental science courses. Curricula and teaching techniques may be shaped by the study, including the obstacles undergraduates encounter during practical application. Environmental and public health groups may use the findings to push for legislation and awareness campaigns about indoor air quality. The relationship between design, mindfulness, and well-being is explained in detail in the paper (Cuce et al., 2019). Businesses in the textile and construction material industries may improve indoor air quality with their goods by using bio-inspired design concepts. These items will serve several functions. Raising public awareness about the importance of indoor air quality for human health can only help. The study presents a story that more people can understand, urging us to all do our part to make our homes healthy (Antonov et al., 2020). When drafting rules and standards for building design and construction, experts in city planning and policymaking may consider the study's findings. Overall, this has the potential to make city dwellers' lives better. The current situation may be changed to promote healthier homes and communities by sharing the information obtained from this study with various stakeholders.

There are several essential ways in which the research advances the profession and the field: The study develops bio-inspired design concepts for better indoor air quality by modeling nest behavior after that of the mother blue tit bird. Not only does this provide a new use case for bio-inspiration in textile design, but it also enhances the discipline as a whole. To help experts in the industry incorporate features inspired by nature into their products, practical standards for bio-inspired design have been established (Abdullah et al., 2019). These guidelines give a realistic framework and actionable insights. Sustainability and health-conscious design are both advanced by this. Beyond theoretical frameworks, the research provides evidence of how bio-inspired textile objects raise consciousness and improve well-being via adoption trials in households. It encourages a new crop of ecologically aware and inventive designers by teaching them the advantages and disadvantages of bio-inspired design to improve indoor air quality (Shashwat et al., 2023). This research fills a gap by recognizing the mutually beneficial link between health and design. This interdisciplinary approach emphasizes the impact of design choices on the health and well-being of those living in buildings, contributing to a more comprehensive understanding of the constructed surroundings. Studying the challenges faced by undergraduate students in implementing bio-inspired design concepts might provide valuable insights for enhancing our pedagogical approaches. By accurately understanding how theoretical information is used in actual circumstances, you may enhance your preparation for future design assignments (Zhou et al., 2023). Experts and educators may greatly benefit from the comprehensive visual record of Bio-inspired Awareness, a physical artifact that draws natural inspiration. This is a concrete illustration of how to enhance indoor air quality by using bio-inspired design principles in a utilitarian and aesthetically pleasing manner. This study not only improves our theoretical understanding of bio-inspired design but also provides practical advice, empirical data, and pedagogical insights that contribute to the advancement of the field (Wang et al., 2022). It promotes the creation of environmentally conscious design advancements and supports using bio-inspired textiles as a viable solution for indoor air quality problems.

BACKGROUND

The indoor air quality issue has received little attention, with just a handful of residential initiatives attempting to increase awareness about it (Chen et al., 2022). Most projects are public works located in outside areas and aim to increase awareness about the importance of outdoor air. Even in the confines of our homes, microorganisms and toxic substances have the potential to infiltrate our surroundings and compromise the quality of the air we breathe, posing a threat to our well-being. This innovative textile study involves a two-step investigation into bio-inspired fabrics. We undertake a poetic expedition to increase awareness about air quality and empower folks to improve their home settings (Hubert et al., 2022). The nesting activities of the female blue tit bird inspire our approach to creating interactive textile things. Our data analysis and iterative adoption tests reveal these artifacts' immense potential to make homes healthier and happier places to live. The second phase of undergraduates' practical application is guided by principles for bio-inspired design that arise in reaction to these insights. This chapter provides a comprehensive strategy for dealing with indoor air quality by demonstrating the interplay between bio-inspiration, optimization, and decision-making.

Worldwide, 4.2 million people die yearly from breathing polluted indoor air (World Health Organization, 2022). Respiratory infections, cardiovascular illness, and cancer are among the many health concerns associated with exposure to indoor air pollution. Because their immune systems and lungs are still maturing, children are more susceptible to the negative impacts of indoor air pollution. According to Arora and McIntyre (2021), indoor airborne microbes may exacerbate respiratory conditions, including asthma and allergies. Vocs emitted by everyday household products may irritate the eyes, nose, and throat, producing nausea, headaches, and fatigue. Estimates put the global biomimicry industry's value at $35.1 billion by 2025 because of rising interest in applying bio-inspired solutions to environmental problems (Zhu et al., 2019). Medicine, energy, and materials science are just a few areas that have discovered the benefits of bio-inspired design. Li et al. (2023) cite recent studies that show bio-inspired design might improve IAQ. According to a 2019 study conducted by the American Heart Association, 70% of Americans were unaware that indoor air pollution poses health hazards. The amount of time individuals spend inside, where air quality may be much worse than outside, needs to be addressed (Rajagopalan et al., 2020). Innovative approaches are necessary to educate the general population on the significance of indoor air quality and provide them with the necessary resources to enhance it. Our seemingly safe shelter significantly contributes to indoor air pollution, which often goes unrecognized. Chemicals and bacteria that harm human health are sneaking into our homes. Despite the undeniable influence on well-being, more effective awareness campaigns and practical solutions regarding indoor air quality are needed (Amoatey et al., 2020). To address this need, our study will uncover hidden threats and provide the groundwork for a bio-inspired, aesthetically pleasing solution for people to enhance their homes.

Method

In this study, the foundation of our exploration rested upon the rich tapestry of existing literature. We delved into the intricate worlds of biology, design, and awareness campaigns, unraveling threads of knowledge that informed our bio-inspired approach. Data collected, a mosaic of interviews and personal journals, underwent meticulous analysis. Patterns emerged, guiding the evolution of our textile artifacts and culminating in the formulation of precise design guidelines. One field that looks to nature and living things for design ideas is bio-inspiration, which is the subject of this literature study. The etymology of this term may be traced back to the Greek word "bios," which denotes the concept of life. Artists, designers, and engineers have used the method since the late 15th century. The following figure 1 illustrates the specific method.

Figure 1. The specific method

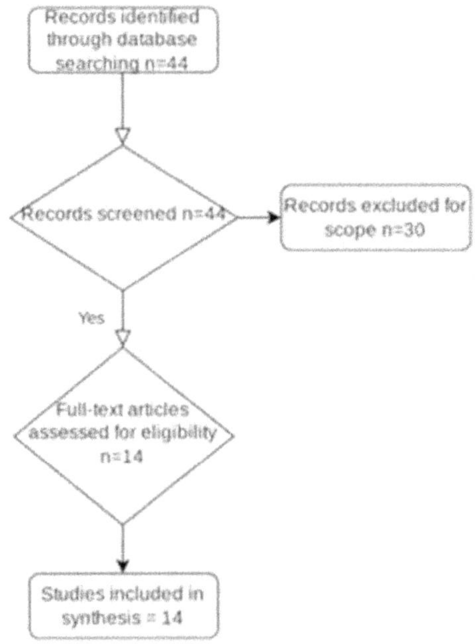

The field known as bionics studies artificial systems that mimic or share properties with biological systems. "biomimetics" refers to the study of synthetic processes that aim to replicate the structure and function of naturally occurring substances and materials and biological systems and processes (Liu et al., 2021). Bionics and biomimetics are synonyms but not synonyms with biomimicry or bioinspiration. Bionics and biomimetics deliver sustainable solutions, but they do not aim to preserve nature. Biomimicry, on the other hand, focuses on technical application, while bio-inspiration does not. The literature review provides a deeper understanding of bio-inspiration and its historical and contemporary context. The word "biomimicry" was used to describe a deliberate attempt to model human problem-solving after the innovative strategies used by nature (Shi et al., 2020). This piece presents a fresh approach to design that seeks inspiration from nature after visualizing the perfect solution. This thinking advocates looking to nature for guidance in all aspects of life, not only modeling. Bio-inspiration, often known as bio-inspired design, is an umbrella word for various design practices that draw inspiration from biological, environmental, and biologically-based sources. It covers everything from a scientific comprehension of function to a more surface-level imitation of form. Many articles in academic journals focus on bio-inspired design as a procedure, with subjects covering everything from how it works to proposing a novel way to use biological phenomena in idea development. Many scientists popularized the concept of biophilia, which is the foundation of biophilic design (Uchiyama et al., 2020). As Makram and Abou (2019) elucidate, gardening or walking demonstrates our inextricable bond with the living Earth. The extent to which a person is connected to nature determines their significance and purpose in life, as per the concept of biophilia. Biophilic design, biomimicry, and bio-inspired design are design concepts that have emerged to provide sustainable solutions for human challenges (Bajçinovci, 2019). Design that integrates biophilia and biomimicry concepts may lead to more inventive and ecologically advantageous solutions.

UNRAVELING INDOOR AIR QUALITY THROUGH BIO-INSPIRED TEXTILES

This section explores the urgent need for immediate action to address the severe air quality problem (Sinha et al., 2020). Smartphones have revolutionized how we track environmental changes, enabling people to improve their health habits. On the other hand, initiatives highlighting the importance of air quality via textiles are few and far between. Rain Palette is an example of a project employing rainfall to represent air quality visually through natural red cabbage dye. Although most of these projects use cutting-edge tech, designers are given much leeway regarding tactics and forms. This analysis emphasizes the importance of textile designs that use a bio-inspired approach to increase awareness of indoor air quality. According to the research on indoor air pollution, one suitable design method is to make people more aware of the problem via their interactions with textile objects (Manisalidis et al., 2020). The research primarily focused on designs that draw attention to the problem of air pollution, examining existing methods in design for air quality. The literature research identified the primary factors responsible for indoor air pollution and its impact on human health. It emphasized the most significant obstacle to enhancing indoor air quality via design (Al-Kindi et al., 2020). A practical approach to reducing domestic air pollution is to increase public awareness of the problem. Numerous studies have shown the positive effects of nature on human health; for example, seeing peaceful natural settings may help alleviate symptoms of stress and mental exhaustion. By influencing one's emotional state, these settings also improve one's ability to solve creative problems and perform higher-order cognitive functions (Tran et al., 2020). According to Fuller et al. (2022), subjective well-being is the state of mind a person experiences due to interaction with various stimuli and events. Biophilic design is an architectural approach that aims to enhance the connection between building inhabitants and the natural environment. It is vital to achieve this goal so that people may live and work in conditions that promote health, well-being and decreased stress. There is scientific proof that getting outside may boost mental health, creativity, and stress levels. Therefore, my strategy is based on that. Incorporating natural materials into buildings with biophilic design principles might provide therapeutic spaces (Saini et al., 2020). People may recover from mental exhaustion and stress more rapidly and entirely in restorative situations, and there is evidence that built-environment images of nature reduce stress. Unfortunately, there is a lack of data on the combined effects of biophilic design features; the only accessible data concerns the usage of wood in such contexts (Kuddus et al., 2020). There needs to be more investigation into the possibility of evoking a feeling of well-being by appealing to many senses simultaneously, such as sight, sound, and smell. While some research has shown that plants with a subtle scent are particularly healing, other studies have zeroed in on specific components, including plants, environmental imagery, and natural light. Biophilic design may greatly enhance human well-being by bringing people in closer contact with nature and using natural components in its designs (Magazzino et al., 2020). The biophilic design philosophy aims to restore or incorporate bio-inspired features into artificial spaces so that they more closely resemble their natural counterparts. Organic and vernacular design are the two sides of this approach. Organic design draws inspiration from nature in its use of light, air, and forms, while vernacular design emphasizes the importance of place in bridging cultural, historical, and ecological gaps (Jain & Sharma, 2020). Our investigation focuses on the serious problem of poor indoor air quality, which is a constant but unseen danger to human health that seeps into our houses. Standard methods of dealing with this problem are insufficient since they do not have the visual appeal and effectiveness to attract and involve the locals. Within this environment, our research seeks to shed light on these hidden dangers and, more importantly, to change how people think about raising awareness and finding solutions (He et al., 2020). Our study paves the way for a bio-inspired, visually beautiful paradigm by acknowledging the shortcomings of current approaches. A fresh strategy like this one aims to reconcile the opposing views of houses as secure refuges and places of possible health risks. By observing the blue tit mother bird as she tends her nest, our research hopes to go beyond just making practical textile goods. We aim to produce an immersive sensory and cognitive experience beyond standard awareness campaigns. The essence of our study demonstrates the profound capacity of a bio-inspired, visually appealing methodology ready to revolutionize our understanding and resolution of the widespread indoor air quality problem.This work aims to design bio-inspired objects that can provide an indoor ambiance that closely resembles nature (Yang et al., 2020). By doing so, the mediator may take a mental or physical break from their daily lives and get hypnotized by their sensations, emotions, and ideas. According to Canbazoğlu et al. (2021), who advocates using nature as a guide, standard, and example, biomimicry and bio-inspiration are conceptually related. This is because biomimetics and bionics are considered in this connection. The creative industries utilize nature as a model in bio-inspiration (design-driven innovation), whereas engineering-driven innovation draws from nature. This is the main distinction between bionics/biomimetics and bio-inspiration. Biomimicry may take either an engineering- or a design-driven approach. The principle of biomimicry is to model human design after living organisms to produce long-lasting, environmentally friendly products. Biomimicry is a method for creating sustainable designs by taking cues from living things and comparing them to their principles (Imani & Vale, 2022). These principles include being responsive to local conditions, using chemistry that is friendly to living things, making efficient use of resources, integrating development with growth, and evolving to survive.Collaborating with nature does not need judging the designs according to the laws of nature. The established technique aims to make home decor items that do not add to indoor air pollution. Because of this, we try to minimize the potential harmful impacts of the products and procedures we use on the environment. The findings support the idea of "well-adapted" design, which focuses on making eco-friendly items that blend in with their natural environment to improve quality of life (Sommese et al., 2022). The idea behind bio-inspiration is to look to nature for ideas on how to make the world a better place via product and solution design. Designing for a better world is all about taking cues from nature and making models that mimic its structures and functions. However, bioinspiration opens up a more expansive view of life by constructing and developing a concept influenced by nature; this, in turn, suggests a less dogmatic approach to understanding biological events. According to this study, bio-inspiration is defined as drawing ideas for problem-solving from natural sources, with the implication that one should take cues from nature while also allowing one's creative interpretation of its processes to inform one's work (Jamei & Vrcelj, 2021). Utilizing natural imagery and materials to fabricate items is intended to prompt contemplation of the origins of these resources. This trait alludes to the metaphorical encounter with nature, suggesting that people may use nature to facilitate communication and cognitive processes. Biodesign, bio-integrated design, and bio-utilization are all components of environmentally responsible design. Biodesign proponents propose using nature as a material for design rather than only studying it for inspiration (Khelil & Zemmouri, 2019). A new curriculum called "bio-integrated design" has been developed by the Bartlett School of Architecture and the Biochemical Engineering Department at University College London in the UK (Robinson et al., 2021). This curriculum combines science with multidisciplinary approaches. Going beyond merely copying nature to genuinely exploiting it as a medium for design is key to their approach, which is analogous to that of Natarajan and Short (2023). The major emphasis of bio-utilization is the direct utilization of nature for beneficial reasons. Benyus outlines three categories of "bio" in her writings: biomimicking, which involves simulating natural processes; bio-assisted technologies, which include rearing organisms; and bio-utilization, which refers to the extraction of products (Vardanyan et al., 2022). Biophilic design refers to intentionally incorporating and imitating natural components in the design process. The phrase "nature" embraces the entire biosphere, from plants and animals to tiny beings. Biodesign aims to replicate natural processes and use natural materials, resulting in some convergence between biodegradable and biomimetic designs (Jatoi et al., 2023). Designers have found inspiration in the ever-changing bio-inspired design technique, which mostly applies to textiles. Around three millennia ago, the Chinese attempted to fabricate artificial silk, marking the first recorded occurrence of biomimetic textiles. Smart Textiles, a fastening method that replicates the hook and loop mechanism found in burdock burrs and served as the official commencement of bio-inspired use in textiles (Sajovic et al., 2023). Physical materiality, including improved manufactured fibers, surfaces, and finishes, has dominated bioinspired textile concepts since then.Material scientists in the textile industry have been studying natural phenomena for clues on creating high-performance fabrics that mimic the properties of living things. Examples include Aquapel, Kevlar, Polymer Opal, Morphotex, Stomatex, and Polymer Opal. These bio-inspired fabrics take their cues from the effective solutions that naturally occurring organisms like plants, insects, and animals have perfected over the ages (Rosetta et al., 2023). Their fabrics are generally modeled after pinecones, which are known for their sensitive nature and ability to open and shut in reaction to variations in humidity and temperature. To alleviate the physical pain of city travel, smart fabrics like Metropolitan Comfort imitate how pinecones' form may alter when exposed to moisture. Made entirely of organic materials, Jane Scott's responsive textiles for knitted architecture react to variations in relative humidity (Scott, 2023). One of many smart architectural surfaces, Techno Naturology is an interactive textile that may open and shut in reaction to variations in humidity and temperature, much like a pinecone.Entropy carpets, for example, are patterned like woodland floors; the tiles blend attractively and can be changed one by one in case of stains or tears. The cradle-to-cradle approach, developed by William McDonough and Michael Braungart, is a biomimicry strategy for designing products considering the whole life cycle and minimizing their environmental impact (Kacprzak, 2022). This method is exemplified by Climatex Lifecycle Fabrics, which are created from all-natural ingredients and treated using only non-toxic chemicals; however, some fabrics have been specifically developed with a utilitarian function in mind. The choices regarding the materials and procedures used were influenced by the role that the textile was required to fulfill (Dicks, 2019). While the materials and procedures used to make these textiles give them their aesthetic features, these attributes do not affect how the product interacts with the user when used for its intended purpose. The following table 1 illustrates the summary of bio-inspired textiles..

On the other hand, the study does not try to mitigate or reverse the harmful impacts of home air pollution; instead, it draws inspiration for awareness-raising artifacts from the model's method of operation (Eguiluz et al., 2020). By outlining the existing state of practice and drawing attention to the knowledge gap, this mapping exercise sought to discover bio-inspired solutions to air pollution. Sustainable carpet tiles, fabric coloration via surface structure, reduced noise from high-speed trains, and responsive architectural structures are just a few of the many issues bio-inspiration addresses in the textile, product, vehicle, and architectural design fields (Lee et al., 2020). Indoor air pollution is another issue that bio-inspiration aims to resolve. An example of a fabric that addresses this problem is Aquapel, which has hydrophobic characteristics. The removal of formaldehyde from PureBond wood adhesive, which is a glue made from soy, aids in the reduction of air pollution. Eastgate Centre is an additional instance of a bio-inspired structure that effectively reduces interior air pollution (Turner et al., 2020). It does this via excellent ventilation without traditional heating or air conditioning systems.

Table 1. Summary of bio-inspired textiles

Aspect	Summary
Bio-inspired Textile Designs	Emphasizes the importance of bio-inspired textile designs to raise awareness of indoor air quality issues, drawing attention to pollution.
Impact on Human Health	Indoor air pollution affects health; designs should increase awareness and address obstacles to improving air quality indoors.
Biophilic Design Benefits	Biophilic design enhances human well-being by connecting with nature, providing therapeutic spaces that reduce stress and mental exhaustion.
Bio-inspired Objects for Indoor Ambiance	Designing bio-inspired objects to mimic nature indoors aims to provide therapeutic experiences and improve well-being.
Biomimicry and Bioinspiration	Biomimicry and bioinspiration draw from nature for sustainable design, focusing on mimicking natural processes and materials to minimize environmental impact.
Bio-utilization for Eco-friendly Design	Bio-utilization aims to utilize nature directly for beneficial purposes, emphasizing eco-friendly design that blends with the environment.
Biodesign and Biophilic Design	Biodesign replicates natural processes in design, while biophilic design intentionally incorporates natural elements to improve quality of life.
Smart Fabrics and Architectural Surfaces	Smart fabrics and surfaces mimic natural phenomena like pinecones' responsiveness to humidity and temperature changes, offering comfort and adaptability in architectural design.
Cradle-to-Cradle Approach	The cradle-to-cradle approach, exemplified by Climatex Lifecycle Fabrics, considers the entire life cycle of products, minimizing environmental impact through sustainable materials.
Utilitarian Functionality in Textiles	Textile materials and processes are chosen based on intended functions, with attention to aesthetics and user interaction.

Products, vehicles, and structures that draw inspiration from nature are all part of the modern practice review. Through the development of goods that improve people's lives, these designs embody realistic solutions derived from natural models. Take, for instance, Pax Water's Mixer Impeller 46, which takes design cues from the calla lily's petal-like bracts; Dawn Haleta's Biomimicry of the Sun 47, a clock that uses LED technology and software to simulate the sun's physical effects; Mercedes-Benz's conceptual Bionic Car, which draws design cues from the yellow boxfish; and the Gerkin Tower, Shinkansen, and Talgo trains, among others (Ukaogo et al., 2020). Biomimicry's renowned solution-based approach results in developing novel or improved products that effectively reduce or eliminate a problem. Ecologically aware designs are needed to tackle the problem of indoor air pollution. The issue of air pollution may have practical solutions that are bio-inspired and rely on natural principles. These designs may be used in various industries, including clothing, transportation, and construction, and they help bring attention to the problem (Amato et al., 2020).

Designing with bio-inspiration in mind allows us to make longer-lasting, eco-friendly products and services that help keep our planet habitable. Product design, architectural design, biomimicry, and other domains have all used the idea of bioinspiration. It has generated ground-breaking designs that challenge conventional architecture and consumer goods wisdom. The issue of indoor air pollution has been highlighted via bioinspiration. Researchers García et al. (2020) are exploring the idea of responsive architecture influenced by biology in this project. In order to probe and test ideas, the project's spatial structure may move or be moved by stimuli from the outside world. The review's essential readings include the significance of physical function in decision-making, the purpose of creating goods that imitate biological models to fulfill the same function, and the emphasis on engineering and design (Qamar., 2022). As a solution-based approach, bio-inspiration is often used to design new or better products that target the causes or consequences of a problem, therefore reducing or eliminating it. Since bio-inspiration primarily serves to guide the design of works that eradicate pollution sources, it is seldom used as a tactic in the creation of speculative works. Although bio-inspiration is not a new strategy for raising awareness about home air quality, it is an unconventional use of textiles to combat the problem of indoor air pollution (Park et al., 2022). The bio-inspired design method aims to derive guidance for optimum systems architecture, functional components, and recipe formulation from the natural world. Biomimicry is the scientific study and replication of patterns, processes, and strategies in the natural world. Biomimicry, suggested by Baumeister et al. (2020), is a consultancy that draws inspiration from nature to inform design. They propose two methods for integrating biology into design: a problem-driven approach, which seeks solutions by studying nature, and a solution-driven approach, where inspiration is derived from nature. The less common biology-to-design method looks to natural systems for inspiration before figuring out how to use such systems. One of the most well-known methods is the "design-to-nature" strategy, which involves looking to nature for a comparable issue and a potential solution to the design challenge.

The Genius of Place framework explores how the strategies and designs of living species and ecosystems impact the creation of human-made environments to create durable and regenerative settings (Hayes et al., 2020). This is achieved by converting biological information into design principles, which are brought to life via illustrations, application concepts, and solutions. Following these phases is the whole bio-inspired process: first, figuring out what needs doing (what is the desired outcome), and second, asking, "How does nature...?" to biologize the issue (Sharma & Sarkar, 2022). One definition of "bio-inspiration" is drawing ideas for new scientific and technological endeavors from real-world biological events. According to Eggermont and Paul (2020), observation is a critical component of bioinspiration as it is the most accessible and cost-effective method for comprehending biological processes. Since this definition of bio-inspiration suggests that there is no one "correct" approach to mimic the behaviors seen in biological systems, it opens up new possibilities for creativity. According to popular belief, Sandak and Butina's (2023) bioinspiration process consists of three stages: (1) observing the behavior or function of a living organism; (2) The process involves simplifying the operation of the live creature by using its talents and imitating some aspects of its functioning. Ultimately, it aims to imitate the operation of the living body. The World Health Organisation (WHO) has identified indoor air pollution as a significant health risk, which serves as a compelling context for our inquiry (World Health Organization 2021). According to the World Health Organization, indoor air pollution worsens allergies, respiratory ailments, and overall health. The claim highlights how serious and pressing the problem is since people's health is put at risk even in the supposed haven of their homes. There must be a paradigm shift in thinking about the home safety paradox and the hidden health risks people face there (Balmes, 2019). The authors are driven to uncover new ways that bring attention to the issue of poor indoor air quality and give people the tools they need to reduce the risks that come with it. Even while there are awareness initiatives on indoor air quality, they only sometimes succeed in making a big difference. The authors are prompted to seek beyond standard approaches by this study's premise that a paradigm change is necessary. The author suggests a change towards a more bio-inspired strategy, taking cues from the way blue tit mothers tend to their nests. More than just a representation of nature's artistic genius, this bird becomes a blueprint for manufacturing helpful textile objects (Zhang & Srinivasan, 2020). Crafted with an eye toward natural accuracy, these objects function as home probes—creative instruments that may improve the aesthetics of interiors while also investigating and resolving the complex dynamics of indoor air quality. Our goal is to show how these textile objects inspired by nature may change people's lives via two home-based iterative adoption trials. Beyond the domain of theory, the tests prove their ability to increase knowledge about indoor air quality, provide people with the tools to make educated choices, and, ultimately, make homes healthier and more pleasant places to live (Megahed & Ghoneim, 2021). This perspective emphasizes the transformative potential of bio-inspired design, which combines form and function to alter our relationship with and understanding of the places we call home.

This study provides practical recommendations for implementing bio-inspired design concepts, drawing on insights from our empirical investigations beyond theoretical frameworks (Vardoulakis et al., 2020). The adoption trials provided the data that inspired these recommendations, which go beyond simple theory. Their main contribution is a set of practical instructions for using bio-inspired design principles in everyday life. Most importantly, these rules are proven correct when used in undergraduate design classes. The study helps shape a realistic grasp of applying bio-inspired ideas by exposing students to the obstacles of turning theoretical knowledge into practical, functioning solutions (Gonzalez et al., 2021). As a result, the story goes from being a theoretical investigation into a practical manual, teaching the next generation of designers how to solve critical problems like poor indoor air quality with creative, eco-friendly approaches. This transition from theory to execution represents a significant and influential advancement for the industry, solidifying bio-inspired design as more than just a philosophical notion but a concrete and achievable approach to improving the quality of people's lives (Azuma et al., 2020).

Moreover, the extensive visual documentation of Bio-inspired Awareness provides persuasive proof of the concrete influence of our bio-inspired products (Tainio et al., 2021). This embodiment showcases the successful transformation of abstract design concepts into functional, aesthetically pleasing, and utilitarian things. The visual record offers a comprehensive depiction of the whole process, starting with the idea's inception and culminating in its finalization, showcasing the transformative capacity of bio-inspired design. "Bio-inspired Awareness" demonstrates the transformation of an item into a visual representation that combines its physical attributes with its functional purpose. This exemplifies the harmonious combination of functionality and aesthetic appeal derived from nature. This chapter is a comprehensive documentation of accomplishments and an excellent tool for educators, producers, and anybody interested in exploring the connections between design, awareness, and environmental well-being. This exemplifies that bio-inspired design is not only a theoretical concept but an aesthetically pleasing and practical approach to addressing tangible issues, such as the urgent problem of inadequate indoor air quality.

SOLUTIONS AND RECOMMENDATIONS

Building regulations and standards should include bio-inspired design concepts based on our research. By recognizing the potential of aesthetically pleasing, nature-inspired solutions, policymakers can incentivize the adoption of such designs in architectural and interior practices. This proactive policy approach can improve indoor environments and public health outcomes. Beyond research, we advocate for innovative and practical solutions applicable in clinical, educational, and community settings. Make healthcare facilities more conducive to healing by using textile innovations inspired by nature. Embed educational programs that teach individuals to integrate bio-inspired principles in their homes, promoting self-sufficiency in maintaining optimal indoor air quality. Community initiatives can include creating green spaces and bio-inspired urban planning, reinforcing the connection between nature and well-being. By endorsing these practical solutions, we envision a seamless translation of research into transformative real-world applications.

Practical Implementation: Pilot Projects: Launching pilot projects in real-world settings to demonstrate the feasibility and effectiveness of bio-inspired design solutions. This could involve partnering with architects, designers, and local authorities to implement small-scale interventions and monitor their impact over time. Monitoring and Evaluation: Implementing robust monitoring and evaluation frameworks to assess the effectiveness of bio-inspired solutions. This includes collecting data on indoor air quality, occupant well-being, and energy consumption to measure the impact of interventions accurately. Stakeholder Engagement: Engaging with stakeholders at every stage of the implementation process. This includes involving building owners, occupants, policymakers, and community members to ensure that interventions are tailored to their needs and preferences. Scalability and Replicability: Designing solutions that are scalable and replicable across different settings and contexts. This involves identifying key success factors and best practices that can be applied to similar projects elsewhere.

FUTURE RESEARCH DIRECTIONS

What is the subsequent course of action? Additional research is required to analyze the impact of bio-inspired textile products on the long-term welfare of residents and indoor air quality. In order to comprehensively assess their efficacy, it would be advantageous to explore the potential for extending these solutions to other geographical regions and socioeconomic contexts. Furthermore, the potential for enhancing bio-inspired textile designs might be achieved by investigating the feasibility of integrating advanced technology, such as intelligent sensors. Ultimately, doing a comprehensive analysis of the broader effects of bio-inspired design on the conservation of natural resources and the advancement of sustainable environmental conditions would significantly improve the depth and effectiveness of the discourse. The author proposes potential avenues for further investigation that expand the scope of this study's conclusions. Investigate the long-term impact of bio-inspired materials on the well-being of building occupants and the overall air quality. Explore the possibility of expanding these concepts to tackle diverse socioeconomic and geographical contexts for a more well-rounded impact... Additionally, research avenues could delve into integrating technology, such as smart sensors, to enhance the functionality of bio-inspired designs. By explicitly highlighting these potential research directions, we encourage the continuous evolution of knowledge and practices, contributing to a sustainable and health-focused future.

CONCLUSION

In conclusion, this investigation into bio-inspired fabrics as a poetic means of bringing attention to the issue of indoor air quality is a paradigm-shifting voyage. We have unveiled the silent threats to well-being posed by compromised indoor air quality, emphasizing the need for innovative solutions. Studying the nesting behavior of female blue tit birds has shown the possibility of textile items being transformed by a mix of drawing inspiration from biology, focusing on aesthetics, and ensuring practicality. The pervasive yet silent threat of compromised indoor air quality necessitates a shift in our approach. This study champions a bio-inspired, aesthetically pleasing paradigm, drawing inspiration from nature to revolutionize awareness and solutions. The nesting behavior of the female blue tit bird serves as an inspiration, encouraging us to design practical textile artifacts that go beyond conventional awareness campaigns. We propose actionable policy solutions and recommendations to enhance our findings' real-world impact. Healthcare policies should integrate bio-inspired textiles into building standards to improve indoor air quality, promoting public health.

Furthermore, intervention strategies can involve educational programs that raise awareness about the benefits of bio-inspired design in enhancing well-being. Practical solutions extend to community initiatives, fostering a collective commitment to healthier living environments. These recommendations aim to provide tangible guidance for policymakers and practitioners.

REFERENCES

Abdullah, A., Said, I. B., & Ossen, D. R. (2019). A sustainable bio-inspired cooling unit for hot arid regions: Integrated evaporative cooling system in wind tower. *Applied Thermal Engineering*, *161*, 114201. doi:10.1016/j.applthermaleng.2019.114201

Al-Kindi, S. G., Brook, R. D., Biswal, S., & Rajagopalan, S. (2020). Environmental determinants of cardiovascular disease: Lessons learned from air pollution. *Nature Reviews. Cardiology*, *17*(10), 656–672. doi:10.1038/s41569-020-0371-2 PMID:32382149

Amato-Lourenço, L. F., dos Santos Galvão, L., de Weger, L. A., Hiemstra, P. S., Vijver, M. G., & Mauad, T. (2020). An emerging class of air pollutants: Potential effects of microplastics to respiratory human health? *The Science of the Total Environment*, *749*, 141676. doi:10.1016/j.scitotenv.2020.141676 PMID:32827829

Amoatey, P., Omidvarborna, H., Baawain, M. S., Al-Mamun, A., Bari, A., & Kindzierski, W. B. (2020). Association between human health and indoor air pollution in the Gulf Cooperation Council (GCC) countries: A review. *Reviews on Environmental Health*, *35*(2), 157–171. doi:10.1515/reveh-2019-0065 PMID:32049656

Antonov, Y. I., Frandsen, K. M., Jensen, R. L., & Møldrup, P. (2020). Simulation of moisture transfer through bio-inspired materials using independent measurements of water vapor sorption and diffusivity. In *RM4L 2020 International Conference* (pp. 115-119). Academic Press.

Arora, A., & McIntyre, J. R. (2021). Biogeneration: Bio-Inspired Architecture for Regenerative Built Environments. *J. Civ. Eng. Archit*, *6*, 1–16.

Azuma, K., Yanagi, U., Kagi, N., Kim, H., Ogata, M., & Hayashi, M. (2020). Environmental factors involved in SARS-CoV-2 transmission: Effect and role of indoor environmental quality in the strategy for COVID-19 infection control. *Environmental Health and Preventive Medicine*, *25*(1), 1–16. doi:10.1186/s12199-020-00904-2 PMID:33143660

Bajçinovci, B. (2019). Biomimicry and Biophilic Design: Multiple Architectural Precepts. *Journal of Science, Humanities, and Arts*, 1-10. doi:10.17160/josha.6.3.544

Balmes, J. R. (2019). Household air pollution from domestic combustion of solid fuels and health. *The Journal of Allergy and Clinical Immunology*, *143*(6), 1979–1987. doi:10.1016/j.jaci.2019.04.016 PMID:31176380

Baumeister, D., Zari, M. P., & Hayes, S. (2020). Biomimicry: An opportunity for buildings to relate to place. In Ecologies Design (pp. 85-95). Routledge. doi:10.4324/9780429279904-11

Belotti, J. T., Castanho, D. S., Araujo, L. N., da Silva, L. V., Alves, T. A., Tadano, Y. S., Stevan, S. L. Jr, Corrêa, F. C., & Siqueira, H. V. (2020). Air pollution epidemiology: A simplified Generalized Linear Model approach optimized by bio-inspired metaheuristics. *Environmental Research*, *191*, 110106. doi:10.1016/j.envres.2020.110106 PMID:32882238

Brebenel, E. (2020). Bioinspired textiles that raise awareness about domestic air pollution. In Textiles, Identity and Innovation: In Touch (pp. 297-304). CRC Press. https://doi.org/ doi:10.1201/9780429286872-45

Canbazoğlu Bilici, S., Küpeli, M. A., & Guzey, S. S. (2021). Inspired by nature: An engineering design-based biomimicry activity. *Science Activities*, *58*(2), 77–88. doi:10.1080/00368121.2021.1918049

Chen Austin, M., Solano, T., Tejedor-Flores, N., Quintero, V., Boya, C., & Mora, D. (2022). Bio-inspired approaches for sustainable cities design in tropical climate. In *Bionics and Sustainable Design* (pp. 333–365). Springer Nature Singapore. doi:10.1007/978-981-19-1812-4_11

Cuce, E., Nachan, Z., Cuce, P. M., Sher, F., & Neighbour, G. B. (2019). Strategies for ideal indoor environments towards low/zero carbon buildings through a biomimetic approach. *International Journal of Ambient Energy*, *40*(1), 86–95. doi:10.1080/01430750.2017.1372807

Dicks, H. (2019). The Biomimicry Revolution in Environmental Epistemology. *Ethics and the Environment*, *24*(2), 43–66. doi:10.2979/ethicsenviro.24.2.03

Eggermont, M., & Paul, R. (2020). Developing holistic engineering competencies in a bio-inspired design course. *Proceedings of the Canadian Engineering Education Association*. 10.24908/pceea.vi0.14131

Eguiluz-Gracia, I., Mathioudakis, A. G., Bartel, S., Vijverberg, S. J., Fuertes, E., Comberiati, P., Cai, Y. S., Tomazic, P. V., Diamant, Z., Vestbo, J., Galan, C., & Hoffmann, B. (2020). The need for clean air: The way air pollution and climate change affect allergic rhinitis and asthma. *Allergy*, *75*(9), 2170–2184. doi:10.1111/all.14177 PMID:31916265

Fu, S. C., Zhong, X. L., Zhang, Y., Lai, T. W., Chan, K. C., Lee, K. Y., & Chao, C. Y. (2020). Bio-inspired cooling technologies and the applications in buildings. *Energy and Building*, *225*, 110313. doi:10.1016/j.enbuild.2020.110313

Fuller, R., Landrigan, P. J., Balakrishnan, K., Bathan, G., Bose-O'Reilly, S., Brauer, M., Caravanos, J., Chiles, T., Cohen, A., Corra, L., Cropper, M., Ferraro, G., Hanna, J., Hanrahan, D., Hu, H., Hunter, D., Janata, G., Kupka, R., Lanphear, B., ... Yan, C. (2022). Pollution and health: A progress update. *The Lancet. Planetary Health*, *6*(6), e535–e547. doi:10.1016/S2542-5196(22)00090-0 PMID:35594895

García-Mayagoitia, S., Pérez-Hernández, H., Medina-Pérez, G., Campos-Montiel, R. G., & Fernández-Luqueño, F. (2020). Bio-nanomaterials in the air pollution treatment. In *Nanomaterials for air remediation* (pp. 227–248). Elsevier. doi:10.1016/B978-0-12-818821-7.00012-9

Gonzalez-Martin, J., Kraakman, N. J. R., Perez, C., Lebrero, R., & Munoz, R. (2021). A state-of-the-art review on indoor air pollution and strategies for indoor air pollution control. *Chemosphere*, *262*, 128376. doi:10.1016/j.chemosphere.2020.128376 PMID:33182138

Hayes, S., Toner, J., Desha, C., & Gibbs, M. (2020). Enabling biomimetic place-based design at scale. *Biomimetics*, *5*(2), 21. doi:10.3390/biomimetics5020021 PMID:32443598

He, G., Pan, Y., & Tanaka, T. (2020). The short-term impacts of COVID-19 lockdown on urban air pollution in China. *Nature Sustainability*, *3*(12), 1005–1011. doi:10.1038/s41893-020-0581-y

Hubert, T., Dugué, A., Vogt Wu, T., Bruneau, D., & Aujard, F. (2022). Exploiting the Potential of Nature for Sustainable Building Designs: A Novel Bioinspired Framework Based on a Characterization of Living Envelopes. In Bionics and Sustainable Design (pp. 289-331). Singapore: Springer Nature Singapore. doi:10.1007/978-981-19-1812-4_10

Imani, N., & Vale, B. (2022). Biomimetic Design for Building Energy Efficiency 2021. *Biomimetics*, *7*(3), 106. doi:10.3390/biomimetics7030106 PMID:35997426

Jain, S., & Sharma, T. (2020). Social and travel lockdown impact considering coronavirus disease (COVID-19) on air quality in megacities of India: Present benefits, future challenges and way forward. *Aerosol and Air Quality Research*, *20*(6), 1222–1236. doi:10.4209/aaqr.2020.04.0171

Jamei, E., & Vrcelj, Z. (2021). Biomimicry and the built environment, learning from nature's solutions. *Applied Sciences (Basel, Switzerland)*, *11*(16), 7514. doi:10.3390/app11167514

Jatoi, A. S., Ahmed, J., Akhter, F., Sultan, S. H., Chandio, G. S., Ahmed, S., Hashmi, Z., Usto, M. A., Shaikh, M. S., Siddique, M., & Maitlo, G. (2023). Recent Advances and Treatment of Emerging Contaminants Through the Bio-assisted Method: A Comprehensive Review. *Water, Air, and Soil Pollution*, *234*(1), 49. doi:10.1007/s11270-022-06037-2

Kacprzak, M. (2022). Cradle to Cradle Marketplace. *Biodegradable Waste Management in the Circular Economy: Challenges and Opportunities*, 13-18. https://doi.org/ doi:10.1002/9781119679523.ch2

Khelil, S., & Zemmouri, N. (2019). Biomimetic: A new strategy for a passive sustainable ventilation system design in hot and arid regions. *International Journal of Environmental Science and Technology*, *16*(6), 2821–2830. doi:10.1007/s13762-018-2168-y

Kuddus, M. A., Tynan, E., & McBryde, E. (2020). Urbanization: A problem for the rich and the poor? *Public Health Reviews*, *41*(1), 1–4. doi:10.1186/s40985-019-0116-0 PMID:31908901

Lee, K. K., Bing, R., Kiang, J., Bashir, S., Spath, N., Stelzle, D., Mortimer, K., Bularga, A., Doudesis, D., Joshi, S. S., Strachan, F., Gumy, S., Adair-Rohani, H., Attia, E. F., Chung, M. H., Miller, M. R., Newby, D. E., Mills, N. L., McAllister, D. A., & Shah, A. S. (2020). Adverse health effects associated with household air pollution: A systematic review, meta-analysis, and burden estimation study. *The Lancet. Global Health, 8*(11), e1427–e1434. doi:10.1016/S2214-109X(20)30343-0 PMID:33069303

Li, Y., Zhang, R., Wen, F., Li, M., Li, W., Li, L., Zhou, Y., Rencus-Lazar, S., Tao, K., Gazit, E., Wu, W., Ying, Z., & Wang, G. (2023). Bioinspired supramolecular arrayed heterojunction-based room-temperature sensor for high-performance gas detection. *Sensors and Actuators. B, Chemical, 396*, 134641. doi:10.1016/j.snb.2023.134641

Liu, G., Wong, W. S., Kraft, M., Ager, J. W., Vollmer, D., & Xu, R. (2021). Wetting-regulated gas-involving (photo) electrocatalysis: Biomimetics in energy conversion. *Chemical Society Reviews, 50*(18), 10674–10699. doi:10.1039/D1CS00258A PMID:34369513

Magazzino, C., Mele, M., & Schneider, N. (2020). The relationship between air pollution and COVID-19-related deaths: An application to three French cities. *Applied Energy, 279*, 115835. doi:10.1016/j.apenergy.2020.115835 PMID:32952266

Makram, A., & Abou Ouf, T. (2019). Biomimetic and Biophilic Design as an approach to innovative sustainable architectural design. *Architecture & Urbanism... A Smart Outlook©*, 509-518.

Manisalidis, I., Stavropoulou, E., Stavropoulos, A., & Bezirtzoglou, E. (2020). Environmental and health impacts of air pollution: A review. *Frontiers in Public Health, 8*, 14. doi:10.3389/fpubh.2020.00014 PMID:32154200

Megahed, N. A., & Ghoneim, E. M. (2021). Indoor Air Quality: Rethinking rules of building design strategies in post-pandemic architecture. *Environmental Research, 193*, 110471. doi:10.1016/j.envres.2020.110471 PMID:33197423

Natarajan, L., & Short, M. (Eds.). (2023). *Engaged Urban Pedagogy: Participatory practices in planning and place-making*. UCL Press. doi:10.14324/111.9781800081239

Nguyen, T. H., Nguyen, L. V., Jung, J. J., Agbehadji, I. E., Frimpong, S. O., & Millham, R. C. (2020). Bio-inspired approaches for smart energy management: State of the art and challenges. *Sustainability (Basel), 12*(20), 8495. doi:10.3390/su12208495

Park, C. G., Jun, I., Lee, S., Ryu, C. S., Lee, S. A., Park, J., Han, H.-S., Park, H., Manz, A., Shin, H., & Kim, Y. J. (2022). Integration of Bioinspired Fibrous Strands with 3D Spheroids for Environmental Hazard Monitoring. *Small, 18*(22), 2200757. doi:10.1002/smll.202200757 PMID:35521748

Qamar, S. A., Qamar, M., Basharat, A., Bilal, M., Cheng, H., & Iqbal, H. M. (2022). Alginate-based nano-adsorbent materials-Bioinspired solution to mitigate hazardous environmental pollutants. *Chemosphere, 288*, 132618. doi:10.1016/j.chemosphere.2021.132618 PMID:34678347

Rajagopalan, S., Brauer, M., Bhatnagar, A., Bhatt, D. L., Brook, J. R., Huang, W., Münzel, T., Newby, D., Siegel, J., & Brook, R. D. (2020). Personal-level protective actions against particulate matter air pollution exposure: A scientific statement from the American Heart Association. *Circulation, 142*(23), e411–e431. doi:10.1161/CIR.0000000000000931 PMID:33150789

Robinson, J. M., Watkins, H., Man, I., Liddicoat, C., Cameron, R., Parker, B., Cruz, M., & Meagher, L. (2021). Microbiome-Inspired Green Infrastructure: A bioscience roadmap for urban ecosystem health. arq. *Architectural Research Quarterly*, *25*(4), 292–303. doi:10.1017/S1359135522000148

Rosetta, G., Macaire, L., Butters, M., & Finlayson, C. E. (2023). Dial-In Synthesis of 'Polymer Opal' Core-Interlayer-Shell Composite Nanoparticles. *Polymers*, *15*(17), 3507. doi:10.3390/polym15173507 PMID:37688133

Saini, J., Dutta, M., & Marques, G. (2020). A comprehensive review on indoor air quality monitoring systems for enhanced public health. *Sustainable Environment Research*, *30*(1), 1–12. doi:10.1186/s42834-020-0047-y

Sajovic, I., Kert, M., & Boh Podgornik, B. (2023). Smart Textiles: A Review and Bibliometric Mapping. *Applied Sciences (Basel, Switzerland)*, *13*(18), 10489. doi:10.3390/app131810489

Sandak, A., & Butina-Ogorelec, K. (2023). Bioinspired building materials-lessons from nature. *Frontiers in Materials*, *10*, 1283163. doi:10.3389/fmats.2023.1283163

Scott, J. (2023). Digital Fabrication and Fabric Innovation. In FABRIC [ated] (pp. 28-39). Routledge. doi:10.4324/9781003138471-4

Sharma, S., & Sarkar, P. (2022). Knowledge capture and its representation using concept map in bio-inspired design. *International Journal on Interactive Design and Manufacturing*, 1-13. doi:10.1007/s12008-022-01069-8

Shashwat, S., Zingre, K. T., Thurairajah, N., Kumar, D. K., Panicker, K., Anand, P., & Wan, M. P. (2023). A review on bioinspired strategies for an energy-efficient built environment. *Energy and Building*, *296*, 113382. doi:10.1016/j.enbuild.2023.113382

Shi, W., Guo, Y., & Liu, Y. (2020). When flexible organic field-effect transistors meet biomimetics: A prospective view of the internet of things. *Advanced Materials*, *32*(15), 1901493. doi:10.1002/adma.201901493 PMID:31250497

Sinha, A., Sengupta, T., & Alvarado, R. (2020). Interplay between technological innovation and environmental quality: Formulating the SDG policies for next 11 economies. *Journal of Cleaner Production*, *242*, 118549. doi:10.1016/j.jclepro.2019.118549

Sommese, F., Badarnah, L., & Ausiello, G. (2022). A critical review of biomimetic building envelopes: Towards a bio-adaptive model from nature to architecture. *Renewable & Sustainable Energy Reviews*, *169*, 112850. doi:10.1016/j.rser.2022.112850

Tainio, M., Andersen, Z. J., Nieuwenhuijsen, M. J., Hu, L., De Nazelle, A., An, R., ... de Sá, T. H. (2021). Air pollution, physical activity and health: A mapping review of the evidence. *Environment International*, *147*, 105954. doi:10.1016/j.envint.2020.105954 PMID:33352412

Tran, V. V., Park, D., & Lee, Y. C. (2020). Indoor air pollution, related human diseases, and recent trends in the control and improvement of indoor air quality. *International Journal of Environmental Research and Public Health*, *17*(8), 2927. doi:10.3390/ijerph17082927 PMID:32340311

Turner, M. C., Andersen, Z. J., Baccarelli, A., Diver, W. R., Gapstur, S. M., Pope, C. A. III, Prada, D., Samet, J., Thurston, G., & Cohen, A. (2020). Outdoor air pollution and cancer: An overview of the current evidence and public health recommendations. *CA: a Cancer Journal for Clinicians*, *70*(6), 460–479. doi:10.3322/caac.21632 PMID:32964460

Uchiyama, Y., Blanco, E., & Kohsaka, R. (2020). Application of biomimetics to architectural and urban design: A review across scales. *Sustainability (Basel)*, *12*(23), 9813. doi:10.3390/su12239813

Ukaogo, P. O., Ewuzie, U., & Onwuka, C. V. (2020). Environmental pollution: causes, effects, and the remedies. In *Microorganisms for sustainable environment and health* (pp. 419–429). Elsevier. doi:10.1016/B978-0-12-819001-2.00021-8

Vardanyan, A., Vardanyan, N., Aâtach, M., Malavasi, P., & Gaydardzhiev, S. (2022). Bio-Assisted Leaching of Non-Ferrous Metals from Waste Printed Circuit Boards-Importance of Process Parameters. *Metals*, *12*(12), 2092. doi:10.3390/met12122092

Vardoulakis, S., Giagloglou, E., Steinle, S., Davis, A., Sleeuwenhoek, A., Galea, K. S., Dixon, K., & Crawford, J. O. (2020). Indoor exposure to selected air pollutants in the home environment: A systematic review. *International Journal of Environmental Research and Public Health*, *17*(23), 8972. doi:10.3390/ijerph17238972 PMID:33276576

Wang, T., Wang, X. X., Wen, J., Shao, Z. Y., Huang, H. M., & Guo, X. (2022). A bio-inspired neuromorphic sensory system. *Advanced Intelligent Systems*, *4*(7), 2200047. doi:10.1002/aisy.202200047

World Health Organization. (2021). *WHO global air quality guidelines: particulate matter (PM2. 5 and PM10), ozone, nitrogen dioxide, sulfur dioxide and carbon monoxide*. World Health Organization.

Yang, M., Zou, W., Guo, J., Qian, Z., Luo, H., Yang, S., Zhao, N., Pattelli, L., Xu, J., & Wiersma, D. S. (2020). Bioinspired "skin" with cooperative thermo-optical effect for daytime radiative cooling. *ACS Applied Materials & Interfaces*, *12*(22), 25286–25293. doi:10.1021/acsami.0c03897 PMID:32378874

Zhang, H., & Srinivasan, R. (2020). A systematic review of air quality sensors, guidelines, and measurement studies for indoor air quality management. *Sustainability (Basel)*, *12*(21), 9045. doi:10.3390/su12219045

Zhou, W., Wu, T., Li, Y., Wei, Y., Han, L., Li, Y., ... Du, S. (2023). A bioinspired vine-like hierarchically structured PET/CA composite nanofibrous membrane with superhydrophobic and superoleophilic surface for high-efficiency cooking fumes capture. *Separation and Purification Technology*, *125517*. Advance online publication. doi:10.1016/j.seppur.2023.125517

Zhu, Q., Tang, X., Feng, S., Zhong, Z., Yao, J., & Yao, Z. (2019). ZIF-8@ SiO2 composite nanofiber membrane with bioinspired spider web-like structure for efficient air pollution control. *Journal of Membrane Science*, *581*, 252–261. doi:10.1016/j.memsci.2019.03.075

KEY TERMS AND DEFINITIONS

Awareness: The state or level of consciousness about a particular subject, issue, or fact, often involving the recognition and understanding of its significance.

Bio-Inspired Design: The practice of deriving innovative solutions for design challenges by drawing inspiration from patterns, processes, and systems found in nature.

Indoor Air Quality: The measurement of the cleanliness and healthiness of the air within indoor environments, particularly in buildings and residences, with a focus on minimizing pollutants and promoting occupant well-being.

Textile Artifacts: Objects or products crafted from textiles involving the use of fibres and fabrics, which may serve functional, aesthetic, or symbolic purposes in the context of this study.

Well-Being: The overall state of health, happiness, and prosperity of individuals, encompassing physical, mental, and social dimensions.

Compilation of References

Abad, A. R. B., Ghorbani, H., Mohamadian, N., Davoodi, S., Mehrad, M., Aghdam, S. K. Y., & Nasriani, H. R. (2022). Robust hybrid machine learning algorithms for gas flow rates prediction through wellhead chokes in gas condensate fields. *Fuel*, *308*, 121872. doi:10.1016/j.fuel.2021.121872

Abad, A. R. B., Mousavi, S., Mohamadian, N., Wood, D. A., Ghorbani, H., Davoodi, S., ... Shahbazi, K. (2021). Hybrid machine learning algorithms to predict condensate viscosity in the near wellbore regions of gas condensate reservoirs. *Journal of Natural Gas Science and Engineering*, *95*, 104210. doi:10.1016/j.jngse.2021.104210

Abdullah, A., Said, I. B., & Ossen, D. R. (2019). A sustainable bio-inspired cooling unit for hot arid regions: Integrated evaporative cooling system in wind tower. *Applied Thermal Engineering*, *161*, 114201. doi:10.1016/j.applthermaleng.2019.114201

Abiodun, O. I., Jantan, A., Omolara, A. E., Dada, K. V., Mohamed, N. A., & Arshad, H. (2018). State-of-the-art in artificial neural network applications: A survey. *Heliyon*, *4*(11), e00938. doi:10.1016/j.heliyon.2018.e00938 PMID:30519653

Adhikar, M., & Amgoth, T. (2019). An intelligent water drops-based workflow scheduling for IaaS cloud. *Applied Soft Computing*, *77*, 547–566. doi:10.1016/j.asoc.2019.02.004

Agarwal, B., & Mittal, N. (2012). Categorical probability proportion difference (CPPD): a feature selection method for sentiment classification. *Proceedings of the 2nd workshop on sentiment analysis where AI meets psychology,* 17-26.

Agarwal, B., & Mittal, N. (2013a). Optimal feature selection for sentiment analysis. In *International Conference on Intelligent Text Processing and Computational Linguistics.* Springer Berlin Heidelberg. 10.1007/978-3-642-37256-8_2

Agarwal, B., & Mittal, N. (2016). Machine Learning Approach for Sentiment Analysis. In *Prominent Feature Extraction for Sentiment Analysis* (pp. 21–45). Springer International Publishing. doi:10.1007/978-3-319-25343-5_3

Agarwal, B., Mittal, N., & Cambria, E. (2013c). Enhancing sentiment classification performance using bi-tagged phrases. *IEEE 13th International Conference on Data Mining Workshops*, 892-895. 10.1109/ICDMW.2013.80

Agarwal, B., Poria, S., Mittal, N., Gelbukh, A., & Hussain, A. (2015). Concept-level sentiment analysis with dependency-based semantic parsing: A novel approach. *Cognitive Computation*, *7*(4), 487–499. doi:10.1007/s12559-014-9316-6

Agarwal, B., Sharma, V. K., & Mittal, N. (2013b). Sentiment classification of review documents using phrase patterns. *International Conference on Advances in Computing, Communications and Informatics (ICACCI),* 1577-1580. 10.1109/ICACCI.2013.6637415

Agbehadji, I. E., Millham, R. C., Abayomi, A., Jung, J. J., Fong, S. J., & Frimpong, S. O. (2021). Clustering algorithm based on nature-inspired approach for energy optimization in heterogeneous wireless sensor network. *Applied Soft Computing*, *104*(107171), 1–15. doi:10.1016/j.asoc.2021.107171

Aggarwal, C. C. (2018). Neural networks and deep learning. Springer. doi:10.1007/978-3-319-94463-0

Aggarwal, C. C., & Aggarwal, C. C. (2018). Machine learning with shallow neural networks. *Neural Networks and Deep Learning: A Textbook*, 53-104.

Agrawal & Kapoor. (2021). A comparative study on geographic-based routing algorithms for flying ad-hoc networks. *Concurrency ComputatPractExper*. doi:10.1002/cpe.6253

Ahmad, M., Ullah, F., Wahid, I., Khan, A., Irfan Uddin, M., Alharbi, A., & Alosaimi, W. (2021). A Bio-Inspired Routing Optimization in UAV-enabled Internet of Everything. *Computers, Materials & Continua*, *67*(1), 321–336. Advance online publication. doi:10.32604/cmc.2021.014102

Ahmad, S. R., Bakar, A. A., & Yaakub, M. R. (2015). Metaheuristic algorithms for feature selection in sentiment analysis. In *Science and Information Conference (SAI)* (pp. 222–226). IEEE. doi:10.1109/SAI.2015.7237148

Alam, M. M., & Moh, S. (2022). Survey on Q-Learning-Based Position-Aware Routing Protocols in Flying Ad Hoc Networks. *Electronics (Basel)*, *11*(7), 1099. doi:10.3390/electronics11071099

Alam, S., Zhao, X., Niazi, I. K., Ayub, M. S., & Khan, M. A. (2023). A comparative analysis of global optimization algorithms for surface electromyographic signal onset detection. *Decis. Anal. J.*, *8*, 100294. doi:10.1016/j.dajour.2023.100294

Alazab, M., Venkatraman, S., Watters, P., & Alazab, M. (2011). Zero-day malware detection based on supervised learning algorithms of API call signatures. *Proceedings of the Ninth Australasian Data Mining Conference*, 121, 171-182.

Alejo-Reyes, Mendoza, & Olivares-Benitez. (2020). Inventory replenishment decision model for the supplier selection problem using metaheuristic algorithms. *Openaire*.

Alghamdi, T. A. (2021). Parametric analysis on optimized energy-efficient protocol in wireless sensor network. *Soft Computing*, *25*(6), 4409–4421. doi:10.1007/s00500-020-05449-8

Alibardi, L. (2003). Ultrastructural autoradiographic and immunocytochemical analysis of setae formation and keratinization in the digital pads of the gecko Hemidactylus turcicus (Gekkonidae, Reptilia). *Tissue & Cell*, *35*(4), 288–296. doi:10.1016/S0040-8166(03)00050-8 PMID:12921711

Al-Kindi, S. G., Brook, R. D., Biswal, S., & Rajagopalan, S. (2020). Environmental determinants of cardiovascular disease: Lessons learned from air pollution. *Nature Reviews. Cardiology*, *17*(10), 656–672. doi:10.1038/s41569-020-0371-2 PMID:32382149

Alsaffar, A., & Omar, N. (2014). Study on feature selection and machine learning algorithms for Malay sentiment classification. *International Conference on in Information Technology and Multimedia (ICIMU),* 270-275. 10.1109/ICIMU.2014.7066643

Alwan, H. B., & Ku-Mahamud, K. R. (2012). Optimizing support vector machine parameters using continuous ant colony optimization. *7th International Conference on in Computing and Convergence Technology (ICCCT),* 164-169.

Amato-Lourenço, L. F., dos Santos Galvão, L., de Weger, L. A., Hiemstra, P. S., Vijver, M. G., & Mauad, T. (2020). An emerging class of air pollutants: Potential effects of microplastics to respiratory human health? *The Science of the Total Environment*, *749*, 141676. doi:10.1016/j.scitotenv.2020.141676 PMID:32827829

Amoatey, P., Omidvarborna, H., Baawain, M. S., Al-Mamun, A., Bari, A., & Kindzierski, W. B. (2020). Association between human health and indoor air pollution in the Gulf Cooperation Council (GCC) countries: A review. *Reviews on Environmental Health*, *35*(2), 157–171. doi:10.1515/reveh-2019-0065 PMID:32049656

Amponis, G., Lagkas, T., Sarigiannidis, P., Vitsas, V., Fouliras, P., & Wan, S. (2021). A survey on FANET routing from a cross-layer design perspective. *Journal of Systems Architecture*, *120*, 102281. doi:10.1016/j.sysarc.2021.102281

Anand, R., & Chawla, P. (2016, March). A review on the optimization techniques for bio-inspired antenna design. In *2016 3rd International conference on computing for sustainable global development (INDIACom)* (pp. 2228-2233). IEEE.

Anand, R., Arora, S., & Sindhwani, N. (2022, January). A miniaturized UWB antenna for high speed applications. In *2022 International Conference on Computing, Communication and Power Technology (IC3P)* (pp. 264-267). IEEE. 10.1109/IC3P52835.2022.00063

Anand, R., & Chawla, P. (2020). Optimization of inscribed hexagonal fractal slotted microstrip antenna using modified lightning attachment procedure optimization. *International Journal of Microwave and Wireless Technologies*, *12*(6), 519–530. doi:10.1017/S1759078720000148

Anand, R., & Chawla, P. (2022). Bandwidth optimization of a novel slotted fractal antenna using modified lightning attachment procedure optimization. In *Smart Antennas: Latest Trends in Design and Application* (pp. 379–392). Springer International Publishing. doi:10.1007/978-3-030-76636-8_28

Anand, R., Jain, V., Singh, A., Rahal, D., Rastogi, P., Rajkumar, A., & Gupta, A. Clustering of Big Data in Cloud Environments for Smart Applications. In *Integration of IoT with Cloud Computing for Smart Applications* (pp. 227–247). Chapman and Hall/CRC. doi:10.1201/9781003319238-14

Anitha, N., Anitha, B., & Pradeepa, S. (2013). Sentiment classification approaches–A review. *International Journal of Innovations in Engineering and Technology*, *3*(1), 22–31.

Antonov, Y. I., Frandsen, K. M., Jensen, R. L., & Møldrup, P. (2020). Simulation of moisture transfer through bio-inspired materials using independent measurements of water vapor sorption and diffusivity. In *RM4L 2020 International Conference* (pp. 115-119). Academic Press.

Anuprathibha, T., & Kanimozhi Selvi, C. S. (2014). Opinion mining for camera reviews. *International Journal of Advanced Research in Data Mining and Cloud Computing*, *2*(5), 1-9.

Arora, A., & McIntyre, J. R. (2021). Biogeneration: Bio-Inspired Architecture for Regenerative Built Environments. *J. Civ. Eng. Archit*, *6*, 1–16.

Asbeck, A., Dastoor, S., Parness, A., Fullerton, L., Esparza, N., Soto, D., Heyneman, B., & Cutkosky, M. (2009). Climbing rough vertical surfaces with hierarchical directional adhesion. *Proceedings of the 2009 IEEE International Conference on Robotics and Automation*, 2675–2680. 10.1109/ROBOT.2009.5152864

Asghar, M. Z., Khan, A., Kundi, F. M., Qasim, M., Khan, F., Ullah, R., & Nawaz, I. U. (2014). Medical opinion lexicon: An incremental model for mining health reviews. *International Journal of Academic Research*, *6*(1), 295–302. doi:10.7813/2075-4124.2014/6-1/A.39

Autumn, K., Majidi, C., Groff, R. E., Groff, R. E., Dittmore, A., & Fearing, R. (2006). Effective elastic modulus of isolated gecko setal arrays. *The Journal of Experimental Biology*, *209*(18), 3558–3568. doi:10.1242/jeb.02469 PMID:16943496

Autumn, K., Niewiarowski, P. H., & Puthoff, J. B. (2014). Gecko adhesion as a model system for integrative biology, interdisciplinary science, and bioinspired engineering. *Annual Review of Ecology, Evolution, and Systematics*, *45*(1), 445–470. doi:10.1146/annurev-ecolsys-120213-091839

Autumn, K., & Peattie, A. M. (2002). Mechanisms of adhesion in geckos. *Integrative and Comparative Biology*, *42*(6), 1081–1090. doi:10.1093/icb/42.6.1081 PMID:21680391

Autumn, K., Sitti, M., Liang, A. Y., Peattie, A. M., Hansen, W. R., Sponberg, S., Kenny, T. W., Fearing, R., Israelachvili, J. N., & Full, R. J. (2002). Evidence for van der Waals adhesion in gecko setae. *Proceedings of the National Academy of Sciences of the United States of America*, *99*(19), 12252–12256. doi:10.1073/pnas.192252799 PMID:12198184

Azad, A. H., & Hassaanien, A.-E. (2016). *Retinal Blood Vessels Segmentation Based on Bio-Inspired Algorithm*. Springer. doi:10.1007/978-3-319-21212-8_8

Azuma, K., Yanagi, U., Kagi, N., Kim, H., Ogata, M., & Hayashi, M. (2020). Environmental factors involved in SARS-CoV-2 transmission: Effect and role of indoor environmental quality in the strategy for COVID-19 infection control. *Environmental Health and Preventive Medicine*, *25*(1), 1–16. doi:10.1186/s12199-020-00904-2 PMID:33143660

Azzizi, N., & Zaatri, A. (2016). A Learning Process of Multilayer Perceptron for Speech Recognition. *International Journal of Pure and Applied Mathematics*, *107*(4), 1005–1012. doi:10.12732/ijpam.v107i4.18

Babalola, S. A., Mishra, D., Dutta, S., & Murmu, N. C. (2023). In-situ workpiece perception: A key to zero-defect manufacturing in Industry 4.0 compliant job shops. *Computers in Industry*, *148*, 103891. doi:10.1016/j.compind.2023.103891

Baccianella, S., Esuli, A., & Sebastiani, F. (2014). Feature selection for ordinal text classification. *Neural Computation*, *26*(3), 557–591. doi:10.1162/NECO_a_00558 PMID:24320850

Bagheri, A., Saraee, M., & De Jong, F. (2013). Care more about customers: Unsupervised domain-independent aspect detection for sentiment analysis of customer reviews. *Knowledge-Based Systems*, *52*, 201–213. doi:10.1016/j.knosys.2013.08.011

Bahloul, N. E. H., Boudjit, S., Abdennebi, M., & Boubiche, D. E. (2017). Bio-inspired on demand routing protocol for unmanned aerial vehicles. *2017 26th International Conference on Computer Communications and Networks, ICCCN 2017*. 10.1109/ICCCN.2017.8038487

Bajçinovci, B. (2019). Biomimicry and Biophilic Design: Multiple Architectural Precepts. *Journal of Science, Humanities, and Arts*, 1-10. doi:10.17160/josha.6.3.544

Bakhshipour, M., Ghadi, M. J., & Namdari, F. (2017). Swarm robotics search & rescue: A novel artificial intelligence-inspired optimization approach. *Applied Soft Computing*, *57*, 708–726. doi:10.1016/j.asoc.2017.02.028

Balmes, J. R. (2019). Household air pollution from domestic combustion of solid fuels and health. *The Journal of Allergy and Clinical Immunology*, *143*(6), 1979–1987. doi:10.1016/j.jaci.2019.04.016 PMID:31176380

Banati, H., & Bajaj, M. (2012). Promoting products online using firefly algorithm. In *2012 12th International Conference on Intelligent Systems Design and Applications (ISDA)* (pp. 580-585). IEEE. 10.1109/ISDA.2012.6416602

Bangotra, D. K., Singh, Y., Kumar, N., Singh, P. K., & Ojeniyi, A. (2022). Energy-Efficient and Secure Opportunistic Routing Protocol for WSN: Performance Analysis with Nature-Inspired Algorithms and Its Application in Biomedical Applications. *BioMed Research International*, *2022*, 1–13. doi:10.1155/2022/1976694 PMID:35372577

Bansal, R., Gupta, A., Singh, R., & Nassa, V. K. (2021, July). Role and impact of digital technologies in E-learning amidst COVID-19 pandemic. In *2021 Fourth International Conference on Computational Intelligence and Communication Technologies (CCICT)* (pp. 194-202). IEEE. 10.1109/CCICT53244.2021.00046

Basari, A. S. H., Hussin, B., Ananta, I. G. P., & Zeniarja, J. (2013). Opinion mining of movie review using hybrid method of support vector machine and particle swarm optimization. *Procedia Engineering*, *53*, 453–462. doi:10.1016/j.proeng.2013.02.059

Baumeister, D., Zari, M. P., & Hayes, S. (2020). Biomimicry: An opportunity for buildings to relate to place. In Ecologies Design (pp. 85-95). Routledge. doi:10.4324/9780429279904-11

Bearman, M., Nieminen, J. H., & Ajjawi, R. (2023). Designing assessment in a digital world: An organising framework. *Assessment & Evaluation in Higher Education*, *48*(3), 291–304. doi:10.1080/02602938.2022.2069674

Beegum. (2023). *Optimized Routing of UAVs Using Bio-Inspired Algorithm in FANET: A Systematic Review.* doi:10.1109/ACCESS.2023.3244067

Belotti, J. T., Castanho, D. S., Araujo, L. N., da Silva, L. V., Alves, T. A., Tadano, Y. S., Stevan, S. L. Jr, Corrêa, F. C., & Siqueira, H. V. (2020). Air pollution epidemiology: A simplified Generalized Linear Model approach optimized by bio-inspired metaheuristics. *Environmental Research*, *191*, 110106. doi:10.1016/j.envres.2020.110106 PMID:32882238

Bharany, S., Sharma, S., Bhatia, S., Rahmani, M. K. I., Shuaib, M., & Lashari, S. A. (2022). Energy Efficient Clustering Protocol for FANETS Using Moth Flame Optimization. *Sustainability (Basel)*, *14*(10), 6159. doi:10.3390/su14106159

Bhonde, S. B., & Prasad, J. R. (2015). Sentiment Analysis-Methods, Applications & Challenges. *International Journal of Electronics Communication and Computer Engineering*, *6*(6), 634.

Bishop, C. M., & Nasrabadi, N. M. (2006). *Pattern recognition and machine learning* (Vol. 4). New York: Springer.

Bousbaa, F. Z., Kerrache, C. A., Mahi, Z., Tahari, A. E. K., Lagraa, N., & Yagoubi, M. B. (2020). GeoUAVs: A new geocast routing protocol for fleet of UAVs. *Computer Communications*, *149*, 259–269. https://doi.org/https://doi.org/10.1016/j.comcom.2019.10.026. doi:10.1016/j.comcom.2019.10.026

Brahim, R. A., Ewees, A. A., & Oliva, D. (2019). Improved salp swarm algorithm based on particle swarm optimization for feature selection. *Journal of Ambient Intelligence and Humanized Computing*, *10*(8), 3155–3169. doi:10.1007/s12652-018-1031-9

Brebenel, E. (2020). Bioinspired textiles that raise awareness about domestic air pollution. In Textiles, Identity and Innovation: In Touch (pp. 297-304). CRC Press. https://doi.org/ doi:10.1201/9780429286872-45

Brindha, G. R., & Santhi, B. (2012). A novel opinion mining technique for product review based on preferences. *Research Journal of Applied Sciences, Engineering and Technology*, *4*(23), 5084–5088.

Buche, A., Chandak, D., & Zadgaonkar, A. (2013). Opinion mining and analysis: A survey. *International Journal on Natural Language Computing*, *2*(3), 40–48. doi:10.5121/ijnlc.2013.2304

Bujari, A., Palazzi, C. E., & Ronzani, D. (2017). FANET application scenarios and mobility models. *DroNet 2017 - Proceedings of the 3rd Workshop on Micro Aerial Vehicle Networks, Systems, and Applications, Co-Located with MobiSys 2017,* 43–46. 10.1145/3086439.3086440

Bülbül, M. A. (2023). Optimization of artificial neural network structure and hyperparameters in hybrid model by genetic algorithm: iOS–android application for breast cancer diagnosis/prediction. *The Journal of Supercomputing*, 1–21.

Butt, S. A., Ercan, T., Binsawad, M., Ariza-Colpas, P.-P., Diaz-Martinez, J., Piñeres-Espitia, G., De-La-Hoz-Franco, E., Melo, M. A. P., Ortega, R. M., & De-La-Hoz-Hernández, J.-D. (2023). Prediction based cost estimation technique in agile development. *Advances in Engineering Software*, *175*, 103329. doi:10.1016/j.advengsoft.2022.103329

Cai, Y., Xiao, L., Kazman, R., Mo, R., & Feng, Q. (2019). Design Rule Spaces: A New Model for Representing and Analyzing Software Architecture. *IEEE Transactions on Software Engineering*, *45*(7), 657–682. doi:10.1109/TSE.2018.2797899

Canbazoğlu Bilici, S., Küpeli, M. A., & Guzey, S. S. (2021). Inspired by nature: An engineering design-based biomimicry activity. *Science Activities*, *58*(2), 77–88. doi:10.1080/00368121.2021.1918049

Chai, Y., Shi, W., & Shi, T. (2017). Load-aware cooperative hybrid routing protocol in hybrid wireless mesh networks. *AEÜ. International Journal of Electronics and Communications*, *74*, 135–144. doi:10.1016/j.aeue.2017.02.002

Chandrakala, S., & Sindhu, C. (2012). *Opinion Mining and sentiment classification asurvey.* ICTACT Journal on Soft Computing.

Chan, L., Chavez, K. G., & Rudolph, H. (2020). Hierarchical routing protocols for wireless sensor network: A compressive survey. *Wireless Networks*, *26*(5), 3291–3314. doi:10.1007/s11276-020-02260-z

Chaudhari, M., & Govilkar, S. (2015). A survey of machine learning techniques for sentiment classification. *International Journal on Computational Science & Applications*, *5*(3), 13–23. doi:10.5121/ijcsa.2015.5302

Chavan, Kulkarni, & Chikode. (2019) *IBeeCup: An Energy Efficient Bio Inspired Clustering Method for Homogeneous and Heterogeneous in WSN.* Academic Press.

Chen Austin, M., Solano, T., Tejedor-Flores, N., Quintero, V., Boya, C., & Mora, D. (2022). Bio-inspired approaches for sustainable cities design in tropical climate. In *Bionics and Sustainable Design* (pp. 333–365). Springer Nature Singapore. doi:10.1007/978-981-19-1812-4_11

Cheng, C. M., Hsiao, P. H., Kung, H. T., & Vlah, D. (2007). Maximizing throughput of UAV-relaying networks with the load-carry-and-deliver paradigm. *IEEE Wireless Communications and Networking Conference, WCNC.* 10.1109/WCNC.2007.805

Chen, R. (2015). A Gecko-Inspired Electroadhesive Wall-Climbing Robot. *IEEE Potentials*, *34*(2), 15–19. doi:10.1109/MPOT.2014.2360020

Cho, S. W., Cha, M. S., Kim, S. Y., Song, J. C., & Sohn, K. A. (2014). Investigating temporal and spatial trends of brand images using twitter opinion mining. *International Conference on Information Science & Applications (ICISA),* 1-4. 10.1109/ICISA.2014.6847417

Choi, Hussein, Park, & Kim. (2018). *Geolocation-based Routing Protocol for Flying Adhoc Networks (FANETs).* IEEE.

Choi, J., Kim, D., Kim, S., Lee, J., Lim, S., Lee, S., & Kang, J. (2012). Consento: a new framework for opinion based entity search and summarization. *Proceedings of the 21st ACM international conference on Information and knowledge management*, 1935-1939. 10.1145/2396761.2398547

Chriki, A., Touati, H., Snoussi, H., & Kamoun, F. (2019). FANET: Communication, mobility models and security issues. *Computer Networks*, *163*, 106877. doi:10.1016/j.comnet.2019.106877

Chui, B. W., Kenny, T. W., Mamin, H. J., Mamin, H. J., Terris, B. D., & Rugar, D. (1998). Independent detection of vertical and lateral forces with a sidewall-implanted dual-axis piezoresistive cantilever. *Applied Physics Letters*, *72*(11), 1388–1390. doi:10.1063/1.121064

Cleghorn, C. W., & Engelbrecht, A. P. (2015). Particle swarm variants: Standardized convergence analysis. *Swarm Intelligence*, *9*(2-3), 177–203. doi:10.1007/s11721-015-0109-7

Cuce, E., Nachan, Z., Cuce, P. M., Sher, F., & Neighbour, G. B. (2019). Strategies for ideal indoor environments towards low/zero carbon buildings through a biomimetic approach. *International Journal of Ambient Energy*, *40*(1), 86–95. doi:10.1080/01430750.2017.1372807

Daneshvar, S. M., Alikhah Ahari Mohajer, P., & Mazinani, S. M. (2019). Energy-efficient routing in WSN: A centralized cluster-based approach via grey wolf optimizer. *IEEE Access : Practical Innovations, Open Solutions*, *7*, 170019–170031. doi:10.1109/ACCESS.2019.2955993

Darmawan, A. (2024). Evaluating proactive and reactive strategies in supply chain network design with coordinated inventory control in the presence of disruptions. *Journal of Industrial and Production Engineering,* 1-17.

De Rango, F., Tropea, M., & Fazio, P. (2019). Bio-Inspired Routing over FANET in Emergency Situations to Support Multimedia Traffic. In *Proceedings of ACM Mobihoc (CATANIA'19)*. Association for Computing Machinery.

De Rango, F., Potrino, G., Tropea, M., Santamaria, A. F., & Fazio, P. (2019). Scalable and highway bio-inspired coordination protocol for FANET in precision agriculture applications. *Computers & Electrical Engineering*, *74*, 305–318. doi:10.1016/j.compeleceng.2019.01.018

Deb, S., Gao, X. Z., Tammi, K., Kalita, K., & Mahanta, P. (2021). Nature-inspired optimization algorithms applied for solving charging station placement problem: Overview and comparison. *Archives of Computational Methods in Engineering*, *28*(1), 91–106. doi:10.1007/s11831-019-09374-4

Decerle, J., Grunder, O., Hassani, A. H., & Barakat, O. (2019). A hybrid memetic-ant colony optimization algorithm for the home health care problem with time window, synchronization and working time balancing. *Swarm and Evolutionary Computation*, *46*, 171–183. doi:10.1016/j.swevo.2019.02.009

Delshad, M. M., Chobar, A. P., Ghasemi, P., & Jafari, D. (2024). Efficient Humanitarian Logistics: Multi-Commodity Location–Inventory Model Incorporating Demand Probability and Consumption Coefficients. *Logistics*, *8*(1), 9. doi:10.3390/logistics8010009

Devassy, D., Johnraja, J. I., & Getzi, J. L. P. (2022). NBA: Novel bio-inspired algorithm for energy optimization in WSN for IoT applications. *The Journal of Supercomputing*, *78*(14), 1–18. doi:10.1007/s11227-022-04505-4

Dicks, H. (2019). The Biomimicry Revolution in Environmental Epistemology. *Ethics and the Environment*, *24*(2), 43–66. doi:10.2979/ethicsenviro.24.2.03

Dixit, A., & Singh, S. K. (2023). BMUDF: Hybrid Bio-inspired Model for fault-aware UAV routing using Destination-aware Fan shaped clustering. *Internet of Things : Engineering Cyber Physical Human Systems*, *22*, 100790. doi:10.1016/j.iot.2023.100790

Durai, S. K., & Benadict Raja, J. (2003). *A bio-inspired fall webworm optimization algorithm for feature selection and support vector machine optimization for retinal abnormalities detection*. Multimedia Tools.

Dushyant, K., Muskan, G., Gupta, A., & Pramanik, S. (2022). Utilizing Machine Learning and Deep Learning in Cybesecurity: An Innovative Approach. *Cyber Security and Digital Forensics*, 271-293.

E., Z., & Atef, M. (2017). Performance Evaluation of AODV, DSR and OLSR in MANET using Opnet Simulator. *International Journal of Computer Applications, 163*(11), 23–30. doi:10.5120/ijca2017913775

Eggermont, M., & Paul, R. (2020). Developing holistic engineering competencies in a bio-inspired design course. *Proceedings of the Canadian Engineering Education Association.* 10.24908/pceea.vi0.14131

Eguiluz-Gracia, I., Mathioudakis, A. G., Bartel, S., Vijverberg, S. J., Fuertes, E., Comberiati, P., Cai, Y. S., Tomazic, P. V., Diamant, Z., Vestbo, J., Galan, C., & Hoffmann, B. (2020). The need for clean air: The way air pollution and climate change affect allergic rhinitis and asthma. *Allergy*, *75*(9), 2170–2184. doi:10.1111/all.14177 PMID:31916265

Eslamloueyan, R., Khademi, M. H., & Mazinani, S. (2011). Using a multilayer perceptron network for thermal conductivity prediction of aqueous electrolyte solutions. *Industrial & Engineering Chemistry Research*, *50*(7), 4050–4056. doi:10.1021/ie101513z

Famila, S., Jawahar, A., Sariga, A., & Shankar, K. (2019). Improved artificial bee colony optimization-based clustering algorithm for SMART sensor environments. *Peer-to-Peer Networking and Applications*, 1–9.

Farra, N., Challita, E., Assi, R. A., & Hajj, H. (2010). Sentence-level and document-level sentiment mining for Arabic texts. *IEEE International Conference on in Data Mining Workshops (ICDMW),* 1114-1119. 10.1109/ICDMW.2010.95

Fathi, M., Khakifirooz, M., Diabat, A., & Chen, H. (2021). An integrated queuing-stochastic optimization hybrid Genetic Algorithm for a location-inventory supply chain network. *International Journal of Production Economics*, *237*, 108139. doi:10.1016/j.ijpe.2021.108139

Firat, M. (2023). Integrating AI applications into learning management systems to enhance e-learning. *Instructional Technology and Lifelong Learning*, *4*(1), 1–14.

Forsmann, J. H., Hiromoto, R. E., & Svoboda, J. (2007). A time-slotted on-demand routing protocol for mobile ad hoc unmanned vehicle systems. *Unmanned Systems Technology*, *9*, 6561. doi:10.1117/12.719355

Fuller, R., Landrigan, P. J., Balakrishnan, K., Bathan, G., Bose-O'Reilly, S., Brauer, M., Caravanos, J., Chiles, T., Cohen, A., Corra, L., Cropper, M., Ferraro, G., Hanna, J., Hanrahan, D., Hu, H., Hunter, D., Janata, G., Kupka, R., Lanphear, B., ... Yan, C. (2022). Pollution and health: A progress update. *The Lancet. Planetary Health*, *6*(6), e535–e547. doi:10.1016/S2542-5196(22)00090-0 PMID:35594895

Fu, S. C., Zhong, X. L., Zhang, Y., Lai, T. W., Chan, K. C., Lee, K. Y., & Chao, C. Y. (2020). Bio-inspired cooling technologies and the applications in buildings. *Energy and Building*, *225*, 110313. doi:10.1016/j.enbuild.2020.110313

García-Mayagoitia, S., Pérez-Hernández, H., Medina-Pérez, G., Campos-Montiel, R. G., & Fernández-Luqueño, F. (2020). Bio-nanomaterials in the air pollution treatment. In *Nanomaterials for air remediation* (pp. 227–248). Elsevier. doi:10.1016/B978-0-12-818821-7.00012-9

Geng, H., Xu, K., Zhang, Y., & Zhou, Z. (2023). A classification tree and decomposition based multi-objective evolutionary algorithm with adaptive operator selection. *Complex & Intelligent Systems*, *9*(1), 579–596. doi:10.1007/s40747-022-00812-8

Gen, M., & Lin, L. (2023). Genetic algorithms and their applications. In *Springer handbook of engineering statistics* (pp. 635–674). Springer London. doi:10.1007/978-1-4471-7503-2_33

George, B., & Wooden, O. (2023). Managing the strategic transformation of higher education through artificial intelligence. *Administrative Sciences*, *13*(9), 196. doi:10.3390/admsci13090196

Ghoseiri, K. (2006). *A new idea for train scheduling using ant colony optimization* (Vol. 88). WIT Transactions on The Built Environment. doi:10.2495/CR060591

Ghosh, P. (2022a). Deep learning to diagnose diseases and security in 5g healthcare informatics. In *Machine Learning and Deep Learning Techniques for Medical Science* (pp. 279–331). CRC Press. doi:10.1201/9781003217497-16

Ghosh, P. (2022b). Timely Diabetes Possibility Prediction using AI Techniques. *Journal of Artificial Intelligence Research & Advances*, *9*(2).

Ghosh, P., & Ghosh, S. (2020). IoT and machine learning in green smart home automation and green building management. *J Altern Energy Sourc Technol*, *10*(3), 8–36.

Ghosh, P., Roy, R., Mandal, S., Chowdhary, M., & Bokshi, S. (2023). Data mining approach to predict academic performance of students. *BOHR International Journal of Computer Science*, *2*(1), 21–31. doi:10.54646/bijcs.2023.21

Gill, R. K., Chawla, P., & Sachdeva, M. (2014). Wireless sensor network: threat models and security issues. *International Conference on Communication, Computing & Systems (ICCCS-2014),* 30-33.

Gonzalez-Martin, J., Kraakman, N. J. R., Perez, C., Lebrero, R., & Munoz, R. (2021). A state-of-the-art review on indoor air pollution and strategies for indoor air pollution control. *Chemosphere*, *262*, 128376. doi:10.1016/j.chemosphere.2020.128376 PMID:33182138

Gravish, N., Wilkinson, M., Sponberg, S., Parness, A., Esparza, N., Soto, D., Yamaguchi, T., Broide, M., Cutkosky, M., Creton, C., & Autumn, K. (2010). Rate-dependent frictional adhesion in natural and synthetic gecko setae. *Journal of the Royal Society, Interface*, *7*(43), 259–269. doi:10.1098/rsif.2009.0133 PMID:19493896

Gu, D. L., Pei, G., Ly, H., Gerla, M., & Hong, X. (2000). Hierarchical routing for multi-layer ad-hoc wireless networks with UAVs. *Proceedings - IEEE Military Communications Conference MILCOM, 1*. 10.1109/MILCOM.2000.904964

Guo, J., Long, K., Yang, K., Jiang, K., Lu, L., & Wang, C. (2023). A novel prediction method for vulnerability outbreak trend. *Computers & Electrical Engineering*, *108*, 108743. doi:10.1016/j.compeleceng.2023.108743

Gupta, A., Kaushik, D., Garg, M., & Verma, A. (2020, October). Machine learning model for breast cancer prediction. In *2020 fourth international conference on I-SMAC (IoT in social, mobile, analytics and cloud)(I-SMAC)* (pp. 472-477). IEEE. 10.1109/I-SMAC49090.2020.9243323

Gupta, A., Singh, R., Nassa, V. K., Bansal, R., Sharma, P., & Koti, K. (2021, October). Investigating application and challenges of big data analytics with clustering. In *2021 international conference on advancements in electrical, electronics, communication, computing and automation (ICAECA)* (pp. 1-6). IEEE.

Gupta, N. K., Yadav, R. S., & Nagaria, R. K. (2020). 3D geographical routing protocols in wireless ad hoc and sensor networks: An overview. *Wireless Networks*, *26*(4), 2549–2566. Advance online publication. doi:10.1007/s11276-019-01983-y

Habib, S., Saleem, S., & Saqib, K. M. (2013). Review on MANET routing protocols and challenges. *Proceeding - 2013 IEEE Student Conference on Research and Development, SCOReD 2013*, 529–533. 10.1109/SCOReD.2013.7002647

Hadi, H. J., Cao, Y., Nisa, K. U., Jamil, A. M., & Ni, Q. (2023). A comprehensive survey on security, privacy issues and emerging defence technologies for UAVs. *Journal of Network and Computer Applications*, *213*, 103607. doi:10.1016/j.jnca.2023.103607

Hameed, Alyahya, Minhas, Habib, Nawaz, Ahmed, Ishtiaq, Islam, & Khan. (2021). *Link and Loss Aware GW-COOP Routing Protocol for FANETs*. doi:10.1109/ACCESS.2021.3101361

Hansen, W. R., & Autumn, K. (2005). Evidence for self-cleaning in gecko setae. *Proceedings of the National Academy of Sciences of the United States of America*, *102*(2), 385–389. doi:10.1073/pnas.0408304102 PMID:15630086

Hayes, S., Toner, J., Desha, C., & Gibbs, M. (2020). Enabling biomimetic place-based design at scale. *Biomimetics*, *5*(2), 21. doi:10.3390/biomimetics5020021 PMID:32443598

Heaton, J. (2018). Ian Goodfellow, Yoshua Bengio, and Aaron Courville: Deep learning: The MIT Press, 2016, 800 pp, ISBN: 0262035618. *Genetic Programming and Evolvable Machines*, *19*(1-2), 305–307. doi:10.1007/s10710-017-9314-z

He, G., Pan, Y., & Tanaka, T. (2020). The short-term impacts of COVID-19 lockdown on urban air pollution in China. *Nature Sustainability*, *3*(12), 1005–1011. doi:10.1038/s41893-020-0581-y

Hema & Sankar. (2016). Energy efficient cluster-based protocol to extend the RFID network lifetime using dragonfly algorithm. In *International conference on communication and signal processing (ICCSP)* (pp. 530-534). IEEE.

Himmelblau, D. M., Barker, R. W., & Suewatanakul, W. (1992). Fault classification with the aid of artificial neural networks. In Fault Detection, Supervision and Safety for Technical Processes 1991 (pp. 541-545). Pergamon. doi:10.1016/B978-0-08-041275-7.50085-5

Hirsch, T., & Hofer, B. (2022). Using textual bug reports to predict the fault category of software bugs. *Array (New York, N.Y.)*, *15*, 100189. doi:10.1016/j.array.2022.100189

Hosseinzadeh, M., Tanveer, J., Ionescu-Feleaga, L., Ionescu, B.-S., Yousefpoor, M. S., Yousefpoor, E., Ahmed, O. H., Rahmani, A. M., & Mehmood, A. (2023). A greedy perimeter stateless routing method based on a position prediction mechanism for flying ad hoc networks. *Journal of King Saud University. Computer and Information Sciences*, *35*(8), 101712. doi:10.1016/j.jksuci.2023.101712

Huber, G., Mantz, H., Spolenak, R., Mecke, K., Jacobs, K., Gorb, S. N., & Arzt, E. (2005). Evidence for capillarity contributions to gecko adhesion from single spatula nanomechanical measurements. *Proceedings of the National Academy of Sciences of the United States of America*, *102*(45), 16293–16296. doi:10.1073/pnas.0506328102 PMID:16260737

Hubert, T., Dugué, A., Vogt Wu, T., Bruneau, D., & Aujard, F. (2022). Exploiting the Potential of Nature for Sustainable Building Designs: A Novel Bioinspired Framework Based on a Characterization of Living Envelopes. In Bionics and Sustainable Design (pp. 289-331). Singapore: Springer Nature Singapore. doi:10.1007/978-981-19-1812-4_10

Hu, P., Pan, J. S., & Chu, S. C. (2020). Improved binary grey wolf optimizer and its application for feature selection. *Knowledge-Based Systems*, *195*, 105746. doi:10.1016/j.knosys.2020.105746

Hussain, Khan, Nazir, Hussain, & Ullah. (2021). Taking Drones to Next Level: The Performance Evaluation of MAA with BCO Routing Protocols for Flying Ad-hoc Networks (FANETs). *Advances in Distributed Computing and Artificial Intelligence Journal, 10*(4), 321-337. doi:10.14201/ADCAIJ2021104321337

Hyeon, S. U., Kim, K., & Yang, S. W. (2010). A new geographic routing protocol for aircraft ad hoc networks. *AIAA/IEEE Digital Avionics Systems Conference - Proceedings*. doi:10.1109/DASC.2010.5655476

Iii, R. D., Parness, A., & Spenko, M. (2014). Improving controllable adhesion on both rough and smooth surfaces with a hybrid electrostatic/gecko-like adhesive. *Journal of the Royal Society, Interface*, *11*(93), 20131089. doi:10.1098/rsif.2013.1089 PMID:24451392

Imani, N., & Vale, B. (2022). Biomimetic Design for Building Energy Efficiency 2021. *Biomimetics*, *7*(3), 106. doi:10.3390/biomimetics7030106 PMID:35997426

Jacquet, P. , Uhlethaler, P. M., Clausen, T., Laouiti, A., Qayyum, A., & Viennot, L. (2001). Optimized link state routing protocol. *IEEE INMIC'01,* 62–68.

Jafar, M., Moghaddam, H., Kalam, A., Nowdeh, S. A., Ahmadi, A., Babanezhad, M., & Saha, S. (2019). Optimal sizing and energy management of stand-alone hybrid photovoltaic/wind system based on hydrogen storage considering LOEE and LOLE reliability indices using flower pollination algorithm. *Renewable Energy*, *135*, 1412–1434. doi:10.1016/j.renene.2018.09.078

Jain, S., & Sharma, T. (2020). Social and travel lockdown impact considering coronavirus disease (COVID-19) on air quality in megacities of India: Present benefits, future challenges and way forward. *Aerosol and Air Quality Research*, *20*(6), 1222–1236. doi:10.4209/aaqr.2020.04.0171

Jamei, E., & Vrcelj, Z. (2021). Biomimicry and the built environment, learning from nature's solutions. *Applied Sciences (Basel, Switzerland)*, *11*(16), 7514. doi:10.3390/app11167514

Jatoi, A. S., Ahmed, J., Akhter, F., Sultan, S. H., Chandio, G. S., Ahmed, S., Hashmi, Z., Usto, M. A., Shaikh, M. S., Siddique, M., & Maitlo, G. (2023). Recent Advances and Treatment of Emerging Contaminants Through the Bio-assisted Method: A Comprehensive Review. *Water, Air, and Soil Pollution*, *234*(1), 49. doi:10.1007/s11270-022-06037-2

Jia, X., Zhou, X., Bao, J., Zhai, G., & Yan, R. (2023). Fusion Swarm-Intelligence-Based Decision Optimization for Energy-Efficient Train-Stopping Schemes. *Applied Sciences (Basel, Switzerland)*, *13*(3), 1497. doi:10.3390/app13031497

Johnson, D. L., Ntlatlapa, N., & Aichele, C. (2008). A simple pragmatic approach to mesh routing using BATMAN. *IFIP International Symposium on Wireless Communications and Information Technology in Developing Countries*. http://downloads.open-mesh.net/batman/misc/batman_ifip.pdf

Johnson, D., & Maltz, D. (2007). The Dynamic Source Routing Protocol (DSR) for Mobile Ad Hoc Networks for IPv4. *Vasa*, *21*(5–6), 1–107. http://medcontent.metapress.com/index/A65RM03P4874243N.pdf

Jumani, T. A., Mustafa, M. W., Alghamdi, A. S., Rasid, M. M., Alamgir, A., & Awan, A. B. (2020). Swarm intelligence-based optimization techniques for dynamic response and power quality enhancement of AC microgrids: A comprehensive review. *IEEE Access : Practical Innovations, Open Solutions*, *8*, 75986–76001. doi:10.1109/ACCESS.2020.2989133

K G, A., & K, D. S.K G. (2017). Dynamic Routing For Flying Ad Hoc Networks. *International Journal of Advanced Research in Computer and Communication Engineering*, *6*(4), 161–170. doi:10.17148/IJARCCE.2017.6430

Kacprzak, M. (2022). Cradle to Cradle Marketplace. *Biodegradable Waste Management in the Circular Economy: Challenges and Opportunities*, 13-18. https://doi.org/ doi:10.1002/9781119679523.ch2

Kala, R. (2023). Mission planning on preference-based expression trees using heuristics-assisted evolutionary computation. *Applied Soft Computing*, *136*, 110090. doi:10.1016/j.asoc.2023.110090

Kamali, S., & Opatrny, J. (2008). A position based ant colony routing algorithm for mobile ad-hoc networks. *Journal of Networks*, *3*(4), 31–41. doi:10.4304/jnw.3.4.31-41

Kandi, H., Mishra, D., & Gorthi, S. R. S. (2017). Exploring the learning capabilities of convolutional neural networks for robust image watermarking. *Computers & Security*, *65*, 247–268. doi:10.1016/j.cose.2016.11.016

Karp, B., & Kung, H. T. (2000). *GPSR: Greedy Perimeter Stateless Routing for Wireless Networks*. doi:10.1145/345910.345953

Kartha, G. P., Anjali, C., Nair, R. V., & Venkateswari, S. (2017). Prediction of defect susceptibility in object Oriented Software. *2017 International Conference on Networks & Advances in Computational Technologies (NetACT)*, 467–472. 10.1109/NETACT.2017.8076817

Karthick & Palanisamy. (2019). Optimized cluster head selection using krill herd algorithm for wireless sensor network. *Automatika: časopiszaautomatiku, mjerenje, elektroniku, računarstvoikomunikacije, 60*(3), 340-348.

Kashyap, K. K., & Agrawal, A. (2018). FANET : Survey on Design Challenges. *Application Scenario and Communication Protocols.*, *5*(04), 1024–1032.

Kaur & Singh. (2018). Nature-Inspired Optimization Techniques in VANETs and FANETs: A Survey. Springer. doi:10.1007/978-981-10-8237-5_63

Khan, Aftab, & Zhang. (2019). *BICSF: Bio-Inspired Clustering Scheme for FANETs*. doi:10.1109/ACCESS.2019.2902940

Khan, S., Khan, M. Z., & Khan, P. (2022). An Ant-Hocnet Routing Protocol Based on Optimized Fuzzy Logic for Swarm of UAVs in FANET. Hindawi Wireless Communications and Mobile Computing.

Khan, A., Khan, S., Fazal, A. S., Zhang, Z., & Abuassba, A. O. (2021). Intelligent cluster routing scheme for flying ad hoc networks. *Science China. Information Sciences*, *64*(8), 182305. doi:10.1007/s11432-019-2984-7

Khan, M. A., Khan, I. U., Safi, A., & Quershi, I. M. (2018). Dynamic routing in flying Ad-Hoc networks using topology-based routing protocols. *Drones (Basel)*, *2*(3), 1–15. doi:10.3390/drones2030027

Khan, M. F., Yau, K.-L. A., Noor, R. M., & Imran, M. A. (2020). Routing Schemes in FANETs: A Survey. *Sensors (Basel)*, *20*(1), 38. doi:10.3390/s20010038

Khelil, S., & Zemmouri, N. (2019). Biomimetic: A new strategy for a passive sustainable ventilation system design in hot and arid regions. *International Journal of Environmental Science and Technology, 16*(6), 2821–2830. doi:10.1007/s13762-018-2168-y

Khishe, M. M. (2020). Chimp optimization algorithm. Expert Systems with Applications. Elsevier.

Kim, T. W., & Bhushan, B. (2008). The adhesion model considering capillarity for gecko attachment system. *Journal of the Royal Society, Interface, 5*(20), 319–327. doi:10.1098/rsif.2007.1078 PMID:17594962

Kim, T. W., & Bhushan, B. (2010). A review of adhesion and friction models for gecko feet. *International Journal of Precision Engineering and Manufacturing, 11*(1), 171–186. doi:10.1007/s12541-010-0020-5

Kim, T., Lee, S., Kim, K. H., & Jo, Y.-I. (2023). FANET Routing Protocol Analysis for Multi-UAV-Based Reconnaissance Mobility Models. *Drones (Basel), 7*(3), 161. doi:10.3390/drones7030161

Kizilkan, Z. B., Sivri, M. S., Yazici, I., & Beyca, O. F. (2022). Neural Networks and Deep Learning. In *Business Analytics for Professionals* (pp. 127–151). Springer International Publishing. doi:10.1007/978-3-030-93823-9_5

Klinmalee, S., Naenna, T., & Woarawichai, C. (2020). Application of a genetic algorithm for multi-item inventory lot-sizing with supplier selection under quantity discount and lead time. *International Journal of Operational Research, 38*(3), 403–421. doi:10.1504/IJOR.2020.107540

Ko, J., Mahajan, A., & Sengupta, R. (2002). A network-centric UAV organization for search and pursuit operations. *IEEE Aerospace Conference Proceedings,* 6. 10.1109/AERO.2002.1036111

Konak, F., Bülbül, M. A., & Türkoğlu, D. (2024). Feature Selection and Hyperparameters Optimization Employing a Hybrid Model Based on Genetic Algorithm and Artificial Neural Network: Forecasting Dividend Payout Ratio. *Computational Economics*, 1–21. doi:10.1007/s10614-023-10530-z

Kout, Bouaita, B., Beghriche, A., Labed, S., Chikhi, S., & Bourennane, E.-B. (2023). A Hybrid Optimization Solution for UAV Network Routing" engineering. *Technology & Applied Science Research, 13*(2), 10270–10278. doi:10.48084/etasr.5661

Krahn, J. M., Abraham, A. G. P., & Menon, C. (2014). Polymeric electro-dry adhesives for use on conducting surfaces. *Proceedings of the Institution of Mechanical Engineers. Proceedings Part L, Journal of Materials: Design and Applications, 228*(2), 109–114. doi:10.1177/1464420713509376

Krahn, J., & Menon, C. (2012). Electro-dry adhesion. *Langmuir, 28*(12), 5438–5443. doi:10.1021/la2048882 PMID:22397643

Kuddus, M. A., Tynan, E., & McBryde, E. (2020). Urbanization: A problem for the rich and the poor? *Public Health Reviews, 41*(1), 1–4. doi:10.1186/s40985-019-0116-0 PMID:31908901

Kumar, Raw, & Bansal. (n.d.). Minimize the routing overhead through 3D cone shaped location-aided routing protocol for FANETs. *Int. J. Inf. Tecnol.* doi:10.1007/s41870-020-00536-3

Kumari, S., Awasthi, Y. K., Bansal, D., & Anand, R. (2023). The Design Mechanisms of Multiband Antennas from 1G to 5G: A Comprehensive Review. *Digital Transformation–Modernization and Optimization of Wireless Networks*, 77.

Kumar, S., Kaiwartya, O., Rathee, M., Kumar, N., & Lloret, J. (2020). Toward energy-oriented optimization for green communication in sensor enabled IoT environments. *IEEE Systems Journal, 14*(4), 4663–4673. doi:10.1109/JSYST.2020.2975823

Kurade, S. S., & Latpate, R. (2021). Demand and deterioration of items per unit time inventory models with shortages using genetic algorithm. *Journal of Management Analytics*, *8*(3), 502–529. doi:10.1080/23270012.2020.1829113

Larabi-Marie, Sainte, & Saswan. (2021). *Emerging Applications of Bio-Inspired Algorithms in Image Segmentation.* MDPI.

Lavanya, N., & Shankar, T. (2019). Energy Efficient Cluster Head Selection using Hybrid Squirrel Harmony Search Algorithm in WSN. *Energy*, *10*, 477–487.

Leberruyer, N., Bruch, J., Ahlskog, M., & Afshar, S. (2023). Toward Zero Defect Manufacturing with the support of Artificial Intelligence—Insights from an industrial application. *Computers in Industry*, *147*, 103877. doi:10.1016/j.compind.2023.103877

Lee, H., & Bhushan, B. (2012). Fabrication and characterization of hierarchical nanostructured smart adhesion surfaces. *Journal of Colloid and Interface Science*, *372*(1), 231–238. doi:10.1016/j.jcis.2012.01.020 PMID:22285098

Lee, J., Bush, B., Maboudian, R., & Fearing, R. S. (2009). Gecko-inspired comined lamellar and nanofibrillar array for adhesion on nonplanar surfaces. *Langmuir*, *25*(21), 12449–12453. doi:10.1021/la9029672 PMID:19856986

Lee, K. K., Bing, R., Kiang, J., Bashir, S., Spath, N., Stelzle, D., Mortimer, K., Bularga, A., Doudesis, D., Joshi, S. S., Strachan, F., Gumy, S., Adair-Rohani, H., Attia, E. F., Chung, M. H., Miller, M. R., Newby, D. E., Mills, N. L., McAllister, D. A., & Shah, A. S. (2020). Adverse health effects associated with household air pollution: A systematic review, meta-analysis, and burden estimation study. *The Lancet. Global Health*, *8*(11), e1427–e1434. doi:10.1016/S2214-109X(20)30343-0 PMID:33069303

Leonov, A. V. (2016). Application of bee colony algorithm for FANET routing. *International Conference of Young Specialists on Micro/Nanotechnologies and Electron Devices, EDM*. 10.1109/EDM.2016.7538709

Leonov, A. V. (2017). Applying bio-inspired algorithms to routing problem solution in FANET. *Bulletin of the South Ural State University*, *17*(2), 5–23.

Li, X., & Huang, J. (2017). ABPP: An adaptive beacon scheme for geographic routing in FANET. *Parallel and Distributed Computing, Applications and Technologies, PDCAT Proceedings*. 10.1109/PDCAT.2017.00055

Li, F., Yue, Q., Liu, Y., Ouyang, H., & Gu, F. (2024). A fast density peak clustering based particle swarm optimizer for dynamic optimization. *Expert Systems with Applications*, *236*, 121254. doi:10.1016/j.eswa.2023.121254

Li, L., Wang, B., Feng, P., Li Liu, D., He, Q., Zhang, Y., Wang, Y., Li, S., Lu, X., Yue, C., Li, Y., He, J., Feng, H., Yang, G., & Yu, Q. (2022). Developing machine learning models with multi-source environmental data to predict wheat yield in China. *Computers and Electronics in Agriculture*, *194*, 106790. doi:10.1016/j.compag.2022.106790

Lin, L., Sun, Q., Wang, S., & Yang, F. (2012). A geographic mobility prediction routing protocol for Ad Hoc UAV Network. *2012 IEEE Globecom Workshops. GC Wkshps*, *2012*, 1597–1602. Advance online publication. doi:10.1109/GLOCOMW.2012.6477824

Liu, K., Zhang, J., & Zhang, T. (2008). The clustering algorithm of UAV networking in near-space. *ISAPE 2008 - The 8th International Symposium on Antennas, Propagation and EM Theory Proceedings*. 10.1109/ISAPE.2008.4735528

Liu, B. (2012). Sentiment analysis and opinion mining. *Synthesis Lectures on Human Language Technologies*, *5*(1), 1–167. doi:10.1007/978-3-031-02145-9

Liu, F., & Chang, Y. (2019). *An energy aware adaptive kernel density estimation approach to unequal clustering in wireless sensor networks.* IEEE Access. doi:10.1109/ACCESS.2019.2902243

Liu, G., Wong, W. S., Kraft, M., Ager, J. W., Vollmer, D., & Xu, R. (2021). Wetting-regulated gas-involving (photo) electrocatalysis: Biomimetics in energy conversion. *Chemical Society Reviews*, *50*(18), 10674–10699. doi:10.1039/D1CS00258A PMID:34369513

Li, X., Keegan, B., & Mtenzi, F. (2016). Energy efficient hybrid routing protocol based on the artificial fish swarm algorithm and ant colony optimisation for WSNs. *Sensors (Basel)*, *18*(10, no. 10pp), 3351. doi:10.3390/s18103351 PMID:30297606

Li, X., Keegan, B., Mtenzi, F., Weise, T., & Tan, M. (2019). *Energy-efficient load balancing ant-based routing algorithm for wireless sensor networks.* IEEE Access. doi:10.1109/ACCESS.2019.2934889

Li, Y., Krahn, J., & Menon, C. (2016). Bioinspired dry adhesive materials and their application in robotics: A review. *Journal of Bionic Engineering*, *13*(2), 181–199. doi:10.1016/S1672-6529(16)60293-7

Li, Y., Zhang, R., Wen, F., Li, M., Li, W., Li, L., Zhou, Y., Rencus-Lazar, S., Tao, K., Gazit, E., Wu, W., Ying, Z., & Wang, G. (2023). Bioinspired supramolecular arrayed heterojunction-based room-temperature sensor for high-performance gas detection. *Sensors and Actuators. B, Chemical*, *396*, 134641. doi:10.1016/j.snb.2023.134641

Luis Antonio, L. F. (2021). Q-FANET: Improved Q-learning based routing protocol for FANETs. *Computer Networks*, *198*, 108379. doi:10.1016/j.comnet.2021.108379

Lytos, A., Lagkas, T., Sarigiannidis, P., Zervakis, M., & Livanos, G. (2020). Towards smart farming: Systems, frameworks and exploitation of multiple sources. *Computer Networks*, *172*, 107147. doi:10.1016/j.comnet.2020.107147

Magazzino, C., Mele, M., & Schneider, N. (2020). The relationship between air pollution and COVID-19-related deaths: An application to three French cities. *Applied Energy*, *279*, 115835. doi:10.1016/j.apenergy.2020.115835 PMID:32952266

Mahapatra, Payal, & Chopra. (2020). Swarm intelligence based centralized clustering: A novel solution. *Journal of Intelligent Manufacturing*, 1–12.

Mahjoob, M., Fazeli, S. S., Milanlouei, S., Tavassoli, L. S., & Mirmozaffari, M. (2022). A modified adaptive genetic algorithm for multi-product multi-period inventory routing problem. *Sustainable Operations and Computers*, *3*, 1–9. doi:10.1016/j.susoc.2021.08.002

Makram, A., & Abou Ouf, T. (2019). Biomimetic and Biophilic Design as an approach to innovative sustainable architectural design. *Architecture & Urbanism… A Smart Outlook©*, 509-518.

Manisalidis, I., Stavropoulou, E., Stavropoulos, A., & Bezirtzoglou, E. (2020). Environmental and health impacts of air pollution: A review. *Frontiers in Public Health*, *8*, 14. doi:10.3389/fpubh.2020.00014 PMID:32154200

Mauša, G., Grbac, T. G., & Bašić, B. D. (2014). Software defect prediction with Bug-Code analyzer - A data collection tool demo. *2014 22nd International Conference on Software, Telecommunications and Computer Networks (SoftCOM)*, 425–426. 10.1109/SOFTCOM.2014.7039122

Mayo Clinic. (2023). *Preventing and treating disease to save your eyesigh* (3rd ed.).

Meena, R. S., Talukdar, R., Kannadasan, B., Nageswara Rao, G., Shukla, K. A., Anand, R., & Gupta, A. (2023). PID Control and Estimation of the Attitude Model Applied to Geostationary Satellites. In *Advances in Signal Processing, Embedded Systems and IoT: Proceedings of Seventh ICMEET-2022* (pp. 631-642). Singapore: Springer Nature Singapore. 10.1007/978-981-19-8865-3_56

Megahed, N. A., & Ghoneim, E. M. (2021). Indoor Air Quality: Rethinking rules of building design strategies in post-pandemic architecture. *Environmental Research*, *193*, 110471. doi:10.1016/j.envres.2020.110471 PMID:33197423

Mishra, P. K., Karmakar, S., & Guhathakurta, P. (2016). A broad literature survey of development and application of artificial neural networks in rainfall-runoff modelling. In *Proceedings of Fifth International Conference on Soft Computing for Problem Solving: SocProS 2015, Volume 2* (pp. 691-710). Springer Singapore. 10.1007/978-981-10-0451-3_62

Moawad, A. W., Fuentes, D. T., ElBanan, M. G., Shalaby, A. S., Guccione, J., Kamel, S., Jensen, C. T., & Elsayes, K. M. (2022). Artificial intelligence in diagnostic radiology: Where do we stand, challenges, and opportunities. *Journal of Computer Assisted Tomography*, *46*(1), 78–90. doi:10.1097/RCT.0000000000001247 PMID:35027520

Moghadassi, A., Parvizian, F., & Hosseini, S. M. (2010). Application of Artificial Neural Network for Prediction of Liquid Viscosity. *Indian Chemical Engineer*, *52*(1), 37–48. doi:10.1080/00194501003759688

Moncayo–Martínez, L. A., & Mastrocinque, E. (2016). A multi-objective intelligent water drop algorithm to minimize cost of goods sold and time to market in logistics networks. *Expert Systems with Applications*, *64*, 455–466. doi:10.1016/j.eswa.2016.08.003

Mondal, A. K., Schneider, K. A., Roy, B., & Roy, C. K. (2022). A survey of software architectural change detection and categorization techniques. *Journal of Systems and Software*, *194*, 111505. doi:10.1016/j.jss.2022.111505

Monga, Sharma, & Sharma. (2022). A comprehensive meta-analysis of emerging swarm intelligent computing techniques and their research trend. *J. King Saud Univ. - Comput. Inf. Sci.*, *34*(10), 9622–9643. . doi:10.1016/j.jksuci.2021.11.016

Mood & Javidi. (2019). Energy-efficient clustering method for wireless sensor networks using modified gravitational search algorithm. *Evolving Systems*, 1–13.

Murphy, M. P., Kim, S., & Sitti, M. (2009). Enhanced adhesion by gecko-inspired hierarchical fibrillary adhesives. *ACS Applied Materials & Interfaces*, *1*(4), 849–855. doi:10.1021/am8002439 PMID:20356011

Nadeem, A., Mehmood, A., & Siddiqui, M. S. (2018). A Review and Classification of Flying Ad-Hoc Network (FANET) Routing Strategies. *International Journal of Sciences: Basic and Applied Research, 8*(3), 1–8. www.textroad.com

Nadeem, Alghamdi, Yawar, Mehmood, & Siddiqui. (2018). A Review and Classification of Flying Ad-Hoc Network (FANET) Routing Strategies. *Journal of Basic and Applied Scientific Research*, *8*(3), 1–8.

Natarajan, L., & Short, M. (Eds.). (2023). *Engaged Urban Pedagogy: Participatory practices in planning and place-making*. UCL Press. doi:10.14324/111.9781800081239

Nguyen, T. H., Nguyen, L. V., Jung, J. J., Agbehadji, I. E., Frimpong, S. O., & Millham, R. C. (2020). Bio-inspired approaches for smart energy management: State of the art and challenges. *Sustainability (Basel)*, *12*(20), 8495. doi:10.3390/su12208495

Nielsen, M. A. (2015). *Neural networks and deep learning* (Vol. 25). Determination press.

Oren, G., Barenboim, L., & Levin, H. (2017). Adaptive Distributed Hierarchical Sensing algorithm for reduction of wireless sensor network cluster-heads energy consumption. *13th International Wireless Communications and Mobile Computing Conference (IWCMC)*, 980-986. 10.1109/IWCMC.2017.7986419

Oubbati, O. S., Atiquzzaman, M., Lorenz, P., Tareque, M. H., & Hossain, M. S. (2019). Routing in flying Ad Hoc networks: Survey, constraints, and future challenge perspectives. *IEEE Access : Practical Innovations, Open Solutions*, *7*, 81057–81105. doi:10.1109/ACCESS.2019.2923840

Oubbati, O. S., Lakas, A., Zhou, F., Güneş, M., & Yagoubi, M. B. (2017). A survey on position-based routing protocols for Flying Ad hoc Networks (FANETs). *Vehicular Communications*, *10*, 29–56. doi:10.1016/j.vehcom.2017.10.003

Padmaja, S., & Fatima, S. S. (2013). Opinion Mining and Sentiment Analysis–An Assessment of Peoples' Belief: A Survey/ *International Journal of Adhoc. Sensor & Uboquitos Computing*, *4*(1), 21.

Pal, V., Singh, G., & Yadav, R. P. (2015). Cluster head selection optimization based on genetic algorithm to prolong lifetime of wireless sensor networks. *Procedia Computer Science*, *57*, 1417–1423. doi:10.1016/j.procs.2015.07.461

Pancholi, P. D., & Patel, S. J. (2021). Literature Survey for Applications of Artificial Neural Networks. *Applications of Artificial Neural Networks for Nonlinear Data*, 1-17.

Pandey, A., Rajan, A., & Nandi, A. (2018). Lifetime enhancement of wireless sensor networks by using sine cosine optimization algorithm. In *2018 7th International Conference on Reliability, Infocom Technologies and Optimization (Trends and Future Directions) (ICRITO)* (pp. 1-7). IEEE. 10.1109/ICRITO.2018.8748649

Park, C. G., Jun, I., Lee, S., Ryu, C. S., Lee, S. A., Park, J., Han, H.-S., Park, H., Manz, A., Shin, H., & Kim, Y. J. (2022). Integration of Bioinspired Fibrous Strands with 3D Spheroids for Environmental Hazard Monitoring. *Small*, *18*(22), 2200757. doi:10.1002/smll.202200757 PMID:35521748

Park, V. D., & Corson, M. S. (2019). Temporally-Ordered Routing Algorithm. *Journal of Chemical Information and Modeling*, *53*(9).

Parness, A., Soto, D., Esparza, N., Gravish, N., Wilkinson, M., Autumn, K., & Cutkosky, M. (2009). A microfabricated wedge-shaped adhesive array displaying gecko-like dynamic adhesion, directionality and long lifetime. *Journal of the Royal Society, Interface*, *6*(41), 1223–1232. doi:10.1098/rsif.2009.0048 PMID:19324664

Pasandideh, F., da Costa, J. P. J., Kunst, R., Islam, N., Hardjawana, W., & Pignaton de Freitas, E. (2022). A Review of Flying Ad Hoc Networks: Key Characteristics, Applications, and Wireless Technologies. *Remote Sensing (Basel)*, *14*(18), 1–25. doi:10.3390/rs14184459

Pati, B., Sarkar, J. L., & Panigrahi, C. R. (2017). ECS: An energy-efficient approach to select cluster-head in wireless sensor networks. *Arabian Journal for Science and Engineering*, *42*(2), 669–676. doi:10.1007/s13369-016-2304-2

Peattie, A. M., Majidi, C., Corder, A., & Full, R. J. (2007). Ancestrally high elastic modulus of gecko setal β-keratin. *Journal of the Royal Society, Interface*, *4*(17), 1071–1076. doi:10.1098/rsif.2007.0226 PMID:17374591

Pedersen, M. E. H., & Chipperfield, A. J. (2010). Simplifying particle swarm optimization. *Applied Soft Computing*, *10*(2), 618–628. doi:10.1016/j.asoc.2009.08.029

Pereira, J. D., Ivaki, N., & Vieira, M. (2021). Characterizing Buffer Overflow Vulnerabilities in Large C/C++ Projects. *IEEE Access : Practical Innovations, Open Solutions*, *9*, 142879–142892. doi:10.1109/ACCESS.2021.3120349

Perkings, C., Belding-Royer, E., & Das, S. (2003). Ad hoc On-Demand Distance Vector (AODV) Routing. *IETF RFC, 3561*, 1–37. http://tools.ietf.org/pdf/rfc3561.pdf

Perkins, C. E., & Bhagwat, P. (1994). Highly dynamic destination-sequenced distance-vector routing (DSDV) for mobile computer. *Proceedings of the Conference on Communications Architectures, Protocols and Applications, SIGCOMM 1994,* 234–244. 10.1145/190314.190336

Piotrowski, A. P., Napiorkowski, J. J., & Piotrowska, A. E. (2024). To what extent evolutionary algorithms can benefit from a longer search? *Information Sciences*, *654*, 119766. doi:10.1016/j.ins.2023.119766

Polo-Mendoza, R., Martinez-Arguelles, G., & Penabaena-Niebles, R. (2023). A multi-objective optimization based on genetic algorithms for the sustainable design of Warm Mix Asphalt (WMA). *The International Journal of Pavement Engineering*, *24*(2), 2074417. doi:10.1080/10298436.2022.2074417

Prabha, C. L., & Shivakumar, N. (2020). Software Defect Prediction Using Machine Learning Techniques. *2020 4th International Conference on Trends in Electronics and Informatics (ICOEI),* (48184), 728–733. 10.1109/ICOEI48184.2020.9142909

Prakash, N., Rajalakshmi, M., & Nedunchezhian, R. (2020). Optimized Energy Aware Routing Based on Suitable Based Antlion Group with Advanced Algorithm (SA-AOA) in Wireless Sensor Network. *Wireless Personal Communications*, *113*(1), 59–77. doi:10.1007/s11277-020-07178-5

Pritchard, N. J., Wicenec, A., Bennamoun, M., & Dodson, R. (2023). A Bibliometric Review of Neuromorphic Computing and Spiking Neural Networks. *arXiv preprint arXiv:2304.06897.*

Puthoff, J. B., Prowse, M. S., Wilkinson, M., & Autumn, K. (2010). Changes in materials properties explain the effects of humidity on gecko adhesion. *The Journal of Experimental Biology*, *213*(21), 3699–3704. doi:10.1242/jeb.047654 PMID:20952618

Qamar, S. A., Qamar, M., Basharat, A., Bilal, M., Cheng, H., & Iqbal, H. M. (2022). Alginate-based nano-adsorbent materials-Bioinspired solution to mitigate hazardous environmental pollutants. *Chemosphere*, *288*, 132618. doi:10.1016/j.chemosphere.2021.132618 PMID:34678347

Qiuet, M., Ming, Z., Li, J., Liu, J., Quan, G., & Yongxin Zhu, Y. (2013). Informer homed routing fault tolerance mechanism for wireless sensor networks. *Journal of Systems Architecture*, *59*(4-5), 260–270. doi:10.1016/j.sysarc.2012.12.003

Rabani, S. T., Ud Din Khanday, A. M., Khan, Q. R., Hajam, U. A., Imran, A. S., & Kastrati, Z. (2023). Detecting suicidality on social media: Machine learning at rescue. *Egypt. Informatics J.*, *24*(2), 291–302. doi:10.1016/j.eij.2023.04.003

Radoglou-Grammatikis, P., Sarigiannidis, P., Lagkas, T., & Moscholios, I. (2020). A compilation of UAV applications for precision agriculture. *Computer Networks*, *172*, 107148. doi:10.1016/j.comnet.2020.107148

Raghavan, R., Verma, D. C., Pandey, D., Anand, R., Pandey, B. K., & Singh, H. (2022). Optimized building extraction from high-resolution satellite imagery using deep learning. *Multimedia Tools and Applications*, *81*(29), 42309–42323. doi:10.1007/s11042-022-13493-9

Rahmani, A. M., Ali, S., Yousefpoor, E., Yousefpoor, M. S., Javaheri, D., Lalbakhsh, P., Hassan Ahmed, O., Hosseinzadeh, M., & Lee, S.-W. (2022). OLSR+: A new routing method based on fuzzy logic in flying ad-hoc networks (FANETs). *Vehicular Communications*, *36*, 100489. doi:10.1016/j.vehcom.2022.100489

Rajabi, M., Beheshtian, S., Davoodi, S., Ghorbani, H., Mohamadian, N., Radwan, A. E., & Alvar, M. A. (2021). Novel hybrid machine learning optimizer algorithms to prediction of fracture density by petrophysical data. *Journal of Petroleum Exploration and Production Technology*, *11*(12), 4375–4397. doi:10.1007/s13202-021-01321-z

Rajagopalan, S., Brauer, M., Bhatnagar, A., Bhatt, D. L., Brook, J. R., Huang, W., Münzel, T., Newby, D., Siegel, J., & Brook, R. D. (2020). Personal-level protective actions against particulate matter air pollution exposure: A scientific statement from the American Heart Association. *Circulation*, *142*(23), e411–e431. doi:10.1161/CIR.0000000000000931 PMID:33150789

Ramasubramanian, V., Haas, Z. J., & Sirer, E. G. (2003). SHARP: A hybrid adaptive routing protocol for mobile ad hoc networks. *Proceedings of the International Symposium on Mobile Ad Hoc Networking and Computing (MobiHoc)*, 303–314. 10.1145/778415.778450

Ramirez-Pedraza, R., Vargas, N., Sandoval, C., Luis del Valle-Padilla, J., & Ramos, F. (2020, January). A bio-inspired model of behaviour considering decision-making and planning, spatial attention and basic motor commands processes. *Cognitive Systems Research*, *59*, 293–303. doi:10.1016/j.cogsys.2019.10.006

Ray, A., & De, D. (2016). Energy efficient clustering protocol based on K-means (EECPK-means)-midpoint algorithm for enhanced network lifetime in wireless sensor network. *IET Wireless Sensor Systems*, *6*(6), 181–191. doi:10.1049/iet-wss.2015.0087

Rizzoli, Oliverio, Montemanni, & Gambardella. (2004). *Ant Colony Optimisation for vehicle routing problems: from theory to applications*. Academic Press.

Rizzo, N. W., Gardner, K. H., Walls, D. J., Keiper-Hrynko, N. M., Ganzke, T. S., & Hallahan, D. L. (2006). Characterization of the structure and composition of gecko adhesive setae. *Journal of the Royal Society, Interface*, *3*(8), 441–451. doi:10.1098/rsif.2005.0097 PMID:16849272

Roberts, D. A., Yaida, S., & Hanin, B. (2022). *The principles of deep learning theory*. Cambridge University Press. doi:10.1017/9781009023405

Robinson, J. M., Watkins, H., Man, I., Liddicoat, C., Cameron, R., Parker, B., Cruz, M., & Meagher, L. (2021). Microbiome-Inspired Green Infrastructure: A bioscience roadmap for urban ecosystem health. arq. *Architectural Research Quarterly*, *25*(4), 292–303. doi:10.1017/S1359135522000148

Rong, Z. X., Zhou, Y. M., Chen, B. G., Robertson, J., Federle, W., Hofmann, S., Steiner, U., & Goldberg-Oppenheimer, P. (2014). Bio-inspired hierarchical polymer fiber-carbon nanotube adhesives. *Advanced Materials*, *26*(9), 1456–1461. doi:10.1002/adma.201304601 PMID:24327478

Rosati, S., Kruzelecki, K., Traynard, L., & Rimoldi, B. (2013). Speed-aware routing for UAV ad-hoc networks. *2013 IEEE Globecom Workshops. GC Wkshps*, *2013*, 1367–1373. doi:10.1109/GLOCOMW.2013.6825185

Rosa, W., & Jardine, S. (2023). Data-driven agile software cost estimation models for DHS and DoD. *Journal of Systems and Software*, *203*, 111739. doi:10.1016/j.jss.2023.111739

Rosetta, G., Macaire, L., Butters, M., & Finlayson, C. E. (2023). Dial-In Synthesis of ‘Polymer Opal’Core-Interlayer-Shell Composite Nanoparticles. *Polymers*, *15*(17), 3507. doi:10.3390/polym15173507 PMID:37688133

Ruibal, R., & Ernst, V. (1965). The structure of the digital setae of lizards. *Journal of Morphology*, *117*(3), 271–293. doi:10.1002/jmor.1051170302 PMID:5883924

Sahana, S. K., Jain, A., & Mahanti, P. K. (2014). Ant Colony Optimization for Train Scheduling: An Analysis. *International Journal of Intelligent Systems and Applications*, *2*(2), 29–36. doi:10.5815/ijisa.2014.02.04

Sahingoz, O. K. (2013). Flying Ad-Hoc Networks (FANETs): A survey. *Ad Hoc Networks*, *11*(3), 1254–1270. doi:10.1016/j.adhoc.2012.12.004

Saini, J., Dutta, M., & Marques, G. (2020). A comprehensive review on indoor air quality monitoring systems for enhanced public health. *Sustainable Environment Research*, *30*(1), 1–12. doi:10.1186/s42834-020-0047-y

Sajovic, I., Kert, M., & Boh Podgornik, B. (2023). Smart Textiles: A Review and Bibliometric Mapping. *Applied Sciences (Basel, Switzerland)*, *13*(18), 10489. doi:10.3390/app131810489

Sakhaee, E., Jamalipour, A., & Kato, N. (2006). Aeronautical ad hoc networks. *IEEE Wireless Communications and Networking Conference, WCNC*, *1*, 246–251. 10.1109/WCNC.2006.1683472

Sandak, A., & Butina-Ogorelec, K. (2023). Bioinspired building materials-lessons from nature. *Frontiers in Materials*, *10*, 1283163. doi:10.3389/fmats.2023.1283163

Sang, Q., Wu, H., Xing, L., & Xie, P. (2020). Review and Comparison of Emerging Routing Protocols in Flying Ad Hoc Networks. *Symmetry*, *12*(6), 971. doi:10.3390/sym12060971

Santos, D., Heyneman, B., Kim, S., Esparza, N., & Cutkosky, M. R. (2008). Gecko-inspired climbing behaviors on vertical and overhanging surfaces. *2008 IEEE International Conference on Robotics and Automation*. 10.1109/ROBOT.2008.4543355

Scott, J. (2023). Digital Fabrication and Fabric Innovation. In FABRIC [ated] (pp. 28-39). Routledge. doi:10.4324/9781003138471-4

Seerat, B., & Azam, F. (2012). Opinion mining: Issues and challenges (a survey). *International Journal of Computer Applications*, *49*(9), 42–51. doi:10.5120/7658-0762

Shah, G. J., & Sitti, M. (2004). Modeling and design of biomimetic adhesives inspired by gecko foot-hairs. *Proceedings of the 2004 IEEE International Conference on Robotics and Biomimetics*, 873–878. 10.1109/ROBIO.2004.1521899

Sharma, S., & Sarkar, P. (2022). Knowledge capture and its representation using concept map in bioinspired design. *International Journal on Interactive Design and Manufacturing*, 1-13. doi:10.1007/s12008-022-01069-8

Sharma, A., & Dey, S. (2012). Performance investigation of feature selection methods and sentiment lexicons for sentiment analysis. *IJCA Special Issue on Advanced Computing and Communication Technologies for HPC Applications*, *3*, 15–20.

Sharma, N. R., & Chitre, V. D. (2014). Opinion mining, analysis and its challenges. *International Journal of Innovations & Advancement in Computer Science*, *3*(1), 59–65.

Sharma, R., Vashisht, V., & Singh, U. (2020). eeTMFO/GA: A secure and energy efficient cluster head selection in wireless sensor networks. *Telecommunication Systems*, *74*(3), 1–16. doi:10.1007/s11235-020-00654-0

Shashwat, S., Zingre, K. T., Thurairajah, N., Kumar, D. K., Panicker, K., Anand, P., & Wan, M. P. (2023). A review on bioinspired strategies for an energy-efficient built environment. *Energy and Building*, *296*, 113382. doi:10.1016/j.enbuild.2023.113382

Shi, H., Song, Z., Bai, X., Hu, Y., Li, T., & Zhang, K. (2023). A novel digital twin model for dynamical updating and real-time mapping of local defect extension in rolling bearings. *Mechanical Systems and Signal Processing*, *193*, 110255. doi:10.1016/j.ymssp.2023.110255

Shirani, R., St-Hilaire, M., Kunz, T., Zhou, Y., Li, J., & Lamont, L. (2012). On the delay of reactive-greedy-reactive routing in unmanned aeronautical ad-hoc networks. *Procedia Computer Science*, *10*, 535–542. doi:10.1016/j.procs.2012.06.068

Shi, W., Guo, Y., & Liu, Y. (2020). When flexible organic field-effect transistors meet biomimetics: A prospective view of the internet of things. *Advanced Materials*, *32*(15), 1901493. doi:10.1002/adma.201901493 PMID:31250497

Shukla, V., Pandya, V., Bandyopadhyay, M., & Pandey, A. (2021). Plasma Density Prediction for Helicon Negative Hydrogen Plasma Source using Decision Tree and Random Forest Algorithm. In *Congress on Intelligent Systems: Proceedings of CIS 2020,* Volume 2 (pp. 357-368). Springer Singapore. 10.1007/978-981-33-6984-9_29

Shukla, V., & Bandyopadhyay, M. (2023). Optimization of input parameters of ANN–driven plasma source through nature-inspired evolutionary algorithms. *Intelligent Systems with Applications*, *18*, 200200. doi:10.1016/j.iswa.2023.200200

Shumeye Lakew, D., Sa'Ad, U., Dao, N. N., Na, W., & Cho, S. (2020). Routing in Flying Ad Hoc Networks: A Comprehensive Survey. *IEEE Communications Surveys and Tutorials*, *22*(2), 1071–1120. doi:10.1109/COMST.2020.2982452

Siddiqua, A., Shah, M. A., Khattak, H. A., Din, I. U., & Guizani, M. (2019). iCAFE: Intelligent Congestion Avoidance and Fast Emergency services. Academic Press.

Sindhwani, N., Anand, R., Nageswara Rao, G., Chauhan, S., Chaudhary, A., Gupta, A., & Pandey, D. (2023). Comparative Analysis of Optimization Algorithms for Antenna Selection in MIMO Systems. In *Advances in Signal Processing, Embedded Systems and IoT: Proceedings of Seventh ICMEET-2022* (pp. 607-617). Singapore: Springer Nature Singapore. 10.1007/978-981-19-8865-3_54

Sindhwani, N., Anand, R., George, A. S., & Pandey, D. (Eds.). (2024). *Robotics and Automation in Industry 4.0: Smart Industries and Intelligent Technologies*. CRC Press.

Singh, H., & Singh, D. (2016). Taxonomy of routing protocols in wireless sensor networks: A survey. In *2016 2nd International Conference on Contemporary Computing and Informatics (IC3I)* (pp. 822-830). IEEE. 10.1109/IC3I.2016.7918796

Singh, H., Veeraiah, V., Khan, H., Singh, D. K., Talukdar, V., Anand, R., & Sindhwani, N. (2024). Investigating Scope and Applications for the Internet of Robotics in Industrial Automation. In Robotics and Automation in Industry 4.0 (pp. 132-151). CRC Press.

Singh, S. K., Thakur, R. K., Kumar, S., & Anand, R. (2022, March). Deep learning and machine learning based facial emotion detection using CNN. In *2022 9th International Conference on Computing for Sustainable Global Development (INDIACom)* (pp. 530-535). IEEE. 10.23919/INDIACom54597.2022.9763165

Singh, S., & Gupta, B. (2016). OSEECH: Optimize scalable energy efficient clustering hierarchy protocol in wireless sensor networks. *Advances in Computing, Communications and Informatics (ICACCI), 2016 International Conference on*, 1441-1446.

Singh, P. K., & Husain, M. S. (2014). Methodological study of opinion mining and sentiment analysis techniques. *International Journal of Soft Computing*, *5*(1), 11–21. doi:10.5121/ijsc.2014.5102

Sinha, A., Sengupta, T., & Alvarado, R. (2020). Interplay between technological innovation and environmental quality: Formulating the SDG policies for next 11 economies. *Journal of Cleaner Production*, *242*, 118549. doi:10.1016/j.jclepro.2019.118549

Sommese, F., Badarnah, L., & Ausiello, G. (2022). A critical review of biomimetic building envelopes: Towards a bio-adaptive model from nature to architecture. *Renewable & Sustainable Energy Reviews*, *169*, 112850. doi:10.1016/j.rser.2022.112850

Soni, M., Gomathi, S., Kumar, P., Churi, P. P., Mohammed, M. A., & Salman, A. O. (2022). Hybridizing convolutional neural network for classification of lung diseases. *International Journal of Swarm Intelligence Research*, *13*(2), 1–15. doi:10.4018/IJSIR.287544

Srivastava, P. R. (2015). A cooperative approach to optimize the Printed Circuit Boards drill routing process using Intelligent Water Drops. *Computers & Electrical Engineering*, *43*, 270–277. doi:10.1016/j.compeleceng.2014.10.005

Sulaiman, M. H., & Mustaffa, Z. (2023). Using the evolutionary mating algorithm for optimizing the user comfort and energy consumption in smart building. *Journal of Building Engineering*, *76*, 107139. doi:10.1016/j.jobe.2023.107139

Suneetha, Naaz. Dubey, & Panwar. (2023). Classification of inherited Retinal Conditions with Machine Learning and Bio-inspired Algorithms. *International Journal of Intelligent Systems and Applications in Engineering*.

Sun, M., Zhou, L., Yu, Y., & Gu, J. (2021). Ant colony optimization based polymorphism-aware routing algorithm for AdHoc UAV network. *Xi Tong Gong Cheng Yu Dian Zi Ji Shu. Journal of Systems Engineering and Electronics*, *43*(9). Advance online publication. doi:10.12305/j.issn.1001-506X.2021.09.24

Tainio, M., Andersen, Z. J., Nieuwenhuijsen, M. J., Hu, L., De Nazelle, A., An, R., ... de Sá, T. H. (2021). Air pollution, physical activity and health: A mapping review of the evidence. *Environment International*, *147*, 105954. doi:10.1016/j.envint.2020.105954 PMID:33352412

Tan, N. D., Kim, H.-S., Le Ngoc, B. L., Nguyen, D. A., & You, S.-S. (2024). Optimization and inventory management under stochastic demand using metaheuristic algorithm. *PLoS One*, *19*(1), e0286433. doi:10.1371/journal.pone.0286433 PMID:38180984

Tao, D. S., Wan, J., Pesika, N. S., Zeng, H. B., Liu, Z. Y., Zhang, X. J., Meng, Y. G., & Tian, Y. (2015). Adhesion and friction of an isolated gecko setal array: The effects of substrates and relative humidity. *Biosurface and Biotribology*, *1*(1), 109–114. doi:10.1016/j.bsbt.2015.02.002

Tomelie, J., Chary, S., & Turner, K. L. (2013). Optimal articulation strategy for a microfabricated gecko-inspired controllable adhesive. *2013 Transducers & Eurosensors XXVII: The 17th International Conference on Solid-State Sensors, Actuators and Microsystems (TRANSDUCERS & EUROSENSORS XXVII).*

Tran, V. V., Park, D., & Lee, Y. C. (2020). Indoor air pollution, related human diseases, and recent trends in the control and improvement of indoor air quality. *International Journal of Environmental Research and Public Health*, *17*(8), 2927. doi:10.3390/ijerph17082927 PMID:32340311

Tropea, M., Santamaria, A. F., De Rango, F., & Potrino, G. (2019). Reactive Flooding versus Link State Routing for FANET in Precision Agriculture. *2019 16th IEEE Annual Consumer Communications and Networking Conference, CCNC 2019*. 10.1109/CCNC.2019.8651744

Turner, M. C., Andersen, Z. J., Baccarelli, A., Diver, W. R., Gapstur, S. M., Pope, C. A. III, Prada, D., Samet, J., Thurston, G., & Cohen, A. (2020). Outdoor air pollution and cancer: An overview of the current evidence and public health recommendations. *CA: a Cancer Journal for Clinicians*, *70*(6), 460–479. doi:10.3322/caac.21632 PMID:32964460

Uchiyama, Y., Blanco, E., & Kohsaka, R. (2020). Application of biomimetics to architectural and urban design: A review across scales. *Sustainability (Basel)*, *12*(23), 9813. doi:10.3390/su12239813

Ukaogo, P. O., Ewuzie, U., & Onwuka, C. V. (2020). Environmental pollution: causes, effects, and the remedies. In *Microorganisms for sustainable environment and health* (pp. 419–429). Elsevier. doi:10.1016/B978-0-12-819001-2.00021-8

Ullah, Z. (2020). A Survey on Hybrid, Energy Efficient and Distributed (HEED) Based Energy Efficient Clustering Protocols for Wireless Sensor Networks. *Wireless Personal Communications*, *112*(4), 1–29. doi:10.1007/s11277-020-07170-z

Unver, O., Uneri, A., Aydemir, A., & Sitti, M. (n.d.). Geckobot: a gecko inspired climbing robot using elastomer adhesives. *Proceedings 2006 IEEE International Conference on Robotics and Automation, 2006. ICRA 2006*. 10.1109/ROBOT.2006.1642050

Usmana, Chughtaia, Nawaz, Kaleema, Khaliqb, & Nguyen. (n.d.). A Reliable Link-adaptive position-based routing protocol for Flying ad hoc Network. *Mobile Networks and Applications, 26*(4), 1801-1820.

Vardanyan, A., Vardanyan, N., Aâtach, M., Malavasi, P., & Gaydardzhiev, S. (2022). Bio-Assisted Leaching of Non-Ferrous Metals from Waste Printed Circuit Boards-Importance of Process Parameters. *Metals*, *12*(12), 2092. doi:10.3390/met12122092

Vardoulakis, S., Giagloglou, E., Steinle, S., Davis, A., Sleeuwenhoek, A., Galea, K. S., Dixon, K., & Crawford, J. O. (2020). Indoor exposure to selected air pollutants in the home environment: A systematic review. *International Journal of Environmental Research and Public Health*, *17*(23), 8972. doi:10.3390/ijerph17238972 PMID:33276576

Vasičkaninová, A., & Bakošová, M. (2009). Neural network predictive control of a chemical reactor. *Acta Chimica Slovenica*, *2*(2), 21–36.

Veeraiah, V., Khan, H., Kumar, A., Ahamad, S., Mahajan, A., & Gupta, A. (2022, April). Integration of PSO and deep learning for trend analysis of meta-verse. In *2022 2nd International Conference on Advance Computing and Innovative Technologies in Engineering (ICACITE)* (pp. 713-718). IEEE. 10.1109/ICACITE53722.2022.9823883

Venkata & Sreenivasu. (2019a). *Foolproof Decision Support System for Melanoma Cancer Detection (FDSSMCD).* INDIA Patent# 201941005828.

Venkata & Sreenivasu. (2019b). Edge AI System for Pneumonia and Lung Cancer Detection. *International Journal of Innovative Technology and Exploring Engineering, 8*(9).

Venkata & Sreenivasu. (2019c). End to End System for Pneumonia and Lung Cancer Detection Using Deep Learning. *International Journal of Engineering and Advanced Technology, 8*(6).

Venkata & Sreenivasu. (2019d). Efficient CNN for Lung Cancer Detection. *International Journal of Recent Technology and Engineering, 8*(2).

Venkata & Sreenivasu. (2019e). Integrated Clinician Decision Supporting System for Pneumonia and Lung Cancer Detection. *International Journal of Innovative Technology and Exploring Engineering, 8*(8).

Vinodhini, G., & Chandrasekaran, R. M. (2012). Sentiment analysis and opinion mining: A survey. *International Journal (Toronto, Ont.)*, *2*(6).

Vives, V., & Ruiz-Fernandez, D. (2021). *Diabetic retinopathy detection through convolutional neural networks with synaptic metaplasticity* (Vol. 20-6). Elsevier.

Vrchota, J., Pech, M., & Švepešová, I. (2022). Precision Agriculture Technologies for Crop and Livestock Production in the Czech Republic. *Agriculture*, *12*(8), 1080. doi:10.3390/agriculture12081080

Walikar, G. A., & Biradar, R. C. (2017). A survey on hybrid routing mechanisms in mobile ad hoc networks. *Journal of Network and Computer Applications, 77*(October), 48–63. doi:10.1016/j.jnca.2016.10.014

Wang, H. J., Mei, T., Wang, X. H., & Lin, X. M. (2005). Interaction and simulation analysis between the biomimetic gecko adhesion array and rough surface. *Proceedings of the IEEE International Conference on Mechatronics & Automation*, 1063–1068.

Wang, J., Jiang, C., Han, Z., Ren, Y., Maunder, R. G., & Hanzo, L. (2017). Taking Drones to the Next Level. *IEEE Vehicular Technology Magazine*, *12*(3), 73–82. doi:10.1109/MVT.2016.2645481

Wang, J., Zhang, Z., Xia, F., Yuan, W., & Lee, S. (2013). An energy efficient stable election-based routing algorithm for wireless sensor networks. *Sensors (Basel)*, *13*(11), 14301–14320. doi:10.3390/s131114301 PMID:24284767

Wang, T., Wang, X. X., Wen, J., Shao, Z. Y., Huang, H. M., & Guo, X. (2022). A bio-inspired neuromorphic sensory system. *Advanced Intelligent Systems*, *4*(7), 2200047. doi:10.1002/aisy.202200047

Weigand, Wiedner, & Andre. (2022). Position-based Routing in Flying Ad Hoc Networks. *Seminar IITM WS 21/22, Network Architectures and Services.*

Wheeb, A. H., Nordin, R., Samah, A. A., Alsharif, M. H., & Khan, M. A. (2022). Topology-Based Routing Protocols and Mobility Models for Flying Ad Hoc Networks: A Contemporary Review and Future Research Directions. *Drones (Basel)*, *6*(1), 9. doi:10.3390/drones6010009

World Health Organization. (2021). *WHO global air quality guidelines: particulate matter (PM2. 5 and PM10), ozone, nitrogen dioxide, sulfur dioxide and carbon monoxide*. World Health Organization.

Wu, Liu, Hsu, Ho, & Lee. (2021). Performance and Limitation of Machine Learning Algorithms for Diabetic Retinopathy Screening: Meta-analysis. JMIR Publications.

Xi, F., Pang, Y., Liu, G., Wang, S., Li, W., Zhang, C., & Wang, Z. L. (2019). Self-powered intelligent buoy system by water wave energy for sustainable and autonomous wireless sensing and data transmission. *Nano Energy*, *61*, 1–9. doi:10.1016/j.nanoen.2019.04.026

Xue, Y., Zhu, H., Liang, J., & Słowik, A. (2021). Adaptive crossover operator based multi-objective binary genetic algorithm for feature selection in classification. *Knowledge-Based Systems*, *227*, 107218. doi:10.1016/j.knosys.2021.107218

Xu, Q., Wang, L., & Sansgiry, S. S. (2020). A systematic literature review of predicting diabetic retinopathy, nephropathy and neuropathy in patients with type 1 diabetes using machine learning. *Journal of Medical Artificial Intelligence*, *3*, 1–15. doi:10.21037/jmai.2019.10.04

Yang, H., & Liu, Z. (2019). An optimization routing protocol for FANETs. *EURASIP Journal on Wireless Communications and Networking*, *2019*(1), 120. doi:10.1186/s13638-019-1442-0

Yang, M., Zou, W., Guo, J., Qian, Z., Luo, H., Yang, S., Zhao, N., Pattelli, L., Xu, J., & Wiersma, D. S. (2020). Bioinspired "skin" with cooperative thermo-optical effect for daytime radiative cooling. *ACS Applied Materials & Interfaces*, *12*(22), 25286–25293. doi:10.1021/acsami.0c03897 PMID:32378874

Yasdi, R. (2000). A literature survey on applications of neural networks for human-computer interaction. *Neural Computing & Applications*, *9*(4), 245–258. doi:10.1007/s005210070002

Yuan, J., Liu, H.-L., & Yang, S. (2024). An adaptive parental guidance strategy and its derived indicator-based evolutionary algorithm for multi- and many-objective optimization. *Swarm and Evolutionary Computation*, *84*, 101449. doi:10.1016/j.swevo.2023.101449

Yue, Y., You, H., Wang, S., & Cao, L. (2021). Improved whale optimization algorithm and its application in heterogeneous wireless sensor networks. *International Journal of Distributed Sensor Networks*, *17*(5). doi:10.1177/15501477211018140

Yu, H., Song, J., Chen, C., Heidari, A. A., Liu, J., Chen, H., Zaguia, A., & Mafarja, M. (2022). Image segmentation of Leaf Spot Diseases on Maize using multi-stage Cauchy-enabled grey wolf algorithm. *Engineering Applications of Artificial Intelligence*, *109*, 104653. doi:10.1016/j.engappai.2021.104653

Yu, Z., Shi, Y., Luo, A., Tao, J., & Yang, S. X. (2018). Research on Landing Collision Experiment of Gecko Robot with Bio-inspired Dry Adhesive. *2018 IEEE International Conference on Information and Automation (ICIA)*. 10.1109/ICInfA.2018.8812558

Zang, C., & Zang, S. (2011). Mobility prediction clustering algorithm for UAV networking. *2011 IEEE GLOBECOM Workshops. GC Wkshps*, *2011*, 1158–1161. Advance online publication. doi:10.1109/GLOCOMW.2011.6162360

Zhang, E., Nie, Z., Yang, Q., Wang, Y., Liu, D., Jeon, S. W., & Zhang, J. (2023). Heterogeneous cognitive learning particle swarm optimization for large-scale optimization problems. *Information Sciences*, *633*, 321–342. doi:10.1016/j.ins.2023.03.086

Zhang, H., & Srinivasan, R. (2020). A systematic review of air quality sensors, guidelines, and measurement studies for indoor air quality management. *Sustainability (Basel)*, *12*(21), 9045. doi:10.3390/su12219045

Zhao, B. X., Pesika, N., Zeng, H. B., Wei, Z., Chen, Y., Autumn, K., Turner, K., & Israelachvili, J. (2009). Role of tilted adhesion fibrils (Setae) in the adhesion and locomotion of gecko-like systems. *The Journal of Physical Chemistry B*, *113*(12), 3615–3621. doi:10.1021/jp806079d PMID:19673126

Zheng, W., Tan, L., & Liu, C. (2021). Software Defect Prediction Method Based on Transformer Model. *2021 IEEE International Conference on Artificial Intelligence and Computer Applications (ICAICA)*, 670–674. 10.1109/ICAICA52286.2021.9498179

Zheng, Y., Wang, Y., Li, Z., Dong, L., Jiang, Y., & Zhang, H. (2014). A mobility and load aware OLSR routing protocol for UAV mobile AD-HOC networks. *2014 International Conference on Information and Communications Technologies, ICT 2014*. 10.1049/cp.2014.0575

Zhou, J., Chen, Y., Leong, B., & Sundaramoorthy, P. S. (2010). Practical 3D geographic routing for wireless sensor networks. *SenSys 2010 - Proceedings of the 8th ACM Conference on Embedded Networked Sensor Systems*, 337–350. 10.1145/1869983.1870016

Zhou, Y., Cheng, N., Lu, N., & Shen, X. (2015). Multi-UAV-Aided Networks. *IEEE Vehicular Technology Magazine*.

Zhou, M., Pesika, N., Zeng, H. B., & Israelachvili, J. (2013). Recent advances in gecko adhesion and friction mechanisms and development of gecko-inspired dry adhesive surfaces. *Friction*, *1*(2), 114–129. doi:10.1007/s40544-013-0011-5

Zhou, W., Wu, T., Li, Y., Wei, Y., Han, L., Li, Y., ... Du, S. (2023). A bioinspired vine-like hierarchically structured PET/CA composite nanofibrous membrane with superhydrophobic and superoleophilic surface for high-efficiency cooking fumes capture. *Separation and Purification Technology*, *125517*. Advance online publication. doi:10.1016/j.seppur.2023.125517

Zhou, Z. H. (2021). *Machine learning*. Springer Nature. doi:10.1007/978-981-15-1967-3

Zhu, Q., Tang, X., Feng, S., Zhong, Z., Yao, J., & Yao, Z. (2019). ZIF-8@ SiO2 composite nanofiber membrane with bioinspired spider web-like structure for efficient air pollution control. *Journal of Membrane Science*, *581*, 252–261. doi:10.1016/j.memsci.2019.03.075

About the Contributors

Ramkumar Jaganathan currently serves as an Assistant Professor in the esteemed Department of Information Technology & Cognitive Systems at Sri Krishna Arts and Science College in Coimbatore, India. His academic journey culminated in the completion of his Ph.D. degree from Bharathiar University, underlining his commitment to scholarly pursuits. With a prolific research career, he has authored and contributed to over 38 research papers, published in distinguished International Journals and Conferences, including SCOPUS and SCIE publications. His research endeavours primarily focus on ad-hoc networks, route optimization, decision support systems, and the Internet of Things, showcasing a diverse range of interests and expertise. Beyond his research contributions, he actively engages in various roles within the academic community. He has served as a Technical Committee Member, Scientific Committee Member, Advisory Board Member, and Reviewer for more than 413 International Conferences and 42 Refereed Journals. This extensive involvement underscores his commitment to advancing knowledge and the academic peer-review process. His multifaceted contributions to research, coupled with his dedication to the academic community, exemplify his standing as a respected professional in the field of Information Technology and Cognitive Systems.

Shilpa Mehta has completed her PhD degree from Auckland University of Technology, New Zealand. She has five years of teaching experience from different reputed colleges and universities of India. Currently, she is working as a Teaching Assistant at Auckland University of Technology (AUT), Auckland, New Zealand. She was awarded Summer Doctoral Research Scholarship for her PhD research. She has worked on various interdisciplinary research projects and her research interests include Radio Frequency Integrated Circuits, RF front ends, Optimization, Internet of Things, Wireless Communication, Artificial Intelligence, Healthcare, Radars, and Software-defined Radios, Smart Cities. As an editor, she has edited four books with IGI Global and one with Nova Science Publishers. She is also working on different edited books to be published by IGI Global, Apple Academic Press, Scrivener-Wiley, Cambridge, and Springer Nature, respectively.

Ram Krishan is presently working as Assistant Professor and Head, Department of Computer Science, Mata Sundri University Girls College, Mansa, Punjab, India (A Constituent College of Punjabi University, Patiala). Dr. Ram obtained his Ph.D in Computer Science and Engineering from Guru Kashi University, Talwandi Sabo in 2017 and M.Tech. in Computer Engineering from Punjabi University, Patiala in 2009. He has rich teaching experience of more than 15 years. He has authored two academic books and also published more than 40 research papers in various International/National Journals, Conference Proceedings and Book Chapters. Dr. Ram has also edited eight research books in the field of wireless communication and computing. His research areas include wireless communication, cloud computing and antenna design.

* * *

Rohit Anand is currently working as an Assistant Professor in the Department of Electronics and Communication Engineering at G.B.Pant Engineering College (Government of NCT of Delhi), New Delhi, India. He has teaching experience of more than 21 years including UG and PG Courses. He is a Life Member of Indian Society for Technical Education (ISTE). He has published 16 book chapters in reputed books and 18 papers in Scopus/SCI Indexed Journals. He has chaired many sessions in International Conferences. His research areas include Electromagnetic Field Theory, Antenna Theory and Design, Wireless Communication, Image Processing, Optical Fiber Communication, IoT, etc.

Suchitra B. is an Assistant Professor with 13 + years of experience successfully contributing to Computer Science Courses. Enthusiastic professional with background in academic advisement. Evident as a Passionate teaching instructor and mentor who has an inclination towards exploring technical concepts with an ability to adapt them well and cascading it for providing innovative teaching solutions. Completed my Ph.D. in computer Science (Data mining) from Bharathiar University . Published Papers in International and National level journals and Conferences. Published various Book Chapters. Acting as a Reviewer in Reputed Journals including Scopus, SCI and a member in IFERP. Authored 2 Books and contributed 3 Patents. Interest in Research.

Partha Ghosh, is an Assistant Professor at Department of Computer Science and Engineering, Govt. College of Engineering & Ceramic Technology. He holds a Ph.D. degree in Computer Science and Engineering. Prior to his doctoral studies, he earned his M.Tech. (Computer Science and Engineering), B.E. (Computer Science and Engineering) and a B.Sc. (Honours) degree in Physics from University of Calcutta. He has teaching experience of about 16 years. His current areas of interest include Machine Learning, Image Processing and Computer Vision. He has contributed several research papers in national and international journals and conferences.

Suradhuni Ghosh, is an Assistant Professor at Department of Geography, Government Girls General Degree College. She earned her M.Sc. (Geography with specialization in Cartography), from University of Calcutta. She has teaching experience of about 16 years. Her current areas of interest include Remote Sensing, GIS and Image Processing. She has contributed several research papers in national and international journals and conferences. She has Submitted Ph.D. Thesis in December, 2022.

J. Viji Gripsy, with an experienced 17-year teaching background, currently works as an Associate Professor in Computer Science at PSGR Krishnammal Science College for Women, Coimbatore. Her expertise is in Mobile Ad-hoc and Wireless Sensor Networks, and she has made significant contributions with over 25 research publications in national and international journals and books. Notably, she has authored 13 books and holds 4 patents, highlighting her notable contributions to the academic and research community. Actively involved in mentoring, she guides 4 research scholars in the dynamic domains of Mobile Networks and Data Mining. As a dedicated professional, she is a life member of esteemed organizations such as the International Association of Computer Science and Information Technology (IACSIT), the International Association of Engineers (IAENG), and the Indian Society for Technical Education (ISTE).

Ankur Gupta has received the B.Tech and M.Tech in Computer Science and Engineering from Ganga Institute of Technology and Management, Kablana affiliated with Maharshi Dayanand University, Rohtak in 2015 and 2017. He is an Assistant Professor in the Department of Computer Science and Engineering at Vaish College of Engineering, Rohtak, and has been working there since January 2019. He has many publications in various reputed national/ international conferences, journals, and online book chapter contributions (Indexed by SCIE, Scopus, ESCI, ACM, DBLP, etc). He is doing research in the field of cloud computing, data security & machine learning. His research work in M.Tech was based on biometric security in cloud computing.

K. S. Jeen Marseline, M.C.A, M.Phil, Ph.D., Dean Computer Science and Mathematics, Sri Krishna Arts and Science College has been a persistent and incessant in her teaching portfolio. She has 25 years of consistent teaching experience in Computer Science stream. As an eminent subject expert, she has vibrantly published more than 45 research papers in both national and international conferences. She has strongly endeavored with her authoritative excellence by being the Controller of examinations in Sri Krishna Arts and Science College in the year 2014 as well as in Sri Krishna College of Engineering and Technology from 2015-2017. She has been strategically in heading the Department of Information and Computer Technology from 2009 to till date that has been genuinely accomplished. She was bestowed with the best faculty Award from the renowned CTS corporate company. Her inspiration to achieve innovative modifications in her subject expertise has made her to visit countries like UAE, Thailand and Malaysia and update with educational upliftment. She has been a distinguished Board of Studies committee member in several colleges.

M. Sasi Kala, M.Sc., M.Phil., Ph.D., is currently working as an Assistant Professor in the Department of Computer Science (PG), PSGR Krishnammal College for Women, Coimbatore. She is having 16+ years of experience in various academic institutions. she has completed her Doctoral Degree in Computer Science from Bharathiar University. Her area of specialization includes computer Networks, Network Security, Cloud Computing and IoT. She is also an author of the Book entitled Software Engineering and Software Project Management and Computer Networks. She has published various papers in international Conferences and Journals. She has been awarded Honorary Degree of Doctor of Letters (D.Litt.) by University of South America recommended by S. Radhakrishnan Research & Development Center, India. She is a proud recipient of Innovative Research & Dedicated Academician Award given by Innovative Scientific Research Professional Malaysia.

Rita Komalasari is a lecturer at YARSI University. Her current work is focused on Biospheric Reverie: Unraveling Indoor Air Quality through Bio-Inspired Textiles, Awareness, and Decision-Making.

Ebenezar Jebarani M. R. is working as a Professor, Department of Electronics and Communication Engineering, School of Electrical and Electronics, Sathyabama Institute of Science and Technology, Sholinganallur, Chennai–600119, Tamil Nādu, India. She has more than 20 years of teaching experience. Her current area of research interest includes Computer Networks, Wireless Sensor Networks, Wireless and Mobile Communication, Embedded systems, IoT, Microprocessor and Microcontrollers and Image Processing. She has published more papers in reputed Journals and Conferences. She was a life member of ISTE and IEI. She was being a reviewer for reputed journals.

D. R. Medhunhashini is a passionate educator with a deep-seated curiosity in the Department of Information Technology and Cognitive Systems, Sri Krishna Arts and Science College. With 13 years of experience she has been dedicated to explore Software Engineering field through research, writing, and practical applications. She has contributed to various publications and conferences, aiming to bridge the gap between academic insights and real-world implications. She continues to engage herself in fostering a commitment to advancing knowledge and sharing valuable insights with the Software Engineering community.

Kavipriya P. obtained her Bachelor's in Engineering (B.E) in the year 2000 from AVC College of Engineering, Bharathidasan University. She received her Master's degree in Applied Electronics, first class with distinction, from Sathyabama University, Chennai in 2005 and also she obtained her doctorate in the field of wireless networks and communication in the year of 2015. Her current area of interest is Wireless networks, Wireless communication, Wireless Sensor Networks and Circuit Analysis. She joined as a teaching faculty in the year 2001 and presently working as a Professor in Sathyabama Institute of Science and Technology, Chennai, Tamil Nadu, India. She had published more research articles in reputed Journals and Conference Proceedings. She taught a wide variety of courses for both Under Graduate and Post Graduate levels over a period of twenty years.

Sabyasachi Pramanik is a professional IEEE member. He obtained a PhD in Computer Science and Engineering from Sri Satya Sai University of Technology and Medical Sciences, Bhopal, India. Presently, he is an Associate Professor, Department of Computer Science and Engineering, Haldia Institute of Technology, India. He has many publications in various reputed international conferences, journals, and book chapters (Indexed by SCIE, Scopus, ESCI, etc). He is doing research in the fields of Artificial Intelligence, Data Privacy, Cybersecurity, Network Security, and Machine Learning. He also serves on the editorial boards of several international journals. He is a reviewer of journal articles from IEEE, Springer, Elsevier, Inderscience, IET and IGI Global. He has reviewed many conference papers, has been a keynote speaker, session chair, and technical program committee member at many international conferences. He has authored a book on Wireless Sensor Network. He has edited 8 books from IGI Global, CRC Press, Springer and Wiley Publications.

N.T. Renukadevi received the M.C.A and M.Phil Degrees in Computer Science from Bharathiar University, India in 2003 and 2008 respectively. She received Ph.D. degree in Computer Applications from Anna University, India in 2014. Since 2008, she is working as an Assistant Professor in the Department of Computer Technology, Kongu Engineering College. Her research interests include Data Mining and Image Processing. She is also a reviewer in reputed journals. She has published 20 research works in referred journals and presented 12 papers in International Conferences.

Nandhini S. is currently an Assistant Professor in the Department of Information Technology and Cognitive Systems, Sri Krishna Arts and Science College, Coimbatore. She has teaching experience of more than 20 years. She has presented research papers in International Conferences and published more than 15 research articles. Her areas of interest include ad-hoc networks, route optimization, virtualization and cloud computing.

S. Nandhinidevi received the M.Sc and M.Phil Degrees in Computer Science from Bharathiar University, India in 2004 and 2008 respectively. She qualified SET and NET in Computer Science in 2017 and 2024. Since 2008, she is working as an Assistant Professor in the Department of Computer Technology, Kongu Engineering College. She is pursuing her research in Deep Learning. She has published 8 research works in referred journals and presented 10 papers in International Conferences.

Nitin Sakhare has completed his PhD in Computer Science and Engineering. He has Published 10 Journal, 5 Conference papers and 8 book chapters indexed in SCI/WoS/Scopus. He has also published 120 text books for Pune, Mumbai and North Maharashtra University.

K. Saraswathi received the MSc Degree in Computer Science from Bharathiar University and M.Phil Degree in Computer Science from Bharathidhasan University, India in 2004 and 2006 respectively. She received Ph.D. degree in Computer Applications from Anna University, India in 2018. Since 2008, she is working as an Assistant Professor in the Department of Computer Technology, Kongu Engineering College. Her research interests include Data Mining and Machine Learning. She has published 20 research works in referred journals and presented 10 papers in International Conferences.

Index

www.ingramcontent.com/pod-product-compliance
Lightning Source LLC
LaVergne TN
LVHW080647011026
849160LV00014B/1346